A CULTURAL HISTORY OF HAIR

VOLUME 6

A Cultural History of Hair
General Editor: Geraldine Biddle-Perry

Volume 1
A Cultural History of Hair in Antiquity
Edited by Mary Harlow

Volume 2
A Cultural History of Hair in the Middle Ages
Edited by Roberta Milliken

Volume 3
A Cultural History of Hair in the Renaissance
Edited by Edith Snook

Volume 4
A Cultural History of Hair in the Age of Enlightenment
Edited by Margaret K. Powell and Joseph Roach

Volume 5
A Cultural History of Hair in the Age of Empire
Edited by Sarah Heaton

Volume 6
A Cultural History of Hair in the Modern Age
Edited by Geraldine Biddle-Perry

A CULTURAL HISTORY OF HAIR

IN THE MODERN AGE

VOLUME 6

Edited by

Geraldine Biddle-Perry

BLOOMSBURY ACADEMIC
LONDON • NEW YORK • OXFORD • NEW DELHI • SYDNEY

BLOOMSBURY ACADEMIC
Bloomsbury Publishing Plc
50 Bedford Square, London, WC1B 3DP, UK
1385 Broadway, New York, NY 10018, USA
29 Earlsfort Terrace, Dublin 2, Ireland

BLOOMSBURY, BLOOMSBURY ACADEMIC and the Diana logo are trademarks of Bloomsbury Publishing Plc

First published in Great Britain 2021
Paperback edition published 2022

Copyright © Bloomsbury Publishing, 2022

Geraldine Biddle-Perry has asserted her right under the Copyright, Designs and Patents Act, 1988, to be identified as Editor of this work.

Series design: Raven Design
Cover image: Woman in Cloche Hat and Pink Dress in Gold Frame
© Science and Society Picture Library

All rights reserved. No part of this publication may be reproduced or transmitted in any form or by any means, electronic or mechanical, including photocopying, recording, or any information storage or retrieval system, without prior permission in writing from the publishers.

Bloomsbury Publishing Plc does not have any control over, or responsibility for, any third-party websites referred to or in this book. All internet addresses given in this book were correct at the time of going to press. The author and publisher regret any inconvenience caused if addresses have changed or sites have ceased to exist, but can accept no responsibility for any such changes.

A catalogue record for this book is available from the British Library.

A catalog record for this book is available from the Library of Congress.

ISBN:	HB:	978-1-4742-3211-1
	HB set:	978-1-4742-3212-8
	PB:	978-1-3502-8589-7
	PB set:	978-1-3502-8751-8
	ePDF:	978-1-3501-2283-3
	eBook:	978-1-3501-2282-6

Series: The Cultural Histories Series

Typeset by Integra Software Services Pvt. Ltd.
Printed and bound in Great Britain

To find out more about our authors and books visit www.bloomsbury.com and sign up for our newsletters.

CONTENTS

LIST OF FIGURES	vi
GENERAL EDITOR'S PREFACE	xii
Introduction: Modern Hair in a Modern Age *Geraldine Biddle-Perry*	1
1 Religion and Ritualized Belief *Yudit Kornberg Greenberg and Hanna Cody*	9
2 Self and Society Part I: The Social Dynamics of Hair *Elisha P. Renne*	25
Self and Society Part II: Fashioning Social Hair *Royce Mahawatte*	41
3 Fashion and Adornment *Alice Beard*	57
4 Production and Practice *Kim Smith*	75
5 Health and Hygiene *Paul R. Deslandes*	93
6 Gender and Sexuality *Chelsea Johnson and Kristen Barber*	111
7 Race and Ethnicity *Shirley Anne Tate*	129
8 Class and Social Status *Geraldine Biddle-Perry*	143
9 Cultural Representations *Nathalie Khan*	163
NOTES	181
BIBLIOGRAPHY	214
CONTRIBUTORS	228
INDEX	232

LIST OF FIGURES

INTRODUCTION

I.1 "Modern Hairstyle," ca. 1956. Photo: Barrett Street Trade School Archive. Reproduced by permission of University of the Arts London: London College of Fashion.   2

CHAPTER ONE

1.1 Lord Shiva. Bazaar Art Poster 1940s. Source: Columbia.edu. Wikimedia/Public Domain.   11

1.2 Male Tuareg, Libya. Photo: David Stanley from Nanaimo, Canada—Tuareg Man, CC BY 2.0, Wikipedia Commons/Public Domain.   14

1.3 Israel, Jerusalem. An Orthodox Jew woman in the Old City. Naeblys/Alamy Stock Photo.   16

1.4 Iranian official offering instruction on suitable hairstyles for young men. Photo: Mohsen Rezai/Mehr News/Getty Images.   20

1.5 Leah Michaelson, Director of Special Projects at Hatshuva. Photo: Courtesy www.breakingisraelnews.com.   21

1.6 Moslema in style fashion show, 2012. Photo: Firdaus Latif—Moslema in style, CC BY-SA 2.0. Wikimedia Commons.   22

CHAPTER TWO PART I

2.1.1 Turkey, late 1980s. Anatolian village bride, with long braids during marriage ceremony. Photo: Carol Delaney. From Delaney, "Untangling the Meanings of Hair in Turkish Society," *Anthropological Quarterly* 67, no. 4 (1994), p. 166. Reproduced by permission of Carol Delaney.   28

2.1.2 Painted barbershop storefront (*kinyozi*), Tanzania, advertising trendy, global hairstyles for men at the Classic of Paris Hair Cutting Salon. Photo: Harry Hook/Getty Images.   31

2.1.3 Four elderly men wearing traditional Ainu garments sitting in foreground with large group of men wearing western-style coats and hats. Ainu village, Japan, 1931–1932. Carl Etter Collection, National Anthropological Archives, Smithsonian Institution, National Museum of Natural History.   33

2.1.4 Hair collected at Auschwitz concentration camp. When the camp was liberated by the Red Army on January 27, 1945, they found piles of hair from the prisoners in the Auschwitz camp in Oświęcim, Poland. Photo: Spiegl/ Ullstein Bild/Getty Images. 34

2.1.5 Preparation for the performance of the traditional Bunu Yoruba marriage ritual known as *gbe obitan*. The bride's hair will be woven into many tiny braids (*e dirun obitan*), which are then decorated with safety pins to make her look new and shiny. Janet Ogunibi, Apaa-Bunu, December 1987. Photo: E.P. Renne. Reproduced by permission of E.P. Renne. 36

2.1.6 A Chinese bride and groom pose for a professional photographer. Photo: Alto/James Hardy/Getty Images. 37

2.1.7 Funeral basin filled with the hair of family mourners for the Nsoko queen mother, who had recently died. Nsoko, Brong Ahafo, Ghana, 1980. Photo: Raymond Silverman. Reproduced by permission of Raymond Silverman. 38

CHAPTER TWO PART II

2.2.1 Saturday Evening Post, May 1, 1920. "Bernice Bobs Her Hair" appears in this issue. Saturday Evening Post/Wikipedia Commons/Public Domain. 42

2.2.2 Publicity photo of Jean Harlow, 1930s. Photo: studio (Celebrities Stars). Wikimedia Commons/Public Domain. 46

2.2.3 "The Secret of Lovely White Hair." Supplement to *My Story: The Evan Williams' Shampoo*, published by The Evan Williams Co. Ltd., London, ca. 1920s. Author's own collection. 48

2.2.4 Elvis Presley receives a crew cut on his first full day as a member of the US Army. Photo: Bettmann/Getty Images. 50

2.2.5 Barbie Doll, c. 1970s. Science and Society Picture Library/Getty Images. 52

2.2.6 Barbie Doll, c. 1970s. Science and Society Picture Library/Getty Images. 53

CHAPTER THREE

3.1 Poster for the film *Bobbed Hair* (dir. Thomas Heffron, 1922). By Realart. Wikimedia/Public Domain. 60

3.2 Publicity photo of Louise Brooks. From short biographical sketch-book *Stars of the Photoplay*, 1930. By *Photoplay* magazine. Wikimedia/Public Domain. 61

3.3 Advertisement for Hermo Hair-Lustr with Gloria Swanson and Wallace Reid. By unknown ad agency/photographer—*Photoplay* (February–June 1921). Wikimedia/Public Domain. 63

3.4 Mary Quant, December 1966. Photo: Jac. de Nijs/Anefo. Source: http://www.gahetna.nl/collectie/afbeeldingen/fotocollectie/zoeken/weergave/ detail/q/id/ab08cfb0-d0b4-102d-bcf8-003048976d84, CC BY-SA 3.0 nl. Wikimedia Commons. 66

3.5 A seventeen-year-old "Twiggy" (Lesley Hornby) with garçonne-style bob, February 2, 1967, launching a new range of clothes, bearing the Twiggy label. Keystone Pictures USA/Alamy Stock Photo. 68

3.6 On the runway at the Chanel Haute Couture show, Paris Fashion Week Fall/Winter 2015/2016. Photo: Getty Images/Victor VIRGILE/Gammo-Rapho. 72

CHAPTER FOUR

4.1 "Bobbed Hair's The Thing!" Newspaper article dated September 25, 1920. By Djuna Barnes—Arizona Republican (Phoenix, AZ), September 25, 1920. Chronicling America: Historic American Newspapers. Library of Congress. Wikimedia/Public Domain. 77

4.2 Women in evening dresses at a jazz party in 1926. Science and Society Picture Library. 78

4.3 Permanent-waving machine, 1923, built by Icall for sale by Eugene Suter under the name "Eugene." The twenty-two tubular heaters designed in 1917 by Isidoro Calvete and patented by Suter in 1920, hung from the "chandelier," distributed the weight of the heaters. Louis Calvete/Wikimedia Commons/Public Domain. 81

4.4 Electric hot comb heater and hot comb. Smithsonian National Museum of African American History and Culture. Gift of Linda Crichlow White in honor of her aunt, Edna Stevens McIntyre. 82

4.5 June 4, 1952: Hairdresser Raymond aka "Mr Teasy Weasy" [sic] puts the finishing touches to a hairstyle. Photo: Chaloner Woods. Photo: Bettmann/Getty Images. 85

4.6 November 13, 1954: Hairdresser Mr. Angel Rose works on a gentleman's coiffure in his salon near Tottenham Court Road, central London. Photo: Maurice Ambler/Picture Post. © Getty Images. 86

4.7 1963: Clients under row of hood dryers. Photo: Barrett Street Trade School Archive. Reproduced by permission of University of the Arts London: London College of Fashion. 87

4.8 Fashion designer Mary Quant seen having the finishing touches made to her new hairstyle by Vidal Sassoon, November 12, 1964. Photo: Ronald Dumont/Getty Images. 89

CHAPTER FIVE

5.1 The carefully groomed face of modernity: *Saturday Evening Post*, July 8, 1922. Saturday Evening Post/Wikipedia Commons/Public Domain. 96

5.2 Brylcreem advertisement (1939): "Don't Let Your Daily Dip Cause 'Dry Hair'." The Advertising Archives, London. 97

5.3 Clairol's hair coloring as an antidote to the tyranny and dictatorial powers of gray hair (1943). The Advertising Archives/Alamy Stock Photo. 98

LIST OF FIGURES

5.4	Charlton Heston promoting the hygienic qualities and sex appeal of Jeris Antiseptic Hair Tonic (1953). The Advertising Archives/Alamy Stock Photo.	100
5.5	L'Oréal instructs women how to avoid a poodle-like permanent curl with their products (1950). Author's own collection.	101
5.6	Wella sells its products to men with longer hair in the 1970s (1973). Wikipedia/Creative Commons/Public Domain.	103
5.7	Blue and Sunny: A butch-femme couple in 1950s America with Blue wearing a tie and a pompadour. Photo courtesy Lesbian Herstory Archives.	107
5.8	Black Panther Party members, many wearing "Afros" as forms of political expression, supporting the organization's cofounder Huey P. Newton in Oakland, California (1968). Everett Collection Historical/Alamy Stock Photo.	108

CHAPTER SIX

6.1	Payot on young Hasid man. Wikimedia Commons.	113
6.2	Badge from Madame C.J. Walker Convention. Created by Bastian Brothers Co. Photo: Addison Scurlock. Collection of the Smithsonian National Museum of African American History and Culture, Gift of Dr. Patricia Heaston.	115
6.3	Rayfield McGhee in a zoot suit, Tallahassee, Florida, ca. 1942. Photo: Florida Memory. State Library of Florida/Wikimedia Commons/Public Domain.	117
6.4	"Free Angela Davis!" poster: the Afro as a symbol of Black resistance. Collection of the Smithsonian National Museum of African American History and Culture.	119
6.5	Two hippies at the Woodstock Festival, August 1969. Photo: Derek Redmond and Paul Campbell—Own work, CC BY-SA 3.0, Wikimedia Commons.	120
6.6	Brent Michael Wood. Photo: Nan Palmero. https://www.flickr.com/photos/nanpalmero/sets/72157679848522636	121
6.7	David Bowie's Genderqueer Fashion, onstage at the Hammersmith Odeon in London, 1973. The last Ziggy Stardust concert. Photo: Steve Wood/Express/Getty Images.	122
6.8	The punk trend continues. Punk girls, with shaved heads and dayglo Mohicans, Morecambe, United Kingdom, 2003. Photo: de:Benutzer: Calzinide—Own work, Wikimedia Commons/Public Domain.	123
6.9	A model at Bronner Brothers International Beauty Show Fantasy Competition, 2016 in Atlanta, Georgia. Photo: Paras Griffin/Getty Images.	124
6.10	Tonsure at the Thiruthani Murugan Temple, Thiruttani, India, 2016. Photo: Allison Joyce/Getty Images.	126

CHAPTER SEVEN

7.1 Miss Beatrice Baird, ca. 1930s. Reproduced by permission of the Tate family. 133

7.2 Two young girls with hair in rollers, San Jose de Ocoa, Dominican Republic. Photo: Adam Jones—originally posted to Flickr, CC BY-SA 2.0, Wikimedia Commons. 136

7.3 Preparations for the Saida do Ilê Aiyê, Brazil. Photo: Tatiana Azeviche. https://www.flickr.com/photos/turismobahia/33118404235/in/album-72157680674698726/. 137

7.4 Girl looks on proudly, Notting Hill Carnival, United Kingdom, 1994. Photo: PYMCA/UIG via Getty Images. 140

CHAPTER EIGHT

8.1 "Through these fingers have passed the most beautiful curls in the world." The magic hands of "Antoine de Paris" (Antek Cierplikowski). From *Antoine By Antoine*, published by W.H. Allen, 1946. 146

8.2 "Antoine de Paris" (Antek Cierplikowski) dressed for the White Ball, Paris, 1927. 147

8.3 Front cover *Glamour of Mayfair* by Jean Hope, published by Gramol Publications, 1934. 149

8.4 Two women in a beauty salon getting their hair and nails done, Hollywood, California, ca. 1936. 151

8.5 Women's hairdressing class, Barrett Street Trade School, London, 1928. Photo: Barrett Street Trade School Archive. Reproduced by permission of University of the Arts London: London College of Fashion. 152

8.6 A beauty salon in Harlem, New York, ca. 1933. Photo: General Photographic Agency/Getty Images. 153

8.7 Young punks Ian Holden ("Angel") and John Vick, May 1982. Photo: Science and Society Picture Library. 157

8.8 "Big hair." Melanie Griffith, *Working Girl*, 1988. Moviestore Collection/REX//Shutterstock. 158

8.9 "You wanna be taken seriously, you need serious hair." Melanie Griffith, *Working Girl*, 1988. Moviestore Collection/REX//Shutterstock. 159

CHAPTER NINE

9.1 "'Cristeene' leaning over window ledge." Photo: Eli Schmidt. Reproduced by permission of Paul Soileau. 164

9.2 "Cristeene" with Rick Owens, in *Butt Muscle* (dir. Matt Lambert, 2016). Reproduced by permission of Paul Soileau. 165

9.3	"Cristeene" in green dress. Photo: Michael Sharkey. Reproduced by permission of Paul Soileau.	166
9.4	"Cristeene" in leather. Photo: Eli Schmidt. Reproduced by permission of Paul Soileau.	168
9.5	"Cristeene" in "bath mat" wig. Photo: Michael Sharkey. Reproduced by permission of Paul Soileau.	168
9.6	Rolling Stones' album cover *Some Girls*, 1978. Designed by Peter Corriston. Pictorial Press Ltd./Alamy Stock Photo.	173
9.7	Portrait of Andy Warhol. Moviestore Collection Ltd./Alamy Stock Photo.	174
9.8	"Cristeene" in flight. Photo: Eli Schmidt. Reproduced by permission of Paul Soileau.	177
9.9	"Cristeene" with bruises in pink dress. Photo: Eli Schmidt. Reproduced by permission of Paul Soileau.	178
9.10	"Cristeene's" wig on a stand. Photo: Michael Sharkey. Reproduced by permission of Paul Soileau.	179

GENERAL EDITOR'S PREFACE

A Cultural History of Hair offers an unparalleled examination of the most malleable part of the human body. This fascinating set explores hair's intrinsic relationship to the construction and organization of diverse social bodies and strategies of identification throughout history. The six illustrated volumes, edited by leading specialists in the field, evidence the significance of human hair on the head and face and its styling, dressing, and management across the following historical periods: antiquity, the Middle Ages, the Renaissance, the Age of Enlightenment, the Age of Empire, and the Modern Age.

Using an innovative range of historical and theoretical sources, each volume is organized around the same key themes: religion and ritualized belief, self and societal identification, fashion and adornment, production and practice, health and hygiene, gender and sexuality, race and ethnicity, class and social status, representation. The aim is to offer readers a comprehensive account of human hair-related beliefs and practices in any given period and through time. It is not an encyclopedia. *A Cultural History of Hair* is an interdisciplinary collection of complex ideas and debates brought together in the work of an international range of scholars.

Geraldine Biddle-Perry

Introduction: Modern Hair in a Modern Age

GERALDINE BIDDLE-PERRY

Consider an image of a postiche simply titled "Modern Hairstyle" from 1956 (Figure I.1). The hair is cut short over the ears and into the nape of the neck; it is uniformly colored, and artfully coiffed high off the forehead to form a wreath of curls that frame the angular planes of the mannequin's face. This is the conceptual starting point of this collection of chapters: how does a hairstyle come to be seen as representative of what it is to be and to look "modern" at a particular moment in time.

The ability to adapt the body to shifting conceptions of the self and the experience of living in a particular age, here the modern age, renders the hair on our head a dynamic site of interpretation, for individuals and social groups engaged in the day-to-day rituals of body management, for writers, artists, scientists, designers, hair practitioners, photographers, film-makers, commercial enterprise, actors and performers, and of course for historians and theorists. It is this complex interaction between what hair is, what can—and cannot—be done with it (theoretically, aesthetically, culturally, fashionably), and what it means to different people in different contexts, that the chapters in this volume grapple with. The task in its infinite discursive dimensions is comparable to that of its subject matter. No one historical example can be reduced to a single meaning nor stand for all, nor can every potential variation in practice or interpretation be addressed. Any examples chosen also bring their own historiographical problems. Hairstyles are frequently trapped and trivialized in a version of fashionable clothing's reductive "hemline history" that merely documents the longs and shorts of style trends in clothes and head and facial hair as synonymous with particular epochs. Clearly, a century of change is more complex than a series of hairstyles. Nevertheless, the trends and the mechanisms of popular memory that iconize them are also embodied in social practices that acquire meanings, or to which meanings are attached, through rituals, ideologies, technologies, and beliefs that are relevant to the construction of modern sensibilities and, thus, to an understanding of the modern age itself.

The chapters that follow attempt to overcome or at least negotiate these complexities through a flexible schema of interpretation: key themes—social organization, fashion, race, gender, religion, class, sexuality, hygiene, representation—separately structure each chapter, but these constantly overlap and frequently collide in the analyses of definitively "modern" hair styling innovations—the bob, the perm, the blonde, the Afro—that to a greater or lesser degree inform all of the chapters. The intention is to critically explore

FIGURE I.1: "Modern Hairstyle," ca. 1956. Photo: Barrett Street Trade School Archive. Reproduced by permission of University of the Arts London: London College of Fashion.

hairstyles in a way that allows them to be conceptually and theoretically expanded and developed in an unfolding mix of contextual and thematic alternatives. Chapter by chapter, the interaction of these two impulses, the thematic and the topical, aim to enrich an understanding and the critical potential of a vital cultural form still overlooked in many contemporary histories of the body.

By way of example, each cultural milieu and social context poses different questions for each of the chapters but it is impossible to understand the modern age without addressing in some way the huge impact the "bobbing," that is, cutting short, of women's hair had on every aspect of culture in the interwar period. For some chapters, the style is situated as the symbol of both change and the experience of change expressed through the body, and operates as a catalyst for the arguments that follow. Royce Mahawatte (in Chapter Two, "Self and Society, Part II") begins with Scott Fitzgerald's short story "Bernice Bobs Her Hair" (1920). The bob, or rather the naïve Bernice's decision to enter the barber's shop and cut her hair, is figured as an incendiary act of social indiscretion that casts shockwaves outwards in the small-town community in which she and her more experienced cousin Marjorie are attempting to make their social mark. Mahawatte's chapter looks at the discursive implications of styles like the bob, but also the peroxide blonde, the buzz cut, and the Afro that occupy a politicized mediating role between consumer agency and social institutions. Mahawatte traces how different disciplinary orders interact in the "fashioning" of new kinds of social bodies? How are these embodied in everyday regimes of hair styling and management practiced in new kinds of places and spaces, in modernist literature and Hollywood cinema, in advertising and popular culture, children's toys, and in the hashtag# communities of the twenty-first century?

Alice Beard's chapter (Chapter Three, "Fashion and Adornment") then develops this line of argument. However, the focus here is on the allure and status the latest styles brought to young women and how such concepts were incorporated into a rhetorical narrative of new attitudes to gender and sex roles in a burgeoning film industry, and in all kinds of visual and material culture more broadly. The modern salon, the cinema screen and fashion page, and the contemporary catwalk, Beard argues, offer spectacular forums for the creation and consumption of "the look," a fusion of fashionable clothes and hairstyles that functioned at an ideological level as the symbol of the gender politics of modern femininity in the twentieth century and beyond.

Beard and Mahawatte in their different ways examine how the bob in the 1920s transgressed traditional gender body codes at a time when patriarchal authority and an old social order were seen as under threat, and the tangible historical barriers to fashionable consumerism were beginning to if not disappear then certainly dilute. The figure of "the flapper"—immediately recognizable by her bobbed hair, androgynous silhouette, and morally and physically "fast" lifestyle—signaled youth and new attitudes to the body, particularly the sexual body. At the same time, women's hair was invested with an exaggerated eroticism in sensational accounts of its barbering in the popular press, and in the expanding spectacle of moving pictures aimed at a largely female audience. Beard explores how on and off screen the early stars of the silent era such as Colleen Moore and Louise Brooks offered a spectacular version of a visibly constructed modern femininity endlessly replicated in an expanding popular media and progressively, in salons in every suburban high street and parade. The simply cut bob and the "flapper rage" were in fact short-lived trends, but "the look" became synonymous with a desire for, if not the realization of, wider political and social change. This is significant Beard argues, in that such desires were now perceived as being fulfilled in autonomous acts of modern consumerism that did not just embody radical change but engendered it.

For Kim Smith's chapter (Chapter Four, "Production and Practice"), the transformative qualities of the bob for individuals, wider society, and the hairdressing profession are again the starting point, this time the determination of a young Millie Dillmount (the fictional heroine in the film *Thoroughly Modern Millie* played by Julie Andrews) to acquire the cachet attached to a style seen as both dangerous and fashionable. Smith explores how bobbed hair was a product of the massive social and technological changes wrought by World War I. New attitudes to science and its advantages for modern living provided a huge stimulus to the evolution of modern professional hairdressing practice. The salon is conceptualized by Smith as a new kind of social scientific laboratory, a testing ground for the products of a series of "ages"—mechanical, electric, chemical, plastic— that decade by decade revolutionized hairdressing practice and its cultural status as a site of social and personal transformation. If hair and hairdressing have been overlooked in recent historiography, then critical consideration of the brushes, combs, scissors, dryers, and chemical reagents that transformed the way modern bodies could be managed and manipulated is almost nonexistent. Smith's chapter redresses this oversight.

Modern hairdressing conferred a new kind of status on the hairdresser, particularly those whose reputations were built on the heads and shoulders of the aristocratic and Hollywood celebrities they styled and dressed. Celebrity body and image were aligned with characteristics that were used by films and advertising copy to promote a modern "glamour aesthetic." Visibly bleached blondes like Mae West, Carole Lombard, and Jean Harlow directly promoted fashionable artifice and ornament through spectacle, but their on-screen performances and promotional images offered an aspirational version of modern femininity that was socially acceptable and, thus, highly desirable for young female cinemagoers. The refinement and manufacture of reliable hair bleaches and colorants and their popular cultural dissemination represented a formidable fashion and sociocultural dynamic.

Like the "artificial" silk dresses that transformed the mass manufacture of fashionable clothes and access to style change between the wars, the products of modern hairdressing were equally artificial, accessible, affordable, and highly aspirational. Young women consumers were part of an expanding workforce employed in factories, shops, and indeed hairdressing salons engaged in processing, manufacturing, and retailing consumer goods and services aimed at an expanding mass market, of which these modern workers were an intrinsic part. However, a new geography of elite consumerism emerged in relation to the expansion of the mass market. Geraldine Biddle-Perry's focus on class (Chapter Eight, "Class and Social Status") examines how a progressively more stylistically and socially diverse fashion system emerged that both cut across the old boundaries of class and status recognition and instigated new hierarchies of power and knowledge to contain the threat of incursion. The exclusive "artistry" of celebrity hairdressing auteurs displaced the primacy of a style in itself as an indicator of one's social standing onto a range of coordinates by which one could plot sophistication. Where one's hair was done and by whom became as important as how one's hair was done in the reformulation of old hierarchies of class and status.

Fashions, in hair and clothes, still emanated from Paris, but Hollywood was now central to modern consumerism and this reconfiguration of new kinds of classed, raced, and gendered bodies. In April 1935, the golden doors of the House of Westmore on Sunset Boulevard were opened. The new salon belonged to the Westmore family, father George, and brothers Perc, Ern and Mont, who at one time or another were heads of hair and makeup at all the leading studios. Hollywood stars Kay Francis turned a golden key, Joan Blondell pushed a golden switch that flooded the interior of the salon with dazzling light, and Claudette Colbert in a golden gown then pressed a gold button to light the exterior. The salon featured floor-to-ceiling mirrors in the foyer; peach-blush carpeting; pure white silk draperies with crystal fringes; bronze, coral, and white furniture graced every booth; every cubicle had its own white and gold telephone; and an announcer system crooned softly into each booth. There were babysitters, hot chocolate, and wine flowed freely, and on the second floor Perc's oak-paneled office and a laboratory were furnished with the newest and most modern equipment.[1]

The products of modern hairdressing offered a new technology not just of the body but also of its image. Modern bodies became more glamorous but also more rational, hygienic, and streamlined. Paul R. Deslandes's chapter (Chapter Five, "Health and Hygiene") explores the powerful visual rhetoric of hair health within which body and mind were intertwined in the promotion of corporeal techniques seen to typify the institutions of the modern body politic. Deslandes evidences how hair styling and grooming were promoted as embodied forms of cultural and economic capital that men and women not only could but *had* to invest in for personal and social well-being; hair and its care acquired political significance as a sign of order or disorder, a vehicle for change, and a portent for social discord. Contingent upon a range of variables—national and ethnic identities, race and gender, economic and cultural status—advertisers attached specific meanings to "healthy" hair by linking ideals of physical appearance and hygienic practices to those of personal satisfaction and social acceptance.

Hair's unique "natural" qualities of material plasticity and symbolic potency assumed a new salience in twentieth-century society and culture. The pull of artifice and the push of culture impelled new strategies of identification in socially sanctioned cultural forms—visual, literary, and of course the body and its performance—inextricably connected to conformist or resistant ideas of "the natural" informed by a cultural imaginary dominated by the hegemony of white, western, patriarchy. Consumers and producers had to negotiate the boundaries between constructed ideals of modern "authenticity" and the social, physical, and economic realities of their praxis.

These complexities keyed into wider cultural anxieties around the experiences of the modern age and found expression in the work of a radical artistic avant-garde that emerged after World War I. Drawing on a range of theories around different categories of the fetish (sexual, anthropological, commodity), Nathalie Khan (Chapter Nine, "Cultural Representation") detaches the hair from modern heads and bodies and looks at the powerful, primarily sexual, symbolism of the wig in a series of commodified and eroticized exchanges between subject and object in art, performance, and popular culture. The 1920s are situated as an era of experimentation for Surrealist artists challenging the increasing rationalization of commodified bodies and body ideals. The Surrealists were influenced by Freudian and Marxist theories of the fetish object—frequently in the form of hair, fur, and feathers—and used these to critique contemporary culture by exposing the hidden, unconscious drives that lay beneath the superficial impulses of modern capitalism. In blurring the boundaries between them, the fetish object took on super "natural" qualities through hair's magical capacity for substitution.

Khan then explores this process in the context of contemporary constructions of queer identity in performances and representations that both challenge and conform to gender norms. Part commodity, part cultural construction, part sensual experience, hair in the form of wigs, she argues, bridges the liminal spaces of person and celebrity persona, public and private image. The fetishistic nature of hair as material object and symbolic subject discursively constructs concepts of performative and political agency in its capacity to be visibly, and self-consciously, "played with."

This is particularly significant to Kristen Barber and Chelsea Johnson's chapter (Chapter Six, "Gender and Sexuality") looking at hairstyles that have challenged the boundaries of race, gender, and sexuality over the past hundred years. Throughout the twentieth century, antithetical constructions of hair and hairstyles as "natural" or "artificial" rapidly assumed a new dominance as a politically charged vector of modern subjectivity and the institutional systems of power and knowledge through which their shifting meanings were discursively circulated. Barber and Johnson use an intersectional approach to evidence how the powerful social and sexual symbolism of hair has been exploited by young female consumers, Black beauty culturists, Chicano and Black African American "zoot suiters," and sub- and countercultural groups such as hippies and punks, to confront a world where capitalism, white supremacy, and the male gaze constrain conceptions of self through the construction of normative gender and raced binaries. Choice of hairstyle, they argue, can infer upon individual and communal bodies levels of societal approbation or condemnation that accrue or diminish according to shifting constructions of "authentic" raced, gendered, or sexed subjectivities. The now ubiquitously "safe" bob once represented a considerable challenge to "natural" ideals of gender and femininity in the 1920s, and while political resistance to the hegemony of hair's essential biological "roots" reached an apotheosis with the "Afro" in the 1960s, within months it had become just one of a range of fashionable options for mainstream Black consumers.

However, as Barber and Johnson demonstrate, for other women elsewhere in the world this commodified cultural exchange is experienced a little differently. The human hair trade is now a global concern reliant on a transnational flow of people and hair to meet the demands of a contemporary vogue for elaborate hairpieces and "real" hair extensions. Women and men who purchase hairpieces from salons, beauty supply retailers, and online storefronts in the United States, China, and much of Europe are often unaware of just where their hair comes from. Largely sourced from India and China, hundreds of barbers work day and night cutting the hair of a constant flow of (primarily female) devotees; the shorn hair then undergoes a series of processes of picking, washing, drying, and packing undertaken by poor, poorly paid women in the global south. This raises a number of complex issues about race and gender and the hegemony of western beauty aesthetics.

As Shirley Anne Tate's chapter (Chapter Seven, "Race and Ethnicity") convincingly demonstrates, haunted by the specter of racial difference and prejudice, Black hair can never be considered just organic matter. It is, Tate argues, vulnerable: physically because sensitive and prone to damage from heat, prolonged use of extensions, and chemical reagents; and ideologically, as a primary signifier of a modern Black civil rights movement diametrically opposed to the straight-haired blonde ideals of white supremacist and colonial power *and* the weaves, waves, wigs, and extensions that Black women have employed to arguably conform to such ideals. This concept of "vulnerability" is situated by Tate as the affective symbolic glue that joins "natural" hair to contested bodies of knowledge and different strategies of management and manipulation. Both, she argues, allow a different construction of a sense of an autonomous, self-actualized, authentic Black femininity across the diaspora.

This concept of a gluing together of diverse and sometimes conflicting perspectives brings to mind editor Alf Hiltebeitel's attempts to tease out points of congruence and dissonance in the diverse collection of essays exploring hair symbolism in Asian culture. In his "Introduction," Hiltebeitel acknowledges the impossibility of pinning hair down (or up) to any one meaning or context: "It [hair] gets into everything, but whatever it gets into, it never seems to be explained the same way; rather, it always seems to be used differently to explain something else."[2] He concludes:

> The social body is both a bounded construct and a fluid one. Hair norms and policies are defined around civilizational, cultural, racial, caste, and gender boundaries; and around temporal transitions and spatial frontiers.[3]

For Yudit Greenberg and Hanna Cody (Chapter One, "Religion and Ritual") the impact of fashion change and built-in obsolescence on the rituals and rules of self-presentation assigned to members of comparative religious groups might, at first sight, seem at best minimal, at worst irrelevant. But, as Greenberg argues, religious discourse on men and women's hair is determined by the cultural contexts in which it originates but also those in which beliefs and practices are developed; and this is particularly significant for understanding its cultural history in a modern age. Greenberg maps out how, over the course of the twentieth and twenty-first centuries, believers in the Hindu and Abrahamic faiths have both sustained traditional treatments of hair in ritual contexts and progressively adapted their practice and presentation in response to the new conditions and technologies of modern life, particularly across the diaspora. The modern age is one of expanding secularization that has seen the separation of religious doctrine from modern conceptions of a sexual self, and from the institutions of power that sanction the nature of its moral boundaries, performance, and expression. However, Greenberg's examples explore the continued covering, cutting, and growing of hair for those of faith as a dialectic: an important symbol of piety and a locus for the performance of a faith-based identity whose formal properties and meanings shift and change over time.

In "The Social Dynamics of Hair" (Chapter Two, Part I) Elisha P. Renne's approach is framed by anthropological discourse but also explores the ritualized and fashionable regimes of hair styling and practice as a global social dynamic: the product of various context-specific interventions in western and nonwestern cultures that have come to define the modern age. Hair's rituals, ideologies, and practices from Europe and North America to Burkina Faso, to Rio de Janeiro and Mumbai are unified in this chapter in a shared symbolic schema of social taboos and organization that mediate between the corporeal and the ideal. Traditional practices conform to the security of social conventions relating to group identity, but have progressively incorporated the idiosyncrasies of individual consumer agency implied in fashionable trends that have rippled out and back in global exchanges of economic, social, and cultural capital. Renne evidences how hairstyles and grooming practices are subject to social conventions and taboos that constantly regulate social bodies. Nevertheless, these also always exist in a dialectical relationship between tradition and modernity, continuity, and change. Parallel histories and theories of the social body and its ritualized management offer a schema of strategies that dominate the cultural imaginary from the Lobi of Burkina Faso to the Hindu temples of South Asia, from the Orthodox Jewish communities of New York to the Hindu diaspora in American colleges, from Black Atlantic to the metropolises of London and Paris.

Modern hairdressing heralded a period of transformation in the ways in which the body was thought about and "treated," medically, aesthetically, psychologically, socially, and fashionably. Each decade has seen styles and practices represented in new cultural forms to more and more consumers that would have seemed impossible to a previous generation as the links between hair color, length, and curl and what it was to be and look modern were intensified. New conceptions of what was "natural" were embodied in the performance and representation of classed, gendered, and raced bodies that continuously challenged the boundaries of what went before. This collection of chapters seeks to reflect the expanding discursive parameters of a modern sense of self and the performative agency offered in twentieth- and twenty-first-century bodies and spaces. Iconic styles and the technical advances in professional and domestic hair care these both stimulated and responded to, are privileged in different ways in all the chapters in this volume as harbingers of radical change. Race, class, gender, sexuality, and the differences they entail are central to the discourses and ideologies that symbolically and materially shape modern bodies—at the apex of which is our most malleable and manipulative part: our hair. As a category of analysis hair is highly unstable and subject to constant shifts in material expression, symbolic understanding, and critical interpretation—but this only reinforces the potency and significance of a natural form upon which and through which culture constantly writes and rewrites its meanings.

CHAPTER ONE

Religion and Ritualized Belief

Contemporary Views and Traditional Practices

YUDIT KORNBERG GREENBERG AND HANNA CODY

INTRODUCTION

The discourse on hair and religion reveals the meanings and dialectical relations that exist between the physical body and the "social body."[1] Hair as an extension of male and female bodies has been represented, modified, disciplined, and celebrated in ancient as well as contemporary societies and religious communities. What sets hair apart from the rest of human anatomy is malleability; hair, unlike other body parts, can be visibly physically altered and adapted: it can be grown, cut, shaved, colored, styled, and covered in numerous and creative combinations. Thus, hair becomes an ideal body part for self-expression, a means for publicly expressing one's social and/or religious identity, and because of its perceptibility and material plasticity, an important symbol of sexuality. The juxtaposition of hair and the sexualized body renders its manipulation subject to prescription and control by religious and social institutions alike, but aligned with questions of social status and gender, this dynamic plays a particularly pivotal role in the rituals and rules of self-presentation assigned to members of religious groups.

In this chapter, we examine the paradoxical category of hair in religion and society in the modern age as both a source of beauty and admiration as well as a source of impurity and shame. Hair presentation and maintenance, whether subject to traditional or contemporary religious or cultural influence, is important because hair functions as a means of representing individual and group identity. Religious rituals pertaining to hair, along with contemporary social trends, have continued to shape and construct our physical body and our identity. However, religious discourse on whether hair should be kept, cut, or covered is often determined by the cultural contexts in which the religious beliefs and practices develop. For example, the current banning of certain religious dress codes in some European countries relating to women's hair covering raises questions about veiling as an example of women's oppression and a mechanism for social control imposed by patriarchal social structures.[2] However, it is important to note that discourse on women's hair as found in scriptures such as the Bible and the Qur'an is neither extensive nor prescriptive. Moreover, men too are subject to a range of rules and conventions regarding the control of their hair as a crucial marker of religiosity, masculinity, and patriarchal authority. While again not mandatory, these nevertheless exert considerable pressure to conform.[3]

The state of hair in religion in the modern age is indeed a complicated subject and draws upon various social, cultural, and historical factors that often take on new meanings and significance, particularly in diasporic contexts. Based upon multiple interpretations of hair in several religious traditions—Sikh, Hindu, Jewish, Christian, and Islamic—this chapter explores the shared symbolic potency of distinctive religiously motivated practices relating to head and facial hair. The examples used are not exhaustive and do not include important rituals and conventions relating to the shaving or other management of body hair. Rather, the aim is to examine the scriptural foundations and modern refigurations of head and face hair and its manipulation that continue to mirror and mold traditional and modern faith-based identities. For heuristic purposes, much of the discussion is organized along gender lines, but the emphasis is dialectic: the relational contradistinctions of men's and women's cutting, growing, display, and concealment of their hair; the tension between tradition and modernization; and the emergence of modest fashion as an expanding sector within a global fashion industry.

HAIR AS METAPHOR OF RELIGIOUS/SOCIAL ORGANIZATION AND CONTROL

While differently motivated, men's visible control of their hair across religions and cultures can be located within a symbolic grammar of social interaction central to the institutions of a given society and the establishment and reinforcement of social, religious, and physical boundaries. Anthropologist Paul Hershman in his notable essay on hair symbolism among Punjabi Sikhs and Hindus, organized these coded relational meanings thus:

	PROFANE (non-sacred)		SACRED
PURE	Hindu men hair cut	→	head shaven
IMPURE	Women hair never cut	→	hair loosened[4]

In this context, scholars Hallpike, Leach, and Olivelle have argued that hair in Hinduism is indicative of social control,[5] sexuality, taboo/sacredness,[6] and as a marker of social separation/inclusion, "a multifaceted complex consisting of sexual maturity, drive, potency, and fertility."[7] In Hinduism the god Shiva, from whose head the Ganges is purported to flow, is often depicted seated with his hair arranged with a stream of water flowing onto a *lingam–yoni*—a statue that represents Shiva and his wife, Parvati—that symbolizes the joining of male and female sexual organs. Thus, the arrangement of Shiva's hair is both phallic and the source of his concentrated sexual potency from which life springs.[8] Through this lens, the hair of mortals, especially women's hair, must be revered as well as feared.

Within a relational system of potent hair symbolism, head shaving in South Asia—whether in Hindu, Buddhist, or Jain traditions—serves as an initiatory ritual that involves either a permanent or an extended period of separation and marks the transition into a new phase of life. Hair that is removed or left uncut serves as a marker of celibacy, a detachment from social norms of appearance and the transcendence of the physical and social boundaries they articulate, particularly relating to sexuality.[9] The annual

FIGURE 1.1: Lord Shiva. Bazaar Art Poster 1940s. Source: Columbia.edu. Wikimedia/Public Domain.

liturgical shaving of hair for Hindu ascetics (*sannyasins* or renouncers) reaffirms their commitment to their vows and their spiritual goals. For others, such as sons following the death of a parent, widowers during periods of mourning, and those undergoing initiation ceremonies, the period of separation from society is briefer.[10] Vedic students returning from a period of separation and who have left their hair uncut are ritually shaved prior to a final ceremonial bath in preparation for marriage and the assumption of their new social role and status.[11]

In most if not all religions, shaving practices are central to rites of passage, initiation ceremonies, and rituals relating to the individual's perceived level of purity; their purpose is to signal clear distinctions based on identity, such as affiliation with a religious community, age, sex, gender, or level of social inclusion or exclusion (either temporary or permanent). For example, Muslim men making the *hajj* (pilgrimage) to Mecca are required to shave their head and body hair and cut their nails as a form of ritual cleansing. Having fulfilled their highest religious goal, they are then free to regrow and groom their beards as a symbol of their religious and social authority and sexual maturity.[12]

The growing of young boys' hair prior to its ritual cutting can also be understood within this symbolic framework of social transition and initiation into structures of masculine social control. Since the seventeenth century, the practice of keeping a male infant's hair uncut until the age of three has become popular and remains prevalent in

Hasidic Jewish communities. This hair-cutting ceremony is called *upsherin* (Yiddish: lit. "shear off") and can be related to the injunction in Leviticus 19:23 prohibiting the eating of the fruit that grows on a tree for the first three years. The young boy, like a healthy tree produces fruit, will grow in knowledge and will become a Torah scholar. For the ultra-Orthodox, only the hair on the head is sheared; the earlocks or *pe'ot* (plural)—the hair in front of the ears extending beneath the cheekbone—are kept per the biblical injunction in Leviticus 19:27, "You shall not round off the *pe'at* of your head." For others, both the hair on the head and the sidelocks are cut off during the ceremony. As part of the *upsherin* ceremony, it is also a custom to weigh the shorn hair and donate it to charity.

In the Hindu faith, the ritual of cutting a young boy's hair between the ages of one and three (*chudakarana* or *mundan*) is similarly recognized as an important sacrament (*samskara*).[13] Sometimes, a small patch of hair (*tonsure*) will be left on the back of the head, again as a means of maintaining health and leading to overall longevity in part derived from a statement made by Vasistha (a Vedic sage), "Life is prolonged by tonsure; without it, it is shortened. Therefore, it should be performed by all means."[14]

For laymen of Jewish, Muslim, and Christian faiths, the relational shaving and or growing of the beard is a primary focus because it occupies an important site of incubation for the display of masculinity, virility, and patriarchal authority. The visible control by adult men of their hair symbolizes their public roles as husbands, fathers, and devotees in relation to "others"—unmarried and younger males and male children, women, those of other faiths, and nonbelievers. Such control inflects all other manipulations, and forms the basis from which they derive their meaning and significance.[15]

Anabaptist Mennonite men in North America keep their hair short, their upper lip shaven, and grow full beards to signify their pacifist beliefs, their sexual maturity, and their marital status. In the Bible in Leviticus 19:27, we read about the prohibition applied to all men against shaving their beard with a razor or removing the hair at the corners of the head. The reason for the prohibition of shaving is not stated in the Bible, but the rabbinic authority, Moses Maimonides (1135–1204), comments that this biblical law indicates that the Israelite priests rejected the common practice of "heathen" priests who shaved their beards and Hasidism, the popular mystical movement that originated in eastern Europe in the eighteenth century, adheres to the kabbalistic view of the beard as an earthly symbol of God and, therefore, mandates the maintenance of long beards and sidelocks. However, most westernized Jews do not wear beards, including many Orthodox rabbis, and despite attempts to proscribe shaving with a razor, in recent decades it has also been ruled permissible to remove facial hair with scissors or an electric shaver.

Faegheh Shirazi evidences disagreements between Islamic scholars, clerics, and experts in *sharia* law as to the interpretation of the Qur'an's dictates regarding the treatment of men's facial hair.[16] Each Islamic sect offers different and conflicting perspectives on the wearing of beards and mustaches, desired lengths, and the finer details of grooming depending on the regional geopolitics and cultural traditions extant at different times, but Shirazi argues, "nowhere in the religious literature is it stated that every Muslim man must grow a beard ... while growing a beard is generally recognized a virtuous act, it is *not* mandatory."[17]

Anthropologist Christopher Hallpike understands these socially sanctioned practices in terms of symbolic equivalence: hair control equals social, that is, primarily sexual, control.[18] In most religions, men's head hair is kept short in contrast to women's who, as we shall see, are largely required to keep their hair long and controlled in some way by braiding, knotting, or most notably, covering to symbolize their shared participation in socially sanctioned structures of sexual expression, particularly marriage. There are exceptions. But as Indologist Patrick Olivelle points out, it is these contradictions that illustrate the extremely "loose" nature of hair's cultural grammar and that allows individuals and groups to cross with ease from one symbolic domain to another.[19]

In the Sikh tradition, one of the signs of the Sikh *khalsa*[20] is a commitment to keep one's hair and beard uncut.[21] But, unlike the symbolism of matted hair associated with social withdrawal, Sikh men's hair is carefully washed, oiled, combed, and then enclosed in a turban into which the well-groomed, waxed, and twisted end of beard and mustaches are then tucked. In this way, the Sikh affirms his sexual maturity and status within marriage and society by symbolically expressing the power of his masculine authority and his control of it in the combing and covering of his hair. While both Sikh men and women leave their hair uncut, traditionally only adult men wear the turban.[22]

In Islam, the Prophet Muhammed has been attributed to calling turbans, "The crowns of this people."[23] The Muslim turban was associated as a sign of "strength, power, dignity, and honor" among those who wore it.[24] Harahap's examination of a *fatwa*[25] discusses the turban's role as a means of differentiating Muslims from "nonbelievers," as well as a symbol of reverence, especially when worn in sacred spaces.[26] Indeed, it was customary in the time of the Prophet for men and women in the Arab world to cover their heads with a mantle of some sort.[27] However, Harahap notes, the wearing of a turban is not mandated in the Qur'an; many Muslim men do not wear the turban at all and the choice of whether or not to wear one appears to depend largely upon individual or local interpretation of religious doctrine, and the customs associated with the practitioner's geographic location.[28] Muslim Tuareg men living in northern Africa commonly adopt their own version of a combined turban and veil (called a *tagelmust*; see Figure 1.2) to indicate adherence to religious modesty while also signifying the individual's age, social ranking, gender, relationship status, and ethnicity. Men will not remove the *tagelmust* when in the presence of nonfamily members or those of a higher social ranking than themselves as a sign of modesty and respect.

Male head covering in Judaism is likewise not an explicit commandment, in either the Torah or the Talmud. Nonetheless, the practice has evolved from a custom to an accepted norm required by all observant Jewish males as a sign of reverence. From the Middle Ages through the modern and contemporary period, rabbinic authorities have agreed that prayers cannot be uttered bareheaded, not only in synagogues but also in other sacred spaces, such as cemeteries. It has, therefore, become a universally accepted practice for men to cover their heads during synagogue services, and most men also cover their heads when studying the Torah and the Talmud. The head covering most often used is the skullcap (Hebrew: *Kippah*; Yiddish: *Yarmulke*), and because there are no restrictions on its shape or fabric, various kinds of *kippot* (plural) developed in the contemporary period.

Even though such head coverings conceal men's hair this is not necessarily the central source of concern for those who wear them. Rather, the idea of the male turban as a symbol of sexual maturity, a "crown," or of the skullcap as a sign of reverence is to establish and sustain masculine hierarchical status within one's own community and differences between religious communities. Covering hair is a consequence of the design, in contrast to women's head coverings, whose primary purpose, as we will see, is to symbolize modesty and purity.

FIGURE 1.2: Male Tuareg, Libya. Photo: David Stanley from Nanaimo, Canada—Tuareg Man, CC BY 2.0, Wikipedia Commons, Public Domain.

WOMEN'S HAIR

Hair as a metaphor for social control makes both male and female bodies the subject of manipulation. This dialectical relationship, as the examples above reveal, cannot be understood solely in terms of rigidly gendered binary oppositional hair practices. Hair covering is not confined to women. For example, Muslim women also take part in the *hajj* and sacrifice their hair, and it is predominantly Hindu women that ritually shave their hair at Hindu temples (although some men also participate). Rather, the shaving, cutting, growing, display, and concealment of men and women's hair present a shared symbolic grammar of social and religious organization. Hair in its control and covering embodies patriarchal structures whose purpose is to regulate and control the boundaries of spiritual, physical, and social bodies through the articulation of difference. Whether giving up just a single lock of hair as an affirmation of Muslim feminine piety, or in offering up all one's hair to the deity in Hinduism, the symbolic potency of hair in spiritual contexts is synonymous with the self: "the religious and social order permeates one another" and the social divisions of gendered hair management are sustained.[29] Sexuality—and more generally gender—thus, continues to operate as the major referent in the language of hair.[30] What constitutes modesty and piety for men is expressed in terms associated with qualities such as reverence for God and humility, whereas female modesty is almost exclusively defined in the sexual realm, seen most obviously in the rules of covering and maintaining women's hair.

Many Muslim and most Hindu women do not cut their hair from the onset of puberty. In Muslim communities in rural Turkey, long hair is a symbol of womanhood in relation to something that men do not possess. In other words, "loose" rampant sexuality must be brought under control through braiding and covering.[31] Adult Hindu women too are compelled to keep their hair long and visibly control it in public, although not necessarily by covering it. Loose hair is traditionally confined to domestic spaces—that is, private arenas of informality and sexual intimacy—and for periods of temporary separation from society during menstruation when a woman's hair is left unbound and unwashed.[32] Married women may also redden their hair parting with vermilion—a tradition that some scholars have identified with fertility and childbearing.[33]

While for Muslim women the wearing of head coverings has emerged as a common practice in Islamic culture worldwide, it was not mandated by the Prophet Muhammed and, in fact, the matter of women's veiling is confined in the Qur'an to the following verses:

> "Oh Prophet! Tell thy wives and daughters, and the believing women, that they should cast their outer garments over their persons (when abroad): that is most convenient, that they should be recognized and not bothered …" (33:59)
>
> "And when ye ask them (the Prophet's wives) for anything ye want, ask them from behind a curtain. That is purer for your hearts and for theirs …" (33:53)

Ambiguously referring to veiling as it relates only to the Prophet's wives or more generally to "believing women," these verses leave room for religious and material interpretation embodied in a formal diversity of head coverings that have subsequently developed across the Islamic world. The second verse, though, incorporates the concept of purity and indicates how wearing a veil serves to protect both the wearer and the "other" from impurity, a state thought to be derived from a woman's sexual potency and fertility following the onset of menstruation.[34] Historically, women have been required to remain physically secluded during their menses in accordance with the Qur'an:

> They question thee (O Muhammad) concerning menstruation. Say: It is an illness [*adha*], so let women alone at such times and go not in unto them till they are cleansed. (2:222)[35]

The crux of women's veiling in Islam appears to rest in its function as a means of what anthropologist Hanna Papanek described as this "portable seclusion."[36]

Similarly, there is scant reference to women's hair or women's hair covering in the Hebrew Bible, which may be surprising given the importance of the practice in Orthodox Judaism in later Jewish history and in modern times. Admiring women's hair as an element of her physical beauty is found in the poetic expressions of the Song of Songs: "Your hair is like a flock of goats from Gilead" (Song 6:5). And while the veil is not an explicit requirement in the Bible, there are hints that women veiled themselves, as seen in the following verse: "Your eyes are like doves behind your veil" (Song 4:1). Other references mention Rebekah covering herself upon seeing Isaac, her future husband (Genesis 24:65); Tamar also dons the veil to disguise herself: "When Judah saw her, he took her for a harlot; for she had covered her face" (Genesis, 38:14–15). Because the evidence is sparse, we do not know precisely the extent to which this custom of hair covering was observed historically, but stringent attitudes toward women's hair as a source of sexual temptation intensified in the modern period when the practice of shaving a woman's hair upon marriage became prevalent in European countries such as Hungary. This is evidenced in Rabbi Hatam Sofer's (1762–1839) ruling that a woman must cut her hair after she weds. Hazon Ish (1878–1953), the ultra-Orthodox rabbi who discusses women's hair[37] reiterates the Talmudic reference to women's hair as *ervah*, or erotic stimulus, which must be covered just as other *ervah* or intimate parts of a woman's body.[38]

Whether married Jewish women shave their heads or not, they are at the very least required to cover their hair as a marker of married status (Figure 1.3). From the perspective of Jewish law (*halacha*), only some covering of the hair is required. Nevertheless, in addition to scarves, hats, and snoods, it has also become customary for ultra-Orthodox and Hasidic women to cover their hair with wigs—a practice that was first introduced by French women who began wearing wigs in the 1600s. At first, the local rabbis rejected this practice, because it was a common style among gentiles; furthermore, they claimed that it was immodest to appear in public with beautiful hair, even if it was a wig. Despite its problematic history, the wig practice took hold and is common today in many Hasidic and ultra-Orthodox communities where some women also choose to wear an additional covering such as a hat to visibly emphasize their piety by ensuring that no one mistakes their wig for natural hair.[39]

FIGURE 1.3: Israel, Jerusalem. An Orthodox Jew woman in the Old City. Naeblys/Alamy Stock Photo.

For all women of faith, "The culture of hair is no trivial matter."[40] Discourses of instrumental religious power differently inform the social meanings assigned to gendered hair. These can communicate structures of oppression and inequality, particularly with regard to veiling in Islam, and head covering and hair maintenance in Indian and Jewish traditions. Patriarchal hair norms produce and regulate the self and society by interacting with the shared cultural traditions of ethnic groupings, disguised as natural body standards. Regardless of its form, its motivation, and the faith of women who wear it, the veil separates and "screens off" the individual, especially with respect to sexuality.[41] By covering their heads, women remove a potentially perceived sexual symbol from public view and reserve it exclusively for the sight of their family or spouse.[42] Some theorists have even conceptualized the disciplining/covering of women's hair as a means of metaphorically "beheading" and disempowering women by eroticizing the female head. In his introduction to *Off with Her Head!*, Howard Eilberg-Schwartz suggests the sexual objectification of a woman's body requires coming to terms with the power of her head, "For the head, which is potentially separable from the body, poses special dilemmas when it belongs to a woman."[43]

Critiques are especially waged against Muslim veiling practices, which are seen as being particularly oppressive. However, feminist scholars such as Leila Ahmed understand the nature of imposition, and the meanings and symbolic significance of women's head covering, as much more complex and contested than reductive narratives of coercion might suggest. The wearing of a *hijab* or headscarf is seen as an immediate and unambiguous signal of religious orthodoxy, but mechanisms of identification are historically produced, ironically through the discourses of western colonialism that first determined the meaning of the veil and thereby set the terms for its emergence as a symbol of Muslim resistance.[44]

Practices and attitudes to body, facial, and head hair express the desire for differentiation in symmetrical and oppositional relations between one religion and another.[45] Other communities seek to express strong links to their traditional roots by continuing to observe closely regulated conventions regarding dress and hair coverings. Orthodox Mennonite women in the United States, "put on all of the Church's rules" in the form of long, loose, simple dresses in muted colors and cover their hair to express their submission to the requirements for female modesty.[46] The expansion of Black Pentecostal churches in Britain since the 1990s offers a version of Christianity with its roots in West Africa that is also based on a distinctive set of doctrines and practices, including strict edicts pertaining to women's dress and the covering of hair and flesh as an expression of ritual purity.[47]

Sociologist Anthony Synnott, in theorizing the continued significance of hair symbolism, argues that what is significant is not establishing an "intrinsic meaning" to practices of growing and shaving (for there is none). What is significant is, "the process by which oppositions to social norms are developed and symbolically expressed in the body ... the same hair symbolizes different realities. Conversely different hair styles may symbolize similar values." The quoting of scriptural edicts and interpretations dating back to antiquity might seem out of place in a volume exploring the role of hair in religion and its rituals in the modern age. But it is precisely the continued emphasis on and concepts of tradition and change that have come to mirror and mold the symbolic, social, and material dimensions of modern religious hair practice and a new politics of faith-based identity.

TRADITION AND CHANGE: CONTEMPORARY PERSPECTIVES AND PRACTICES

Barbara Metcalf argues: "The sense of contrast with a past or contrast with the rest of society is at the heart of a self-consciousness that shapes religious style."[48] Thus, tradition as a key part of self-identification is particularly relevant to the construction of diasporic religious identities—for example, Muslims in Manchester in the north of England who are conjoined through a "global sacred geography" with rituals and sacred sites in Pakistan.[49] Hindu communities in North America have similarly reconfigured ritual procedures to make connections between the past and contemporary social interaction with the wider community and with other migrant Hindus from regionally and ethnically distinct traditions.[50]

An interesting response to head covering practices was made by the Jewish Reform movement who issued the following declaration: "We Reform Jews object vigorously to this requirement for women, which places them in an inferior position and sees them primarily in a sexual role."[51] Reframing women's head covering and shifting its rationale from female sexuality to piety, both Conservative and Reform movements encourage women to cover their heads when praying, defining the act as a ritual for men and women alike, and one which symbolizes respect of God. In the contemporary Orthodox world, most rabbis consider hair covering to be an obligation incumbent upon all married women; however, there is variation in the form this takes. Based upon interpretations of rabbinic texts some maintain that women must cover all their hair, for example the Mishnah Beuarah; some maintain that women must cover all their hair because it is forbidden for a man to pray in front of his wife if any of her hair is showing.[52] Other Orthodox rabbinic figures have suggested that hair is no longer defined as erotic in a modern context, because most women in society do not cover their hair in public. It is concluded based on this logic that men are no longer prohibited from praying in the presence of a woman's hair.[53]

In the diasporic Hindu communities explored in Barbara Miller's ethnographic study, the changing hair practices of Indian girls and younger women's health and sexuality is often associated with the appearance and maintenance of her hair.[54] She states that many Indian women believe their hair should remain long, thick, uncut but controlled, that is, neatly secured in either a braid or a bun. To leave hair unbound may suggest a sense of "looseness" of the woman's character; cutting hair may symbolize poor health or a turning away from tradition in favor of equally symbolically loaded western values and styles, which Miller codes as:

> conforming heterosexual/sexy female BABE = head hair[+] hair care[+] leg and underarm hair[−]
> nonconforming nonheterosexual female LESBIAN = head hair[−] hair care[+] leg and underarm hair[+]
> Nonconforming politically resistant female FEMINIST = head hair[=] hair care[−] body hair[+][55]

For the younger members of South Asian culture in diaspora, the negotiation of such ideals reveals "the conflicts that may ensue, and the re-recreation and manipulation of forms in the culture of origin and the culture of immigration."[56] While both codes are limited and simplified, they present a way of understanding how hair in the United States interacts with transcultural symbols of sexuality, ideology, relationship status, and moral values. Short, permed, or dyed hair is rarely seen and younger South Asian women favor ponytails, chin-length cuts, and obviously managed blow-dried styles with a side rather than the usual middle parting; the braid, particularly the traditional oiled braid has been largely abandoned. Nevertheless, Miller concludes, whether in traditional or contemporary Indian, Euro-American, or Indian immigrant culture, whether you wear it long or short, styled or colored, there is still "no way to avoid the message power of hair. Even if you cover it with a hat or scarf it still talks."[57]

The conflicts that arise from such visibility are often ambiguous. In recent decades with the rise of fundamentalism across Islamic cultures it has become increasingly difficult for Muslim men *not* to wear a beard. After seizing Kabul in 1996, strict rules were swiftly imposed by the Taliban relating to the standardization of men's beards and head and body hair (Figure 1.4). These were instituted by force, with some individuals reportedly being whipped and even imprisoned for failing to respect such edicts: beards had to be large enough to be held by all five fingers, head hair was to be kept short, and armpits and pubis were to be shaved.[58] In 2007, barbershops along the Pakistan–Afghanistan border were bombed if their owners refused to stop shaving beards.[59] In this context, some men wore a beard as a safeguard against aggression and ostracism by being marked out as "irreligious." For others, particularly a younger generation, facial hair has assumed a new significance within the body politics of modern religious identification in the Middle and Near East and North Africa, but also in the Muslim diaspora in Europe and North America where revivalism has been central to a transnational expression of modern Islamic identity articulated through the body.

As Stephen Warner notes, "Religious identities often (but not always) mean more to individuals away from home, in their diaspora, than they did before and those identities undergo more or less modifications as the years pass."[60] However, it is important not to overlook the symbolic potential of hair as a cultural form expressive of shared ideals of religious conformity, as well as negotiation and resistance to the institutions of power and control. The relational contradistinctions of hair rituals and practices and their scriptural foundations in Hinduism, Judaism, Christianity, and Islam differently inform men and women's contemporary expressions of modern religious identities. But these coexist with styling trends and shifting interpretations of piety and religious identity that ripple out globally through new faith-based forms of performative expression, particularly with the growth of new media.

Diverse and fashionable hair covering options can be seen in contemporary Jewish communities, especially in Israel where covering one's hair with colorful scarves, a practice known as "wrapping," is becoming increasingly popular. Jewish-based Facebook groups such as "Wrapunzel: The Fangroup" and Judith de Paris – Hairwear "Oui Love to Wrap!" have recently flourished by presenting new and creative ways to wear scarves. Leah Michaelson (Figure 1.5) is passionate about the art of wrapping and the combination of colors in her scarfs. She shared her perspectives in an interview on hair, fashion, modesty, and the orthodox Jewish practice of women's head covering: "If you look at society today, a woman's hair is what gets noticed. Women talk about having 'a bad hair day.' There's lots of emphasis on hair being attractive … but when a woman dresses modestly and is completely covered, what's seen is her inner beauty coming out."[61]

Internet platforms have provided unprecedented opportunities for even the most orthodox of religious women to engage with other faith groups; notions and practices related to modesty have become significant channels through which to communicate and exchange ideas.[62] There is a trend among some Christian women in Israel promoting a return to the practice of head covering during worship.[63] Penina Taylor, internationally

FIGURE 1.4: Iranian official offering instruction on suitable hairstyles for young men. Photo: Mohsen Rezai/Mehr News/Getty Images.

renowned speaker, coach, and author, and representative of Wrapunzel, an online "community that celebrates the art of hair covering," shared two major reasons why Christian women cover their heads. Firstly, a belief that a covered head is a symbol of a woman's submission to her husband or, if she is not yet married, to the authority of her father; secondly, Taylor suggests, some Christians desire to identify with the Jewish tradition and the origins of their faith and "really feel that this is the way to authentically worship God."[64]

This association of head covering, modesty, and piety with the desire to find new forms of expression resonates with similar considerations in contemporary veiling practices among Muslim women. For example, Aheda Zanetti in 2004 invented the "burkini," a full-body swimsuit, for her niece who struggled to play volleyball while

FIGURE 1.5: Leah Michaelson, Director of Special Projects at Hatshuva. Photo: Courtesy www.breakingisraelnews.com

also wearing her *hijab*. According to Zanetti, she designed the burkini as a means of increasing Muslim women's mobility in the public sphere without sacrificing observance of their religious beliefs.[65] Described as "Another win for the modest fashion movement," in 2016, Anniesa Hasibuan, a Muslim woman from Indonesia, became the first fashion designer to present a *hijab* collection during New York Fashion Week (Figure 1.6).[66] Cultural theorist Reina Lewis explores the proliferation of fashionable trends in "modest dressing" that have emerged, stimulated by the demands of predominantly youthful consumers, and fueled by the opportunities offered by the Internet and new media as a platform for performative expression and debate.[67] Lewis observes:

> The emergence of modest fashion as a niche sector within the global fashion industry is not just about clothes: it simultaneously stimulates interest in and validates modesty as a sphere of personal and community activity.[68]

Unlike previous generations, these designers and consumers do not understand or experience consumer culture as antithetical to religion, ethnic culture, or tradition versus fashion. Rather, they interpret "modesty" through an engagement with mainstream contemporary trends.⁶⁹ High-end and mainstream styles are now disseminated within a diverse community of consumers committed to the values of modesty, complemented by bloggers and "hijab fashionistas" offering online tutorials on how to tie, wrap, and style hair and makeup. The founder of one such site declared, "My motto is: one should never underestimate the haircut of a girl in a hijab. And I don't just say that because I had a Mohawk last month."⁷⁰ Online shopping and the variety of platforms for rapid style exchange provided by social media have de-territorialized faith and modest fashion and allowed the creation of new communities of consumers from different faiths and secular backgrounds who are reinterpreting modesty and religiosity.⁷¹

In October 2016, Conde Nast International launched *Vogue Arabia*, initially as an online edition with a print magazine anticipated in spring 2017. One of the first articles that appeared in this landmark publication was Khaoula Ghanem's "How to Style Your Hair under a Hijab." The piece features French-Algerian abaya designer Faiza Boughessa and Saufeeya Goodson, "Feeeeya," a modest fashion blogger with 2.5 million followers on Instagram.⁷²

Christian Bromberger describes how women in prosperous urban areas of Tehran must hide their hair (so too plastic mannequins in shop windows) but continue to bleach and style their hair and particularly their eyebrows according to fashion. He argues, "Everywhere, hairstyles mark the limit between submission and disobedience."⁷³ In Iran, discourses of concealment and patriarchal authority are reproduced in the private spaces of the female salon and beauty parlor where clients are literally screened from the eyes of the outside world by a white sheet covering the front windows and a heavy thick curtain

FIGURE 1.6: Moslema in style fashion show, 2012. Photo: Firdaus Latif—Moslema in style, CC BY-SA 2.0. Wikimedia Commons.

through which they enter for threading, eyebrow plucking, haircutting, and coloring before reemerging in their ample black *manteaus* topped with the latest fashion in lacy *chador*.[74]

CONCLUSION: UNTANGLING HAIR AND RELIGION IN THE MODERN AGE

Decisions to cut or grow or cover one's hair in the modern age in socioreligious contexts rest at the crossroads between law and custom, personal choice and community identification, and tradition and change. The rise of religious fundamentalism in the Middle East and Asia since the 1980s has raised the stakes and had an indirect effect on other diasporic Muslim communities and on other orthodox faiths by promulgating "so called" traditional customs and laws as the centerpiece of a radical Islamic political agenda. Over the course of the twentieth and into the twenty-first centuries, the symbols of religious identity articulated through hair and the body in general, have emerged as a key element in the discourse of geopolitical western colonialism and its resistance. Orthodox and traditional forms of expression are easy to classify according to a rigid oppositional hierarchy of piety, but the juxtaposition of feminism, religious renewal movements, and the growing influence of new media have also opened up new spaces for men and women of faith to perform and legitimize alternative, more hybridized models of identification that are equally significant.

Each religion has its own formal and informal rituals, explicit commandments, and implicit unspoken codes pertaining to such practices, and whose interpretations are often disputed. However, notions surrounding what hair means and how it should be presented have continuously evolved in the modern age. Comparative studies of social and political change within the major religions show that, while each brings different resources to the encounter with modernity, they all confront similar predicaments.[75]

Contemporary discourses on the interaction between gender, religion, and fashion bolster the new dynamism of religious expression. Religious comportment and its interpretations are continually in flux in response to evolving political, technological, and social realities, including the openness to interfaith and cross-cultural engagements. In the modern age, the presence of the Internet, as well as the shifting geopolitical landscape, has allowed religious practitioners to continue to adapt and disseminate new ways of expressing their spirituality. Within such contexts, reconceptualizing and redressing hair are an important means of expressing one's identity as an individual and as a member of a social and a religious group, and negotiating the social and physical boundaries of the two, both in conformity and in resistance.

CHAPTER TWO

Self and Society Part I: The Social Dynamics of Hair

ELISHA P. RENNE

INTRODUCTION

The meaning of hair for individuals within any given society varies according to their particular social position, gender, race, and age, just as the meaning of hair more generally in a particular society may differ in others, in both place and time. Thus, the meaning of the long hair of a Tamil *sādhu* priest in Coimbatore, India, differs from the long hair of a village bride in Anatolia, Turkey, with the former suggesting the priest's celibate withdrawal from the sexual conventions of social life and the latter, the young bride's introduction to them.[1] For as anthropologist Carol Delaney observes, head, facial, and body hair—its cutting, growing, styling, and shaving—may have similar meanings in different societies, but the "specific cultural context" of these practices and related beliefs about hair are quite particular.[2] It is indeed, often unassuming, small details concerning hair that are revealing of underlying social mores and suggest the ways that changes in women's and men's hair practices and hairstyles are related to and reflective of larger historical and social processes. Hair is frequently considered unimportant, but "Une société nous dit beaucoup d'elle-même par ses franges" (A society tells us a good deal about itself by its fringes [my translation]).[3]

Arguments about whether the meaning of hair is best understood psychologically as a symbol of sexuality and/or sociologically as a sociocultural form have been raised in the anthropological literature. Edmund Leach's influential arguments about the phallic symbolism of "Magical Hair"(1958) are based on the separation of public from private symbolic motivation.[4] Like Leach, Paul Hershman (1974) relates hair's symbolic potency to a process of unconscious genital substitution but, in contrast to Leach, concludes that hair's social meanings may have other sources beyond the sexual.[5] Gananath Obeyesekere's study of female ascetics in India also concludes that hair symbolism may well be motivated by unconscious erotic urges but further expands the links between public symbolism and personal experience in the creation of cultural meaning: "Personal symbols must be related to the life experience of the individual and the larger institutional context in which they are embedded."[6]

Delaney's cultural anthropological approach reflects her ethnographic experiences living in a small rural village in Anatolia, Turkey. There she participated in everyday and ceremonial affairs, made friends, learned the language, and asked incessant questions, and wrote extensive fieldnotes. In other words, her knowledge of the social dimensions of this village was based on "being there."[7] Therefore, Delaney emphasizes the need to acknowledge that, "While hair cutting may be used cross-culturally to symbolize some relation to sexuality, the actual meaning of that relation cannot be deduced from universal 'facts,' but must be empirically investigated in specific cultural contexts."[8] This chapter takes to heart Delaney's admonition and applies it to the discussion of hair, self, and social identity in the modern age more generally. The aim is to explore the interconnectedness of hair's symbolic and material potency as a key strategy of social identification and organization in distinctive twentieth-century cultures. The chapter draws on a range of ethnographic evidence, from Burkina Faso, China, the Dominican Republic, England, Ghana, India, Nigeria, Poland, Singapore, Sri Lanka, Tanzania, and the United States, to explore themes concerning hair—of the body, of the face, and primarily of the head— and social identity, including discussions of sacred and taboo aspects of hair; hair and social organization; hair and rites of passage; and hair, power, and marginalization. Hair's "extraordinary" topicality, anthropologist Alf Hiltebeitel argues, cannot be reduced to polarized boundaries and differences; even if such tropes are strategic to the specificities of certain contexts, they intersect in a social body that is, "both a bounded construct and a fluid one."[9]

A focus on western hair styling and dressing predominates in other chapters in this volume. The aim of this chapter is not to counter or contest these with an alternative perspective on "other" traditional or ritualized practices that challenge the normative value system of western modernity, but to offer a wider conceptual and analytical framework for understanding the interconnectedness of the diverse examples and various thematic contexts explored in this collection. The emphasis here is on hair itself as a key strategy of social identification and organization wherever it is cut or grown, shaved, and styled, or covered, dressed, manipulated, or left untended. In this chapter, individual bodies across cultures, their hair, and its grooming are seen as subject to social conventions that reflect wider social values and beliefs about the moral world but that yet exist in a dialectical relationship between continuity and change. Indeed, as German sociologist and philosopher Georg Simmel theorizes, it is this continual tension between the acceptance of social demands and conventions and individual subversion of them that drives the formulation of an essentially contradictory modern social mentalité.[10]

For Simmel, "Fashion includes ... the charm of novelty coupled to those of transitoriness," but an individual must look "within" him- or herself and look "without" to society.[11] Individuals seeking to distinguish themselves from the larger society through fashionable hairstyles need to continually be alert to new possibilities in order to maintain structures of social distinction over time. The chapter's focus is not on the implications of hair-styling fashion and style trends per se as a motivational force in the discourse of modernity—but on the ways in which an individual's actions always reflect both personal inward-looking predilections and preferences and outward-looking social strictures. It is this interplay that defines social practice and suggests a dynamic by which group practices operate to buttress continuity but may also change over time. The many meanings that people attribute to hair, how they think about hair in relation to the body and hair's various treatments as an aspect of propriety and fashion, as well as the ways that hair is used in ritual practices, all provide "une fenêtre privilégiée pour humer l'air du temps et observer les mouvements des sociétés et de l'histoire" (a privileged window for assessing the mood of the times and observing the movements of societies and of history [my translation]).[12]

HAIR, THE BODY, AND SOCIAL IDENTITY

Across cultures, the social dynamic of conforming to the comforts and security of social conventions which relate to a group identity, be it age, gender, ethnic, religious, or national group, is consistently counterbalanced by individual idiosyncrasy and agency, a dialectical relationship of social identification, wherein:

> The individual is contained in sociation and, at the same time, finds himself confronted by it ... he exists both for society and for himself ... The "within" and the "without" between individual and society are not two unrelated definitions but define together the fully homogenous position of man as a social animal.[13]

Distinctive and changing hairstyles reflect shifts in family relations, social organization, and radical social and political changes relating to cultural concepts of gender, race, and ethnicity. The 1920s, the period that signifies the start of the modern age that this volume examines, witnessed considerable changes in social life in many parts of the world, related to the end of World War I and the return to civilian life of men and women exposed to both the horrors and the technological advances of modern warfare, but also to life elsewhere. This led to new techniques of the body reflected in,[14] for example, the desire for more streamlined, modern hairstyles for men and particularly for women. Thought by some historians to have been introduced by military nurses returning home after the war, the "bob" hairstyle was associated with the "new woman," who had a more active, urban life.[15] In the United States, new gendered ideals of fashionable modernity stimulated the expansion of beauty salons, where hair stylists needed to learn how to use new electrical equipment and new methods of dyeing and straightening hair. The confluence of social and technological change embodied in the production and consumption of such styles was associated with the mass production of the Ford Model T motor car (which began limited production in 1913 but by 1920 had produced over a million vehicles) and the construction of motorable highways; and the development of electric-generating plants and high-voltage transmission lines which provided urban residents with the luxury of light.

Other regions of the world have equally witnessed changes in hair-cutting practices, reflecting increasing global trade and mobility as well as varying forms of colonial rule, mainly by European governments, in many parts of Africa and Asia. The tension between those seeking to preserve local identities and related hair-styling practices in the face of western ways associated with modernity is a theme that has continued throughout the twentieth century and beyond, reflected in recent years in countries such as Iran and Turkey where majority Muslim populations have been encouraged to cover their head hair (women) or style their head and facial hair (men) in prescribed ways.[16]

Delaney's study of rural Turkish society in the 1980s, exemplifies how the specific treatments of hair during the lifetimes of women and men reflect continuities and shifts in social and cultural understandings of gender roles and relationships. As infants and young children, both boys and girls dress similarly and have their hair cut, although boys' hair is cut more often and girls' hair is often long and tangled. However, after puberty—around twelve years of age—boys' head hair is cut short, reflecting their future social control of their own bodies and sexuality as well as that of their wives and daughters. Girls' head hair, which continues to grow, suggests a luxuriant sexuality that must be covered with a headscarf. Delaney argues that the dangerous allure of young girls and women's uncovered hair (which should only be seen by their husbands) is hidden for fear of causing other men to lose their self-control.[17] The importance of women's hair and their sexuality for their husbands (and the perpetuation of his family) is underscored in the treatment of their head and body hair in preparation for marriage (Figure 2.1.1). Body hair is assiduously plucked, after which the bride's long hair (uncut since puberty) is washed and then combed and braided. The bride is then dressed in her wedding finery and brought to her husband's house. Forty days after the wedding, her braids are cut, signifying her new social role as wife and, it is hoped, new mother.

Men's hair continues to be cut short, although there are some distinctions made between men regarding beards. While young men may grow beards, socially they are proscribed from doing so as beards are the prerogative of older Anatolian village men who have performed the pilgrimage to Mecca. However, some young men, particularly in urban areas, have begun to wear beards as part of a more authentic Islamic identity and also as a counter to the Turkish government's support for western forms of dress and hairstyles. Similarly, while some urban Turkish elite women (particularly those who may

FIGURE 2.1.1: Turkey, late 1980s. Anatolian village bride, with long braids during marriage ceremony. Photo: Carol Delaney. From Delaney, "Untangling the Meanings of Hair in Turkish Society," *Anthropological Quarterly* 67, no. 4 (1994), p. 166. Reproduced by permission of Carol Delaney.

have studied abroad) do not cover their heads and wear western hairstyles, this practice is challenged by other younger urban elite women who seek to emphasize a Muslim, rather than western ("modern"), identity by covering their hair with headscarves.[18] Unlike the Turkish village women described by Delaney whose veiling reflects concerns about gender identity and sexuality related to being modest Muslims, urban university women wear headscarves not only to delineate gender but also to assert a proper moral order in the face of western influence.

HAIR AND SOCIAL ORGANIZATION

Thinking about hair and social identity in different societies clearly requires acknowledging hair as a "natural symbol," an inherent part of the human body but one that through societal actions communicates a range of meanings expressive of the social system in which it is found.[19] Such meanings are shaped by the social ideals passed down and cultural constraints imposed by the social body, while the social body in turn constrains the way the physical body is perceived. Thus, there is "a continual exchange of meanings between the two kinds of bodily experience so that each reinforces the categories of the other."[20] Many recent studies of African American treatments of hair evidence its importance in addressing racial discrimination and racism in US society.[21] The "Afro" hairstyle, where hair was left "nappy," that is, not straightened, and then carefully teased and trimmed into a halo of curls, emerged in the early 1960s as a marker of African American racial pride and beauty. The style became inextricably associated with the demand for equal rights in education, housing, and employment pioneered by prominent Black women, such as Odetta and Abbey Lincoln.[22] Wearing one's hair "naturally" came to symbolize a new Black American identity that made a visible connection with its African roots. The first Miss Black American beauty contest, which took place in August 1968 was won by Saundra Williams, who wore her crown "nestled in her Afro hairstyle."[23]

Nevertheless, the decision to adopt the style was not always easy; there were intergenerational conflicts and there was a gendered aspect to this style as well. A "natural" look was considered scandalous by many, often older, African American women and also by some men, who saw straightened hair as a symbol of racial dignity and good grooming. One woman described a girlfriend "whose mother actually went into fits when her daughter walked in with an Afro."[24] Many Black men rejected the American normative values associated with existing styles and adopted the Afro as part of their participation in the civil rights and Black Power movements of the late 1960s and early 1970s. However, the practical aspects of the style and its trimming and maintenance required adaptation rather than radical changes in masculine barbershop and personal hair-styling practices. Some older men still straightened (or "conked") their hair with oil and a hot metal comb (a style popularized in the1940s), but they were in the minority, and most men had their hair cut in conservative, closely trimmed hairstyles that could be gradually grown out, trimmed, and shaped into Afros. For many Black women, however, merely finding someone to cut one's hair was a challenge as African American beauty salons specialized in hair straightening. Some women went to barber shops but were teased by Black community members and referred to as "boys" or "mistakenly" referred to as "sir" by white shop owners.

Maxine Craig examines the bases for these attitudes as well as the rise and subsequent demise of Afro hairstyle fashions in favor of a return to relaxed/straightened wavy long hairstyles.[25] Craig's interviews with Black women and men in the early 1990s suggest a complex interplay between conformity to group expectations of racial propriety evidenced in straightened groomed hair and ideals of racial pride associated with Afro styles that rejected white European beauty ideals as the standard upon which all others were judged. However, this relationship between questions of identity and conforming and challenging strategies of hair styling is highly ambiguous. Many Black women, rather than rejecting the Afro, began to use an expanding range of improved hair products and experiment with fashionable, more flexible hairstyles and hair-related practices such as the recent fashion for styles of braided hair worn by African American women (inspired by African women's hairstyles) that equally reflect changing ideas about race and gender that ripple back and forth globally in the modern age.

In the city of Kathmandu, Nepal, for example, salons began to appear in the 1950s and 1960s, although they were initially associated with domestic space and catered for elite women consumers. Shrijana Ram, one of the first women in Kathmandu to have her hair cut and styled (this was in 1958 after having attended hairstyling school in New Delhi, India), used a room in her family house to establish her beauty salon. Ram provided a model for other women in Kathmandu to follow and by the early 1960s, public beauty salons began to appear and this affected another aspect of the social life of Kathmandu. Whereas hairstyles in the past had previously defined a Nepali woman's different class, caste, and ethnic identity, by the 1990s these visually distinctive identities based on hairstyles began to change as a more socially diverse range of Nepali women attended for styling and dressing and at times, hair cutting.[26] However, like the Afro, the adoption and adaptation of such styles cannot be understood as an unambiguous rejection of previous traditions symptomatic of intergenerational conflict. As Julia Thompson notes, "although Kathmandu women often looked to the outside world for new gender models and identities, these new forms are incorporated into their lives in distinctly Nepalese ways."[27] Thus, while younger women experiment with different styles of haircuts associated with western fashions, they have also retained aspects of long-standing, local hair-styling practices. For example, many—but not all—young brides continue to grow their hair long to suit their husbands and mothers-in-law, although this does not preclude elaborate and diverse wedding hairstyles.

The growth of western-style beauty parlors and the adoption of new hairstyles and hair-styling techniques that incorporate local ideas about beauty and propriety into new social identities have taken a different direction in the Dominican Republic. Here, demand for frequent attendance linked to racialized concepts of what constitutes "good" and "bad" hair (*pelo bueno* and *pelo malo*) has driven the widespread growth of beauty salons.[28] Gerald Murray and Martina Ortiz estimate that more than 55,000 salons are now operating in the Dominican Republic in contrast to the early 1960s when there were less than a hundred.[29] Based on interviews with women from different social backgrounds attending one hundred beauty salons in Santo Domingo (the country's capital) it was found that women categorized good hair as *pelo lacio* (lit. "limp hair"—straight, soft hair) associated with European/white women's hair; and bad hair as *pelo crespo* (lit. "crisp hair")—frizzy, hard hair) associated with African/Black women's hair. In the Dominican Republic, if a woman has "one drop" of European blood as evidenced by straight hair, she is identified as *blanco* (white). Thus, Dominican women, the vast majority of whom are "mixed race," go to salons weekly and use a range of hair straightening products to make sure that their hair is "good."[30] The valorization of this identity is related to the strained political and economic relations that exist between the Dominican Republic and Haiti, which are both located on the island of Hispanola.[31] However, as in Kathmandu

FIGURE 2.1.2: Painted barbershop storefront (*kinyozi*), Tanzania, advertising trendy, global hairstyles for men at the Classic of Paris Hair Cutting Salon. Photo: Harry Hook/Getty Images.

and the salons of the Black Atlantic, concepts of resistance and oppression related to racial or ethnic identity are ambiguously embodied; women's weekly visits to the salon might serve to guarantee a respectable "white" identity, but they also offer practitioners and consumers a discrete space of feminine expression. An expanding hair care and beauty industry provides a source of income for women hairdressers, reflects the growing economic independence of women who attend them, and clearly impacts on changing aspects of social organization.

Women's negotiation of modernization in relation to the opportunities for economic enterprise and independence associated with hairdressing consumption and practice is mirrored in the global expansion of barbershops for men. For example, in Tanzania, in East Africa, the demand for keeping one's hair trim has provided many underemployed young men with work. The ending of the socialist government of Julius Nyerere in 1985 opened up the country to a range of imported commodities that included radios, televisions, cosmetics, hair clippers, and barbering equipment. By the late 1990s, the city of Arusha, which is located near the border with Kenya, abounded with barbershops. As Brad Weiss observes, "it is no exaggeration to say that there were hundreds of barbershops in the center of the city alone."[32] These barbershops are easy to spot, with their displays of painted signboards indicating the range of hairstyles available to customers (Figure 2.1.2).[33] Yet the hairstyles depicted, for example, the shaved heads of the American basketball star, Michael Jordan, or the hip-hop artist, Tupac Shakur, are not often worn by the young male patrons of these shops, who prefer a short trimmed haircut. In fact, it could be dangerous for young men to wear shaved head hairstyles—punished by principals if they were in school or viewed with suspicion by police. Similarly, dreadlocks, referred to as the Rasta hairstyle, while fashionable among young African American men, could even result in young Tanzanians being arrested. The images displayed in the colorful signage rather suggest the global connections of barbershop owners, barbers, and their clients with the wider world and the extent to which Tanzanian men are cognizant of the context in which they live: a decline in government services, public schools, and jobs, and widespread exposure to western consumerism. Simply copying the ideal, Weiss argues, would conflate the aspirational fantasy of an alternative lifestyle with reality—a situation that underscores the "tension in the relationship between 'customary' and 'timely' hair fashion."[34] This continuing concern with prior hairstyles underscores the ways that social order is related to bodily conventions, which, despite changes associated with the West, persist and seek to maintain a prevailing moral cadence.

MATERIALIZATION OF POWER AND ITS SPIRITUAL DIMENSIONS: SOCIAL INCLUSION, PUNISHMENT, AND MARGINALIZATION

Tensions between local practices and imported (often, western) practices regarding the styling and management of men's and women's hair reflects its power as a cultural force invested with symbolic meanings that change over time and are related to wider shifts in systems of status recognition and ethnic and racial identification linked to social and political change. Yet for some who identify with timeless religious ideals or seek to associate with sacred spaces outside of everyday time during the performance of life-cycle rituals—that is, rites of passage—the meaning of hair and hair practice differs. Arnold van Gennep observes, "To cut the hair is to separate oneself from the previous world; to dedicate the hair is to bind oneself to the sacred world and more particularly to a deity or a spirit with whom kinship is established."[35] The ritual cutting or sacrificing of hair at a shrine may imply lifelong dedication to a deity, while the shorn heads of widows represent their separation from past marital existence. Hair may be both a source of spiritual power and a marker of it, and this power is embodied in an ambiguous range of growing, cutting, and shaving rituals.

For the Lobi of Burkina Faso, West Africa, "hair is considered to be the strongest part of an individual ... there is a close relationship between an individual's hair and his/her *thuú* (vital principle [soul]), the only part that subsists after death."[36] In southwestern Nigeria, children born with particular characteristics are treated as sacred beings with special rituals performed in their honor and given names that refer to these conditions; "Dada," one of the most well-known of these, is bestowed on children of either sex who are born with a full head of hair.[37] The hair of these babies, it is said, has been braided in heaven (before they were born); they are believed to bring wealth and good fortune to their parents as demonstrated in the praise poem (*oriki*) for Dada that begins with the phrase, "The one who wears a crown of money."[38] Unlike other infants whose hair is cut at naming ceremonies, Dada children's hair may be washed but not cut until they are older when special rituals may be performed to enable this procedure.[39]

In Sri Lanka, the appearance of uncut hair similarly has a spiritual meaning although this differs in terms of chronology. Rather than appearing at birth, the growth of long, matted locks are part of the process whereby priests and priestesses confirm their identity as devotees of the Hindu supreme lord, Isvara. These matted locks may not be cut during their lifetime as one woman explained:

I treat the locks as the god Isvara himself. I wash them and lime them when I bathe. I hold incense on them because I think it is not my thing, it is a thing of the god Isvara. I serve them. I don't permit anyone to touch them. People sometime ridicule me, but I tolerate it and tell them it's Isvara's gift to me.[40]

In this cultural context, long, matted hair no longer belongs to an individual but rather marks the presence of the deity himself. Elsewhere, however, it may have less socially positive meanings. Ainu men of Hokkaido, Japan with untrimmed beards and long hair were ostracized in the 1920s as "animal-like" and categorized by the Chinese anthropologist Chen Yinghuang as "ape-men, who had never left the lowest rungs of evolutionary ladder" (Figure 2.1.3).[41] Similarly, in the rural Cantonese village near the Hong Kong–Chinese border, destitute men with dirty, long hair and nails terrified villagers who avoided what they believed were the partially decomposed corpses or "hungry ghosts" of suicides or people who had died without children. Viewed as tabooed beings, even the passive presence of these men was considered dangerous; women turned their heads and refused to look at or speak to them and children were hidden from their view.[42]

The connection between the power to define social categories of people in relation to hair growing and hair-cutting techniques associated with social marginalization and even death may also be clearly seen in the treatment of those newly arrived at Nazi death camps such as Auschwitz, in Oświęcim, Poland, in the early 1940s (Figure 2.1.4). The heads of those who were to be used as camp laborers were immediately shorn. For those sent to the gas chambers, their hair was first cut from their lifeless heads by these laborers, who then moved it to curing rooms and finally packed it into bales in preparation for sale

FIGURE 2.1.3: Four elderly men wearing traditional Ainu garments sitting in foreground with large group of men wearing western-style coats and hats. Ainu village, Japan, 1931–1932. Carl Etter Collection, National Anthropological Archives, Smithsonian Institution, National Museum of Natural History.

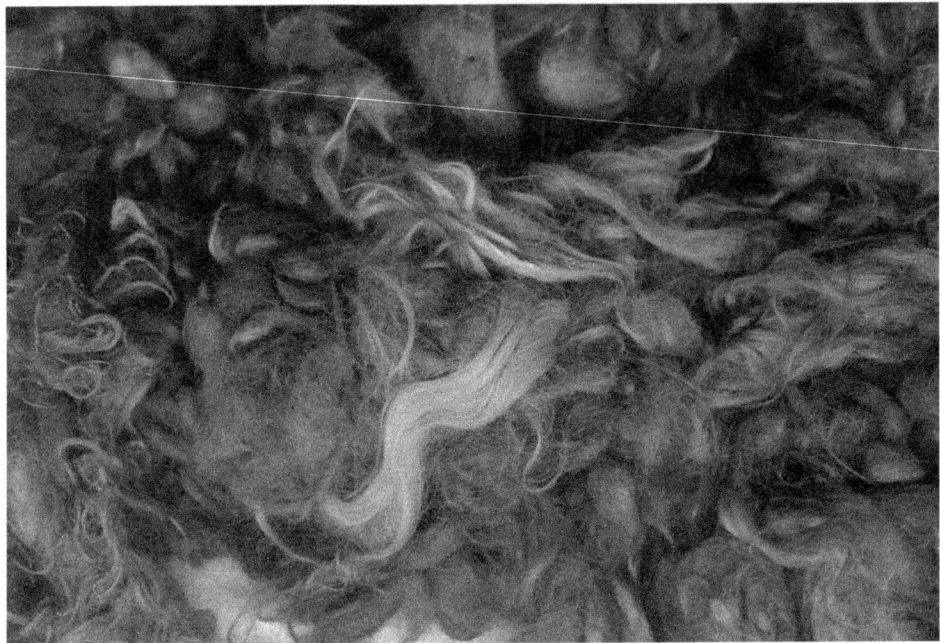

FIGURE 2.1.4: Hair collected at Auschwitz concentration camp. When the camp was liberated by the Red Army on January 27, 1945, they found piles of hair from the prisoners in the Auschwitz camp in Oświęcim, Poland. Photo: Spiegl/Ullstein Bild/Getty Images.

to German felt and textile manufacturers who used it to produce "thread, rope, cloth, carpets, mattress stuffing, lining stiffeners for uniforms, socks for submarine crews, and felt insulators for the boots of railroad workers."[43] Human hair was used as a vehicle to disempower and to dehumanize through "social death" by emphasizing the "thing-ness" of death camp victims who became a source of raw materials for manufactured products.

HAIR PRACTICE AND CULTURAL RITES OF PASSAGE

As may be seen in these examples of hair practices in relation to power, there may be negative consequences for those whose hair is seen as different from prevailing social ideals and practices. Yet there are singular events—specifically, birth, marriage, and death in the human life cycle—in which hair is treated in ways that intentionally distinguish those who are the center of these events—the newborn, the bride (and groom), and the dead (and close family members). Referred to as rites of passage,[44] these rituals follow a similar tripartite format, even as the cultural details that constitute each stage differ. The format includes firstly, the separation of the individual from a previous social status or group; secondly, a liminal period in which the individual is "betwixt and between" two different social identities; and finally, the incorporation of an individual into a new social group.

During the ritual for an expectant new mother in Lobi society, the mother's head hair is shorn to mark the official entry of herself and her child into her husband's family (patrilineage).[45] This ritual begins in the middle of the night; a woman from the husband's patrilineage (usually his sister) will come and spit cold water on the expectant mother's head, saying that she accepts the woman and her child—whether a girl or boy—for their family.[46] At dawn, an old woman from the husband's family will then shave the head of the mother-to-be; she takes the hair and hides it in the rafters of the family granary. By doing so, she separates the new mother from her own family and puts the mother and the child that she will bear under the protection of the husband's family.

Hair may also play an important role in facilitating birth, which can be thought of as a rite of passage for a newborn. In rural Malaysian society, during the liminal period after labor has begun but before the infant is born, if the infant's head is seen but appears to be stuck in the birth canal, the midwife may oil the mother's hair. She lifts strands of hair from the area around where the mother's fontanelle (the soft spot on a newborn's head) used to be, relating the birth of the child to the mother's own (successful) birth. As the midwife does so, she recites: "If this hair is slippery, you will slip right out; if this hair is not slippery, you will not slip out."[47] In instances when the child cannot be delivered by a midwife, *bomoh* (religious specialists) may be called to recite Qur'anic verses or Malay prayers; they may also loosen the woman's hair, just as they open windows and doors in the hope that these actions will facilitate the birth of the child into the world.[48]

Once a child is safely born, however, it may be some time before naming ceremonies or other rituals that officially celebrate the presence of the newborn into the human community are performed. Hindu parents continue to perform a ritual for young children called *mundan sanskar*, which includes shaving the child's head. *Mundan sanskar* literally means "shaving of the head ceremony" and it is performed when the child is between one and three years of age.[49] In India, a priest is consulted to determine an auspicious date and family and friends are invited to attend. When the day arrives, the mother or father holds the child on her or his lap while the priest recites a *mundan sanskar* mantra and partially shaves the child's head, which is completed by a barber ritual specialist. (In some families, the father cuts the hair.) The hair is then offered to a Hindu deity or to a sacred river such as the Ganges.[50] There are several reasons given for the performance of this tonsure ritual. Traditionally it was believed to cleanse the baby from its past life and prepare it for a new one. Some also believe that its performance will provide the infant with protection, both physically and spiritually. In some parts of India, however, in the case of a special child whose parents had difficulties in conception, the child's hair is not cut or combed as a way of making it unattractive and thus providing extra protection against the evil eye of those who would wish to harm it.[51]

The hair of new brides in many parts of the world also receives special treatment to mark their new social status as married women. In the confluence area of central Nigeria, Bunu Yoruba women practice a form of traditional marriage called *gbe obitan* ("bringing a wife") that entails a ritual and that requires a special hairstyle to separate a young woman from her unmarried age-mates (Figure 2.1.5). During a two-hour period, the bride's hair is plaited by her age-group members into the tiny braids worn only by new wives in the practice known as *e dirun obitan*. When the braiding is completed, many small safety pins are attached to the braids at the back of the head, which women say makes the bride look shiny and new.[52] This hair arrangement remains during the transitional three months when the bride has been taken to her husband's house but has not been entirely separated from her own family. After a final ritual return to her family's house that concludes in her return to her husband's house, she may remove the safety pins from her hair; the pins are then distributed to other married women in the village.

FIGURE 2.1.5: Preparation for the performance of the traditional Bunu Yoruba marriage ritual known as *gbe obitan*. The bride's hair will be woven into many tiny braids (*e dirun obitan*), which are then decorated with safety pins to make her look new and shiny. Janet Ogunibi, Apaa-Bunu, December 1987. Photo: E.P. Renne. Reproduced by permission of E.P. Renne.

In Singapore, young urban brides must also have their hair elaborately styled as part of a marriage ritual that includes a series of formal studio photographs (Figure 2.1.6).[53] These bridal photographs, taken by professional photographers, conform to a certain formula: the bride and groom appear in sumptuous costumes and with flawless hairdos, posed in front of carefully prepared background scenery either in a studio setting or at an exterior scenic site. The uncomfortable staging of the photography session, which occurs

FIGURE 2.1.6: A Chinese bride and groom pose for a professional photographer. Photo: Alto/James Hardy/Getty Images.

several months before the actual marriage ceremony, is an integral part of the marriage process. It is a time when the bride's spectacular coiffure and heavy makeup as well as the groom's special hair treatment and dress separate them from their everyday lives, transforming them into a film-star-like couple who "celebrates the ideal modern ideology of romantic love and imagines the triumph of couple-hood over family."[54]

Distinctive hair treatments frequently mark the different stages of an individual's social life, including the end of an earthly existence. Mourners in Lobi society (in Burkina Faso), particularly widows, observe a number of hair-related rituals. While her husband's body is laid out, the widow's head is completely shaved. During the period between burial and a second funeral ceremony, her hair must remain uncut reflecting ideas about the presence of her husband's spirit. It is only after the mourning period that her hair is again shaved off, marking her new status distinct from her husband's spirit.[55] In Ghana, to the south of Burkina Faso, family members of one large ethnic group, the Asante, shave their heads when mourning a prominent or royal family member.[56] In this case, their hair is put in a specially designed basin positioned near the deceased person's grave.

In 1967, Roy Sieber visited Nsoko (a village in west central Ghana) where, in a passageway opposite the deceased queen mother's shrine, he viewed a basin filled with hair from the shaved heads of relatives mourning her death (Figure 2.1.7).[57] By depositing their hair in this basin, family mourners both marked their respect for the passing of their mother and left their hair in a place where it would be safe from those who might use it for nefarious purposes.

FIGURE 2.1.7: Funeral basin filled with the hair of family mourners for the Nsoko queen mother, who had recently died. Nsoko, Brong Ahafo, Ghana, 1980. Photo: Raymond Silverman. Reproduced by permission of Raymond Silverman.

CONCLUSION

Hair provides a unique perspective for examining processes whereby ideas about self and social identity are constituted and changed, in relation to both specific and shifting social, cultural, political, economic, and historical contexts. The social use of hair practices across cultures exposes common concerns—about gender and sexuality, about race and ethnicity, about power, social inequality, and political disfranchisement. In societies such as rural Turkey, the valorization of men's authority and their control of women play out in the management of hair. Village men's hair is cut short and controlled; additional facial hair such as mustaches are forbidden while only older men may wear beards to reinforce a social hierarchy based on age and achievement; women's long hair, like their sexuality, must be covered and controlled. Alternately, young men's long hair, beards, and mustaches signified the countercultural social mores of the West in the 1960s; while women's growing socioeconomic autonomy and sexual freedom, as well as demands for gender equality, were reflected in very short hairstyles, which both downplayed gender distinctions and signaled a playful sexual attractiveness emphasizing youthfulness as a challenge to traditional feminine ideals.

Across cultures, the development of beauty salons has similarly influenced hair-styling practices that embody individual and collective responses to and demands for wider social change. Hair and hair-related practices are indicative of racial identity and social hierarchies relating to race, as in the Dominican Republic where women's straightened hair provides them with "good hair," the limp, straight hair associated with Europeans. Equally, some Europeans also evaluated social groups on the basis of hair type, notably with the rise of fascism where blond Germans were elevated as an idealized Aryan race and dark-haired Jews denigrated as almost subhuman.[58] This stigmatization was taken to the extreme in Nazi concentration camps, when the shaved hair of camp laborers and those destined for the gas chambers was turned into a commodity for sale, obliterating the intimate relationship of hair to individuals.

The tension between individuals' desires for new styles and social group conventions often embody intergenerational conflicts in terms of not only gender, but also race and ethnicity. This dynamic was clearly seen in the discussion of young African American women's decision to wear their hair as Afros in a natural style, while their mothers often despaired of this improper hair practice. Yet their actions in the 1960s and 1970s led to the expansion of other possibilities associated with the civil rights movement and also to a related diversity of traditional and contemporary hair styling practices. This dialectical relationship between individuals pushing for change and the larger social group seeking to maintain the status quo suggests how the dynamics of conformity and transgression in society and in the treatment of hair may occur simultaneously. When Shrijana Rana opened up a beauty salon in her house in the late 1950s in Kathmandu where some Nepali women had their hair cut, there was resistance from older women who saw such behavior as improper and disrespectful. Yet by the 1990s, the demands of younger women for shorter hairstyles led to a compromise of sorts. Although young unmarried women frequently cut their hair, they let it grow before their marriages so as not to challenge traditional gender ideals but also indulged in elaborate hair-styling practices.

Hair may be styled, managed, and manipulated in ways that underscore specific social identities, but hair practices and the operational borders between those they define may also be quite muted. What is significant is a shared impulse to manage, style, and groom human body, head, and face hair to communicate social meanings that locate bodies as individuals in different relationships with particular groupings. Indologist Patrick Olivelle stresses the dialectical nature of hair symbolism: socially significant meanings pertaining to the manipulation of hair originate in a multiplicity of sources, while any one symbol may simultaneously contain multiple meanings and, moreover, acquire new meanings "that may go beyond and thereby transform the earlier meaning."[59] For Olivelle, hair symbolism impels cultural action through a generative "grammar" of hair practices as tight or as loose as the material practices it defines and describes. This chapter has sought to explore hair-related social practices beyond differences between East and West, traditional and modern. Many practices have changed in the world since the 1920s, but the use of hair both in asserting a new individual identity and in maintaining aspects of an older basis of social organization persists.

Self and Society Part II: Fashioning Social Hair

ROYCE MAHAWATTE

In May 1920, the *Saturday Evening Post* published F. Scott Fitzgerald's "Bernice Bobs Her Hair."[1] This short story tells of the awkward Bernice's visit to her more confident cousin Marjorie, as they both try to make their way in society that season. Bernice is described as "pretty, with dark hair and high color, but ... no fun on a party"; nonetheless, after some strict instruction from her cousin, she soon becomes a social sensation.[2] Her newfound popularity arises in no small part from her carefully rehearsed line that she will soon cut her long hair into a bob—a revolutionary short hairstyle favored by a fashionable avant-garde and the so-called "new woman." Considered a daring act by her new friends, Bernice's "tonsorial intentions were strictly dishonorable," her threat was only an attention-seeking ploy.[3] The ploy works of course, especially with Warren McIntyre, the previously spurned but constant devotee of Marjorie. Indeed, Bernice ends up being in such demand at dances that Marjorie begins to feel upstaged and while they are out with friends one day in the town, she coolly calls her cousin's bluff, demanding that Bernice makes good her threat. Caught up in a tide of social anxiety, peer pressure, and bravado, Bernice walks into the barbershop, asks the barber to cut her hair, and emerges with it hanging "in lank lifeless blocks on both sides of her suddenly pale face. It was ugly as sin—she had known it would be ugly as sin" (Figure 2.2.1).[4]

With her aura of danger gone, not only do the boys lose interest but Bernice is also asked not to attend an important dance to take place the following day. Realizing her jealous cousin has tricked her, she winces as Marjorie "tossed her own hair over her shoulders and began to twist it slowly into two long blonde braids."[5] Bernice immediately decides to leave town that night, but before she goes she steals into the sleeping Marjorie's room and shears off her cousin's braids close to her neck. On the way to catch the last train she throws the plaits into Warren's front porch "where they landed with a slight thud." Her final words are: "scalp the selfish thing!"[6]

The bob in this story is a rich symbol for exploring social and cultural change in the early twentieth century. The hairstyle has unstable meanings, as both cousins discover. The cutting of Bernice's hair into a short and increasingly popular style would seem like the logical extension of a young woman's rise in society in 1920. Indeed, other contemporary writers with more faith in the social system might have presented a woman cutting her hair in this way as a liberating act. To quote historian Caroline Cox, the style exemplified "everything believed to be modern about the New World Order after the

FIGURE 2.2.1: *Saturday Evening Post*, May 1, 1920. "Bernice Bobs Her Hair" appears in this issue. Saturday Evening Post/Wikipedia Commons/Public Domain.

carnage of the First World War."[7] Fitzgerald, in contrast, uses the act of "bobbing" of both girls as a way of exploring the volatile economy of modern female beauty at a time of radical social change. Unfortunately for the naïve and gauche Bernice, the bob did not catch on as a mainstream hairstyle in the United States until the mid-1920s. In the story, set in a town that was not quite eastwards enough to be free of its provincial restrictions, short hair was still socially a step too far. The cutting of Bernice's hair becomes a spectacle, like a public deflowering, a violent act of psychosexual mutilation designed by Marjorie to diminish the competition. Yet it is an act that transforms Bernice; her retaliatory bobbing of Marjorie's hair is an act of independence and her most decisive in the whole story.

Analyzing a short story in this way could be viewed as an intellectual contrivance, but Fitzgerald's exploration of contemporary social mores demonstrates how responses to hair can become a significant feature of cultural criticism. The events in the narrative are propelled not only by emotional responses. For a writer like Fitzgerald, who came to vividly explore the relationship between social climbing and precarity, resistance and conformity, the fashioned social body is a crucial literary tool. The cutting and styling of hair had become an index of sociocultural change in several quite complex ways. Change was not, perhaps, always marked so dramatically as in Bernice's visit to the barber and the resulting aftermath. From this period, however, hair fashions and social identities became linked to each other via a number of developing institutions and technologies, which in turn, as they advanced, brought about sociocultural change on the body further.

Styles themselves are ephemeral, so it is understandable that cultural historians have often overlooked the significance of fashioned hair to the construction of social meaning, though much work has been done from an anthropological perspective.[8] The aim of this chapter is not to give a chronology of hairstyles and haircuts, work largely been done by Caroline Cox and Richard Corson.[9] Instead, the critical impetus is to explore some of the major features of hair fashion in the modern age, following fashion theorist Joanne Entwistle, as "situated bodily practices," that is, an outcome of both social factors and individual actions embodied in forms of body adornment.[10] Entwistle suggests, such an approach

> requires moving between, on the one hand, the discursive and representational aspects of dress and the way the body/dress is caught up in relations of power, and on the other, the embodied experience of dress and the use of dress as a means by which individuals orientate themselves to the social world.[11]

Fashion is a material and bodily experience predicated on temporal and spatial relationships. Adopting a particular fashion or style can bring eligibility or exclusion to or from social groups. Historian Gilles Lipovetsky describes fashion as one of "the organizing principles of modern collective life" and his view can also allow us to see the fashioning of hair as a structuring social principle.[12] Innovations in hair styling and styling technologies—bobbing, the use of peroxide dyes, the mechanization of barbering, curling and straightening techniques—are explored in this chapter as situated practices through which the self, the body, and social and economic forces came to act together to embody and define the modern age.

HAIR AS A SOCIAL METAPHOR

As a part of our bodies, hair is a site of meaning and a place of conflict. It intersects with our biological identity, and hence what we consider to be "natural." At the same time, and perhaps more importantly, hair has to conform to cultural standards. Arguably, the most common way that we understand social hair is in terms of how it is cut, styled, and maintained. This is the first concept of that which I would like to introduce: an understanding of fashionable hair as a metaphor for both the self and the effect of social norms. The work of anthropologist Mary Douglas is useful here because it articulates the complex position of the body as being part biological and part social organisms shaped by social forces. In her groundbreaking study *Purity and Danger*, Douglas presents the body as:

a model which can stand for any bounded system. Its boundaries can represent any boundaries which are threatened or precarious ... We cannot possibly interpret rituals concerning excreta, breast milk, saliva and the rest unless we are prepared to see in the body a symbol of society, and to see the powers and dangers credited to social structure reproduced in small on the human body.[13]

Douglas explores the interrelationship that exists between the lived experience of the body and its function as a natural symbol of selfhood. The boundaries between the physical and the social operate as a set of ordered relations constantly under threat of contamination from "matter out of place," uncleanness and dirt, that is, bodily waste products, which must be ritually controlled.[14] Although it is perceived as being potentially less dangerous than other bodily fluids, hair represents a problematic emanation: "every head hair has a disgusting character even when it seems to be in place."[15]

In western society this concept of "pollution" according to Douglas is largely a matter of aesthetics, hygiene, or etiquette which "only becomes grave in so far as it may create social embarrassment" and thus becomes subject to social sanctions: "contempt, ostracism, gossip, perhaps even police action."[16] The threat of pollution is managed at two levels: firstly, instrumental—influences that reinforce social pressures and uphold moral values and social rules defined by beliefs in the dangers of contagion; secondly, expressive—the "symbolic load" that such beliefs carry with them.[17] So it would follow that the fashioning of social hair, in most of its forms, stands to correct the metaphorically precarious and threatening nature of the social and physical body's boundaries, or at least managing such anxieties. Hair is ordered, tied down, and treated so that it lies flat against the head. It is often cut so that it gives the impression of structure and balance and hence an ordered "situation." Curls are brought together and defined, as opposed to being loose and "frizzy" or kept short or tied up. Even when hair is permed curly, or styled to look unkempt as with the "grunge" fashions of the 1990s, its presentation invariably follows rules of balance and structure in some way to reinforce notions of cultural intervention rather than biological heritage.

In *Natural Symbols* Douglas wrote explicitly about not just the contemporary social politics of hair, but also about the culture that surrounded it in the late 1960s:

> Shaggy hair, as a form of protest against resented forms of social control, is a current symbol in our own day ... Take the general run of stockbrokers, of academics, stratify the professional sample by age; be careful to distinguish length of hair from unkempt hair; relate the incidence of shagginess in hair to sartorial indiscipline ... Those which are aiming at the centre top, public relations, or hair dressing, those which have long been fully committed to the main morality, chartered accountants and the law, they are predictably against the shaggy option and for the smooth drink, hair style, or restaurant. Artists and academics are potentially professions of comment and criticism on society: they display a carefully modulated shagginess according to the responsibilities they carry. But how shaggy can they get? What are the limits of shagginess and bodily abandon?[18]

Of course, Douglas' reading of hair is of its time —in the current cultural climate there is an increasing "professionalization" of academia, while there is a rise in "alternative" financial services that might allow for more countercultural hairstyles. The nature of hair symbolism is clearly not fixed, nor is it exactly fetishized; it is relational. Hair stands for different things at different times: the self, volition, or sexuality, for example. How we fashion hair is a representation of how we deal with these abstractions of the self in relation to the group. The potency of "natural symbols" lies in the continual exchange of meanings that exist between physical bodies constrained by social conventions and the physical conditions that in turn sustain a particular view of society. Representations of straight and curly hair in the modern age often emphasize or manipulate the metaphor of apparent order and chaos. Race concepts clearly also have a particular bearing on the dichotomy of Douglas's notion of the "main morality": hair that is raced as nonwhite, particularly the hair of Black people, has often been placed outside the culturally constructed criteria that Douglas alludes to.

Because hair is physically "rooted" in the biological body, it is frequently drawn upon to provide explanations for arbitrarily constructed social bodies and what they mean. One thing that is clear is that *actual* natural hair—hair that is uncut, uncombed, and unwashed—is a social impossibility. Hair that is natural in this way indicates circumstances such as poverty or illness, religious or subversive beliefs, and attitudes or various formations of "otherness" that are invariably viewed as socially excluding. Hair we describe as "natural" has to display qualities deemed to be natural, or at least *representative* of it. Within Douglas's powerful dialectic, the social fashioning *of* hair and fashions *in* hair are not a matter of mere cause and effect. Concepts of the innate (biological) and the superficial (cultural) are interrelated in ritualized hair practices in western culture that took on a new salience with the technological and social changes of the twentieth century.

"... AS NATURAL AS ANY BLONDES"

In the 1920s, the advent of the bob, as we have seen, signified a radical break from gender ideals that for centuries equated long hair with feminine beauty and morality.[19] Bernice's bobbing at the barbershop equally marked an evolutionary point in the history of modern hair styling and grooming practices. Traditional hair "dressing" skills became increasingly redundant and only barbers were thought to possess the relevant skills and "artistry" to successfully cut hair. Hundreds of women waited in line to be clipped by the famous New York barber Signor Raspanti—hailed as "the high priest of bobdom ... [who] turned bobbing into a science."[20] Barbers such as Raspanti sought to capitalize on the trend and established dedicated ladies' hair salons, progressively offering a range of styling techniques and beauty products aimed at a female clientele to "offset the perceived harshness and potentially threatening masculinity" of the merely short-cut look.[21] The radical social and political agenda that having one's hair bobbed so potently symbolized was defused through more "natural" strategies of feminine artifice such as "Marcel,"[22] and progressively "permanent" waving, and in particular, the development of hydrogen peroxide as a reliable bleaching agent.

Stephen Gundle and Ellen Tremper have discussed hair bleaching techniques used on Hollywood actresses in the early 1930s and the emergence of glamour as a new media aesthetic.[23] Orthochromatic film stock was insensitive to yellow and so back-lit hair colored white blonde shot particularly well, bringing out an ethereal halo effect and making pronounced contrasts between darks and lights dramatically apparent.[24] The glamour of the "platinum blonde," to use the popular moniker for screen star Jean Harlow was packaged in narratives that appealed to a new generation of cinemagoers. Harlow's otherworldly beauty was a key element of her promotional persona but was countered by screen roles concerned with social climbing: the day-to-day experiences of modern aspirations and the role that smart talking and sexual politics might play in the achievement of them

(Figure 2.2.2).²⁵ If the natural blonde was an indicator of purity and unworldliness, the peroxide blonde was an indicator of a modern woman who could metaphorically manage her physical and social "situation" by means of the latest beauty treatments.

Jean Harlow more than any other star at this time was a product of what Gundle defines as "studio alchemy," that is, the ability to mingle illusion and reality. Rather than just turning them into god-like beings, the studio system synthesized "natural" beauty and artifice, with "the most obvious point of synthesis being hairstyling."²⁶ The standardized aspect of Harlow's image—colored hair, drawn eyebrows, false eyelashes, deep mascara and lipstick, white satin dress, and mask-like retouched skin—was "always more important than her individuality."²⁷ Even in films where Harlow wore her hair dark or red, there is a sense that the color change is a playful manifestation of the screen star's volition.²⁸ Contemporary female cinemagoers were different from their mothers and also

FIGURE 2.2.2: Publicity photo of Jean Harlow, 1930s. Photo: studio (Celebrities Stars). Wikimedia Commons/Public Domain.

from the fashionable aristocrats that graced the society pages: they were a new class of consumers for whom self-determination via artifice was both natural and achievable.[29]

Modern ideals of "natural" blonde hair moved rapidly from being a symbol of cinematic fantasy to a routine styling practice requiring care, repetition, and of course the purchasing of products. Blurring the boundaries between nature and culture, an article in the *Washington Post* of 1935, titled "Blondee Loveliness needs Great Care," opens with a conversation between three women, a blonde, a redhead, and a brunette, in which each desires the color of the other. The blonde, however, has the most fatigue, albeit feigned, when it comes to discussing her hair-care regime, declaring, "If you only knew the time and labor I spent on being blonde!" Her perplexed friends ask whether she is a natural blonde. She responds, "A natural blonde? Oh yes, as natural as any blondes ..."[30] The article delivers beauty tips for the maintenance of blonde hair, outlines various "natural" hair treatments as alternatives to the continuous use of damaging bleaching tints, and suggests procedures to lighten the skin to complement, or help compensate for a lack of, the desired blonde attributes. The reader is advised to select from "natural" bleaches such as cucumber juice and cornmeal and buttermilk, or to use ready-made skin bleaches, but, the author cautions, "follow the instructions carefully."

It is impossible to look at this emerging culture of chemical hair-lightening practices without considering how the white raced body was constructed in this period and the "white supremacist" bias inherent to screen culture (Figure 2.2.3).[31] The *Washington Post* article is not exceptional in linking hair bleaching to the bleaching of skin to conform to a cultural construction of beauty that always had the ideal of the "white" body as its objective. Such practices made a "white phenotype" in order to emphasize or even enhance a presumed "white genotype."[32] Set against the rise of fascism in Europe, the blonde-haired and blue-eyed ideal in the 1930s was a marker of racial superiority connected in the United States to anxieties about immigration to America from southern Europe, and the increased mobility of some African Americans.

Race concepts, like those of gender, have a particular bearing on the moral dichotomy Douglas poses in her theories of "natural symbolism." Natural symbols are socially created meanings that naturalize particular understandings of the human body in a binary structure of physical and social inclusion and exclusion. The idealization of white raced blonde hair was correlative to the production and consumption of new and improved chemical hair relaxants and other technological innovations for straightening Black hair and bleaching skin to conform to white normative values.[33] The idea of "race" is arguably the most extensive bodily metaphor of the modern age. The surface of the body, and hair in particular, articulates an *all-pervading* and historically hierarchical situation originating in part in the colonial encounter.[34] Most relevant for us here, however, is the idea that beauty follows power, or at least subscribes to its narratives. Michel Foucault did not write about fashion, let alone the styling of hair, but his ideas of "governmentality" can be richly applied to the motivations that play a part in hair and its management as embodied social practices.[35]

HAIR LENGTH AND GOVERNMENTALITY

Foucault's idea of a disciplinary society was exemplified by the image of the nineteenth-century prison, "the Panoptican,"[36] an institutional structure, where inmates were under constant surveillance by guards in a central tower, who in turn were observed by the

FIGURE 2.2.3: "The Secret of Lovely White Hair." Supplement to *My Story: The Evan Williams' Shampoo*, published by The Evan Williams Co. Ltd., London, ca. 1920s. Author's own collection.

inmates.[37] Under this "carceral" system of visibility, power, and knowledge, subjects were socialized and order maintained through both the obligation to self-regulate and the formation of group identities through shared disciplinary practices that align "docile bodies" to discourses of institutional power in the operation of a "normative gaze."[38] Social institutions, be they formal or informal, harness the Foucauldian concept of "biopower," that is, the imposition of formally and informally coded practices that need to be repeated with both frequency and with regularity as a function of social forces and obligations: for example, the cutting and styling of hair using chemical agents, clipping machines, heat treatments, and ways of setting hair, of braiding hair, of applying hair pieces, or shaving or plucking facial hair. Rather than being simply an expression of individuality or personality, hairstyles enforce group identity through systems of surveillance and disciplinary practices through which social bodies are both watched and problematized.[39]

Returning to "Bernice Bobs Her Hair" we can see how hair stands as an important marker of the disciplinary regimes of self-regulation and group identity. Small-town conformity dictated that women's hair must be controlled so that bobbing one's hair had metaphorical and more material implications. Asked if she believed in bobbed hair, Bernice responded gravely, "I think it's unmoral."[40] The idea of bobbing offered a fantasy of freedom from the social and physical boundaries that long hair embodied, but once physically enacted Bernice's social boundaries become precarious: "It was quite a new look for Bernice and it carried consequences."[41] And, as Marjorie makes clear to Bernice, she has other hair that also requires both constant surveillance and discipline:

> You never take care of your eyebrows. They're black and lustrous, but by leaving them straggly they're a blemish. They'd be beautiful if you'd take care of them in one-tenth the time you take doing nothing. You're going to brush them so that they'll grow straight ... When a girl feels that she's perfectly groomed and dressed she can forget that part of her. That's charm. The more parts of yourself you can afford to forget the more charm you have.[42]

The upkeep and management of hair is a disciplining process for these young women, for which docility or its rejection has rewards and penalties. The Foucauldian docile body is a governable body and haircuts—be they raced or gendered; military or civilian; avant-garde or mainstream—encourage social order. In the twentieth century, this was particularly important at a time when old social boundaries were becoming more blurred. To style one's hair is to bring the self into a social process. The end results are various, as the naïve Bernice discovered, but the act of fashioning social hair is always a metaphor for how closely people are associated with the center or periphery of power.

Fashioned hair as both a mass movement and as a socializing practice owed much to what Foucault defines as new "technologies of self" that in this context accompanied innovations in the cutting and styling of hair in the twentieth century. Sleek, short hair for both men and women signified a generational desire to move away from the past and incorporated new demands for political emancipation and contemporary anxieties about health and hygiene in a fashionable, pared down design aesthetic. However, while in many ways emancipatory in motivation, the spatial reorganization of modern hairdressing along gender lines also reinforced the boundaries of patriarchal authority. The introduction of the Wahl electric hair clipper in 1919 allowed not just precision cutting and clipping, but also speeded up the process to conveyor-belt-like rapidity. Linked to varying modern practices associated with masculine self-presentation in the mid-twentieth century, particularly in the United States, a clean-shaven face and short clipped hair enforced narrow ideas of maleness, values of efficiency, cleanliness, and, of course with growing nationalism, military prowess (Figure 2.2.4).[43]

Barbers could cut men's hair with ease and, most importantly, into a standardized style that could be easily and endlessly repeated. While there were variations between styles, especially for men of different ages and occupation, in the United States the "buzz cut" (the name was taken from the characteristic buzzing sound of the vibrating blades) became characteristic of hegemonic, and military, masculinity and the incorporation of the American male body into processes of institutionalized embodiment. The haircut initiated young men into American male adulthood. The introduction of conscription in America from 1940 to 1973 meant that most young men who came of age at these times, including rock 'n' roll legend Elvis Presley, would have encountered governmental measures to incorporate their bodies into a disciplinary, normative bodily structure. In

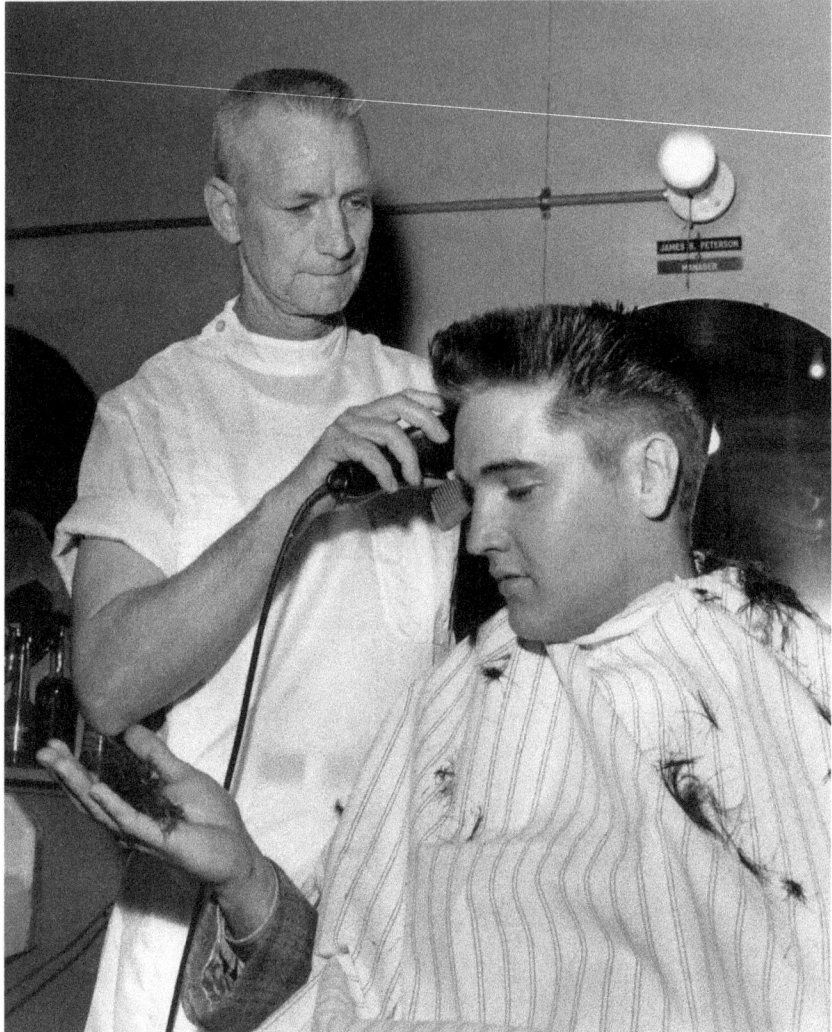

FIGURE 2.2.4: Elvis Presley receives a crew cut on his first full day as a member of the US Army. Photo: Bettmann/Getty Images.

return, docility conferred group membership. Barber's shop boards advertised haircuts in serried ranks that emphasized not just the regularity of the style, but also the pull of social conformity. Whether the clipped hair of the American male in institutional contexts can be seen as a strictly "fashioned" one is semantic. This was fashioning as social control.

CURLING AND STRAIGHTENING

The disciplinary role of fashioned hair in the construction of social bodies can be explored often in unlikely places. The role of hair styling in child's play and in doll manufacturing in particular reveals some interesting assumptions. Dolls, "can tell us much about the creation and significance of self-image in the context of group identities … toys become the vehicles for play through which different aspect of the world can be encountered."[44] In his piece on "Toys," published in 1956, literary theorist Roland Barthes tried to unpack the social role of play and the social conditioning that underlay the contemporary design of toys, for instance:

> dolls which urinate; they have an oesophagus, one gives them a bottle, they wet their nappies; soon, no doubt, milk will turn to water in their stomachs. This is meant to prepare the little girl for the causality of house-keeping, to "condition" her to her future role as mother.[45]

Teenage fashion dolls targeted at young girls became an important part of gendered play after World War II. Of interest here are the ways in which these dolls, in particular "Barbie" manufactured by Mattel since 1959, encouraged children to style, but also sometimes cut, apply wigs to, or change the length of their dolls' hair. Girls' grooming toys "enjoy perennial popularity, from fashion dolls to ponies with manes for combing."[46] However, the introduction of teenage fashion dolls with hair-styling features marked the intersection between children's cultures and the desire to style and fashion hair according to particular normative ideals in new ways.[47]

Reflecting popular hair styling trends was always a key part of updating Barbie's image. In the 1960s, Barbie sported a "bubble cut" like Jackie Kennedy's,[48] and Mattel market-tested a new "Mod" doll "Francie" (Barbie's fifteen-year-old British cousin) with her hair in a straight, flicked-back style to complement her new wardrobe, "stripes, paisley prints, London lace, and granny gowns."[49] In 1968, the *Washington Post* ran a feature positively discussing the politics and styling of the "Afro" and concluded: "Whatever the fashion outcome, all of these women know that they will express themselves instead of following the fashion standards."[50] In the same year, the first Black Barbie was released: "Colored Francie," a Black version of the Francie doll line. This doll had the same features, hairstyle, and body as the raced white version, but while the raced white Francie line sold well, the Black raced one did not. This was most likely because of being called "colored" on the packaging, which was clearly regressive during the rise of the civil rights movement. At the end of 1968, Mattel replaced her with a new Black fashion doll called Christie, who in her first incarnation supported a short, quasi-afro-come-bubble-cut while subsequent lines had long straight hair. This doll sold well.[51]

Mattel in 1981 explicitly responded to a desire to style and restyle dolls' hair with the introduction of "Magic Curl Barbie" who came with long, tightly curled hair that became straighter (although still wavy) when a "Magic Mist" solution was applied and rigorously brushed in. The doll belongs to the "superstar" generation of post-1977 Barbie dolls (see for example Figure 2.2.5) and marked the revival and revamping of the toy, after a mid-1970s decline in quality and sales.

Incorporating the fashionable dynamics of curling and styling into gendered *and* racialized play, the Magic Curl range of dolls was manufactured in two forms: a raced white one that was the most common and, a more rare, raced Black doll. Magic Curl Barbie looked very different from most of the Barbie dolls introduced over the previous four years and sold in the major territories: in both raced forms, Barbie had curly hair.

In the television advert for the white raced Magic Curl doll, one of the two girls pictured playing states that Ken, Barbie's boyfriend, likes straight hair while Barbie likes her hair curly. The magic mist solution is applied and Barbie's hair—and metaphorically Barbie herself—is "straightened out," at least temporarily. Barbie, of course, can move between the two styles as she chooses, presenting racial and gender identification as a

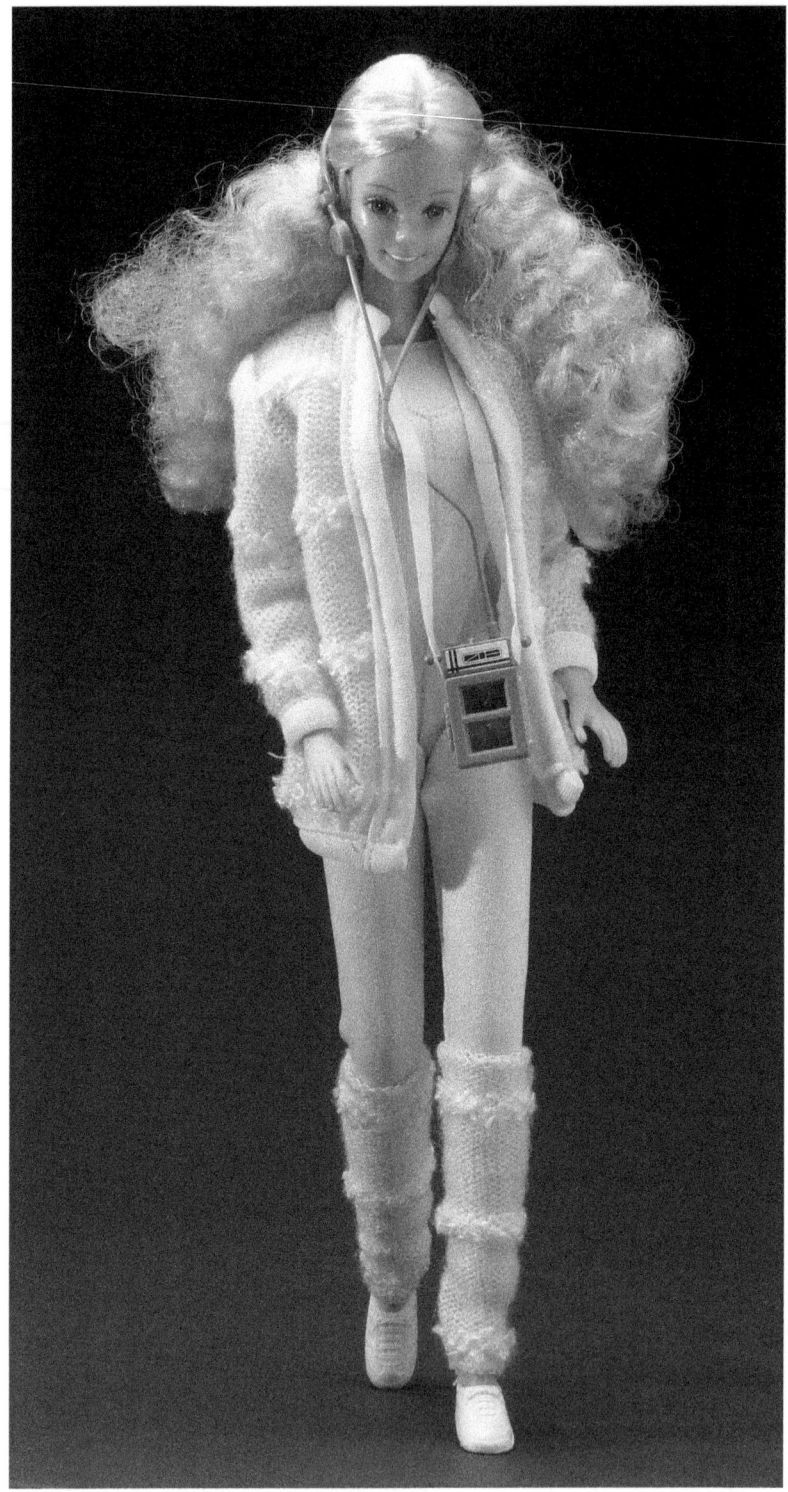

FIGURE 2.2.5: Barbie Doll, ca. 1970s. Science and Society Picture Library/Getty Images.

FIGURE 2.2.6: Barbie Doll, ca. 1970s. Science and Society Picture Library/Getty Images.

"magical process" of choice and mobility, played out through hair fashions. However, read against the range of scholarly opinions on the styling of African American hair in the twentieth and twenty-first centuries, with regard to the Black raced Magic Curl doll the issue of hair straightening in the late 1970s is more complex.[52] In a country with a history of slavery, this form of disciplinary hair fashioning presented as play is, knowingly or not, antithetically situated in the culture of chemical "relaxers" and thus takes on a political significance in relation to historical white supremacist attitudes to hair and beauty practices *and* strategies of Black resistance iconized in "the Afro" or "natural" as it was sometimes referred to.

Tensions between the biological and the natural bodies are expressed here in the "magic" of hair styling Black and white raced Barbie dolls. These toys reflect boundaries of natural beauty or normative values formulated in relation to cultural constructions of gender, race, or any other signifiers of self or "otherness" that are at any one time in no way rigid. Indeed, it is the spectacular dimensions of hair's symbolic potency that allow it to be *played with*.[53] Slowly from the late 1970s, Mattel started labeling their Black Barbie ranges as simply "Barbie," implying that the doll has exponents in all ethnicities and that the brand was not restricted to raced whiteness; nevertheless, the majority of Black Barbie dolls continued to have long, straight, or wavy hair (Figure 2.2.6).[54]

PLAYING WITH HAIR

Fashioned hair as an expression of individual agency has a complex and contradictory relationship to how the self conforms to the group. What characterizes the fashioning of hair as an embodied social practice in the modern age is this recurring interplay between resistance and conformity. The threats posed by the female bob as a symbol of female emancipation in the 1920s were defused by the spatial reorganization of professional practice along gender lines. The masculine look was "feminized" through constant innovations in technical and styling practices that in turn by the 1930s embodied new attitudes to modern selfhood, and Hollywood glamour reconfigured "artifice" by redrawing the symbolic and social boundaries of idealized femininity. When viewed as a bodily metaphor and as a socializing practice, dyed blonde hair rapidly moved from being a controversial representation of 1930s aspirational American modernity to a widespread and highly disciplinary beauty practice. In between the extremes of early platinum styles and contemporary techniques of discreet, multitonal "natural" highlights, the status and meaning of blonde hair have fluctuated over the decades.[55] If synonymous with the golden age of Hollywood then the "bottle blonde" has also become associated with concepts of feminine immorality and social impropriety. "Brassy," that is, yellowing, peroxide blonde hair and untouched-up dark roots connote vulgarity and even monstrosity; for example, the sullen face and coarse bleached bubble cut of child killer Myra Hindley in 1965 came to signify "all that was cheap, nasty and, in the public's imagination, ultimately evil about the look."[56]

The political uses of hair, perhaps most famously embodied in the Afro, were part of a wider subcultural and countercultural movement in Europe and North America that challenged hegemonic power structures representative of institutional incursions on the body. In the United States, this dichotomy of authenticity in relation to "natural" styles has come to have a particular resonance. Bruce Tyler outlines the different positions on hair straightening as being either "assimilationist" or "nationalist": the former endorsing the use of chemical relaxers to straighten hair, the latter seeing such practices as a form of self-loathing.[57] If African American women were once taught that their untreated "nappy" hair was not presentable, untreated straight hair could also take on negative connotations by signaling a mixed rather than "pure" Black African racial heritage or a lack of political consciousness. The aesthetics of the "the natural" confronted white raced ideals that dated back from the nineteenth century but, as Robin D. Kelley argues, its political and aesthetic genealogy is complex and nuanced. The style is not simply a part of the Black Power movement but an older articulation of avant-garde fashions from the 1950s for short to medium compact styles not teased outwards (as with "Afros") but which avoided chemical relaxers for an "*au naturel*" look and feel.[58] Others such as cultural historian Kobena Mercer[59] and Maxine Craig[60] and sociologist Shirley Tate[61] are also critical of polarized interpretations and their work highlights the complex ways in which people style their hair, which may involve irony, creativity, an appreciation of contemporary styles, and of course play itself.

Technically, the Afro was a long hairstyle in that the actual strands of hair were long and picked out with the "Afro comb," or augmented with weaves or wigs,[62] in this sense it is analogous to strategies of self-presentation adopted by other political movements in the 1960s that also challenged the clipped and disciplined styles of raced "respectability." Since the rise of professional dress for men in the 1830s, the business suit and short, visibly groomed hair were markers of professionalism, socialization, and docility. From the mid-twentieth century onward, hair that extended below the nape of the neck, or more controversially from the crown of the head to beyond the nape of the neck, was associated with lassitude, Regency politics, and in the modern era, unconventionality and political dissidence. In the 1950s the oversized quiffs of the "Teddy boys" in postwar Britain and the unclipped long (by contemporary standards) hair and beards of the "Beat" generation in Europe and North America marked a cultural change. Over the course of the next decade, men's hairstyles began to represent a mainstream youth counterculture mediated on the rise of popular youth music and the imagery that accompanied it. Their uneasy reception by mainstream society demonstrates how much the challenge to the buzz cut and other short men's styles was symbolic of wider threats to normative, white male authority.

The construction of self through style is not the same as self-determination, Celia Lury writes, but a relation organized by consumer culture: "it is the different kinds of stylized relation enabled by consumer culture that are helping to shape the *specific* kinds of belonging to the social groupings of class, gender, race and age that are characteristic of contemporary society."[63] In the modern age, mainstream men and women's hairstyles have frequently developed from avant-garde designs and processes. In the postmodern era, the aesthetics of functionality have evolved into ones of pastiche, while at the same time hair reflects social identity more and more.

Since the 1970s, head and facial hairstyles and grooming practices associated with traditional ideals of gender, race, and sexuality, and even age, have been exploited by different social groups to fashion alternative "authentic" identities. Hair clipped "short back and sides" and buzz cuts, so symbolic of white patriarchal authority, military masculinity, and the protestant work ethic, have been appropriated by "skinheads," a working-class subculture in Britain,[64] and by gay men and women, to redefine the performative boundaries of class and sexuality respectively.[65] The figure of the "New Lad" brought the fashionable resurgence of the "crew cut," while the shaved head in the 1990s celebrated a sense of maleness perceived as lost after feminism and the nostalgic "yuppie" styles of the preceding decade. In the late twentieth century, the bleaching of hair blonde was revived as a symbol of female empowerment by ironizing and playing with traditional and white supremacist ideals of feminine sexuality and beauty, particularly in popular music imagery. Female artistes such as Madonna, Mary J. Blige, Annie Lennox, Salt-N-Pepa, and Beyoncé have self-consciously moved through different shades of blonde to explore and question the artificial and procedural nature of such constructs.

What is perhaps most striking about our contemporary moment is the role that digital technology is now playing in bringing about new social formations correlational to hair styling trends. A current fashion for young women is to dye their hair gray, appropriating a color associated with old age as a self-conscious aesthetic with styles that vary and combine with new "dip dyes" and the shaded and textured "ombré" style (where mid-length and long hair is dyed halfway along the shaft, giving a two-tone effect as if the hair were dipped in color, like a paint brush). The self-conscious dyeing of hair gray reconfigures the boundaries of the natural and the artificial and marks a resistance to the fetishism of youthful appearance and disciplinary beauty norms embodied in the need for gray hair or roots to be colored or covered. As significantly, the fashion can be seen as an example of a "network-style subculture": a group that share certain styling practices but who connect via virtual space and not necessarily the physical. The social networking picture-sharing platform Instagram allows members to post and share hairstyles, and, for example, #GrannyHair has received, to date, over 100,000 posts from a wide range of ethnicities. This suggests the rise of social networking and digital fashion cultures more broadly has also reinscribed political possibilities into contemporary modes of self-presentation.

CONCLUSION

As with many bodily practices, hair styling as an embodied social practice in the modern age has occupied a vacillating cultural position. On the one hand, hairdressing practices can reinforce hegemonic structures of order and adherence to contemporary codes of class, race, or gender performance. On the other, hairstyles have demonstrated their power as strategies that reject normative values, and continue to do so. We can place a preoccupation with styling over the twentieth and twenty-first centuries, and even understand major cultural movements and paradigms (modernism, postmodernism, "post-Internet" modernity) in terms of how the hirsute social and physical body is manipulated and managed. The styling of hair in the twentieth century charts the descent of modernism (characterized by functional, geometric hair designs on women) into postmodern approaches (often, though not always, characterized by full and "big" hair or by revisitations of geometric styles). Hair styling, as distinct from traditional "hairdressing" in the first part of the twentieth century, fell in line with ideas of minimalism, artifice, and functionality while in postmodernity, fashionable hairstyles can articulate irony and nostalgia. Both seek to construct a "natural" appearance according to what is considered "natural" at the time. While this may seem like a depoliticization of hair fashioning, it also heralds an opening up of the discussion about the roles and meanings of socially fashioned hair as a powerful agent of reflexivity in the modern age.

CHAPTER THREE

Fashion and Adornment

ALICE BEARD

INTRODUCTION

Gilbert Foan noted in 1931, in his comprehensive study that was to become the modern professional hairdressers' "bible," that it was often bizarre events such as a recent exhibition of Botticelli paintings in London that stimulated trends in hairstyles.[1] Fashions, he suggested, were no longer decreed by royalty, nor hairdressers and society obliged to capitulate to their regal diktat; fashions were now initiated by milliners, dressmakers, artists, and advertising experts; the bandeau as featured by Mlle. Lenglen the famous tennis player; and by stage and cinema stars "whose haircuts have all had quite a vogue among cinema 'fans'."[2] Individuality was the order of these new modes, but surely Foan asked, "fashions in hair are the special interest of hairdressers, who should therefore, be leaders rather than the followers of fashion?"[3]

This chapter explores how such trendsetting aspirations for modern hairdressing developed after World War I. Previous historical and numerous practice-based studies have described and chronologically detailed succeeding fashions in hair over hundreds of years, but there have been few analyses of hair styling and its practitioners as a significant generative force in the mechanisms of the modern fashion system. This chapter explores how in the 1920s fashions in hair styling and their representation became a key intermediary in the construction of "The Look," a new version of fashionable femininity synonymous with ideals of what it was to be and to look "modern."[4] Since the nineteenth century, clothing styles had been promoted on the printed page through fashion magazines and illustrated fashion plates in newspapers and journals; by the early twentieth society, with the advent of popular cinema, style was increasingly staged on the screen and spread through the medium of the moving image in dramatically different ways.

Part One of this chapter examines how the cinematic image of femininity directly appealed to young working women who were both the producers and the consumers of new products aimed at a mass audience. They contributed to the phenomenon by buying the clothing, makeup, and hair products, magazines, and movie tickets that together constructed the latest "look."

The chapter then traces the impact of evolving high-end and mainstream hairdressing production and consumption practices in relation to wider shifts in the mechanisms of style change in the first half of the twentieth century. Gilbert Foan observed that, "In some subtle way," the emancipation of women connoted "the emancipation of the hairdresser" from the traditional status and practices of barbering and the personal dressing of hair. The nature of the profession had changed he argued, from that of "craft labour" to a form of "specialist modern art" in response to customer demand for the latest styles and an expanding range of goods and services.[5]

Part Two develops these ideas in the context of the 1960s and the emergence of a new kind of attitude to hairdressing as an autonomous system of creative innovation and toward hairdressers as a culturally vital element in initiating style change. Vidal Sassoon's reinvention of the bob in 1963 drew on the clean, graphic crop of the 1920s and created a look that would revolutionize hair styling as an essential component of fashion, and as a key signifier of the new youth culture. The chapter explores how hair was exploited as a new visual grammar by a contemporary fashion media and a new generation of young photographers, journalists, and stylists. Sassoon's innovative intertextual approach demonstrated the capacity of a hairstyle to be both spectacular and transformative, and integral to the overall design of the fashion image on the fashion page, in popular culture, and on the catwalk.

The chapter concludes in Part Three with a focus on the catwalk and the rise of the session stylist. It examines the ways in which hair can play a critical part in the construction of the overall silhouette of each carefully crafted look because it is intrinsic to both the shape and form of the design, and the movement and dynamism of its deportment.

PART ONE: FASHION AND "THE LOOK"

In the 1920s, the revolutionary designs of young Parisian couturiers such as Coco Chanel and Jean Patou stripped away excessive ornamentation with knitted separates and simple dresses and suits that eschewed ostentation. Distinctions in design, cut, and construction continued to operate as a form of sartorial status recognition; but the cachet of fashionable functionality, alongside a popular cultural emphasis on youth, slenderness, and a new kind of sex appeal, offered a much more varied repertoire of fashion choice and accelerated fashion change. The latest "fashions" were still decreed and regularized by Paris but the seasonal rhythms of *haute couture* were increasingly disrupted by the dynamics of modern life and multiple networks of influence from industrial and technical innovation to the mass media, from advertising to ideology, and from new systems of communication to the social sphere.[6] By virtue of such aesthetic and sociocultural heterogeneity what now constituted "fashion" and motivated style trends had radically changed.

Following World War I, America had entered into a period of huge and rapid industrial growth with advances in mass manufacturing, and technological design. Hire purchase schemes ensured more borrowing and an increased demand for new goods and services, while greater numbers of younger women entered the workplace creating more disposable income and a new consumer market. This increase in prosperity signaled social change, and for women, greater social freedom in both work and leisure as they took up what had been understood as masculine leisure pursuits such as smoking, drinking, and cycling. The era came to be defined by the figure of the "flapper" noted for her cropped hair which signaled youth, activity, freedom, liberation, modernity, and symbolized the desires of new women of a new age. As Biddle-Perry and Cheang explain:

> Short or bobbed hair became the antithetical hallmark of the modern woman, and along with other trends in masculine hairstyles such as the garçonne and the Eton crop, formed the apex of a new type of feminine fashionable body freed from ornament and restriction in both under- and outerwear. Shorter-length, tubular, or bias-cut dresses in real or artificial silk favored a boyish, slender silhouette, accentuated by boxier, narrow coats and separates and close-fitting cloche hats.[7]

Wearing one's hair short wasn't new. Before the War, "Blue Stockings" (young female intellectuals) had chosen to wear their hair in shorter simpler styles, and the eponymous Gibson Girls had tied their hair up, away from their faces and shoulders. Easy, fuss-free styles had been taken up enthusiastically by women campaigning for political equality and, after 1914, by those contributing to war work as nurses, in factories, and the land army.[8] But it was Irene Castle's crop, cut short because it suited her career as a dancer, that promoted the look as both practical *and* stylish to a wider, cross-class audience of young women. Short hair complemented women's progressively more active lifestyles after the war and as Karen Stevenson suggests their desire to visibly express this: "As short hair for women had previously been perceived as deviant, punitive, or a self-inflicted denial of sexuality, women who did cut their hair in the 1920s were making a significant cultural statement."[9]

The flapper "rage" ran for a relatively short period, but in challenging both taste and society, clothes and hairstyles were increasingly understood as both a material and a symbolic act of feminine agency, the embodiment of individual stylish self-expression exercised in the creation of a fashionable image. In cutting her hair short and wearing the latest in modern garments, the new woman was configured as one who "bought a symbol of emancipation, glamour and success."[10] Debates in the popular press, particularly those aimed at an expanding cinema audience, reinforced the idea of short dresses and short hair as challenges to both good taste and social stability. In "To bob or not to bob hair—The major dilemma facing women in 1924," *Photoplay* collated newspaper reactions to the style: "It is an incentive to crime!"; "It's a result of the war and falling morals"; "Bobbed hair leads to divorce"; "Shocked husband shoots himself when wife bobs hair!"; "Bobbing your hair will make you go bald!"[11]

At the same time, the decision to adopt such a fashionable image was depicted as an autonomous act of modern consumerism. This image of modern, active femininity as both shocking and desirable was spread through moving and still images, on the silver screen and in the pages of magazines with the promotion of a new generation of silent screen stars such as Colleen Moore and Clara Bow (see Figure 3.1). Their dramatic portrayals of pleasure-seeking young women drinking, dancing, smoking, and seeking sexual adventures were instrumental in disseminating the latest looks to young women audiences. Elizabeth Wissinger suggests "this process made audiences receptive to subtle cues and associations, fuelling consumerism through exposure to Hollywood depictions of luxury and glamour, expressed by objects made desirable by how they were portrayed in film."[12] Moore cut her hair short into a "Dutch-boy" bob for her role as a flapper in *Flaming Youth* (1923).[13] In interviews, she credited the look to her mother (using a Japanese Doll for inspiration), but as Drake Stutesman suggests, it was more likely the work of studio stylist Perc Westmoore, then head of the makeup department at the First National Pictures film company to whom Moore was contracted.[14]

Clara Bow's somewhat messy, tousled curls matched her on-screen characters' bohemian, fun-loving natures and looser morals, while her off-screen hedonistic lifestyle, much to the delight of the tabloids, consolidated the connection. Bow famously starred in, and was the personification of, the *It* girl (1927), a film based on Elinor Glynn's racy popular novel: plucky, impulsive, modern, and—like her hair—somewhat wild.[15] Dark lipstick accentuated her cupid's bow lips, her eyes were ringed with black eyeliner, and she was frequently shown smoking in public. However, this image was countered by the way Bow's image was framed on screen and in publicity stills: posed looking up at the camera to emphasize her wide, child-like eyes and, importantly, her portrayals

FIGURE 3.1: Poster for the film *Bobbed Hair* (dir. Thomas Heffron, 1922). By Realart. Wikimedia/Public Domain.

of "ordinary" girls like her audience who worked as cigarette girls, waitresses, shop assistants, and usherettes.

Perhaps the most striking and iconic example of the cinematic bob was that popularized by Louise Brooks. Her modern geometrical and graphic version, known as the "Japanese Bonnet Style," was sleek, chic, and sophisticated on screen and she was often styled in profile in publicity images to allow the cut to accentuate the fine symmetry of her features (see Figure 3.2). Brooks's roles in the heavily censored *Pandora's Box* (1929) and *Diary of a Lost Girl* (1929) presented the sexually confident and adventurous, progressive images of active femininity which made a direct appeal to young female audiences and constructed a new language of hair with the daring modern cut that signaled and spoke to modern women.[16]

Drake Stutesman suggests: "The clever, sexual, active woman's 'glossy bob' haircut … was arguably the first haircut perfected by and for cinema."[17] Brooks' high-contrast black bob, pale skin, and dark painted lips were the perfect fit for a contemporary German Expressionist film aesthetic. Highly stylized surrealist sets and dramatic chiaroscuro lighting was exploited by cinematographer Günther Krampf in a film form that would pave the way for the visual language of film noir in its symbolic use of light and shade and its unsettling thematic undercurrents of jealousy, murder, intrigue, and suspense. Brooks's wardrobe was credited to art director Gottlieb Hesch, and she wore designs by Jean Patou who also dressed her off screen in a streamlined silhouette of modern knits

FIGURE 3.2: Publicity photo of Louise Brooks. From short biographical sketch-book, *Stars of the Photoplay*, 1930. By *Photoplay* magazine. Wikimedia/Public Domain.

and sportswear. On screen in her backless gowns, revealing expanses of skin, and with a knowing use of her visual and feminine charms, the sharpness of Brooks's bob matched the power of her filmic image to convey a very direct sexuality, with none of the mock coyness of her contemporary Clara Bow.

Fashion and the "Hollywood Look"

As picture theaters opened up across cities and towns in Britain and America, young women were able to enjoy the sophistication and glamour of Hollywood through the medium of the moving image. The cinema functioned as a new kind of vehicle of consumer desire. The large screens conveyed this spectacle magically and seductively, and audiences consumed and relished the smallest details of costume, hair, and makeup in intimate close-up. Part of the huge appeal of the medium was that these new audiences of working girls with ordinary lives could imitate and recreate the magic of these appearances at home on themselves.

New hairstyles and new hair grooming products were widely promoted through film fan magazines. As early as 1921 in *Photoplay* magazine, the National Hair Goods Co. declared, "bobbed hair is fashionable" and offered their bobbed hair pieces for women yet unwilling to commit to the scissors.[18] Hollywood stars were already also commonly used to promote hair and makeup products. In the same issue, a publicity shot of Gloria Swanson accompanied an advertisement for Hermo Hair Lustr (see Figure 3.3), which promised its styling cream:

> keeps the hair dressed ... Adds a charming sheen and lustre, insuring the life and beauty of the hair. Dress it in any of the prevailing styles and it will stay that way. Gives the hair that soft, glossy, well-groomed appearance so becoming to the stars of the stage and screen.[19]

Many stars were reported to provide these services gratis in exchange for publicity, and the fact that they were willing to do so was promoted as further endorsement of the products advertised. Beauty columns were full of "The Secrets of the Stars" aimed at a star-struck audience that "devoured the intimate glimpses they were given into the beauty habits of their favourites."[20]

The development of at-home hair care, washing, and styling, promoted through women's magazines and by celebrities, was set alongside the opening up of more neighborhood salons offering services in dyeing, cutting, and styling to keep up with consumer demand.[21] As an article in *Photoplay* was keen to point out:

> Bobbed hair has introduced the item of "overhead" into the feminine budget ... For the great majority of the bobbed hair sisterhood it's a choice between learning how to use the iron and the tight curlers every night, or spending money for the daily, semi-weekly or weekly marcelle and accompanying trim. Even the permanent marcel wave doesn't take care of itself, but needs regular water-waving to preserve the natural appearance ... Not that the hairdressers are complaining![22]

There was a gradual progression from what Foan describes as the "crude" short bob of the war years to styles longer in appearance such as the contemporary vogue for the "Ten-inch Bob." This shift was marked, he argued, by the need to combine new artistic cutting techniques with technological innovations in waving, curling, and coloring, "all calculated to be more profitable to the hairdressing profession."[23] In response, Foan advised "wise students" of the craft to "cultivate these branches in his own and the profession's interest" and stressed the need for "the progressive hairdresser to keep abreast of the times by carefully noting possible tendencies towards changes in hairdressing fashions."[24]

The 1930s saw the popularization of the bleached blonde, aided by both the technology of the silver screen and the manufacture of domestic hair bleaches and colorants.[25] The visibly dyed hair of rising stars such as Mae West and perhaps the most iconic exemplar, Jean Harlow, became emblematic of "glamour," a new version of fashionable femininity created through the spectacle of modern artifice. In his article for *Photoplay* in 1931, columnist Professor L. Hall described the appearance of Harlow's hair in the film *Hell's Angel* (1930) as "magical ... [it] ripples gracefully over the skull and falls into a torrent

FASHION AND ADORNMENT 63

FIGURE 3.3: Advertisement for Hermo Hair-Lustr with Gloria Swanson and Wallace Reid. By unknown ad agency/photographer—*Photoplay* (February–June 1921). Wikimedia/Public Domain.

of silver down the back of the lady's neck … it is startling hair, bizarre, but on the whole quite beautiful."[26] Harlow's appearance epitomized demonstrably staged femininity: her makeup by Hollywood artist Max Factor made a feature of her pale skin and plucked and penciled her eyebrows, and her dazzling white blonde curls were maintained by weekly appointments with celebrity hairstylist Alfred Pagano who bleached out her hair with a mixture of peroxide, ammonia, clorox, and domestic soap flakes. Harlow's natural hair was eventually so damaged that she had to wear wigs but the look created "platinum fever" as thousands of young cinemagoers raided their chemists to try and replicate it.

In an interview in *Collier's Magazine*, producer Samuel Goldwin predicted that women went to the movies, "one to see the pictures and stars, and two to see the latest in clothes."[27] In Gilles Lipovetsky's historical account of the emergence of the modern fashion system in the late nineteenth century, style change was articulated through two new, mutually constituted modes of production: *haute couture* and industrial mass manufacture. These two industries, he argues, might seem to have little in common:

> Their goals and methods, the articles the produce, and the prestige they earn are undeniably incommensurate; nevertheless, these two industries together form a single configuration, a homogeneous system in the history of the production of ephemera.[28]

The longer length, body-clinging, bias-cut designs in luxuriously soft satin fabrics created by couturier Madame Vionnet in the 1930s were out of reach for most consumers, but not the look itself. Department stores and increasingly local high street multiples such as Marks and Spencer offered copies of the latest fashions, while the inclusion of paper patterns aimed at the domestic home dressmaker became a key feature of an expanding range of popular women's magazines. Direct access to style trends was no longer confined to the exclusive confines of the salon, as Christopher Breward suggests: "Parisian models had become overshadowed by the marketing and publicity prowess of Hollywood."[29] The bridge between the two was the spectacular but replicable body of the film star.

High-end and mainstream hairdressing evolved in tandem with these shifts in the mechanisms of fashion production and fashion change.[30] The rapid rise of mass production techniques that had facilitated the production of acceptable/creditable facsimiles of couture designs and luxury fabrics such as silk were mirrored in hairstyles that involved scientific advances and technological innovations, and professional skills and artistry similarly once the sole preserve of a fashionable elite and now accessible to mainstream consumers. Chanel designed costumes for Gloria Swanson, and Elsa Schiaparelli for Mae West, and the industry developed its own designers, notably Adrian, who created lavish costumes for stars such as Joan Crawford and Barbara Stanwyck. At the same time an elite breed of "couture coiffeurs" such as Antoine of Paris, the Westmore Brothers, and Sydney Guilaroff with salons on New York's Fifth Avenue and Sunset Boulevard in Los Angeles, created styles that were not just accessories to the latest Hollywood looks but a key part of their construction and commodification. Guilaroff, for example, according to the *New York Times*, "started the whole short hair business" when, as a youngster working at the Hotel McAlpin he drastically shortened Louise Brooks's hair. Later head of department at MGM studios, Guilaroff coiffed Claudette Colbert's bangs, and sleekly styled Joan Crawford's dark brunette hair to complement the highly tailored sophisticated dark silk suits with padded shoulders and slinky evening gowns designed for the star by Adrian.[31]

Within a period of two decades, the interrelationship between fashions in clothing and hair styling was transformed in the construction of "the look" on screen, in the salon, in the domestic environment, and most significantly, through consumers' and practitioners' growing expectations and understanding of this interconnectedness. With Hollywood's appropriation of a declining Parisian couture's style leadership (exacerbated by World War II and the Occupation), modern hairdressing was becoming an autonomous creative force not just in stimulating style change but in how such change was experienced and embodied. With the rise and growing cultural dominance of postwar youth movements a new interconnectedness emerged between high-end and popular fashions. *Haute couture* diversified with ready-to-wear collections by young designers such as Pierre Cardin and Yves St. Laurent, and London's Carnaby Street and the King's Road became a cultural hub for British designers including Mary Quant and Barbara Hulanicki. Vidal Sassoon, then a young East End hairdresser, recalled:

> Around me I could see clothes that had a wonderful shape to them and all because of the cutting. I wanted to see hair keeping up with fashion, maybe jumping ahead of it, leading it along a certain line instead of lagging behind it. I wanted to shape heads, as the new young fashion designers were shaping bodies. I wanted to cut hair as they cut cloth.[32]

PART TWO: THE NEW BOB

The revolutionary geometric bob that Sassoon pioneered had been in development for a decade, but one of its first appearances was on the catwalk of young designer Mary Quant, who wanted a swinging alternative to the stiff and lacquered chignons more commonly worn by runway models. Sassoon described how he "tried the cut out on Mary first, cutting her hair like she cut material. No fuss. No ornamentation. Just a neat swinging line. It caught on faster than any line I had done before or have done since."[33] Sassoon cut hair as Quant cut cloth, with a focus on shape and movement, both creating new styles that literally swung. The new bob's five points established hairdressing as design: a dynamic balance of geometry with three angles at the nape of the neck and two at either side of the face (see Figure 3.4). It was an adaptable style that could be cut at different lengths depending on the wearer and provided a dramatic contrast to the fussy demi-waves and set beehives of the previous decade. Sassoon had created a hairstyle that was uniquely modern: both cutting-edge and low-maintenance that young women could wash and care for these new styles at home themselves rather than relying on their salons for a weekly shampoo and set.

Sassoon saw the role of hair as "setting trends rather than following them, creating rather than aping looks on the catwalk."[34] And, while new modes in hairdressing innovation were driven by the catwalk, they were as importantly, disseminated through printed media. As Sassoon has acknowledged, the popularity of the style was in no small part due to an image created in collaboration with fashion photographer Terence Donovan. In 1963, Sassoon was asked to cut actress Nancy Kwan's waist-length hair for her role in *The Wild Affair* (1965).[35] The completed look was shot in black and white by Donovan for British *Vogue* and featured Kwan, dressed in Quant's design, with her hair cut and styled into a short geometric shape, accentuating her high cheekbones and long neck. Donovan's photographs were published in US *Vogue* in September 1963, and a month later in British *Vogue*, and were also used in the film's title sequence, picturing and constructing the bob both in and as a series of fashion images.[36] Sassoon's bob for Kwan reveals the crucial dynamic that was emerging in the 1960s between the platforms of fashion media—from catwalk to screen to photograph—which would lead women to arrive at salon appointments clutching pages torn from their favorite fashion magazines, desperate to recreate "the look."[37]

The seismic shift in hairdressing also changed our understanding of the role of the hairstylist, as Caroline Cox explains: "The hairdresser was now a sculptor and the cut was paramount, no longer the foundation of the hairstyle but the focus."[38] *Vogue* magazine featured a young Grace Coddington who modeled the neo-bob style as a geometric

FIGURE 3.4: Mary Quant, December 1966. Photo: Jac. de Nijs/Anefo. Source: http://www.gahetna.nl/collectie/afbeeldingen/fotocollectie/zoeken/weergave/detail/q/id/ab08cfb0-d0b4-102d-bcf8-003048976d84, CC BY-SA 3.0 nl. Wikimedia Commons.

graduated cut curving into a bowl shape with some height at the crown. The look was applauded by fashion editors, notably Claire Rendlesham of *Queen* magazine who had her hair cut by Sassoon and featured the new style in her fashion pages. In 1965, the *Sunday Times Magazine* described Sassoon as the "Czar of the Scissors," responsible for leading a revolution in English life through his commitment to the idea that style could be simple and functional: "for him the basic hair cut is vital. Elaborate settings are so much frou frou. His simple haircuts almost eliminate the need for setting. And they're practical enough to swing back into shape on their own."[39]

The change in fashion photography away from the studio was symptomatic of wider developments in the technology of photography which allowed "outside" fashion, and which constructed a new feminine ideal: the woman who was "on the move."[40] The "single girl" symbolized a new generation of youthful fashionability and was epitomized in the figure of "Twiggy," seventeen-year-old aspiring model Lesley Hornby whose hair makeover played a key part in her transformation into the 1960s "it" girl and catapulted her into the popular press as the personification of Swinging London. In 1967, at the suggestion of her boyfriend and manager Justin Villeneuve, her hair was cut in a thoroughly modern crop created by Mayfair hairdresser Leonard Lewis (see Figure 3.5). The short cut, clipped close to the face and tapering at the neck reimagined the gamine Eton crop of the 1920s. With her new style, Twiggy emerged as a new model of femininity defined by and for the youth culture from which she emerged. Not since the 1920s were women offered the opportunity to reinvent their selves with a simple haircut. In fashion photography and editorial, hair operated as an intrinsic part of both achieving a particular "look" *and* as a signifier of a new young fashionable consumer.

In the late 1960s and early 1970s, women's magazines offered possibilities of endless design choice and pages of competing fashionable looks, and hair came to play an increasingly important role in the finished product on the fashion page. Responding to the rise of the West End hair salon and the increasing fashionable status of the hairdresser in "Swinging London," magazine fashion and beauty editorial now covered trends in hair fashions and the contribution of the fashion editor and the task of "styling" a model through clothing, and hair and makeup were, therefore, seen as crucial. Fashion journalist Brigid Kennan remarked:

> You can open a newspaper one day and see the Return of the Forties put forward as *the* latest, but one the same day another paper might be promoting moulded plastic clothes or boiler suits or almost anything … The confused state of fashion—the "anything goes"—exists in every sector. Hair can be long, short, curly or straight. Faces can be powdered or shiny, lips can be blood red or non-defined.[41]

The latest "new looks" promoted by beauty editorials were often in fact reworkings of classic styles. In "Profile of a Profile," Penny Vincenzi illustrated the selling points of the "new bob" circa 1972, and in doing so made reference to both the business of hairdressing and the commodification of style and fashion-ability. She observed:

> The profile, classic or otherwise, is making a comeback. For a very long time now it has been obscured by fringes, layers, freak-outs and just plain hair—and very plain a lot of it is, too … Now we have the rebirth of the profile, along with the rebirth of the bob, and people have necks again, which is nice … Hairdressers report a general rush to the scissors; Leonard's are doing 50 bobs a day and at Vidal Sassoon they are bobbing

250 heads a week ... The new bob is angled to the cheek, rather than carved straight into the jaw; it's more flattering and doesn't look like you never got round to growing out your 1960s' version.[42]

Fashion photography in the 1970s often looked back to the past and took stars of the silver screen as direct inspiration with historical references to popular cultural icons made explicit in the accompanying text. As Laird Borrelli points out, "metaphor aids in the visualization of style by linking a look or a garment to a point of reference outside of the world of fashion."[43] For example, in Sarah Moon's editorial work for *Nova* magazine, black and white photos acknowledging the influence of Garbo and Dietrich replicate the image of a 1930s starlet with "fashionably wavy hair and the heavy contrast made-up face right down to black on eyes and lips."[44] Importantly, however, editorials and features articulated the role of the old not in terms of reprise, but as the reference point in the construction of the new in terms of hair, femininity, and fashionable sexuality. For

FIGURE 3.5: A seventeen-year-old Twiggy (Lesley Hornby) with garçonne-style bob, February 2, 1967, launching a new range of clothes, bearing the Twiggy label. Keystone Pictures USA/Alamy Stock Photo.

example, writing in 1973, Caroline Baker stressed how the new styles could be "sleek and smooth like Valentino or cropped and brush-like a la Bowie";[45] or, a year later, how "Maria Schneider, of Last Tango fame, put the big endorsement on the curly look and it threatens to take over, at last, from the long, blonde, Bardot hairdo that has until now been the sexy way to do hair."

Valerie Steele argues that by the 1970s "fashion was not in fashion" but rather became "optional."[46] Instead, there was an emphasis on fashionability defined by individuality, where "style ceases to be a matter of what you are wearing and becomes more the way you wear it."[47] As fashion became less about what was worn and more about *how* it was worn, makeup and hair styling were presented to magazine readers both as a means to achieve a complete "look" and as a way of adding an important mark of individuality. As well as ideas on what to look like, magazines offered advice on how to achieve the new, fashionable hairdos and encouraged an active participation in home styling, through a constructive "Do-It-Yourself" approach that encouraged experimentation. Fashion was defined by the choice of styles and looks on offer in editorials and features promoting specific garments or haircuts that described the fun to be had in "playing" with fashion and the creativity involved in constructing different fashionable personae.

In fashion photography and beauty editorial, a clear and important new kind of relationship emerged between clothing and hair as parts of a fashionable ensemble. In an article from 1973 entitled "Hair Today," designer Caroline Charles made a direct link between clothing and hair styling: "I think you change your hair because with a new fashion it's the first thing that *feels* wrong."[48] How could the fashionable reader be "ahead of hair" when styles seemed to change as often as fashions? According to contemporary fashion columnist Pip Newberry, it was about looking and feeling "right now":

> Take a short cut ... any short cut ... The very brave are sporting convict cuts but more popular is the smooth, shaped head with the hair cut into the nape of the neck and a soft fringe. Short hair is easy to manage but only if you have a real Rolls Royce of a cut in the first place, and you may find that the time and trouble saved by having short hair is soon cancelled out by the frequent visits to the hairdresser ... necessary to keep your cut in trim. Short hair suits everyone—if it feels right it looks right ... right now.[49]

As desire for the image and the product is fashioned here through the relationship between the words and pictures on a page, then so hair styling can be understood not as mere dressing, but as a vital element in the visual grammar of a fashion statement. Getting the right hair like the right clothes was crucial to the achievement of an overall "look" but equally significant in developing an understanding of a way of dressing as a means to a *way of being*.

PART THREE: THE CATWALK

By the 1980s, women's magazines were disseminating the latest fashions in hair via beauty editorial and catwalk reports, highlighting key looks and seasonal changes in styling. These reports conveyed descriptions of both the "feel" and the "look" of the new styles as well as technical details of the cuts themselves, indicating a knowledgeable audience of readers and consumers. Glossies such as *Vogue* were instrumental in bringing catwalk styles and seasonal trends back to the attention of their readers, in the seasonal "Paris News" column the latest European looks were reported: "curly and short are the hair words. Still lots of asymmetric cutting, crew looks, and hair combs."[50] Runway styles were interpreted for readers in editorial such as *Vogue*'s "Hair Report" and key defining details of the styles were signaled through the editorial captions:

> Just one look at the photographs ... snapped as these models walked down the runway at Calvin Klein's fall collections and you see what hair is all about this season. There is a line, a shape, a swing to hair. And there is a shine—you can "read" it in all three pictures. Another change: the turn to a smoother, more controlled look that has lost none of its ease or softness—and just one of the ways of getting the small, neat look you want with the narrowing line of clothes.[51]

At the beginning of the decade *Vogue* had predicted the fashion toward a shorter, stronger, more androgynous and individual style: "This look—and all the other ways your hair will look in the 80s—will depend more and more on the involvement of the wearer, deriving its shape, vitality, and direction not only from the cut—but from simple brush strokes, from hand-combing, from the very personal ways it's worked."[52]

Cut by Dutch hairdresser Christiaan Houtenbos, modeled by Gia Carangi, and photographed by Irving Penn, the new style was cropped and choppy, clipped short on top and finger combed to create texture through longer lengths at the back, resulting in a functional and versatile cut. Importantly, the editorial spread highlights the skill and art of the professional by picturing the hairdresser at work, actually cutting into the hair with his scissors: "One of the keys to the look is in the cutting itself ... where Christiaan sectioned off the top hair, twisted it first, then cut it—jaggedly— some longer, some shorter ... that's what accounts for the 'springiness' you see in the finished cut."[53]

Catwalk hair is a collaboration between hairstylist and designer, part of the network of production at the heart of the fashion image which includes editor, photographer, model, stylists, and makeup artists to name a few. Quant and Sassoon provided one of the first real collaborations between hair stylist and designer, and our contemporary understanding of the work of the "session stylist"—who operates only within the production of fashion media—originates in that moment when Quant's models were sent off dancing down the runway with their fashionably bobbed hair.[54] Before this time, models' hair was styled up off the shoulders and away from the garments worn on the catwalk—usually swept back into a ponytail or a chignon. This simple style was "a reflection of the fact that during this decade many fashion models were responsible for their own hair and makeup styling."[55] As Wissinger points out "the creation of the hair and makeup for the fashion image was simply not a site of investment."[56] As fashion developed as a global business "fashion shows became elaborate spectacles designed for the camera, paving the way for the whirlwind of fashion weeks beamed immediately worldwide."[57] The teams of stylists that emerged as a consequence, "represented an expansion both of the model's work to submit to bodily manipulation and to the economies of producing the model 'look.'"[58]

Working for *Vogue* as a session stylist, and collaborating with designers Yohji Yamamoto and Comme de Garçons, Christiaan Houtenbos would be responsible for the move towards shorter cuts and more simple and graphic styling creating cutting-edge and radical looks including singers Grace Jones's flat top and Debbie Harry's jagged bob. Houtenbos had trained as an apprentice in his family's barber business and his technique incorporated men's hairdressing tools such as razors and clippers to cut into and shave hair in sections to create depth and movement. "Christiaan" (as he was known professionally) perfected the technique of the "undercut," a barbering technique that had its origins in the 1930s where the underneath of the hair was shaved with an electric razor to create a sharp and blunt bobbed cut. Initially cut on model Bonnie Berman for an editorial shoot in *Vogue* March 1983, the fashion editor was unsure of the style and the shaved section remained hidden under the upper layers of the bob in the published photos. However, this new version of the traditional men's "buzz cut" would be showcased in the Comme de Garçons Spring/Summer show of 1984; as they walked the runway the models moved and turned revealing the radical cut and creating an international fashion for the style.

The dissemination of new styles here marks a shift, bringing fashion image-making full circle, and reveals the distinct opportunities each platform provides; the buzz cut, initially too radical for the magazine, is later revealed, through motion on the catwalk, is taken up by fashion insiders who then promote and detail the style in magazine editorial "hair reports," to instruct readers on how to achieve their version of "the look."

Sam McKnight's career has defined our contemporary understanding of the profession of hairdressing. McKnight is recognized as "an image-maker in his own right," and was the subject of a retrospective spanning his career at Somerset House in London in 2016.[59] In the 1980s, he was arguably the first independent session stylist in London working across editorial, advertising, and catwalk shows.[60] As a young hairdresser McKnight was seduced and enthralled by the hair styling he saw on the pages of fashion photography in *Vogue*, and pursued the credits to Molton Brown, an innovative salon in London's West End. Here, he trained with founders Caroline Burstein and Michael Collis, securing his own editorial styling appointment for *Vogue* magazine in 1977 and styling his first catwalk show for the Emanuels in 1979.

McKnight's style is grounded in this early training where he was taught to approach hair more naturally, that is, to feel and work with his hands, and this sensibility characterizes his signature "done/undone" look that has helped to define the particular cool appeal of supermodel Kate Moss. One of McKnight's earliest and most influential looks was his short bleached crop cut which transformed the modeling careers of both Jeny Howorth in the 1980s and Agyness Deyn in 2005, and in doing so, like the flappers of the 1920s, and Twiggy's youthful reinvention of the style in the 1960s, established new images of desirable and fashionable contemporary femininity.

McKnight's collaborations with Vivienne Westwood and Karl Lagerfeld for Chanel depends on this shared understanding of the importance of silhouette and proportion.[61] While in the 1960s the five-point bob established the primary importance of the cut, hairstyling for the contemporary catwalk requires more transitory, ephemeral designs. McKnight has been innovative in his design and use of hairpieces, often styling his wigs as separate sections of hair, recalling the use of bobbed wigs promoted in 1920s. In his styling for photographer Tim Walker's spreads for British *Vogue*, April 2011, McKnight dresses model Lindsey Wixson in a chopped black bob wig, deliberately cut shorter than her natural hair line so her shaved hair is just visible underneath. Like his use of pink candy-colored bobbed wigs on model Cara Delevingne for Chanel's 2013 Cruise Collection, there is no illusion that this style is natural; this is hair as artifice, both changeable and self-consciously "fashioned."

For Chanel's Fall/Winter 2015 show McKnight used bobbed "hair hats" to complete Lagerfeld's vision of his models as "production line androids." The process was a careful and detailed collaboration as McKnight explained: "Karl sent me … a sketch of a very specific sharply angled bob which he felt perfectly accentuated his designs … So we went to work in the studio, cutting and shaping some dark wigs into slightly different lengths and angles."[62] Set in an elaborate casino staged at the Grand Palais in Paris the show was opened by actors and models including Julianne Moore, Vanessa Paradis, and Kristen Stewart, who took up their positions at the gambling tables, each dressed in custom couture and wearing diamond jewelry modeled on Chanel's original 1932 designs. The actress/models arrived almost mechanically in sequence, their makeup by Tom Pecheux conforming to an identical look with rouged cheeks, red lips, and bold brows. McKnight introduced the idea of the wig as a hat, so each model, regardless of her natural hair could be complete in a unified look wearing a dark colored, smooth, and angular bob (see Figure 3.6). The hairpiece acted as a "futuristic accessory" complementing the computer designed collection pieces, and 3-D printed seamless quilted jackets.

FIGURE 3.6: On the runway at the Chanel Haute Couture show, Paris Fashion Week Fall/Winter 2015/2016. Photo: Getty Images/Victor VIRGILE/Gamma-Rapho.

Each wig piece sat higher than the models own natural hairline to create a deliberately "visible little triangle of the front hairline to soften the effect" and then fan out from a center parting, falling forward into two triangular points alongside the models' cheekbones.[63] The wig is cut up shorter at the back revealing the softer curve of the model's own swept-up hair. Under these "wig hats" hair was tightly tied up on top, to give a little height on the crown, exaggerating the angle of the swing of the hair towards the face. The geometry of the bob and its accentuated points, and the sections of visible hair underneath the wig reference both Sassoon's five-point style and Christiaan's shaved undercut.

Reprise, reference, and repetition are constant and continual components of fashion image-making. It is the detail of interpretation that marks the look out as modern, desirable, and cutting-edge, exemplified in McKnight's approach to "modern retro":

> A twist on a classic. A reinvention. Making the old new again. This is what it means to be a creative—taking references from the past and calling upon them to inspire work in the present. As image-makers, we will often purposely reference what has come before to create something new ... In the same way fashion is cyclical so is beauty. It is an ever-developing arena where new icons are being created and becoming part of our cultural tapestry to be later reinterpreted by the next generation of creatives.[64]

In the modern age, hair in fashion photography, on the screen, and on the catwalk is always more than just a superficial finishing touch; its cut, texture, color, and movement are integral to the creation of a complete fashionable "look." Hair styling is more than simple dressing; while subject to constant shifts and changes in the pursuit of the new, it maintains its crucial dynamic in the transformative processes of fashioning desire and identity. Rather than just an accessory to pivotal moments and shifts in style and the iconography of style, hair is always part of the narrative drive of fashion's dynamic and cyclical movement.

CHAPTER FOUR

Production and Practice

Thoroughly Modern Hair: A Century of Technological Progress

KIM SMITH

INTRODUCTION

World War I ushered in a new sense of modernity instigated through the mechanical transformation of warfare on an industrial scale, the impact of which extended beyond the battlefield into every aspect of civilian life. Many inventions attributed to modern warfare in fact had their origins in prewar life, but the war accelerated innovation and stimulated new attitudes toward aesthetic creativity and design technology.[1] Therefore, scientific research was not viewed retrospectively in the same way as other more devastating or directly combative components of the war-machine.[2] Technological advance came to define much of how modern design was implemented, understood, and consumed in cultural terms. This chapter investigates the scientific and technical innovations in a century of "Ages"—Machine, Plastics, Chemical—that underpinned and shaped twentieth-century hairdressing production and practices that defined what it meant to be, and to look, *modern*.

The emergence of modern hairdressing has been carefully detailed in Richard Corson's chronology of historical style trends, techniques, processes, and products,[3] while Caroline Cox's sociohistorical exploration is focused on a narrower field of British hairdressing and styles from the late nineteenth century onward.[4] Wendy Cooper has discussed hair using an anthropological approach, considering its connection and relationship to both the individual and the social body;[5] and Anthony Synnott's texts have considered hair's materiality through sociological theory.[6] The aim of this chapter is to offer an alternative perspective. The focus here is on the invention of new scientific processes and technologies, and the design of new machinery and products with which to implement them, that were adopted and exploited by an expanding modern hair industry.

The desire to achieve or acquire the latest in fashionable hair styling prompted constant modifications and improvements, particularly in the interests of health and safety. The modern hair salon became a place to experiment; effectively it may be likened to a science laboratory as a space of danger and discovery, a place in which to test out new methods and machines appropriate to new modes of professional expertise and of modern consumerism. Unlike some of the subtler innovations that transformed modern dress manufacture and textile production, the fashionable cutting, curling, or coloring of hair was immediately visible as the direct result of technological and scientific advance. This is an area of an emerging modern hairdressing culture, only infrequently analyzed or discussed, that this chapter situates as a key mediator in the fashioning of the modern age.

CUTTING IT IN THE MACHINE AGE

We are living in the age of the machine. Man made the machine in his own image. She has limbs which act; lungs which breathe; a heart which beats; a nervous system through which runs electricity ...[7]

In the opening scene of the film *Thoroughly Modern Millie*, the eponymous heroine Millie Dillmount (Julie Andrews) arrives in New York City fresh from Kansas.[8] It is 1922 and on a street in Manhattan, Millie realizes that her old-fashioned, provincial appearance puts her at a distinct disadvantage in this bustling metropolis. She walks in through a revolving shop door only to magically step out again with her long hair now fashionably shorn. The "bob-cut" was the fastest way to look "modern": the style was all the rage, a signifier of a new type of racy, youthful femininity and of new attitudes to both the past and the future (Figure 4.1). Contemporaneous with Millie's fictional transformation, Monique Lerbier, heroine in the French novel *La Garçonne* (1922), similarly rejects the conventions of her traditional upbringing by leaving home and heads for Paris where, among other things, she cuts her hair very short.[9] Meanwhile in Shanghai, the silent film star Wang Hanlun demonstrates her modernity and break with Chinese tradition by wearing western fashion and famously having her long hair cut into a bob on screen.[10]

Synnott has argued that it is not the ceaseless change of hairstyles but the process of change itself that is important in understanding hair symbolism in the twentieth century as a powerful cultural form.[11] Design historian Cheryl Buckley's discussion of the experience of 1920s modernity emphasizes the importance of women's short hair in this regard, "to be *feminine* depended upon being *modern*."[12] New possibilities of framing the self through fashion were unfurling.[13] The very descriptor "modern" implied a new sensibility and embodied a neoteric feminine identity which embraced the ideals, if not always their realization, of greater political and social freedoms, equality, and public independence.[14] The physical act of cutting off one's hair signified a break with tradition, the immediacy of which startlingly relegated prewar socioculture to a dim and distant past and epitomized a forward-looking fashionable ideal that had no time for nostalgia.

Science, technology, and consumer culture were fused in a "machine aesthetic," a powerful compound of ideas in which machines were imbricated in a potent mythology of "the modern" and incorporated into new strategies of fashionable self-presentation and body management.[15] Artists, designers, and writers articulated the material products and experiences of industrial modernity through increasingly abstract representations of idealized bodies that were endlessly mass-producible.[16] The bob was central to the articulation of this new aesthetic: cut short, square, and sharp, the style complemented a vogue-ish female form that emphasized linearity and angularity.[17] By the late 1920s, one estimate suggested that in New York up to two thousand women were having their hair bobbed every day.[18] The Eton crop, the last incarnation of the solely cut bob, was the shortest of all and appeared in 1926 at exactly the point when skirts were also at their shortest.[19] Associated with a fashionable avant-garde—Josephine Baker, the Black

FIGURE 4.1: "Bobbed Hair's the Thing!" Newspaper article dated September 25, 1920. By Djuna Barnes—Arizona Republican (Phoenix, AZ), September 25, 1920. Chronicling America: Historic American Newspapers. Library of Congress. Wikimedia/Public Domain.

Parisian dancer; society hostess Lady Ottoline Morel; and Radclyffe Hall the lesbian novelist, all famously sported the style—the crop was emblematic of the "flapper," a smoking, hedonistic, emancipated "new woman" whose radical image was one to which many young women aspired.

Jazz music and a hugely popular craze for dancing reflected new body ideals with "a whole new syncopated style of movement ... jerky rhythms expressed a machine consciousness" and incorporated a new morality in dramatically different fashions in dress and hairstyles (see Figure 4.2).[20] The Eton crop's androgynous, exotic "otherness" mirrored the styling of the flapper's male counterpart, the "cake-eater"—a fashionable collegian who wore his hair slicked back close to the head in a shiny, sleek style personified in popular culture by cartoonist John Held.[21] The hairstyle, so popular that songs were written about it, was greased down with pomade or brilliantine, and resembled highly polished leather. Worn with a clean-shaven face, it eradicated the human sense of hair to create a streamlined, robotic but sexualized appearance famously adopted by the silent movie star Rudolf Valentino.[22]

From a practice perspective, short styles recast the spatial and social dimensions of hairdressing and prompted the evolution of the dedicated modern ladies' salon in tandem with that of the modern barbershop. Beards and sideburns were seen as the bygone symbols of an outmoded patriarchal masculinity.[23] Manual clippers had been invented in London in the nineteenth century by a Serbian émigré, Nikola Bizumić; but it was an engineering student from Illinois in the United States, Leo Wahl, who patented the first electric clipper in 1919 and revolutionized men's hairdressing. Men's hair could be clipped and shaved more quickly and in greater numbers creating a conveyor belt of masculine conformity to modern ideals.[24] Traditional ladies' hair practitioners for the most part dressed clients' hair in their own homes and so not only lacked the professional skills and expertise of barbers but also dedicated spaces in which to perform their "art." In response, many barbers, realizing that the trade in ladies' hairdressing was far more

FIGURE 4.2: Women in evening dresses at a jazz party in 1926. Science and Society Picture Library.

lucrative than that of men's, converted some or all of their business to accommodate the influx of female clients wishing to have their hair professionally cut.[25]

Three implements traditionally constituted the basic cutting tools in the barber's arsenal: razor, scissors, and thinning shears. With the shift from the private boudoir to the public salon these tools of the trade formed the foundation of the emerging craft of ladies' hair and established hair cutting as *the* practice of twentieth-century modernity. The razor produced "a cut with very fine ends and a precise contour" and was always carried out on wet hair to prevent hair pulling.[26] Thinning shears—distinguished by having "teeth" rather than a sheer blade—were used to take out bulk where the hair was thick and enable the hairdresser to create the right shape. Hairdressing scissors, recognizable by their single-finger handles, finely tapered blades, and handle spurs, had been adapted from general use to assist in precision cutting in the late nineteenth century. Normally around 8 inches in length, they were used in the "scissor-over-comb" method of cutting—the first example of *graduating* hair that was to become so much a staple of modern hairdressing.[27]

Further advanced modifications appeared in the mid-twentieth century to improve the durability of metal and hairdressing technique. Almost all hairdressers' scissors came from Solingen in Germany rather than Sheffield due to their superior quality and craftsmanship but were finished in British workshops. A move from steel and nickel plate to stainless steel was a new development caused by the effect of waving lotions on ordinary steel blades. The chemicals, which pitted the metal and ruined the scissors as a result, had no such effect on stainless steel versions. At the same time there is evidence that the distinct finger-rest (or spur) on one bow was developed by one British company to alleviate strain. The company also created a model with a stud between the bows to produce a quieter cutting action. Images of standard hair scissors in the late 1950s show neither of these new innovations that were ubiquitous by the end of the century. These advances were particularly notable in men's hairdressing that required more skill, artistry, and creativity even with the basic tools of scissors and comb than the short back and sides had required.[28]

The shared material transformation of emancipatory hair-cutting practices for both men and women, thus, paradoxically reinforced gender differences, spatially and stylistically.[29] Increasing demands by female consumers for specialized bobbing, constant stylistic innovation, and an expanding range of beauty products and services generated the need for a new kind of "feminised space that was chic, sophisticated and a desirable sphere of consumption."[30] The simply cut bobbed style and the ubiquitous cloche hat were suddenly out of fashion; women sought a softer, fuller, more tousled look prompting constant variations of "shingled" styles such as the "bingle" and "mingle" using the technique of "Marcel" waving, a complex technique of *ondulation* using heated tongs which waved hair in a ripple effect.[31]

ELECTRIC JELLYFISH, MONSTER MACHINES, AND A LOT OF HOT AIR

Modern femininity as symbolic of radical change progressively involved ever more complex, expensive, and modern procedures such as perming, setting, and bleaching to control and perfect the latest hairstyles that very visibly promoted the means of their production.[32] Thus, the discovery of synthetic plastics and chemical dyes as well as the electrification of hairdressing gadgets had a crucial impact on the modern hairdressing industry and the expectations of a new generation of modern consumers. From the early twentieth century, several formulae for "permanent waving" solutions and machines to produce longer lasting, tighter curls were being developed to replace the tried and tested Marcel technique. In 1906, the young Carl Nestlé had demonstrated a new machine involving tubes heated by gas that were applied to hair previously prepared with chemical treatment, but real improvements began in World War I when Eugene Suter, a Swiss émigré living in London, adapted a gas machine to electric.[33] In 1919, the introduction of the "appareil Gallia," which resembled a gruesome "electric jellyfish," ushered in a new era of hairdressing technology.[34] However, while innovative, the perming process was, nevertheless, still beset with problems; results were unreliable and posed health hazards. Chemical burns as well as electrocution were just some of the trials endured by women who would have to sit for up to ten hours, at great expense, under different contraptions variously described as "the octopus," "the chandelier,"[35] or "the milking machine" (Figure 4.3).[36]

In the context of these rapid stylistic and technical innovations a modern Black hairdressing industry was also emerging in the United States with new approaches to production, practice, and consumerism. Modern raced-subjectivities were articulated through hair care and styling and salon expansion over the course of the twentieth century in new ways and embodied and engaged with the powerful set of ideas this chapter interrogates. The most significant technology for Black hair culture was the arrival of the electric hot-comb in the 1920s, an important tool in straightening and waving hair and thus considered an essential part of fashionable good grooming for aspirational African Americans who associated it with economic and social advance (Figure 4.4).[37] Often erroneously cited as the invention of Black hair and beauty entrepreneur Madam C.J. Walker, hot combs heated on a stove or hot plate had been in use in Europe and North America since the 1870s and retailed in stores such as Bloomingdale's and Sears.[38] Madame Walker was, however, responsible for introducing the method to Black women as part of a package of affordable and accessible hair straightening and styling products that transformed the styling and management of Black hair. Her "shampoo-press-and-curl" method became the foundation of a rapidly expanding modern Black hairdressing industry that opened up new concepts of beauty to African American women routinely denied the luxury of such rituals.[39] The use of a chemical "reagent," colloquially known as a perm, enabled hair to be styled in the latest fashionable waves that lasted between six and eight weeks and rapidly emerged as the predominant practice of an evolving modern Black hair culture.[40]

For Black men, a modern respectable appearance meant clipping their hair into short simple "buzz cuts"—so called because of the noise made by the electric razor. Many fashionable men also looked to straighten their hair, at first using traditional wave caps and cold curls, then a caustic solution of potatoes, eggs, and lye (a hazardous liquid metal hydroxide) called the congalene, or conk for short, first produced commercially by KKK (Knocks Kinks Krazy), a company based in Los Angeles. The conk was a longer style with soft waves on the crown and shaped with pomades or brilliantine; the craze took hold in the late 1920s, reached a peak in the 1940s, but continued to be popular with some men right into the 1960s.[41] Numerous branded versions of relaxants, bleaches, and other grooming products aimed at both male and female Black consumers were part of the wider growth of the American cosmetic industry and constituted more than 50 percent of advertising in the Black popular press.[42]

FIGURE 4.3: Permanent-waving machine, 1923, built by Icall for sale by Eugene Suter under the name "Eugene." The twenty-two tubular heaters designed in 1917 by Isidoro Calvete and patented by Suter in 1920, hung from the "chandelier," distributed the weight of the heaters. Louis Calvete/Wikipedia Commons/Public Domain.

For all consumers, modern hair and beauty salons were not only the ideal places to experience the latest in technological processes and new products; they were frequently the only places capable of dispensing them, as the concoctions and contraptions were largely unsuitable or unavailable for domestic interiors. Efforts to refine and develop the extremely lengthy permanent waving process and reduce potential problems with frizzing and health risks continued throughout the 1920s. Nevertheless, the cachet of having the time and money to have one's hair professionally treated in this way meant that hairdressing swiftly "became big business."[43]

FIGURE 4.4: Electric hot comb heater and hot comb. Smithsonian National Museum of African American History and Culture. Gift of Linda Crichlow White in honor of her aunt, Edna Stevens McIntyre.

Plastics, together with the expansion of electrically powered professional and domestic equipment in salons and private homes, were also emerging as vital constituents in the design of new forms of hair technology inscribed into notions of fashionable consumerism. Bakelite, the first truly synthetic plastic, appeared in 1907; its heat conductivity and thermosetting properties meant that it became the most widely used material for electrical insulation.[44] This was particularly important when considering health and safety in salons where appliances were increasingly electrically powered. Handheld dryers appeared commercially in the 1920s but were heavy and slow with an output of only 100 watts, and their use was largely confined to barber shops. Made of steel and zinc often with wooden handles, they still posed the risk of electrocution if they came into contact with water, a danger overcome by later models completely housed in Bakelite. The design of seated-hairdryers fell into two categories: metal head coverings and soft bonnet models. The metal models were not uniform in design and styles were many and various. Some fitted closely around the head often in a claw configuration while others were simply giant versions of handheld blow-dryers. Soft bonnet-hood styles were very similar in design: a tall, cloth hood perforated with ventilation holes attached to a pipe blowing warm air into it to dry the hair was placed over the client's head.⁴⁵ However, few salons employed gas-heated mechanical dryers because of safety issues, for example, the risk of carbon monoxide poisoning, while the safer electrically powered alternatives were prohibitively expensive.⁴⁶

BLONDE BOMBSHELLS: COLORING IN THE CHEMICAL AGE

The introduction of reliable, safe synthetic hair dyes was a major innovation and a sister technology to permanent waving. Commercial hair dye was first developed in 1909 by Eugène Schueller, a young graduate chemical engineer, and marketed under the name *Oréal*. According to company history, this was the first chemical hair dye formula, and produced a more varied range of colors than the bright, artificial look achieved by henna or mineral salts.⁴⁷ Nonetheless, many early chemical para dyes were acutely toxic.⁴⁸ There was a lack of prior testing to ensure safety, and there were numerous reports of severe allergic reactions, scalp burns, and even deaths. As a direct result, in Britain the Pharmacy and Poison Act was legislated in 1933.⁴⁹ Less harmful but no less problematic for the consumer, the techniques employed to dye the hair shaft resulted in a block of flat color which gave the appearance of having been painted on and coverage was often uneven and differing in strength.⁵⁰ In addition the use of hair colorants still had a stigmatic reputation as the marker of aging looks or of dubious morals.

These negative psychological and physical associations were progressively countered in the 1930s with Hollywood cinema's depiction of a new kind of modern, fair-haired heroine.⁵¹ The mannerisms and looks of screen idols such as "the blonde bombshell," Jean Harlow, were hugely influential in disseminating fashionable and technological change to women consumers of all classes in the interwar period. Being "permanently" waved and having long-lasting colored hair became crucial symbols of 1930s modernity, reinforced by associating femininity with other modern innovations such as the telephone which became a frequent feature in high-class salons—a relationship often depicted in advertisements and films of the period.⁵² Booming interwar chemical industries in Britain and North America used modern advertising methods and the promotional opportunities opened by cinema and other new forms of popular culture to overcome anxieties about the potential harmful effects of scientific advance.⁵³ Harlow's eponymous image of the "platinum blonde"⁵⁴ promoted the "natural" advantages of blonde-haired femininity *and* the "naturalness" of the scientific innovations that now enabled its achievement. Harlow herself denied that she bleached her hair, protesting that she merely added a little "blue" to the rinsing water when washing.⁵⁵ This was after all Hollywood's golden age and the cinema itself a modern phenomenon selling "celluloid dreams" to its audiences.

BETTER THINGS FOR BETTER HAIR

The outbreak of World War II in 1939 could be seen to mark an interregnum in the development of modern hairdressing. Shortages of raw materials and the demands of the war effort meant that many of the products of interwar scientific and technological advance—either in development or recently enjoyed by consumers—were either rationed or, more often, unavailable. Virtually every aspect of professional and domestic hair care was in some way affected by wartime shortages or subject to statutory proscription.⁵⁶

By early 1941, in Britain, shampoo in liquid and powder form, setting lotion, hair dyes, tonics, and brilliantine were all controlled by a Limitation of Supplies Order, and in 1942 soap was rationed.[57] Yet, as in World War I, World War II acted as a key stimulus rather than an impediment to innovation and scientific advance: modern warfare again encouraged scientific research, product development, and refinements in technological design and manufacture which would eventually filter down to the general public after the war. Many prototypes introduced in the late 1930s were improved with further research and development.

Equally important, new configurations of fashionable modern femininity again emerged at the interface of the machinery of war and traditional gender ideals.[58] During the war there was a huge emphasis on "making do" with what was available, but this should not be seen as a rejection of professional styling or its products and processes. The maintenance of prewar innovations in fashion, hair care, and beauty regimes was constantly encouraged and sustained through home front propaganda and popular culture, particularly the cinema. Despite the British government's emphasis on British cinematic production, Hollywood also continued to offer escape through fashionable consumerism in which hair styling played an important role; even in wartime it represented an affordable, accessible, and achievable entry point to ideals of modern glamour and luxury that would set the standard for postwar femininity.[59]

In terms of hairdressing, as with *haute couture*, the 1950s is retrospectively viewed as a golden age; luxury hair styling enjoyed a period of unrivaled esteem. The great Parisian *coiffeurs* continued to dictate fashionable styles that were interpreted by Mayfair, the British center for sophistication, where several luxury hairdressers were also fast gaining wider reputations for creating prestigiously fashionable hairstyles.[60] Coiffeur Raymond "Teasie Weasie" Bessone one of London's newest stars, firmly believed that after years of privation and austerity what women now wanted was glamour (Figure 4.5).[61] Those in the provinces who could afford it enjoyed the social cachet of an occasional trip to London's Mayfair salons, returning home with visible evidence of their fashionable and social status in the form of hairdos indelibly stamped "exclusive."[62]

However, things were beginning to change. Technical innovations offered by upmarket hairdressing practitioners that were once enjoyed by a privileged few were progressively extended in various ways to the mass market. Encouraged by the new opportunities for business provided by postwar regeneration, Mayfair hairdressers embarked on a process of national expansion in bombed-out provincial cities and towns that raised women's hair-consciousness and the skills of local stylists.[63] Economist Gertrude Williams, writing in the 1950s, described how women living in the suburbs and provinces keenly appreciated the value of escaping domestic drudgery and isolation with a "weekly or fortnightly visit to the nearest big town … [to] have their hair dressed, and meet their friends for meals in much more glamorous surroundings."[64]

As the 1950s unfolded, it became clear that a new age of scientific and technical innovation had arrived; synthetic materials became agents in fulfilling the Du Pont Corporation's promise of providing "Better things for better living—through chemicals."[65] The privations of war had only fueled demand for a wide range of chemically based consumer products from cosmetics to clothing and of course hair care and styling products. The invention of cold wave perming enabled a form of winding hair called *croquinole* that reversed the spiral form by starting at the ends and finishing at the roots, creating far superior curls.[66] The process also introduced a new "DIY" (Do It Yourself) home perm that quickly took off in countries all over the world. For example, Toni

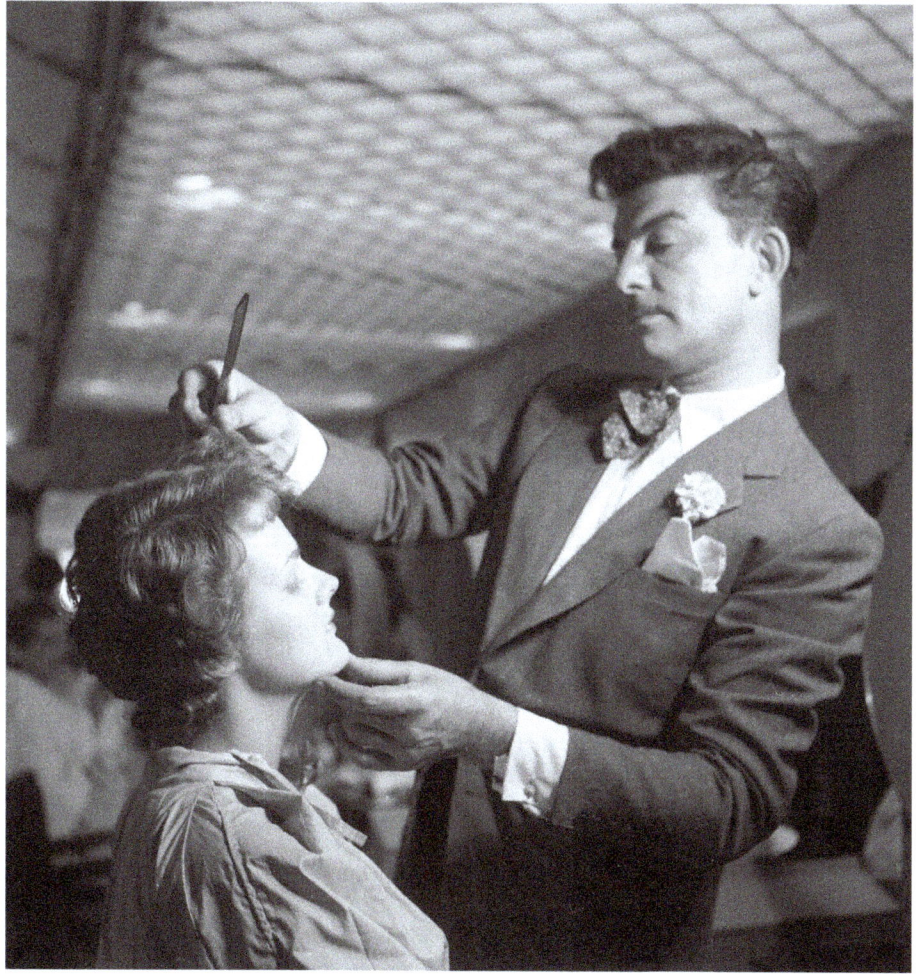

FIGURE 4.5: June 4, 1952: Hairdresser Raymond aka "Mr Teasy Weasy" [sic] puts the finishing touches to a hairstyle. Photo: Chaloner Woods. Photo: Bettmann/Getty Images.

"PROM" home permanents that were introduced from America in 1950 were snapped up by eager consumers at markets throughout postwar austerity Britain. So great was the demand it led to black market forgeries and counterfeit versions.[67]

Breakthroughs in chemical hair-dye technology brought improvements with the introduction of the new "one-solution" method that combined lightener and toner.[68] The discovery that fur industry dyes were also suitable for human hair extensively widened the range of available shades.[69] Semi-permanent color rinses intended to "brighten" mousy hair were introduced aimed at younger rather than older women;[70] the growing teenage market not only was interested in hair colorants but did not seem affected by stigmas once associated with them.[71] As a consequence, the trade in hair coloring tripled in the period 1959–1961.[72]

Better solutions for perming and dyeing were matched by improvements in other chemical technologies, notably nylon—an important factor in the development of those most ubiquitous of hairdressing tools, brushes, and combs. Unlike earlier thermosets such as Bakelite, nylon was a thermoplastic of greater flexibility in its properties and did not shatter if dropped. John (Jack) Denman Dean patented the Denman D3 styling brush in 1939 which separated the brush back from the bristles which were supported on "a rubber or like flexible sheet ... to give a strong brushing action, whilst at the same time allowing desired yielding of the bristles."[73] The brush was further developed when Dean returned to Britain after working for Du Pont during World War II and used ball-ended nylon pins instead of the customary tufted hogs' hair bristles. Drawing on the expertise of a number of hairdressers, including Freddy French of Mayfair, Denman's new lines of brushes were more hygienic as they were completely washable and their association with luxury hairdressing lent an air of prestige—French's clients were able to buy the brushes stamped with his logo and packaged in an elegant tasseled box. Well suited to the new blow-drying and brushing-out practices that were emerging as vital to creating the new silky, swinging styles of the 1960s, the Denman brush would become a singularly important innovation in modern hairdressing.[74]

Nylon, through its ability to be compression molded, also became integral to mass-produced comb manufacture: its flexibility rendered it virtually unbreakable, ideal for a pocket-comb that no longer snapped when sat upon. Despite its ubiquity, the comb became one of the symbols of subcultural "resistance" in postwar Britain with the emergence of the Teddy Boy, a working-class youth typified by his "neo-Edwardian" sartorial choices and fastidious attention to personal grooming. The image of "the Ted" with a carefully coiffed D.A. (Figure 4.6),[75] is as much a trope of his distinctive

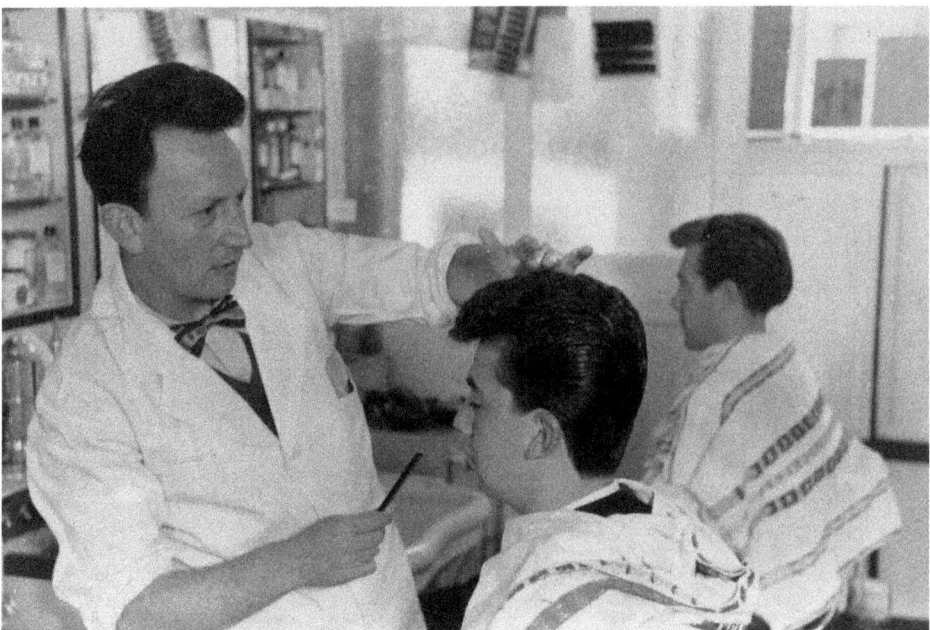

FIGURE 4.6: November 13, 1954: Hairdresser Mr. Angel Rose works on a gentleman's coiffure in his salon near Tottenham Court Road, central London. Photo: Maurice Ambler/Picture Post. © Getty Images.

style as his drape jacket or crepe-soled shoes, and the pocket-comb as much as the notorious flick-knife, the style weapon of choice. In the Teddy Boys' hands, the comb was transformed from the ordinary and functional to an object of spectacular masculine display.

The same might be said of the long-handled tail-comb that became a vital accessory for young women styling their hair in a "beehive," the iconic statement hairdo of the early 1960s. The combination of a short, fine-toothed comb with a long, sharp "tail" was well suited to teasing, backcombing, and styling hair into a dome-like structure held in place with pins and hair spray—another recent innovation in hair care this time derived from a need for insecticide during the Pacific War. Shellac (a natural but volatile plastic) was far too heavy and sticky but in the early 1950s it was found that by dissolving it in alcohol, it could be sprayed from an aerosol to provide a thin protective lasting film.[76]

The beehive in many ways marked the pinnacle of an era of "big hair." Cox persuasively suggests that such styles could be reinterpreted as representing "the apex of 1950s and early 1960s optimism, when the synthetic was praised over the natural," and when a belief in the positive effects of science and technical innovation still held strong.[77] In contrast, Grant McCracken critiques this period as one in which artificiality became a desirable aesthetic that spoke of "highly conventionalized, unchanging selves, of women frozen into place."[78] Salons all over Britain typically contained serried ranks of helmet dryers beneath which sat trapped an army of female consumers (Figure 4.7). Feminist theorist Susan Brownmiller critically examines such practices as a form of "permanent bondage,"

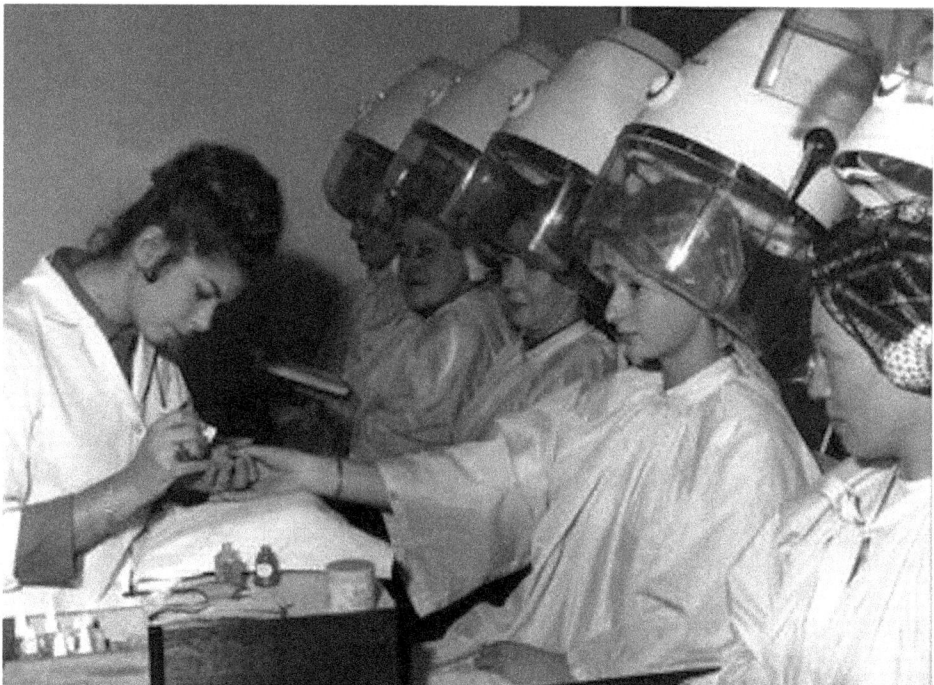

FIGURE 4.7: 1963: Clients under row of hood dryers. Photo: Barrett Street Trade School Archive. Reproduced by permission of University of the Arts London: London College of Fashion.

and describes the limitations she felt imposed on her by having to spend two lunch hours a week having her hair shampooed, curled, and held in place with pins, lotion, rollers, clips, and finally a plastic hair net, before sitting under a hot dryer.[79]

CUTTING IT IN THE [POST]MODERN AGE: "THE ENGLISH CUT"

A younger generation of women in the 1960s, like Brownmiller, felt physically and ideologically constrained by outdated hairdressing practices and styles seen as symbolic of wider social and political inequalities. This effectively brings us back to where we started this chapter: the arrival of a short haircut for women that came to define an era of radical social and fashion change. Like the bob of the 1920s, the inception of young London hairdresser Vidal Sassoon's geometric bob in the 1960s once more transformed the process of hair*dressing* into hair*cutting*. Sassoon simplified the way hair looked with a vision of clean lines and angular contours. The celebrated "Quant bob" of 1963 (after fashion designer Mary Quant; Figure 4.8) was followed by the "V-Shaped," the "Asymmetric," the "Five-Point," and "Ungaro," all within the space of a few years. The precision of these cuts was tested by watching as clients shook their heads and styles fell back perfectly into shape. Referred to as the "English Cut," this type of styling became the consummate criterion of 1960s "Sassoonery" that propelled London hairdressing and other young hairdressers who created a succession of iconic styles—Leonard Lewis (the "Twiggy"), Roger Thompson (the "Isadora"), Trevor Sorbie (the "Wedge"), John Frieda (the "Purdey")—to the summit of international prestige.

For much of the twentieth century, most ladies' hairdressers used a combination of razors, scissors, and thinning shears.[80] Sassoon, a former employee of Raymond Bessone, whom he called "the man who taught Britain to cut," learned to thin, prune, and cut with scissors alone because Raymond would not have razors or thinning shears in his salon.[81] This technique required great skill and dexterity and was difficult to learn; Raymond often cut in salon cubicles hidden from prying eyes and would start the cut on different parts of the head to confuse onlookers. Sassoon took Raymond's technique of "cutting sharp" further in his reinvention of the bob, progressing it with feats of angled precision and by cutting closer to the head using five-and-a-half inch scissors because he "wanted something tiny that would be like an extension of [his] hand" and give him greater control.[82]

This form of styling relied almost entirely on cutting shapes and using handheld dryers with a styling nozzle for concentrated airflow to speedily blow rather than perm, backcomb, set, or lacquer hair into place. However, a notion of simple, "natural" styles belies the continued importance of science and technology to modern practice. Hood dryers remained in use as the only suitable method for treatments such as hot-oil conditioning, coloring, and perming—although old-fashioned fixed forms gave way to portable dryers that could be positioned at the dressing-out tables or alternatively wall-mounted and pulled down when needed. As top London hairdressers Joshua and Daniel Galvin stated, it was a culture of "wash 'n' wear and 'drip-dry'," nevertheless, a different approach to, for example, permed hair, also "opened wide to attract younger women, and men of all ages."[83] There were various revivals of the perming method in response to a demand for fashionable, long-lasting but messier, looser curls, stimulated by style trends such as the wilder, unstructured mid-length permed style, the *Coupe Sauvage* of the 1970s. Even men

FIGURE 4.8: Fashion designer Mary Quant seen having the finishing touches made to her new hairstyle by Vidal Sassoon, November 12, 1964. Photo: Ronald Dumont/Getty Images.

were encouraged to embrace the process when "the footballers perm," spearheaded by Liverpool Football Club and England player Kevin Keegan, became fashionable.[84]

This period also saw a pivotal moment in the evolution of modern hair coloring. Stylist Annie Humphreys, who worked for Sassoon, began the process with her investigations into ideas of color theory first developed by the Bauhaus design movement of the 1920s.[85] With trial and error, Humphreys began to produce startling effects fusing Sassoon's cutting techniques with her own ideas about color.[86] However, it was a fellow Sassoon apprentice Daniel Galvin's invention of the "brickwork" technique that really revolutionized modern coloring practice. Galvin, like Humphreys, realized that the role of color was not simply to cover gray hair, but could be used to create, shape, and enhance a haircut. Forced to experiment and in the absence of any formal training at this time, he arrived at a method of weaving through sections of hair with a tail comb and using several different shades and tones of color to create high- and lowlights that were subtly dispersed and evenly diffracted throughout the hair to produce an overall shimmer. Galvin did not use bleach to lighten hair and, like Humphreys, preferred to mix his own shades, administering them in three stages: "one for cover, one for color, and one for depth."[87] The quality, range, and capacity of modern colorants and techniques of application such as tips, streaks, and flashes to highlight altered the hair-dyeing process out of all recognition.[88] Young consumers were also beginning to experiment with all the colors of the rainbow, deliberately using unnatural shades to create a distinctive appearance. Fashion designer Zandra Rhodes went to Galvin's to have her hair dyed green and introduced him to textiles dyes that Galvin promptly sent to industry chemists to convert into a safe, easy-to-use range of hair colorants called "Crazy Colors."[89]

Political, social, and technological changes since the 1960s were embodied in a whole range of new styles and techniques increasingly open to all consumers. Black women too had greater styling choices, and straightening didn't have to be one of them.[90] Up to the late 1960s, most Black women living in the West straightened their hair. However, Black Bohemianism in the 1950s led by a new generation of African American female artists such as Nina Simone and Miriam Makeba remonstrated against what they saw as a slavish adherence to an acculturation that followed European standards of beauty.[91] Their protest was visibly manifested with their adoption of an "authentic" Black hairstyle, the "Afro" (also known in America as the "Natural"). Much critical discussion has focused on how the style revolutionized Black beauty ideals and became a highly politicized symbol of the Black Power and civil rights movements in the 1960s.[92] Of concern to this chapter is the Afro's stylistic impact as part of a wider trajectory of historical technical innovations in hair-styling production and practices; these played a key role in negotiating new kinds of modern classed, gendered, and raced subjectivities in new ways.

In comparative hairdressing terms, just as the freedom of Sassoon's "wash and go" styles in the 1960s relied on precise and intricate cutting techniques, then so the liberation of "natural" Black hair from alteration required constant and careful attention from new products and processes.[93] The Afro as a construction of Black American resistance was teased into place and maintained with an Afro comb or pick—introduced into the United States by Willie Morrow, a pioneer in modern Black hairdressing. The comb formed a direct link with an African heritage that could be appropriated as an iconic symbol of new Black identities and political struggle.[94] But to achieve the perfect halo shape could also often entail the use of creams, lotions, warm pressing, and large rollers to radiate the hair from the scalp, while electric clippers shaped and perfected the hairline.[95] As Ingrid Banks points out, "Even with traditions, ideas and practices change to accommodate and usher in new generations that put their own spin on customs."[96] Moreover, not everybody wore Afros; many Black men and women continued to straighten or clip their hair, and the meaning of the Afro as an explicitly political statement very swiftly shifted to a mainstream fashion statement subject to constant stylistic adaptation.[97]

By the late 1970s, fashionable hairstyles and the products and practices involved in achieving them were no longer necessarily rigidly defined by divisions of race or gender. Traditional Black styling practices were appropriated by white consumers: the corn/cane row was popularized by blonde, white Hollywood star Bo Derek's appearance in the film *10* (dir. Blake Edwards, 1979) and whose success in turn encouraged Black consumers to once more adopt the style; the Afro was mirrored in the man-perms popularized by white European footballers, while a range of new Black curly man-perms appeared—the "Jherri curl" (named after its inventor, chemist and hairdresser Jherri Redding) being the most popular—that seemed "to revel in their allusions to an ever widening range of stylistic references."[98] In the last decades of the twentieth century, many young Black men in Britain and North America drew on a range of multicultural influences to combine previous styles with new ones. Jazzie B, who spearheaded the British musical group Soul II Soul, mixed the clippered, short sides of the "skiffle" cut (Britain's version of the "buzz cut") with a long crown of nappy locks to create "Funki-Dreds," a distinctively Black British hairstyle.[99] In America, first Larry Blackmon of the band Cameo, then a young Black TV actor, Will Smith (*Fresh Prince of Bel Air*) further adapted the buzz cut with an exaggerated flat top to create the High-Top Fade (a trend revived by Black youths in Britain in 2016). As Synnott argues it is hair's malleability that makes it so apt as a symbol of changes in both group and individual identities.[100]

CONCLUSION

In 2015, the trade journal *American Salon* published a short piece looking back at four historic items of hairdressing technology: a 1910 handheld blow-dryer version with stand; a 1936 electric perming machine; a 1953 Wahl hair clipper; and a 1971 electric "Curve 'n' Comb." The article paired these supposed relics with their modern day equivalents and declared: "Aren't you glad it's 2015?"[101] Strikingly, it is not how different but how similar are the comparative appearance and functions of these historically technically innovative products. The electronically controlled Digital Perm machine is less monstrous than Nestlé's original from a hundred years earlier, but the new technology has brought back permanent waves to the trendy salon where the practice had all but died out.[102] In hair coloring, the latest trend is to "pixelate": hair is dyed in square blocks of vibrant colors to resemble computer pixels. But the process can be seen as the direct legacy of practitioners like Annie Humphrey in the late 1950s and Daniel Galvin in the 1960s who were the catalysts of experimental coloring technologies. The latest innovation from British technology company Dyson, the *Dyson Supersonic*, is a revolutionary blow-dryer driven by a powerful, digital motor repositioned into the handle to minimize fatigue that incorporates a sophisticated microprocessor which automatically senses and regulates the temperature to help prevent extreme heat damage.[103]

This chapter began with the shift from the private boudoir to the public salon in the 1920s and the incorporation of scientific and technological innovations into modern hairdressing that in less than a decade had impacted on every aspect of production from the humblest tools in the hairdressers' kit such as brushes and combs to the latest inventions of a burgeoning chemical industry. Hair salons functioned as experimental laboratories developing and disseminating the latest in modern scientific and technological advance in changing styles and practices that embodied the idea and experience of modernity for practitioners and consumers. The development of safe, reliable, affordable "synthetic" alternatives to traditional and often expensive materials marked a turning point in the everyday lives of its consumers. As plastics became cheaper they could be mass-produced, and their use became almost the hallmark of "modern design."[104] The advent of electricity and the products of the modern chemical industry between the wars combined ideals of modernity with the aspirational desires of those whose daily routines they came to dominate. The nascent technologies were often risky, but for a new generation of mass consumers they were synonymous with "progress" articulated in all kinds of body regimes, but particularly hair care and styling. Pioneering research and subsequent refinements in design and manufacture constantly redefined the nature of modern consumerism. Plastics, chemicals, and electric technology democratized hair, and beauty culture and practices once the sole privilege of the middle and upper classes were now available to all but the poorest in society.

Simultaneously incorporating technologies of science and of self, hairdressing practice and production are often overlooked as *the* intermediary between the material and the symbolic in the modern and now postmodern age. Always at the vanguard of scientific, economic, social, and fashion change, hairdressing production and practice have to keep "ahead."

CHAPTER FIVE

Health and Hygiene

Meanings, Images, and Politics

PAUL R. DESLANDES

In response to a question posed to him in 1939 about his shaving habits, a twenty-nine-year-old Briton responded: "I don't like to see badly shaven or unshaven faces and I always feel very unkempt if I haven't shaved—in fact it gives me a definite inferiority complex."[1] With these simple words, this man highlighted some essential points about the relationship between hair and hygiene in the modern age. While concerns about hygiene have always partly been about the health of the human body, they are also intimately bound up with concerns about physical appearance, social order, and mental satisfaction. In exploring the theme of hair and hygiene in the recent past, this chapter treats the concept of hygiene as expansive, encompassing a broad range of concerns related to physical vitality and fitness, the social meanings of tidy and untidy hair, and psychological well-being. The relationship between hair and hygiene is explored here as a point of access for discussing somatic and mental health (and attempts by the state and other bodies to improve it), but also topics related to the history of visual culture (particularly in the form of advertising), the history of race, and the history of symbols. The intent is to privilege the study of hair not as tangential but as central to human history. To borrow a phrase from the scientist-cum-historian Kurt Stein: "Hair, because of its unique properties, has shaped human evolution, social communication, history, industry, economics, forensics, and art."[2]

As earlier volumes in this series remind us, the relationship between hair hygiene and broader bodily health has a long and complicated history that can be traced to the ancient world. In the twentieth century, though, this was rendered even more complex by the intervention of several key forces. Kathy Peiss in her discussion of the emergence of a modern beauty industry in the United States and historians of other western societies (including France, Germany, and Great Britain) have noted how a new kind of highly commodified beauty and body culture, geared to both women and men, solidified in the decades immediately following World War I.[3] Its development was closely linked to innovations in the production of new chemicals and new grooming products during the Second Industrial Revolution that occurred in the years after 1870.[4] The hair industry, as a component of this emerging modern beauty culture, was also progressively regularized with the growth of professional organizations, trade-specific publications like the *Hairdresser's Weekly Journal* in Great Britain,[5] and increased government oversight.[6]

Furthermore, and of particular significance to this chapter, the twentieth century ushered in new forms of visual culture that placed a growing emphasis on physical appearance as both an explicit marker of modernity and an indicator of health.

In exploring these complex themes, this chapter is organized into two sections. The first examines the discursive rhetoric that emerged around hair and hygiene in the twentieth century, and focuses on how issues such as health, race, and psychological well-being affected how products were promoted in press advertising. The rise of photography in the nineteenth century had altered the ways in which the human face and body were both captured and reproduced; this, and the proliferation of photographically based advertising images it stimulated, had a profound impact on how healthy human hair was depicted. The second section highlights several key moments in twentieth-century history when hair, hair care, and hair hygiene acquired political significance and served as a sign of order or disorder, a tool for political change, or a harbinger of social discord.[7] The impact of these changes is traced to illustrate how an expansive definition of hygiene might be employed to examine issues ranging from the treatment of Nazi collaborators in postwar France to the rise of the Afro in the 1960s. The examples that follow are drawn from a variety of regional contexts to illustrate the pervasiveness of the cultural links between human hair and hygiene. This range of examples is also intended to highlight the fact that concerns about hair and hygiene are simultaneously universal and contingent on a range of variables including national histories, sexual and racial politics, and stages of economic development.

THE PROMOTIONAL RHETORIC OF HEALTH, HAIR, AND HYGIENE IN THE TWENTIETH CENTURY

The twentieth century was characterized, as Jackson Lears notes in his study of American advertising, by a proliferation of new techniques and tropes in promoting ideals of physical perfection: the eradication of unwanted (and unclean) odors, the quest for slimness, and new hairstyles and shaving standards.[8] Emerging forms of modern visual culture in the context of wider social and cultural change established new connections between healthy hair, psychological well-being, and self-esteem.[9] All kinds of advertising and representational media employed an innovative visual language to promote the notion that success in life was predicated on an attractive personal appearance and good hygiene.[10] By attaching specific meanings to this consciously constructed relationship between the possession of an attractive and hygienic physical appearance and levels of personal satisfaction, advertisers placed a high premium on the healthy, clean, and well-groomed body in articulating what they viewed as the ideal modern subject (Figure 5.1).[11]

In the late nineteenth century, advertisers began to privilege the relationship between beautiful full heads of hair and good health. The British company Beetham's, for example, used what Thomas Richards has called "those lovely seaside girls" to sell skin ointments by highlighting their beautiful white skin and luxurious, frequently golden, hair.[12] Good hygiene and careful grooming became the implied dual markers of beauty and racial fitness in archetypal images of white Anglo-Saxon physical vitality and attractiveness. The "Gibson Girl," the notable fictional creation of the Massachusetts-born graphic artist Charles Dana Gibson, featured prominently in popular American magazines like *Colliers* in the years around the turn of the century. The "Gibson Girl" was characterized most visibly by voluminous hair, piled on top of her head in a loose chignon and combed up high away from her face into a large "pompadour" style.[13] A male counterpart to this new model of modern femininity was similarly captured in the popular press by the German-born American illustrator, J.C. Leyendecker, best known for his depictions of the "Arrow collar" man, an idealized vision of the clean-shaven face and perfectly groomed head of hair that would come in this period to epitomize modern masculinity and social status.[14]

The cultural dominance of these white aesthetic standards in the West meant that, more often than not, the relationship between hygienic and beautiful hair was cast in eugenic and racist terms in the interwar period. In 1920, British colonial administrator Harry Hamilton Johnston offered the following commentary in his assessment of the aesthetic impact of the "miscegenation" of the black and white races, paying particular attention to differences in the hair: "the potency of the Negro strain is such that its presence is evident to the discriminating eye for several generations ... The fatal kink in the hair (blond or even red though it be), the tumid lips, the finger nails, reveal the remote relationship to the African."[15] Johnston and others, in keeping with the troubling tenets of racial science, assumed that differences between white people and people of color were always markers of superiority in the first instance and inferiority in the second.[16] Thus, healthy (read white raced hair) served simultaneously as an indicator of racial fitness and a gauge of purity. This point was also made abundantly clear in the 1930s "Breck Girl" campaign of the Springfield, Massachusetts-based Breck Shampoo Company, which promoted their products through depictions (done initially as pastel portraits) of the young white, and frequently blonde, women thought to epitomize the best of interwar American health and beauty.[17]

Advertisers and beauty entrepreneurs seeking to cultivate new mass markets and address modern aesthetic and hygienic standards frequently relied on the authority of medical professionals and other experts to showcase the hygienic properties of their products. Medical authorities, for instance, began to argue that facial hair was a breeding ground for germs.[18] The introduction of the Gillette Safety Razor revolutionized the way men dealt with this newly constructed "problem," and hygienic and fit masculine bodies with streamlined slicked-back hair and closely shaved faces became potent "symbol[s] of modernity."[19]

The vogue for short bobbed hair for women, following World War I, also required a shift in their grooming practices, including more regular cuts and the use of sharp razors to achieve clean and crisp lines. Frequent visits to the hairdresser or, initially for some, the barber, as well as the use of fixatives and tonics ensured that the connections between aesthetic liberation and hygienic and grooming practices were explicit.[20] In 1920, a US company based in Tennessee, La Creole Laboratories, harnessed the power of the American Medical Association to sell its shampoo and other hairdressing products emphasizing that "absolute cleanliness is essential for beautiful, healthy hair," and prescribing that customers shampoo every ten to fourteen days.[21] Numerous popular hair-care manuals equally proselytized the benefits of frequent washing with soap-based shampoos, although, as historian Caroline Cox has observed, this trend took off slowly, especially among working-class women who struggled to get access to hot water.[22]

Around the same time, pioneering entrepreneurs in an emerging African American hair and beauty industry were developing parallel marketing techniques and products motivated not just by the need to mirror white raced ideals of good (i.e. straightened) hair, but also by a desire for consumers to enjoy better hair health and hygiene. Annie Turbo Malone from St. Louis, Missouri founded the Poro company in the early twentieth century and began to manufacture products to counteract hair loss caused by insufficient diets and the poor sanitary conditions experienced by many Black women in Jim Crow

FIGURE 5.1: The carefully groomed face of modernity: *Saturday Evening Post*, July 8, 1922. Saturday Evening Post/Wikipedia Commons/Public Domain.

America. Poro's "Miracle Hair Grower" had the added effect of making Black hair more manageable and easier to comb without the aid of water.[23] Madame C.J. Walker, who revolutionized the use of the hot comb with a range of lotions and other treatments explicitly suited to the care and conditioning of Black hair, also employed innovative advertising techniques. Walker company marketing strategies frequently utilized the rhetoric of health linked to social aspiration to promote the benefits of her "secret formulae," asking in one advertisement from the 1920s: "Have you short, thin unsightly hair? ... Do you want a good job?" and offering a "Haven of Hope For Millions."[24]

Advertisers in many western consumer economies in the 1930s promoting physical hair health drew explicit connections between proper hair care, personal satisfaction, and mental hygiene, especially important in a moment of economic malaise. A 1931 advertisement for Poro emphasized the psychological benefits of grooming and well-dressed hair that might accrue to its customers: "Chasing the Blues Away! Nothing so lifts one out of the 'dumps' as a nice, warm bath … hair properly dressed … and a few minutes' attention to the skin."[25] An emphasis on the achievement of personal attractiveness and peace of mind as contingent upon careful and deliberate hair hygiene was a technique commonly deployed to sell an expanding range of products to a growing mass market. As clean hair achieved through more frequent washing was extensively promoted as part of modern hygienic regimens for women and men alike, so too were nourishing tonics intended to counter the dryness frequent shampooing might cause. One for Brylcreem hair oil from 1939 (Figure 5.2) declared: "Water actually *dries* your hair! And 'Dry Hair,' as you know is the forerunner of dandruff, thinning hair, and ultimate baldness."[26]

The responses that British men and women gave to a series of survey questions in 1939 as part of a large-scale project, known as Mass Observation, are instructive here in understanding how people talked and thought about grooming and self-presentation. Previous research has shown how Mass Observation respondents interpreted the potential benefits of healthy and hygienic grooming practices in response to new ideas in fashion and physical culture circulated in advertising and other forms of popular media.[27] A thirty-seven-year-old London man, for instance, employed language that clearly focused on aspects of psychological fulfillment: "My conscious reasons for trying to look nice are first self-esteem I suppose … When well-groomed I feel more confident and can be at ease with my fellows. I hate to be thought common or rough; & thus I try to look smart & keep my dignity."[28]

FIGURE 5.2: Brylcreem advertisement (1939): "Don't Let Your Daily Dip Cause 'Dry Hair'." The Advertising Archives, London.

Even during World War II, despite shortages and limitations placed on the manufacturing of some consumer goods, hair-care products and toiletries were seen as essential to maintaining the morale of combatant nations. A beauty industry executive noted: "It is our feeling that toiletries are necessary for men and women to maintain their self-confidence and their courage."[29] In 1943, one advertisement employed a propagandist rhetoric to cast gray hair as a "heartless dictator," a tyrant that women should resist and "refuse to tolerate" by using Clairol Shampoo Tint (Figure 5.3).[30]

Characterized by Angela Liljequist as an era that saw the "Shampoo Revolution," the late 1940s and 1950s ushered in the tradition of, at least, weekly hair washing.[31]

FIGURE 5.3: Clairol's hair coloring as an antidote to the tyranny and dictatorial powers of gray hair (1943). The Advertising Archives/Alamy Stock Photo.

Advertisements for shampoos highlighted the ability of products to leave users "overjoyed" and delighted by "the highlights, the lustre, the glorious silkiness."[32] The frequency with which people shampooed increased dramatically with new standards of health and hygiene,[33] as well as the rise of lanolin-based shampoos that replaced harsher soap-based products.[34] One survey reported an increase by 5 percent between 1944 and 1945 in the number of Americans who washed their hair every seven days.[35] In an advertisement for Silvikrin shampoo that appeared in a 1952 issue of *Picture Post* (an enormously popular illustrated weekly in Great Britain), its use was described not only as a healthy tonic but also as the perfect safeguard against the ill effects of the hustle and bustle of modern life. Harkening back to often doom-laden advertisements from the late nineteenth century, the copy warned, "under the conditions of modern life *nobody's* hair health can be taken for granted."[36]

For men seeking to prove their postwar masculine credentials, the crew cut and other close-cropped styles associated with military conformity and both moral and physical cleanliness remained *de rigueur*. In a 1953 advertisement for Jeris's Antiseptic Hair Tonic—the name in and of itself emphasizing the product's hygienic qualities—dandruff was cast as an ugly and unhygienic affliction whose eradication was essential for "femme" or sex "appeal" (Figure 5.4); the copy proclaimed: "Gals love its he-man fragrance. Its clean, crisp, manly scent. With JERIS on your topknot, your femme-appeal's potent."[37]

Explicit connections between physical hygiene and hair health and the risks attached to complacency about following its regimens were not, however, the exclusive preserve of advertisers in this era. Beauty manuals and advice guides also made clear the links between normal physiological functions, beautiful, healthy hair, and "natural" femininity. One British beauty guide by Veronica Dengel that remained popular throughout the late 1940s and 1950s, exhorted readers:

> Unless you establish a regular schedule of bowel elimination, you cannot hope to have shiny hair. Retention of body waste in the large colon is a certain method of ruining your health, youth, and beauty. Failure to respond to the physical urge for a bowel movement is one of the greatest and gravest causes of constipation among civilized peoples.

Clearly ascribing great importance to regular bowel movements, the author went on to provide further advice about lavatory regimens. In addition to committing to time on the toilet each morning, readers of Dengel's guide were instructed to relax, place their feet on a stool, and bend over to mimic a squat. Readers were also reminded to avoid distracting thoughts or actions, such as filing one's nails.[38]

For women consumers in the early 1950s, elaborately curled, colored, and bouffant styles predominated. These required frequent, often weekly, visits to hairdressers but were accompanied by corresponding shifts in personal beauty regimens, hair hygiene practices, and consumer habits. Products like Lustre-Crème shampoo, for example, used an image of immaculately groomed Hollywood star Elizabeth Taylor to promote the product's magical and hygienic properties for the domestic user: "Under the spell of its lanolin-blessed lather, your hair shines, behaves, is eager to curl. Hair dulled by soap abuse ... dusty with dandruff, now is fragrantly clean. Hair robbed of its natural sheen now glows with renewed highlights."[39] Even the most ubiquitous and mundane of hairdressing tasks such as brushing were subject to detailed descriptions in a broad range of advice literature including a 1963 book, published in London, with the title of *Modern Living: Your Looks*.[40]

FIGURE 5.4; Charlton Heston promoting the hygienic qualities and sex appeal of Jeris Antiseptic Hair Tonic (1953). The Advertising Archives/Alamy Stock Photo.

HEALTH AND HYGIENE   101

The growth of an expanded range of hair-care products in the postwar period was dramatic: aerosol hairsprays, new products for treating dandruff, new techniques in coloring and "permanents" that could curl the hair without, literally, frying it at very high temperatures, and a variety of new hair preparations for men.[41] Many were increasingly oriented toward home use.[42] Hair conditioner was introduced to female consumers and home hair coloring and permanents became more commonplace. The French-based, but clearly international, company L'Oréal in 1950 advertised a permanent solution by emphasizing the ability of the product to create a naturally undulating curl rather than an unnatural *frisée* (curl) that resembled the hair of a poodle (Figure 5.5).[43] The makers of "Miss Clairol Hair Color Bath" similarly reassured domestic consumers in 1960 that they too could use the product and achieve the "wholesome good looks" which, the copy continued, were "as much a matter of grooming and fresh, sparkling hair color as of pretty features."[44]

FIGURE 5.5: L'Oréal instructs women how to avoid a poodle-like permanent curl with their products (1950). Author's own collection.

In the decades that followed, the bouffant was cast by a new generation of young hairdressers such as Vidal Sassoon, and by an increasingly important youth market, as symbolic of an older generation: static and reliant on unnatural teasing, styling, and volumes of aerosol hairspray. Sassoon's revolutionary geometric bob, in contrast, relied on precise cutting to produce dramatic cascades of hair that moved naturally and fell back into place easily.[45] As the 1960s gave way to the 1970s, the trend for longer "natural" hairstyles for men and women alike provoked a 28 percent decrease in the number of American barber shops between 1972 and 1982.[46] Wider social and intergenerational tensions were also reflected in conflicting discourses about hair that privileged, depending on the group speaking, artifice or naturalness, stillness or movement, and constraint or freedom.

Curiously, the rejection by younger consumers of the traditional hairdressing profession, "big hair," or crewcut conformity did not necessarily mean a wholesale dismissal of grooming culture, the benefits of consumer society, or the notion that hair health remained important. For many, in fact, the countercultural stance and radical politics associated with long hair relied on an engagement with a hair-care industry that capitalized on these trends and sought to earn profits by promoting new beauty standards. Thus, as we shall see in the next section of this chapter, long hair could be derided by some contemporaries at the same time that it was embraced by the manufacturers of shampoos and other grooming products that sought to counter the potential trichological problems long hair could bring. One example, an advertisement for Wella Balsam Shampoo, that appeared in a 1973 issue of *Playboy* magazine (Figure 5.6), attempted to capitalize on consumer anxieties and an expanding men's market by suggesting: "The longer your hair is, the more chance it has to get thin, broken and dull." This shampoo was situated as an effective and healthful cleanser that also had the effect of making hair easy to comb. For those consumers who needed extra help, Wella instant conditioner was said to allow them to "stay in style but get your head together."[47]

As significantly, self-expression through hair styling and an engagement with healthy grooming techniques were also present in the "me" decade of the 1980s. This era was not, however, one characterized by the hippie-inspired naturalness of the late 1960s and 1970s but, once again, by excess, particularly in the form of "big" hair. The association between voluminous hair and femininity persisted throughout the twentieth century but its exaggerated nature and extension to the realm of male styles meant that it acquired new meanings during an acquisitive decade.[48] While for women like Margaret Thatcher, a coiffed helmet of big hair functioned as both a form of protection and a projection of power, for others big hair symbolized a revival of glamour, an embrace of a style that was popularized in American television programs like *Dynasty* and *Dallas*.[49] Curiously, the tousled and teased hairstyles of the 1980s were not necessarily intended to be artificial and were still seen as the product of good hygiene and visits to the hairdresser for regular cuts and natural-looking permanent waves. Sally Brampton, a fashion journalist writing in the British newspaper *The Observer* in 1982 noted: "Of course, this 'natural' look requires as much art as more contrived styles. Few of us are happy with what nature intended, so the top hairdressers are constantly developing new methods to produce an artless finish that looks as if you simply threw a comb through your hair before going out."[50]

The relationship between good grooming, physical and mental health, and the articulation of social identities in the West continued during the closing decades of the twentieth century. The British social survey Mass Observation was revived in the 1980s and recorded the views of a thirty-eight-year-old male florist who noted the following

FIGURE 5.6: Wella sells its products to men with longer hair in the 1970s (1973). Wikipedia/Creative Commons/Public Domain.

with respect to hair care and hygiene and the impact of advertising in 2001: "I have probably tried every shampoo and conditioner on the market and this is where television advertising comes in. I remember an ad campaign a few years ago for a new shampoo which smelt entirely of apples and for a few weeks I walked around smelling like an orchard!"[51] In addition to commenting on the impact of advertising, many respondents also chose to discuss the relationship between personal satisfaction and good hair hygiene. In language reminiscent of the responses from the late 1930s, another respondent—a sixty-six-year-old male retiree—observed: "I do think it is important to keep ones [sic] hair looking clean and tidy for your own self-respect as much as for any social asset."[52]

THE POLITICS OF HAIR AND HYGIENE IN THE TWENTIETH CENTURY

Over the course of the twentieth century, regimes of hair health and hygiene, while often promoted in terms of personal grooming and adherence to fashionable trends, were imbued with broader political and social significance. This most natural of human attributes possesses tremendous symbolic and signifying potential, as Geraldine Biddle-Perry and Sarah Cheang have asserted: "Hair as fetish or fashion serves as a powerful vehicle for all kinds of anxieties and their social proscription. It presents a narrative of human experience and a significant and historically consistent vocabulary of subjective identification and performative expression."[53] Ranging from the social rebellion embodied in the feminine embrace of short hair and a boyish aesthetic in the 1920s to the political assertions of long hair and Black civil rights associated with the Afro in the 1960s and 1970s, the links between hair and hair hygiene have consistently played a key role in assertions of the self and the articulation of a political or cultural voice. Alternatively, for those interested in repudiating these assertions of selfhood, critiques of these trends over the course of the twentieth century have functioned as attempts to reinforce the normative values as well as white, heterosexual, and patriarchal authority.

In the 1920s, women had their hair cut radically short in a fashionable bob to visibly reject the elaborate, voluminous, and seemingly oppressive coiffures of an older generation. Women's short hair was a dynamic sign of independence and the product of technological innovations before and during World War I.[54] The bob complemented a new fashion aesthetic that was freer in form, boxier, and more masculine and sought to embody new ideals of modern femininity and demands for social change and political equality. In France, as historians Mary Louise Roberts and Steven Zdatny have noted, the style became especially popular after women read Victor Margueritte's 1922 novel *La Garçonne* (a feminized version of the French word for boy).[55] However, women with short hair were subject to intense wider sociopolitical scrutiny in Europe, North America, and elsewhere, including China, Japan, and the Philippines.[56] In Britain, they were frequently pilloried in the popular press and the subject of sometimes humorous, but often vituperative, critiques portraying them in social commentary and caricature as "unhealthy" deviants or misguided fashion victims.[57] Simultaneously, some traditionalists in France argued that the new practice was unhygienic: long hair, it was asserted, protected the scalp from the unhealthy bacteria and germs that might lead to hair loss on the head or, indeed, hair growth on the face.[58]

In a speech delivered in Atlantic City, New Jersey, in 1924 by a vice president of the Wholesale Beauty Trade Association, the threat of women somehow acquiring masculine physical traits through cutting their hair was again highlighted: "The great-granddaughters of the bobbed beauties of the present will be able to twirl jaunty moustaches and trim their beards a la Vandyke. Baldness will be as common among them as among men."[59] For these critics, bobbed hair represented a threat to the gender order, to families, and, most significantly in France, to pronatalist perspectives and policies that sought to increase birth rates. Stories of husbands confining their wives to their houses for cutting their hair or, in one instance, a father killing his daughter for the same infraction abounded.[60] Violence surfaced in other contexts; the *Manchester Guardian* reported in 1925 that Viennese female high school students who wore short hair were attacked by male students for "not being proper Germans."[61]

For some women, the embrace of closely cropped hair and masculine clothing styles enabled them to mark same-sex desiring sexual identities in new ways. The sensational aspects of Radclyffe Hall's lesbian novel *The Well of Loneliness*, published in 1928, were closely associated with the author's physical and fashionable characteristics, especially her closely cropped hair.[62] While these styles were widely circulated within popular culture, the novel was deemed obscene in the trial that followed its publication and a gradual abandonment of masculine fashions by "straight-identified" women ensued as the 1920s gave way to the 1930s.[63] However, the novel raised awareness of the potential expression of gender nonconformity and sexual difference through one's hair and the fashioned body, as reflected in the appearance of the novel's central character—Stephen Gordon. One Mass Observation respondent, a British insurance official, self-identified as "physically female; mentally etc. male," noted how the construction of a masculine identity was rooted, in part at least, in hair hygiene and grooming practices that conformed to the actions of other men. This individual reported in their response to the 1939 Mass Observation directive on physical appearance: "I have my hair cut on the average about once a month." They went on to describe regular trips to the same "man in the City" for regular trims and the use of brilliantine for styling—all techniques that were fairly standard for British men in the 1930s.[64]

Concerns about hair and hair hygiene entered the political realm in other ways in the decades immediately following World War I. Deviance from normative hair ideals, particularly in styles or practices seen as symbolic of moral, racial, and national degeneracy, took on more dangerous implications with the rise of fascism in several European countries and the outbreak of World War II. In fascist Italy, the thin, masculinized women of the 1920s were derided as threats to the nation with their short, sleek hairstyles and potentially sterile bodies, while fuller-figured women with longer, naturally wavy hair (occasionally tied back in kerchiefs) were valorized as symbols of maternal fecundity.[65] The extremist ideology of racial cleansing and fear of contamination also informed the official view of National Socialism, which focused on vilifying foreign French and American fashions and styles through the embrace of natural "Aryan" beauty. The party line incorporated not just ideals of white raced superiority but also a rejection of artifice in the form of makeup or permanent waves and a celebration of long hair, frequently contained by a bun or braids.[66] While never entirely consistent in terms of policy or expectations regarding women's appearance or their engagement with "foreign" fashions, as historian Irene Guether has noted, the Nazi state, nonetheless, saw a connection between the maintenance of a certain type of appearance (and hairstyle), racial ideologies, and economic and cultural goals.[67] In carrying this perspective to its most extreme conclusions, the Nazis shaved the heads of concentration camp prisoners to abuse and humiliate them. This act also sought to dehumanize by denying prisoners the subjective autonomy associated with hair and its management as an intrinsic marker of human identification.[68]

When war broke out in a fractured Europe in 1939, the bodies of soldiers were disciplined to promote military efficiency and good health. Aside from medical inspection to ensure that they met minimum weight and health requirements and were free of venereal disease, the soldier's hair was cut to a regulation length to both highlight conformity and ensure general hygiene.[69] In fact, expectations regarding hygiene were high in the military as reflected in guidebooks for soldiers from a variety of countries. In one handbook for American soldiers from 1941, readers were told: "Now that you have been accepted in the military service it is your duty to our country and yourself to keep well and ready for any service." Avoiding disease and maintaining a clean and tidy appearance were central to these responsibilities. Good hygiene involved not only regular shaving but also "protecting oneself from the vermin that might infest the body hair."[70] The haircut was, of course, part of the hygienic and regulatory rituals that all soldiers in combatant nations underwent upon entering the military during World War II. In one reminiscence of their experiences of this time, the child of a Welsh volunteer who went into service in 1941 told a story of their father's first military haircut. Rather than receiving a "Clark Gable style" or a "Leslie Howard quiff," James Gow watched as the barber pushed "the clippers' metal forks ... through his oiled quiff" and saw a "roll of black hair" fall to ground. He emerged with stubble that, his child noted, "wouldn't have been out of place in the Red Army."[71]

As World War II concluded, the cutting of hair continued to both possess political significance and function as a mechanism of social control and symbolic cleansing.

As the Nazis were defeated throughout Europe in 1944 and 1945, those who had collaborated with the regime, particularly women, were singled out for harsh forms of public punishment. Their heads were shaved in ritual acts of vengeance that were often accompanied by verbal taunts and other forms of physical violence.[72] Notable examples were those of the shorn women of France accused of either direct political collaboration or, more likely, of *collaboration horizontale* (sexual relationships with German officials and soldiers),[73] and thus of infidelity to the nation. One description from the period demonstrates the potency of hair symbolism: "Down on the ground, a woman is defending herself from a wild crowd. 'Friend of the German' someone says. A local hairdresser shears her head. He leaves her a long lock by which she is dragged by some shrieking women."[74] Shaving functioned in these contexts not just as a form of public humiliation, but also as an act intent on forcefully subverting women's sexual allure: the eradication of "natural" feminine hair serving to allay fears of contamination and safeguard the future health of the nation.

The cutting, growing, and display of long and short hair allied to institutional discourses of moral and physical health and hygiene and its regulation took on a growing political significance in the postwar world with the rise of rock and roll, youth subcultures, and increasingly vocal feminist, Black, and gay civil rights movements. As historian Lynne Luciano has observed in relation to Elvis Presley: "Not only would Elvis shock America with his pelvic gyrations, adopt black music styles, and wear flamboyant 'Negro' clothing, he would blur the physical distinctions between men and women with hair that demanded a complicated regimen of fussing and combing."[75] An emphasis on dress and in particular on the styling and grooming of hair was central to articulating lesbian identity in the 1950s and 1960s, especially among those who were part of an emerging butch-femme culture that existed on both sides of the Atlantic (Figure 5.7). One woman that frequented lesbian bars in London observed the hallmarks of a butch identity in the period: "The extremes in dress were fascinating, I mean some of the more butch women. I mean, navy blue suits, immaculate white shirt, you know, ties with a Windsor knot. Short cropped haircuts."[76] Women who aspired to butch looks in New York City, especially when going out at night, as Alex Ginter has observed, transformed fashionably short feminine hairstyles into carefully combed ducktail styles that were punctuated by both the telltale tapered back and "D.A." (duck ass) and often extravagant pompadour tops.[77]

In the 1960s and early 1970s, long rather than short hair on young men and women became ubiquitous as a component of the broader social and political turmoil of the period. Engaged in a generational and political rebellion against the establishment and its normative values, teenagers and young adults asserted their "freedom" to wear their hair in any way they saw fit. The cult musical *Hair*, which opened in New York City in 1968, famously celebrated such freedom with actors appearing on stage naked and proclaiming in song:

Hair ...
Flow it, show it, long as God can grow it, my hair,
I want it long, straight, curly, fuzzy, snaggy, shaggy,
Ratty, matty, oily, greasy, fleecy, shining, gleaming,
    steaming ...
Twisted, beaded, braided, powdered, flowered and
    confettied,
Bangled, tangled, spangled, spaghettied.[78]

FIGURE 5.7: Blue and Sunny: A butch-femme couple in 1950s America with Blue wearing a tie and a pompadour. Photo courtesy Lesbian Herstory Archives.

Similarly in this period, feminist writer and activist Germaine Greer in her groundbreaking study *The Female Eunuch* used standards about hair care to comment on the oppressive dialectic of mass consumerism and feminine beauty ideals: "I'm sick of weighting my hair with a dead mane, unable to move my neck freely, terrified of rain, of wind, of dancing too vigorously in case I sweat into my lacquered curls."[79] Greer, like others in her generation, recognized that regimens of hair care were never simply just an effect of physiological or biological impetus but also a tool of both political oppression *and* potential radicalism.

At the same time, Black women and men in the United States and elsewhere began to reject hairstyles and practices that had historically privileged white raced beauty aesthetics in favor of the more "natural" and voluminous Afro (Figure 5.8). The American novelist, journalist, and educator Bebe Moore Campbell noted the political significance of the style: "In the 1960s and 70s, the afro was more than hair ... It was the symbol of black pride, a silent affirmation of African American roots and the beauty of Blackness." Radical changes, Campbell continued, were needed: "Time to change the definitions of nappy and kinky to mean good. Real good."[80]

Alternative understandings of what constituted the healthy and the "natural" and the assumptions of race, gender, or sexuality that sustained them were thus a key part of the countercultural politics of the 1960s. However, demands for change were expressed in and through the body and strategies of self-presentation in ways that challenged the status quo and fueled intergenerational and social tensions. While running for governor in the late 1960s, the actor-turned-politician and future Republican president Ronald Reagan, equated hair-length with poor hygiene noting, in a now famous joke, that male hippies "dress like Tarzan, have hair like Jane, and smell like Cheetah." Set against the background of US involvement in Vietnam, the superficial gloss of humor masks the underlying social divisions and sense of cultural crisis prevalent at this time. This was more markedly revealed in the moral panic that ensued after the murder of the actress Sharon Tate and others in Los Angeles in 1969 by followers of cult leader Charles Manson. Fear of long hair became palpable in the streets of that city where people worried that every hippie might be a potential killer.[81]

Contested politicized meanings about healthy social and individual bodies symbolically and materially expressed in and through the care and management of their hair did not just disappear because people no longer saw long hair as either remarkable or a threat. In the 1980s and 1990s in the wake of the AIDS crisis, the fit and hairless masculine body was privileged along with clipped and sometimes shaved head hair to both counteract

FIGURE 5.8: Black Panther Party members, many wearing "Afros" as forms of political expression, supporting the organization's cofounder Huey P. Newton in Oakland, California (1968). Everett Collection Historical/Alamy Stock Photo.

negative stereotypes of all gay men as bearers of disease and to highlight health and resilience in an age of devastation. As Allan Peterkin has noted in his study of facial hair, "the shaved face, chest, legs, genitals, and anus on muscled bodies ... reassured men of the object's (or partner's) purity, youth, and by extension, freedom from disease."[82]

CONCLUSION

The discourses about hair and hair care intrinsic to the fashioning of individual and group subjectivities in the modern age are clearly never just about the material aspects of personal grooming and hygiene. Embedded within them are a complex set of ideas about not only the human engagement with the material world but also the intertwined relationship that exists between aesthetics and the construction of individual and social bodies. Exploring the history of hygienic hair-care practice and products and their promotion clearly provides an important point of access for understanding the potent symbolism of hair cleansing and styling rituals. Decisions about the cutting of one's hair or the shaving of one's face or body are never arbitrary nor do they operate exclusively in a vacuum of personal aesthetic choice. Rather, attitudes about grooming, hair care, and bodily hygiene must always be situated within specific national, ideological, economic, or cultural contexts. They must also be understood to betray political perspectives and the relationships of individuals and groups alike to both normative and non-normative cultural beliefs and practices.

This chapter has explored the various interconnections that have existed, at different moments, between social change and personal grooming. As with all choices related to the fashioning of the human body, decisions about hair growth, hair removal, and hair care must be interpreted as meaningful cultural practices. On the one hand, the study of hair care and hair hygiene illustrates the twentieth-century obsession with consumption, the human engagement with visual culture, and emerging discourses of personal hygiene. On the other, it also serves to illuminate just how central the close inspection of the body is to deep considerations of the human experience, the human relationship to nature and the ability to control or transcend it, and, ultimately, the exercise of power.

CHAPTER SIX

Gender and Sexuality

The Gender and Sexual Politics of Hair

CHELSEA JOHNSON AND KRISTEN BARBER

The gendered body is made, not born; it is in constant flux as both local cultural traditions and larger politics shape bodies and ultimately relationships between groups of people. Judith Butler's theories of performativity "made trouble" by suggesting the corporeal disruption of essentialist notions of identity and constraining gender scripts.[1] The flapper of the 1920s, for example, is one of the most controversial images of the modern age: a brash young woman sporting shorter skirts, staying out late at jazz clubs, smoking, drinking, driving, and, infamously lobbing off her hair close to her head in a short, angular style known as "the bob." Emerging on the heels of women's increased entry into the workforce during World War I, women's short hair signaled a sense of freedom from previous moral codes and gender expectations. Aligned with feminist demands for women's suffrage, it threatened the sex-segregated institutions of traditional feminine propriety and the androcentric state.

The management of hair, while often taken for granted as a benign everyday practice or form of personal self-expression, is both politically and socially significant. This chapter considers how gender politics shape what hair looks like and means in different places and at different times—what Butler might describe as the "relationship between how gender appears and what gender signifies."[2] As we move from the 1920s into the present day, it becomes clear that the importance of coiffing is not solely a women's issue. Nor is it one that can be presented in all its complexity without considering how sexuality, race, ethnicity, religion, and global economics inform how we approach hair. Practices involving the styling of hair, the covering of hair, and the growing out or removal of hair are more wholly understood in terms of nationalism, global capitalist exchange, and the politics of exclusion. This is because the wider dimensions of styling make visible the oppressive character of white, Anglo, heteronormative, middle-class, and western norms. Recognizing these norms helps to reveal the political injustices that privilege some at the expense of others and to challenge constructions of "authentic" identities assumed to arise from shared experiences.

OPPOSITIONAL HAIR: MAKING MEN AND WOMEN

In his study on hair symbolism, sociologist Anthony Synnott puts forward a "theory of opposites" that suggests men and women are supposed to have opposite hair; that head and body hair are opposite; and that opposite political ideologies are associated with distinct styles, including hairstyles.³ It is the unique variety and malleability of this oppositional structure that Synnott argues makes hair important in the construction of social norms that affect what sexed and gendered bodies look like in different contexts.⁴ For example, in many cultures while hair on a woman's head is highly valued, women with visible body and facial hair are stigmatized as dirty or monstrous, or as failing to achieve western feminine ideals.⁵ An estimated 99 percent of American women have shaved, waxed, or plucked their auxiliary hair, with 85 percent doing so regularly.⁶ This practice reveals the salience of hetero-cultural expectations that conflate feminine sexiness with corporeal hairlessness.

Because gender is assumed to reflect biological sex, body and facial hair serve as "cultural genitalia" to distinguish men from women.⁷ This is especially important for female-to-male transgender people who navigate sometimes very public gender transitions.⁸ Sociologist Kristen Schilt's research on the experiences of transgender men at work finds that the ability for FTMs (female to male transgender people) to accomplish masculinity is intimately tied to body size, muscular frame, hairstyle, and facial hair growth. Growing facial hair with hormone therapy can take years, and with the absence of facial hair or visible stubble in the early stages of transition, FTMs are frequently mistaken for being years or even decades younger than they are.⁹ Without facial hair, many FTMs fail to access the patriarchal dividends available to other men at work, such as presumed competence, authority, and prestige. In this way, the cultural tendency to tie facial hair to masculinity helps to support the "glass ceiling,"¹⁰ keeping both women and men who don't live up to masculine ideals from career advancement.

For some men in religious contexts, facial hair holds a crucial place in distinguishing themselves from women. For example, Sikhs consider hair God's creation and so eschew cutting their hair and even trimming their beards as a sign of religious and sexual maturity; and for Muslims, beards are an important marker of Islamic masculinity.¹¹ Within these societies, men's grooming practices naturalize the institutions of patriarchy and oppositional gender roles. Oftentimes, women's head hair is seen as a source of temptation and pride, and indicative of sexual maturity or marital status. And so, as men grow their hair out as a sign of authority, women cover their hair to signal feminine virtue and moral probity and privacy.

In many religions around the world, gendered hair is assigned a significant symbolic value because it is imbued with particularly erotic, intimate, or powerful qualities. Married Orthodox women wear head coverings, demonstrate modestly, and some add their hair is especially sacred in religious doctrine, serving as a sign of righteous womanhood and thus a key target for shaming, for example, when priests uncover the hair of a woman suspected of infidelity. Traditional head coverings were largely abandoned by many Jewish women in the 1960s, but sheitel wigs were seen to offer a popular "natural" and more modern alternative to cloth head coverings in ultra-Orthodox but cosmopolitan communities such as the bustling and diverse neighborhood of Crown Heights, Brooklyn, where Orthodox Jewish women support a thriving market for human hair wigs.

The Jewish snood, like the Muslim hijab, has come under fire by some feminist groups for representing a husband's ownership of his wife and casting an unfair burden on women to signal their piety. Other Jewish women argue that covering their hair is a feminist expression of autonomy and faith, a practice that encourages others to see them as more than bodies. Leonard Nimoy, actor and photographer, took a feminist approach to critiquing Jewish representations of women's bodies, highlighting the double standard women experience when they are reduced to their supposed essential (hetero) sensuality. Nimoy spent seven years artistically engaging the Jewish deity Shekhina, from whom Jewish men are supposed to shield their faces or otherwise look away. "Why can't we look?" he asked. He represents Shekhina as a naked female body, capturing the "simultaneous idolization of femininity and invisibility of the female body in religion, specifically in Judaism."[12] In this way, Nimoy highlights the ways veiling women's bodies, hair included, tell us something not only about women's relationships to their own bodies or to a capitalist industry, but also about their roles as cultural symbols for ethnic, gendered, sexual, and religious institutions.

Male devotees also have to navigate tensions around historical religious rules on hair and its various and complex contemporary interpretation. The formal aesthetics of hair styling in different religious contexts are subject to change while the signifying practices remain relatively static. There can thus be many different reasons why men shun the razor (see Figure 6.1).[13] Orthodox Jews cultivate long beards and often times grow out payots—elaborate, curled sideburns. These practices honor ancient Hebrew "beard-

FIGURE 6.1: Payot on young Hasid man. Wikimedia Commons.

preservation laws" that make facial hair a sign of ethnic identity and religious piety. This is an ode to "God's grace," whereby men preserve the presumed authentic self that sets Jewish men up as public specters of the covenant. After World War II, a movement for western European Jewish men to embrace the beard became a nationalist project whereby they claimed association with the Middle East instead of Europe. This is similar to Muslim men for whom "Hair had become the front line in the cultural battle between modernists and traditionalists."[14] Muslim men's beards have recently become politicized in the global north as a narrative of terrorism and fear proliferates around the rejection of western power and culture, and in the preservation of patriarchal relations. The separatist effect of this sort of facial hair has new consequences for men who might experience ethnic and religious suspicion and discrimination as they move about the world.

The institutional structures of gender and ideology are transcultural; and they symbolize religious, political, and sexual social acceptance and idiosyncratic identities—that is, "they are 'made flesh' in the hair as people conform to, or deviate from, the norms, and even deviate from deviant norms."[15] In order to overcome the complexities of almost limitless variations in styles that might have multiple meanings, Synnott suggests focusing on those modes representative of deviations from the norm.[16] The following sections, therefore, explore oppositional hairstyles that, like the bob in the 1920s, make trouble by questioning the traditional binary conventions of gender's supposed biologically rooted performance: Black Club Women, Black and Hispanic Zoot Suiters, civil rights advocates, feminists, hippies, punk rockers, and LBGT communities that are examples of recent social formations that have purposefully politicized hair over and against hegemonic cultural standards.

THE TANGLES OF RESISTANCE: HAIR IN BLACK LIBERATION

For Black women in the United States, hair culture in the modern age has served as a crucial site for reimagining Black femininity, mobilizing antiracist activism, and escaping economic oppression.[17] The salon—or more precisely, the beauty shop—is often a safe place where Black women care for each other and talk about and create looks that engage current gendered racial politics. Here, and at the kitchen table, Black women have long used sartorial means to testify to the struggles of being Black in societies where whites make the rules.[18] This testimony has sometimes been contradictory, but it has always been significant in reflecting the real tensions Black people have faced as they struggle for respect and recognition in their everyday lives. As scholar Audre Lorde notes, "[For] in order to survive, those of us for whom oppression is as American as apple pie have always had to be watchers, to become familiar with the language and manners of the oppressor, even sometimes adopting them for some illusion of protection."[19]

From the 1920s through the 1950s, straightened, ironed, and relaxed Black hair were linked to racial uplift. In a pre-civil rights era that saw a rising tide of Jim Crowism (a system of institutionalized racial apartheid), the careful grooming of hair that conformed to white ideals was strategized, notably by Black Club Women,[20] as a pathway to acceptance by more powerful whites.[21] Pioneering Black entrepreneurs from the turn of the century such as Madam C.J. Walker, Annie Turnbo Malone, and Madam Carter reinforced dominant ideals of feminine beauty by inventing products and technologies to press, or thermally straighten, Afro-textured hair.[22] Black beauty culturists became "global ambassadors for American consumer capitalism," disseminating images of Black women as respectable, upwardly mobile, and fashionable (see Figure 6.2).[23] But these women and their clientele were also often on the front lines of civil rights work.[24] Walker refused to sell skin lighteners and promoted a pride in "Black beauty"; her platform as a successful businesswoman allowed her to work alongside prominent Black leaders such as W.E.B. Du Bois, together petitioning lawmakers to create antilynching laws.

FIGURE 6.2: Badge from Madame C.J. Walker Convention. Created by Bastian Brothers Co. Photo: Addison Scurlock. Collection of the Smithsonian National Museum of African American History and Culture, Gift of Dr. Patricia Heaston.

Middle-class Black women formed local and national reform organizations, such as the National Association of Colored Women (NACW), that aimed to advance Black literacy, health care, and political access through interracial understanding. Black respectability politics intentionally emphasized cultural sameness to shift whites' focus away from essentialist tropes of racial inferiority as explanations for socioeconomic differences. The aim was to challenge racist ideas that circulated in the white imagination about the hypersexualization of Black women as wild and primitive—stereotypes that have been metaphorically mapped on to their bodies by stigmatizing kinky and curly hair.[25] However, while the discourse of respectability was an effective survival strategy of social and economic inclusion for many African American women, it also enforced narrow definitions of femininity on Black women already burdened with the responsibility to represent their race through their bodies.[26]

Black men experienced their own unique conflicts around race, gender, and respectability. In the early 1940s, they became known for their flamboyant, colorful, and oversized zoot suits and extravagantly styled hair at a time when white masculinity shunned sartorial lavishness. Zoot suiters wore their hair deliberately tousled, either combed together into a thick single curl or slicked high into a "pomp" at the front, and combed back from the sides to meet in a center vertical point in the back, resembling a duck's tail (Figure 6.3).[27] Black American men used a wide range of hair-care products to achieve this look, from chemical relaxers to pomades. In his autobiography, civil rights leader Malcolm X reflects on wearing the zoot suit and straightening his hair at home using lye, a caustic solution of sodium hydroxide so strong it burns the scalp. He recalled:

> When Shorty let me stand up and see in the mirror, my hair hung down in limp, damp strings ... I'd seen some pretty conks, but when it's the first time, on your *own* head, the transformation, after the lifetime of kinks, is staggering ... on top of my head was this thick, smooth sheen of shining red hair—real red—as straight as any white man's.[28]

Originally popular among Black men, this look was also adopted by young Mexican *pachucos*[29] in Texas, Arizona, and California in an effort to resist subordinating white middle-class normative masculinity.[30] In the xenophobic atmosphere catalyzed by Pearl Harbor, ideals of masculine respectability were increasingly tied to white American nationalism that *pachuco* style directly contradicted.[31] In response, the style became iconized as an early symbol of Chicano resistance and politics of confrontation. For these men, polished yet ostentatious suits and hairstyles symbolized self-determination in spite of widespread anti-Mexican feelings, racism, punitive border patrol agencies, and mass deportations in the American Southwest.[32] The time, care, and expertise required to successfully craft the look and the indulgent use of excessive amounts of fabric, defied harmful images of Mexicans as rural and backwards.

The aesthetic origins and gendered and racialized meanings of zoot suit style are ambiguous. Zoot suits were not popular among middle- and upper-class white men, particularly when the United States rationed fabric to support the war effort, and the white press painted zoot suits and their wearers as unpatriotic, careless, and thuggish. This accusation was further validated by inflammatory reports of men in zoot suits molesting white women. These tensions erupted into the Zoot Suit Riots of 1942. Despite Americans of all ethnic and racial origins being enlisted in the war, angry white military servicemen and civilians in Los Angeles targeted Mexican, Filipino, and Black men in zoot suits, pinning them down to violently rip off their suits and cut their hair in a

FIGURE 6.3: Rayfield McGhee in a zoot suit, Tallahassee, Florida, ca. 1942. Photo: Florida Memory. State Library of Florida/Wikimedia Commons/Public Domain.

powerful symbolic gesture of cultural imperialism.[33] But not all zoot suiters were men: two Black female gangs, the Slick Chicks and the Black Widows (named for their black zoot suit jackets, short skirts, and fishnet stockings), played an active role in the riots, challenging conventional notions of feminine beauty and sexuality and rebelling against urban poverty and alienation.[34]

For some Black American men, the zoot look symbolized cultural resistance to white masculine supremacy and offered "a tapestry of meaning, where music, politics and social action merged."[35] But for other young Black male activists, coloring and straightening

Afro-textured hair to achieve the look retrospectively became associated with ineffectual strategies of assimilation-as-oppression. Malcolm X came to view his conk as "the first really big step towards self-degradation" it was "ludicrous" for "Black people to adopt their [white] methods of relieving our oppression."[36] A new Black political movement was emerging that used corporeality to reject ethnic oppression. Acculturation and assimilation became seen as problematic and effective tools for realizing social mobility since they assume minority cultures are inferior and undervalue the unique contributions and beauty of marginalized groups.

By the 1960s, many Black men and women in the United States and United Kingdom challenged Eurocentric beauty ideals, and by extension white supremacy in the political, economic, and social spheres; they embraced "natural," kinky hair as a symbol of racial empowerment.[37] Throughout the Black Atlantic, not straightening one's hair, favoring dark skin, and choosing Black lovers were all part of reconnecting to an African homeland and alternative ideals of beauty.[38] Round, picked-out Afros, also referred to as "naturals," signified Black racial pride as part of the civil rights and Black Power movements. "Black is beautiful," the slogan went: liberated hair meant minds and bodies liberated from the colonial legacies associated with "nappy hair" as untamed and indicative of a primitive state.[39] Angela Davis, Kathleen Cleaver, Huey Newton, and Jesse Jackson were key figures in the movement who became cultural icons not just because of their antiracist politics but also because of their hair. When the US Federal Bureau of Investigation pursued and later tried scholar-activist Angela Davis in 1970—alleging kidnapping, murder, and conspiracy—the government and press circulated photographs that highlighted her "rebellious" Afro (see Figure 6.4). During and after the two months in which she was on the "Most Wanted" list and in hiding, Davis estimates that "hundreds, perhaps even thousands, of Afro-wearing Black women were accosted, harassed, and arrested."[40]

However, since the late 1960s, many Black women and men returned to a diverse range of straightening, perming, ironing, relaxing practices, weaves, wigs, and hairpieces. Their motivation for doing so is as varied as the styles they adopted, from following fashion trends or wanting to distance themselves from the Afro's association with militancy, to managing the pressures of working in a white corporate environment or the problems associated with the time, products, and processes required to style an Afro. Historian Kobena Mercer argues that this is precisely why it is a mistake to assign pathological self-hate to Black women who choose to wear weaves, or to consider Afros and dreadlocks as more authentically Black styles.[41] It is important to acknowledge the gendered dimensions of racial "authenticity" imbricated in the categorization of Black hair styling practices as *either* "authentic" or "natural" and thus politically resistant, *or* "unnatural," artificial, and thus conformist and assimilatory.[42]

RESISTING OPPOSITIONAL NORMS: HIPPIES, PUNK ROCK, AND RIOT GRRRLS

Oppositional hair practice implies a sense of agency in exposing the "mundane impersonations by which heterosexual masculinity and femininity are performed and naturalized and undermines their power by virtue of effecting that exposure."[43] Hair that makes trouble critiques prevailing hetero-normative values, making visible the social constructed-ness of its "truths"—that is, ideals of what men and women and "others" should look and behave like. Such concepts became integral to popular and political counter and subcultural strategies of self-presentation in the 1970s that played with gender and sexual norms to contest and reinterpret wider social conflict.

FIGURE 6.4: "Free Angela Davis!" poster: the Afro as a symbol of Black resistance. Collection of the Smithsonian National Museum of African American History and Culture.

At the same time as the Afro became a symbol of protest, many white youths in North America and Europe became members of a counterculture—so-called "hippies"—that rejected the conservative values of their parents. Hippies wore loose, often "ethnically" inspired clothing and beads. They let their hair grow long and sometimes tied it back with headbands or dressed it with flowers. Men grew out their beards and women let their curly or straight hair grow out naturally (see Figure 6.5). This look contrasted sharply with previous ideals of a crisply starched, neatly coiffed housewife and preppy, sweater-vested or flannel-suited man with short, slicked back hair. For young hippies, long hair was rebellious and uninhibited, and a key part of cultivating an aesthetic that explicitly rejected what they saw as the constraints of respectability by doing drugs, not working, and refusing to embed themselves in the commercial market—including the purchase and application of cosmetics and grooming products.⁴⁴ Older generations saw these youths as unpatriotic or anti-American; and anti-hippie protests broke out, with one historical photo showing a man holding a sign that reads: "Long hair is communism."

Young white men embraced long hair—or what historian Julia Willett refers to as "Jesus hair"⁴⁵—as a signifier of a feminized sensitivity and a rejection of narrow gender expectations for men to be strong and aggressive. "Damn the man" was a popular colloquial call to reject government involvement in the US Vietnam War, and to more generally question institutions of authority. Many young men were rethinking and challenging conventional gender scripts that funneled white, middle-class women into the home and their male cohort into the corporation. But others saw this new, softer male aesthetic as an affront to masculinity. For example, a group of Wayne State University fraternity members cut off all their hair in opposition to the "emasculation of American men."⁴⁶ Fears around boys' and men's feminization continue today as transgender politics and a spotlight on LGBT communities create what masculinities scholar Michael Kimmel refers to as a "crisis of masculinity." What is at risk here, he argues, is not just that men might be mistaken for women but also that they may lose their access to unfair privileges rewarded to them within a gender order that devalues both women and femininity.⁴⁷

There is still an emphasis on the importance of professional men coiffing their hair in neat and stylish ways so as to appeal to their clients;⁴⁸ while other studies show that some blue-collar men in construction eschew a sense of caring about how they look for fear of being taken by others as gay.⁴⁹ In contrast, contemporary "hipster" masculinities make it clear that some men care about how they look and are not afraid of new trends

FIGURE 6.5: Two hippies at the Woodstock Festival, August 1969. Photo: Derek Redmond and Paul Campbell—Own work, CC BY-SA 3.0, Wikimedia Commons.

in ambiguously gendered styles such as the "man bun" (Figure 6.6). One advice column suggests men wanting to sport a bun should "think more Indian Sikh than Kardashian at the gym."[50] This suggests that the man bun is as much a fad donned by high-status, straight celebrity men that draws upon the exoticization of ethnic others as it is a rejection of middle-class masculine convention.[51]

Exposing the contradictions of gendered subjectivity is not a substitute for actual social or political change, but it often opens up a performative space of transgression through strategic appropriation.[52] In the 1970s, musicians such as David Bowie and Mark Bolam pushed the boundaries of sexual binaries by wearing makeup, dyeing their hair, and wearing platform boots and exotic costumes (see Figure 6.7). The punk movement that then followed in Britain and the United States equally highlighted the radical potential for clothes and body adornment to critique mainstream culture through "the expression of rage and protest."[53]

Punks embodied an antiestablishment, nonconformist, antifashion ethos with torn jeans, leather jackets, bondage gear, Dr. Marten boots, t-shirts decorated with handwritten slogans, body piercings, and jewelry made from found objects such as pins, razor blades, and even tampons. Punks wore garish makeup, and their hair wildly colored, and sculpted with gel. Many shaved and styled their hair in Mohawks, with a central crest of hair that was sprayed to keep it upright.

Rock musician Iggy Pop, the progenitor of punk in the United States, has long played with gender norms by moving his body and playing with his long hair in ways that blur sexual binaries. But he has also at times engaged an aggressive phallic embodiment that simultaneously

FIGURE 6.6: Brent Michael Wood. Photo: Nan Palmero. https://www.flickr.com/photos/nanpalmero/sets/72157679848522636.

FIGURE 6.7: David Bowie's Genderqueer Fashion, onstage at the Hammersmith Odeon in London, 1973. The last Ziggy Stardust concert. Photo: Steve Wood/Express/Getty Images.

reflects the importance of subcultures for queer expressions of gender and rock's masculine privilege. For women, navigating the male dominated spaces of rock music is both physically and emotionally treacherous but also key in rethinking the limits of femininity.

The underground 1990s feminist hardcore movement Riot Grrrl reclaimed punk's musical subversive ethos and politics of style for a new generation of American women. Riot Grrrl challenged the androcentrism of punk by injecting feminist critique into the punk music, politics, and look. For Riot Grrrls, punk's rejection of mainstream culture and fashion offered a refuge from gender norms of behavior, and hair was an important part of expressing alternative femininities (see Figure 6.8).[54] Riot Grrrls like

FIGURE 6.8: The punk trend continues. Punk Girls with shaved heads and dayglo Mohicans, Morecambe, United Kingdom, 2003. Photo: de:Benutzer:Calzinide—Own work, Wikimedia Commons/Public Domain.

Ani Difranco—who uses her music to promote feminist and antiracist messages[55]—are popularly portrayed as angry women. This is because they seek to reclaim their bodies as well as their sexual and gender identities, and to carve out conspicuous subjectivities by rejecting the idea they should "look like girls."

Riot Grrrls articulated a sense of agency over the cultivation and meaning of women's bodies by parodying feminine artifice, using outrageous makeup, and coloring their hair with vegetable dyes. Punk DIY (do it yourself) fashion and hair styling were aligned with a growing natural hair movement to expose the commercialized nature and limitations of gender norms. The style challenged hetero-feminine definitions of appropriate womanhood that situate women as ideally desirable to cismen.[56] Through a gendered bricolage of studded leather gear, "girly" bows, and cheerleading skirts, Riot Grrrls reclaimed the playfulness of girlhood in ways they felt were missing from second "wave" feminism and those who viewed fashions in clothes, hair styling, and makeup as oppressive to women.[57]

THE GENDER POLITICS OF THE GLOBAL HAIR INDUSTRY

Hair is uniquely malleable, and so its cultural significance and symbolic power are various. Ethnically, racially, and ideologically diverse, old and young, heterosexual, gay, bi, and transgender men and women have appropriated oppositional hairstyles and hair practices. However, while "fashion and dissidence may combine,"[58] Butler makes it clear that an identikit of fashions, including hairstyles, cannot just be "freely" selected from a range of possible options and then "tried on" for size.⁵⁹ Rather, performativity is a system of overlapping tropes of social revelation and disavowal that reveal the compulsory rather than arbitrary means of its production. We are engaged in cultures with symbolic codes that are difficult, if not impossible, to avoid. This sort of compulsion is easy to see in modern western religious, or otherwise ritualized, hair-styling practices that have indeed rippled out globally in the modern age.

Contemporary fashions in the global north, particularly in cosmopolitan contexts, show that it is sometimes acceptable to indulge in seemingly contradictory hair regimes. New trends such as dyeing Black hair platinum blonde or the "man bun" are ambiguously raced, gendered, or sexed.⁶⁰ These hairstyles suggest autonomy from and resistance to proscriptive body norms and the hegemonic structures of oppression of which they are a part. However, structures of inequality do not easily disappear. When white women wear hair extensions, for example, this is generally to accomplish length—think reality TV celebrity and heiress Paris Hilton—rather than when Black women use them to change the texture of their hair. How women wear hair devices reflects historical race, class, and gender hierarchies.

As the brightly colored, intricate, and towering art pieces seen on the streets and in Black hair shows reveal, hair additions are a vehicle for Black cultural innovation, creativity, and commercial enterprise (see Figure 6.9). Grammy nominated rapper/singer Nicki Minaj, for example, plays with pastel-colored weaves and sculptural wigs, mainstreaming working-class Black women's hair culture, and asserting the right to be both a Barbie and a "bad bitch" in the male dominated hip-hop community.⁶¹ But for many Black women, hair texture and its influence on hair-styling practices can still determine one's access to upward mobility via access to employment, social networks, and romantic relationships,

FIGURE 6.9: A model at Bronner Brothers International Beauty Show Fantasy Competition, 2016 in Atlanta, Georgia. Photo: Paras Griffin/Getty Images.

and through negative representation in the media.[62] In 2014, the US Army updated its grooming policy to prohibit dreadlocks, twists, and large cornrows—all hairstyles popular with women of African descent—disparaging them as "matted and unkempt." At the same time, a young waitress, Akua Agyemfra, in Toronto, Canada, was paradoxically sent home from work by management that insisted company policy was for staff members to wear their hair down. She demonstrated that her hair did not fall straight and later argued that "black women at restaurants are forced to wear wigs, weaves or extensions, or are forced to straighten their hair every day."[63]

Clearly, not all hair is equally coveted. Representations of feminine beauty in the global north as young and thin with light skin and long hair are unattainable for most women without help. In the 1980s and 1990s, many Black women turned to weaves and extensions as one alternative to straightening their own hair to meet hegemonic feminine ideals. Wigs and weaves that fetch the highest price are long, straight, and soft—and are made with actual human hair—a preference that reflects the role the hair industry places in the reproduction of hierarchies around women's bodies.[64] The social status and rewards attached to these characteristics encourage especially Black women to spend significant amounts of money and time on hair products and styling. Black women spend $7.5 billion annually,[65] about 80 percent more than the general market, on beautification with most revenue stemming from extensions, wigs, and relaxers to chemically alter the texture of their hair.

The global hair industry is supported by both gendered or ethnic religious rituals—such as those in Judaism and Hinduism—and the commodification and exploitation of poor women's bodies as they provide hair for wigs and labor in sweatshops that produce weaves. In his HBO documentary *Good Hair*, actor and comedian Chris Rock focuses attention on what hair in the Black community means to men and women, how it is styled, and where it comes from.[66] The documentary made headlines by exposing the lived realities of the bodies from which the hair is harvested. Before strands are passed from the hands of auctioneers, manufacturers, distributors, and retailers to the eventual consumer, women sit on rugs for long hours, picking out lice, combing hair, and feeding it into machines that attach the hair to wefts that can be sewn into roots as weaves. The camera follows Rock into the temples, where we watch a child of about two years old wail while an older woman quickly shaves her head with a straight razor in act of reverence to God. Later in the documentary, a middle-aged Indian man in a sharp white, button-down shirt explains to Rock that his factory's global economic success rests on the shoulders of women.

Much of the hair used in wigs and weaves come from India, where it is shorn as an act of spiritual devotion and surrender (see Figure 6.10). In the Temple of Lord Venkateshwara in Tirumala, India, for example, more than five hundred barbers work day and night to keep up with the thousands of Hindus who arrive daily to tonsure, or sacrifice, their hair in exchange for a blessing in accordance with the myth of Vishnu[67]—who is also known as Narayana and Hari, the protector. In the 1990s, tonsuring at temples reached an industrial level to keep up with the dramatic increase in consumer demand for human hair in the United States, China, and much of Europe. By the early 2000s, many temples even began managing and tracking donations using computer systems.[68] A kilo of raw Indian hair sells for around US$200 (or £150) at auction to traders who then clean and process it and sell it overseas for US$75 to US$200 for a three-ounce package.[69] In 1999, the Indian prime minister even presented the National Export Award to Indian Hair Industries (P) Ltd. According to their website, the company's processing department "consists of over 2000 female workers who manually sort, wash, dry, & bundle" human hair for sale overseas.[70]

FIGURE 6.10: Tonsure at the Thiruthani Murugan Temple, Thiruttani, India, 2016. Photo: Allison Joyce/Getty Images.

The human hair trade in India has largely avoided ethical critiques because temple donation-based sourcing is the most visible means of production. Disembodied and distanced from the physical reality of such practices, producers and consumers tend to navigate the moral ambiguities that the commodification of women's hair presents by relying on altruistic and religious rationales. The human hair industry remains largely unregulated by border control agencies and hair is imported and exported with few restrictions. Some postcolonial scholars view these economic relations as disturbingly reminiscent of the British Empire's exploitation of Indian labor and resources during the colonial period.[71] On the other hand, the hair trade in India could also be considered a byproduct of a preexisting practice that economically benefits the temples, as well as the economic growth of India more generally.[72] Either way, the day-to-day labor of manufacturing hair artifice is overwhelmingly the product of poor women of color's exploitation around the world.

CONCLUSION

Throughout the twentieth century, subcultural groups, activists, and creatives have fashioned their bodies in ways that resist mainstream norms. Looking specifically at hair, we can see that people cultivate or remove their hair in terms of the gendered, racial, and global politics of particular times and places. The flapper's bob is an early example of how hair is shaped by a progressive rethinking around gender and sexual binaries. Some styles, such as the Afro and unshorn hippie hair, reveal shifts in how men and women think about their racialized bodies, their relationships to previous generations, and the limits of government intervention in their group life. Others, like the sometimes colorful and spiky hair of Riot Grrrls, explicitly challenge male-dominated social spaces, heteronormativity, and the male gaze by playing with androgyny and "female masculinity."[73] The hair industry is growing via the fetishization of human hair yet wants us to forget from where wigs and weaves come. People in the global north are intimately connected to people living and laboring in the global south, who do not share in the large profits made from their spiritual sactifices. The power of hair's symbolic and material manipulation lies in the capacity to both stabilize and destabilize social regulations of raced, sexed, and gendered bodies according to what is considered to be "authentic" at a particular time and place. As gender norms continue to shift, people will find new and creative ways to reconcile seemingly disparate religious edicts, professional demands, and beauty ideals in ways that affirm and express their lived experiences as gendered but always also racialized, ethnic, and religious people. And they will, therefore, continue to stake their places as consumers and workers in a complicated global market.

CHAPTER SEVEN

Race and Ethnicity

SHIRLEY ANNE TATE

DEBATING "NATURAL/UNNATURAL" BLACK HAIR

It is hair's ability to become, or more accurately to stand in for, the body that orientates us to conflictive ideologies of bodies racialized as "other." Such ideologies stick to hair as the signifier of polarized racial differences: civilized/uncivilized; superior/inferior; citizen/other. Whiteness continues to be at the center of a supposed superiority, with Blackness forever cast as inferior in a relationship of intersubjectivity.[1] In *Black Skin, White Masks* (1986), Frantz Fanon argues that there is no "black task," history, or indeed politics separable from the humanist emancipatory project: the Black body, psyche, and self are made in opposition to others in and through the gaze of white supremacy.[2] Black hair, simply put, is "race" performative, its practices shape bodies and worlds and (re)make subjectivities. The very meaning of Black hair itself, its tangles, textures, and lengths, or lack of them, inflect the discursive spaces of Stuart Hall's "floating signifier," that is, the generative concepts that organize the great classificatory systems of difference that operate in societies at any one time.[3]

For Black women, hair is not merely dead organic matter; it is haunted by specters of racial difference, of racial dis/identifications and of political struggles over Black authenticity. Black hair stylization-as-text invites readings of a materiality that asks us to racialize a normative aesthetic.[4] Colored or uncolored strand, kink, curl, plait, lock, twist, chinee-bump, wave, weave, braid, or wig all imbricate the open, but at the same time complicated, links that exist between stylization technologies and markets, and economies of knowledge and domination that span colonial, postcolonial, and decolonial time and space. Our continuing fascination with what grows out of our heads, what hair does, how it feels, what it looks like, and what we can or cannot do with it continues to inform our affective political attachments and praxis and allied constructions of "race," as well as gender, age, sexuality, and class. However, while explicitly signified, it is this very ubiquity that renders Black hair's instrumental power largely unmarked within our everyday "post-race" lives and issues of "naturalness," vulnerability, and the relational life of Black/white power structures in the contemporary Black Atlantic.

The debate on natural versus unnatural hair and its links to Black authenticity, pride in Blackness, and a positive political and self-identification as Black, has raged in the Black Atlantic since at least the 1930s.[5] The debate continues despite changes in Black women's hair-styling possibilities enabled by an expanding global market in styling technologies from ceramic straighteners to human hair weaves. This chapter explores the natural/unnatural hair divide as arbiter of racialized identity in the twentieth and twenty-first centuries. It examines the power of Black hair-styling and grooming strategies to both conform to and challenge racialized aesthetics and racism in a range of symbolic, political, and material contexts. The discussion questions hair's affective attachment to the Black woman's body in relation to debates generated within both Black Nationalist politics and second wave Black feminist ideology as a response to the "straight hair rule."

Following the phenomenological traditions of Fanon, Frank B. Wilderson understands this fungible, commodified, and externally controlled experiential reality of Blackness as a racialized "libidinal economy"—a system of unconscious *and* material pleasures *and* phobias formulated through the power of racial antagonism rather than as a conflict between equals.[6] Black hair viewed from a phenomenological perspective shifts the focus onto "the importance of lived experience, the intentionality of consciousness, the significance of nearness or what is ready-to-hand, and the role of repeated habitual actions in shaping bodies and worlds."[7] Drawing on this approach, the chapter looks at the material and political vulnerability of Black hair and women's identifications located within the aesthetics of post-second wave Black feminist sensibilities. Black hair is explored as a powerful cultural form that embodies an ambiguous decolonizing potential; its diverse practices enable a reading of racialized power and of resistance to white normative beauty ideals, and an active deconstruction of the norm of naturalness as a rigid prerequisite for Black authenticity within Black antiracist aesthetics.[8]

WHAT IS BLACK HAIR ANYWAY? HAIR'S RACIALIZED LIBIDINAL ECONOMY

Black hair is rooted in Fanon's epidermal racial schema and *l'expérience vécue noir* (the lived experience of Blackness), that is, a sense of selfhood brought into being not just *as* the subject of the white gaze, but by the act of seeing oneself *through* the white-scripted gaze of otherness.[9] Yet it is within this dynamic that Fanon locates the power of Black corporeal resistance. For Fanon, the enslaved accepts servitude because of fear of death and so enables the master to be tyrannical and violent without limitations. However, when the enslaved discover that the oppressor can also be killed, white power is demystified, the mentality of the enslaved is ejected from the Black psyche and this transformation ushers in a belief in the possibility of revolutionary struggle.

Understandings of "natural" Black hair are elemental to transformational politics from the margins that mark the body as an agent in constant revolt against systematic oppression. Growing hair into dreadlocks for Rastafarians in Jamaica, for example, valorizes the beauty of natural Black hair but also has a deeper political purpose as a self-conscious *display* of marginalization whose purpose is to induce dread in the heart of Babylon, that is, the institutions that economically, politically, socially, and aesthetically oppress Black people.[10] It is the centrality of political praxis that makes a Rasta's dreadlocks different from, for example, the pan-Indian Hindu *jata* (long hair matted in locks worn by both male and female ascetics). Both forms of uncut hair are regarded as sacred, but while the latter practice signals a ritualized renunciation of worldly matters,[11] the former engages with the worldly racial politics of Babylon.

Dreadlocks express working-class, urban/rural dispossessed insurrection against the respectable appearance regimes of Jamaican (post)colonial society where darker skinned people of African descent experience colorism.[12]

We cannot be unmoved by the shaved, short or long, straight or curled spectacle of Black hair. We cannot be unmoved because hair speaks of who we are through Michel Foucault's mechanisms of "governmentality," whereby disciplinary body regimes operate as a form of "biopower."[13] Such power extends beyond the politics of state power and its institutions of surveillance and regulation. Through the apparatus of a generative system of institutional and individual power/knowledge, Foucault considers how individuals govern themselves through appropriate "technologies of the self," including an ethics of care of the self. Understood in the context of race, previous research has evidenced the ways in which recognizable cultural constructs of the "I" and the "Other" are discursively disseminated. Regimes of beauty truth are, "about 'race-ing' bodies and being raced by embodied subjects from hairdressers to people in the street."[14] I remember some ten years ago giving a talk in an academic context about the politics of Black hair and being challenged by a member of the audience who as Afrikan refused "Black" as a description of her hair and that of other women of Afrikan descent. She asked a question that is still really apposite today: "What is Black hair anyway?" At the time this was a very politically emotive question suggestive of the fissures extant in Black politics in the late twentieth century: who could legitimately occupy the space of the Afrikan body in the diaspora? It seemed the only body that could be seen as "authentic" was a darker skinned, more "natural" "Afro-haired" one. A decade on, in 2015, in a discussion on beauty I heard a replay of this question of Black authenticity and of the necessity for Black women to have "natural skin and hair." There was no debate about what "natural" meant or the possibility for Black differences in hair texture, issues that clearly impact on both questions of self and correlative styling strategies. The "natural" Afro has remained stubbornly fixed to an idealized head of African descent, perhaps because of the texture necessary for its volume and height. In short, the more kink the better.

Actively engaged in an everyday politics of appearance these women's Black hair "manifestos," based on understandings of naturalness in the twentieth and twenty-first centuries, decenter whiteness as the normative position from which recognition of what counts as hair itself even starts.[15] As "white" hair power is demystified, then so it is revealed as a fundamental technology of racial classification that reframes relations between "nature," artifice, and political struggle. The experience and reality of Blackness is thus shaped at the junction of the political economy of white western capitalism and the libidinal economy of anti-Black racism.[16] This libidinal economy Wilderson argues:

> is linked not only to forms of attraction, affection, and alliance, but also to aggression, destruction and the violence of lethal consumption … it is the whole structure of psychic and emotional life … something more than but inclusive of or traversed by … a "structure of feeling"; it is a dispensation of energies, concerns, points of attention, anxieties, pleasures, appetites, revulsions, phobias capable of great mobility and tenacious fixation.[17]

A phenomenology of racial visualization creates an unconscious system of material and symbolic exchange that can make us approach some bodies and even pass through them, but be repulsed and repelled by others. This is especially so within political contexts where there is a framing of feminine beauty as an elision of Africanness/African descent.

Ginetta Candelario's study of the Dominican Republic and US Dominicans' beauty work in the United States is illustrative here.[18] In a cultural historical context in which a nation imagines itself as *mestizo* (mixed race) there is an erasure of African-ness because of continuing racism against those of African descent *alongside* a negation of Anglo-whiteness in the creation of a national ideal: a mixed *Taino* (Indigenous)–European (Spanish) identity shown through light skin and hair that is not bone straight but curly/wavy.

Black hair's libidinal economy in this way operates in concert with the political economy of racism in terms of attraction, alliance, and affection or a turn to repulsion, violence, hatred, and discriminatory attitudes to appropriative consumption, but it also demonstrates that what constitutes "natural" Black hair is open to question.

WHAT IS "NATURAL" BLACK HAIR ANYWAY?

Over the course of the twentieth century, "natural" Black styles emerged in opposition to the "straight hair rule" that had historically dominated aesthetics and feminine stylization practices reinforced by the emergence of a modern, Black middle class/elite, and an expanding global Black hair and beauty culture. In the 1930s, when Rastafarianism emerged in Jamaica, respectable Black femininity involved straightening hair with a hot comb and curling with curling irons. Both methods were used in my grandmother's house, introduced by Aunt Dora who was training to be a hairdresser. This is hardly surprising given the spread of US styling technologies to the Caribbean and the to and fro of bodies and products. Madame C.J. Walker, the noted pioneer of the US Black hair and beauty industry is known to have visited the Caribbean selling her hair and beauty products.[19] Walker did not invent the straightening comb; Bloomingdale's, with a presumably all-white client base, sold a metal comb called "Dr. Scott's Electric Curler" as early as 1886 while Walker was still picking cotton in Mississippi.[20] Rather, Walker, a "race woman" who suffered from alopecia, developed and sold the comb as part of a hair-care kit of products and techniques specifically suited to not just straightening but fashionably styling and conditioning Black hair.[21] A picture of my mother aged twenty-one shows her with mid-back-length hair, straightened and curled to fulfill the expectations at this time of an appropriate look for accomplished, modern, young, middle-class Black women (Figure 7.1).

When I asked about hair-styling practices in their youth, her sisters, my aunts B and Elsie, spoke of making sure that the coals were not too hot because the comb would burn the hair, using bath soap as shampoo, or the soft flesh of "tuna"—a cactus—to condition the hair, "hair dressings" such as "Apex,"[22] or coconut/castor oil for moisturizer, and using brown paper wrapped around the hair, much like rollers today, to create curls. I remember myself as a child having curls made in my unstraightened hair with strips of brown paper or with chinee-bumps while it was still wet after washing.

Hair is laden with experiential data that mediates our relationships with our race-coded selves and others through the discursive ethical care of the self, concepts of respectability, and the politics of normative appearance that govern our psyches. But what the to and fro of the discussion so far has shown is the relational aspects of Black hair's signifying power and also how hair signifies differently generationally. This problematizes its reading as a rigid text of either Black political commitment or anti-

FIGURE 7.1: Miss. Beatrice Baird, ca. 1930s. Reproduced by permission of the Tate family.

Black sentiment. Indeed, W.E.B. Du Bois writing in 1937 in the *Pittsburgh Courier*, then the United State's leading Black weekly, tackled this head-on when he argued that fashion was fashion and style was style, so hair straightening or curling did not signify Black self-hatred.[23] For my aunts and my mother, in the 1930s and now, straightened hair does not make them less Black but is one in a series of looks that they have adopted throughout their lives. Clearly, however, what, and who, we think we see when we look at hairstyles, textures, and practices can still negatively inform what we feel about ourselves, and others. A very heated debate has raged across the Black Atlantic diaspora as to whether the straightened hair of the former US First Lady Michelle Obama, and that of her daughters, is a form of "race" betrayal.[24]

Like my mother, my aunts, and art historian and writer on the culture of the Black diaspora Kobena Mercer,[25] I see straightening as one of a number of ways in which Black hair can be styled.[26] Straightening her hair does not, *quid pro quo*, make Obama or her daughters less Black, or anti-African American, or "ashamed-of-being-Black-and-wanting-to-be-white" in terms of their politics or their sensibilities. For some Black Nationalists, second wave Black feminists and others who adhere to Black antiracist aesthetics, this viewpoint would be the focus of derision, and of disgust and dismay at a lack of Black political consciousness of antiracist politics. However, it is useful here to reflect upon a comment made by a Black children's book author from Santa Maria in Brazil in the question and answer session of a talk I gave in 2009 around these issues, who asserted that, in a Brazilian cultural context, "only Black women straighten their hair." This suggests that the vexed critique of Michelle Obama's hair is misplaced; it is the specificities of Black stylization that is politically significant. For example, integral to the history of Brazilian *mestiçagem*[27] are assumptions about "good appearance" formulated in a context of continuing anti-dark skin, anti-kinky haired, racist attitudes to those of African descent.[28] Cultural, political, and aesthetic contexts produce many complicated takes on hair which attempt to performatively "fix" us in place as the racialized libidinal economy of skin shade also does its work. Artifice in Brazil makes you Black, while artifice in Dominican hair salons also marks you as "mixed," and idealized concepts of racially "appropriate" hair and hair practices remain central to the continuing debate in the Black Atlantic diaspora about who can occupy the space of "authentic Black woman." Kink, texture, style, curl, wave, color, straightness, weave, extension, and wig continue as contested signifiers of ambiguous ideals of Black identity.

Emanating from the two master signifiers, Blackness and whiteness, but also from within Black Nationalist politics, hair has come to be a central aspect of Black corporeality constituted through the "sticky associations between signs, figures and objects."[29] The natural/unnatural binary persists and points to the continuing impact of and necessity for, Black anti-racist aesthetics. Perhaps this necessity is made even more urgent by the continuing racism of "post-race" times, a racism that extends to aesthetics and what adorns our heads. So, we also might ask, "what is 'natural' black hair anyway?"

The aesthetic, political, and economic traction attached to the Afro and dreadlocks on a Black woman's head demonstrates how the libidinal economy of Black hair works to valorize some styles by connecting them to Black liberation struggles, while producing phobic attachments to hair practices and textures judged inauthentic and thus antipolitical. This latter judgment, with its intimation of willful "whitening/Europeanization" implies an anti-Black orientation on the part of those who change Black hair's texture with heat or chemical or who disguise it by weave, wig, dye, or extension. The continuing need for "natural" homogeneity wrought by Black Nationalist politics has arguably generated its own insidious exclusions: straightened/straight, curled/curly, weaved or wigged styles are seen as fake, inauthentic, and out of place on a Black woman's head. But in response, it is important to understand that, "there are other truths which also exist uncomfortably with the 'truth of being Black' … [C]lass, location and historical moment are determinants of what we do with our hair."[30]

"WHOSE HAIR IS IT ANYWAY?"

Afros and dreadlocks, symbolically understood as politically motivated hair-styling practices, are perceived as "natural" because they are supposedly untouched by the mainstream hair market's stylization technologies and products—but they are never free from some sort of intervention by their wearers. Indeed, I remember the work involved in maintaining an Afro in the 1970s that rendered the hairstyle far from natural. An Afro demands daily attention whether that is moisturizing, wearing plaits/chinee-bumps at night, or constant washing and blowing out, as well as very regular barbershop visits to maintain its shape, size, and texture. Furthermore, in her insightful chapter on the Afro comb, Carol Tulloch argues that while essential to maintaining the Afro style, what we see as a symbol of Black Power had a history imbricated at times with white shampoo combs. The original "natural" Afro shape was created through the use of these combs and also "of warm pressing, chemical blowouts, or diluted sodium hydroxide to soften and lengthen (but not completely straighten) the curls of black hair."[31] Even by the early 1970s the Afro had become "a hairstyle plain and simple."[32] "The natural" as it was originally called sat alongside a range of more traditional nonpoliticized hair-styling practices such as cornrows/canerows, braids, plaits, chinee-bumps, and the politicized dreadlocks.

As politicized expressions of racial pride, Rasta and Afro styles have clearly undergone constant shifts and changes both ideologically and aesthetically, yet the politics of authenticity and naturalness remain doggedly central to the rhetoric of "Black beauty" and the performative strategies of resistance. Angela Davis, a key civil rights activist notably associated with the rise of the 1960s Afro, viewed the version of the style that became popular in the 1990s as, "a pastiche ... the imitation of a particular style ... a neutral practice" without a critical or political edge that, allied to a "fashion-revolutionary glamor" linked to nostalgia, had "survived disconnected from the historical context in which it arose."[33] Located for over a century as a zone of "crisis," some view the transracial, global popularity of locks and cornrows as a superficial, stylized form of cultural appropriation;[34] "real" locks only correctly belong on the heads of "real Rastas."[35] In contrast, others situate the popular dissemination of the Afro and the shift "from statement to style" as a necessary step in the progressive trajectory of Black consciousness: the "natural" has never been natural at all and the ambiguities of Black authenticity have constantly taken on new meanings.[36]

The twenty-first century has witnessed a resurgence of the Afro not necessarily as a marker of Black radicalism but also as a style which speaks of "cool" for contemporary consumers turning en masse to the 1970s for style inspiration. The style's contemporary reincarnation is very gendered, however. Unlike in the era of Angela Davis and Black Power there are far fewer Black women with Afros, and those that are worn also appear, by and large, to be more unstructured than that of their male counterparts in order to maintain a stylistic, rather than a necessarily political, edge. The Afro pick associated with the Black Power movement of the 1960s has also reappeared as a hair accessory shoved into the hair of young Black men in 2016, although its signifying function again operates more as a marker of individual fashionably unruly Black masculinity than of collective Black political activism. Rasta locks similarly entered the global market in hair in the 1990s as a sign of dissent for the urban Black and white cool and those involved in a reggae and Rasta Livity music culture with transracial roots.[37] In this performative (re)production there is a decentering of the idea of normative Black hair as "kinky" and short and white hair as straight and endless. Locks can now as easily appear on the heads of a Japanese band playing at *Reggae Sunsplash* in Jamaica, as they can on the heads of Black Brazilian men in a *bloco afro*, as they can appear as part of the stylization of a white woman community worker in inner-city Manchester, United Kingdom, or on the head of a blonde, white woman commuter on the *sbahn* in Frankfurt. For those Black women who want a more "glamorous" look or desire a style more likely to be admitted through the portals of corporate life, "Sisterlocks" are available—a costly process whereby uniformly thin locks in a wide variety of styles are tightly fixed in place with a special tool in a precise grid across the scalp.

What were once "naturally" grown can be bought as a stylized "off the shelf" look: "rebellious" locks and weaves can be plaited into even overrelaxed hair to immediately achieve the desired "naturalness." The expansion of such practices evidences the continued primacy of locks in global markets in Afro-centric fashion and stylization, but equally the (re)production of shifting concepts of Black authenticity. For example, let us listen to twenty-three-year-old Black British student Ray's take on her synthetic hair which she uses to add volume and length to her own, already ceramic straightener straightened hair to create an elaborate, glamorous up-do:

> Look, right, I bought it so it's my hair. It was one four nine (149) with a decimal point between the one and the four (laughs). I just add it in so it becomes my hair for the night so I can have a more elaborate style. The point is it has to look

FIGURE 7.2: Two young girls with hair in rollers, San Jose de Ocoa, Dominican Republic. Photo: Adam Jones—originally posted to Flickr, CC BY-SA 2.0, Wikimedia Commons.

natural like it comes out of your head even though the volume of it means it's impossible.[38]

"Natural" now is about enhancing and adding color, texture, volume, and length to hair that has to *look* natural even though its weavers, wearers, and watchers know "it's impossible." Natural is not necessarily about being devoid of artifice; rather, styles now embrace the hyperfake—wigs, extensions, and weaves, all of which can also be made from human hair in which there is global traffic.[39] Black women from the African continent to the diaspora can wear hair supplied through the cutting practices of Hindu devotion in India or the hair trade operated by middlemen in Russian towns and villages,[40] or by wearing synthetic hair made in China. We see the impossibility of "natural hair" all across the Black Atlantic as women achieve "spectacular femininities" through weaves from Jamaica[41] to Nigeria.[42] It is a spectacularization of hair which, for cultural historian Carolyn Cooper, has very little to do with whiteness/Europeanness and much more to do with African stylization practices.[43] The rise of a global market in what might be defined as "fake naturalness" makes us reappraise the grounds upon which the discourse of authenticity is founded. Indeed, it makes us begin to see "natural Black hair" as a mobile category made so by the myriad stylization technologies available to performatively (re)produce it, but which simultaneously make it both politically vulnerable and powerful (Figure 7.2).

VULNERABILITY AND POWER

The power of performative and political fluidity is exemplified in the evolution in Brazil of the *blocos afro* (Carnival street bands/parades limited to those of African descent) that sought to counter the hegemonic white/*mulata* beauty ideals and lighter skinned aesthetic of carnival in Rio de Janeiro. Ilê Aiyê, the first *bloco afro* to be established in 1974, clearly reflected the Afrocentric aesthetic references set up by the "Black Is Beautiful" movement.[44] As other *blocos afro* emerged, Bahia's Carnival was re-Africanized through a wide range of constructed diasporic African aesthetics in terms of hair styling such as braids and dreadlocks (Figure 7.3).

As well as stylization there was also a counter discourse on beauty and affirmative identity politics—nicely captured in Angela Figueiredo's (2003) documentary film *Ebony Goddess—24a Black Beauty Night Ilê Ayê*.[45] The film charts the search for the most beautiful contestant in a Black beauty pageant that is not just about the display of Black women's bodies but about how beauty that challenges prevailing Eurocentric ideals is performed *through* hairstyles, clothes, and dances. Hair is central to this concept of Afro-Brazilian beauty as contestant Taís Carvalho, Ebony Goddess 2002, states: "Hair is everything, everything in a woman … if your hair is well done even with your clothes in shreds you are beautiful."

Simone Santos, a 2003 Ebony Goddess contestant, relates the concept of real beauty to African ancestry and natural braided hair that allows your hair to grow in opposition to artificially straightened hair that can make it fall out. However, like Ray, the Black British student cited earlier, there is no separation between using synthetic hair for volume or length, or just wearing what Simone terms "natural braided hair," that is, hair which is

FIGURE 7.3: Preparations for the Saida do Ilê Aiyê, Brazil. Photo: Tatiana Azeviche. https://www.flickr.com/photos/turismobahia/33118404235/in/album-72157680674698726/.

styled and dressed (braided) but has not been straightened. The synthetic "fiber" and her "natural" hair both become "her" braids:

> I believe each one has her own beauty each one chooses her style if one wants to follow our African ancestors. I braid my hair because it feels good. That's mine. I don't want to straighten my hair. My hair is curly and you can see that our hair is sensitive. Some say it's hard but it's sensitive. It's great using braids even with fiber hair. When a Black woman uses products to straighten her hair it only lasts for a while then it begins to fall. If you braid your hair it grows more quickly.[46]

Simone's viewpoint springs from the Afro-aesthetics of the 1970s widely practiced by Black Brazilians as part of their everyday stylization routines; many women stopped straightening their hair and adopted "Afro-looking hairstyles" while men adopted dreadlocks/Afros.[47] However, Simone demonstrates how such practices are subject to continual adaptation motivated by a constant crossover between the symbolic and the material. For Simone, braiding is an essential part of the Ebony Goddess pageant, but she also argues it protects Black women's hair: Black hair is not "hard", its "sensitive".

Traction alopecia is a common form of hair loss caused by frequent straightening and forceful pulling, and from overuse of weaves and braided extensions. Supermodel Naomi Campbell raised awareness of this condition by making headlines around the world in August 2012 when her baldness became obvious as she was photographed climbing back onto the boat of her then partner Vladislav Doronin in the Mediterranean Sea off Ibiza.[48] In response to her critics, in 2013 a spectacularly bewigged Naomi offered a new and sophisticated take on contemporary Black femininity as producer and coach of the reality TV program *The Face* (Sky Living) where contestants vied to become the new face of US cosmetic giant Max Factor. Interestingly, however, within the politicized culture of Black hair styling strategies, as we have seen, to wear a wig implies the evasion at some level of working in, of and on hair that grows "naturally" from the scalp. Black wigs, therefore, continue to attract an interpellating Black gaze, perhaps because of their easy detachability from the head as well as the full coverage of the hair itself. But the "art" of blending the bought with the growing hair shaft in terms of, for example, color and texture also (re)makes artifice as natural as women increasingly disidentify with the natural/unnatural binary and engage instead with stylization's subjective possibilities and complexities. In this disidentification the binary is disassembled, questioned, and (re)constructed: what is bought can become one's own in the act of its remaking. Ebony Goddess Simone's and Naomi Campbell's spectacular negotiation, of the vulnerability of Black hair speaks against any easy categorization within the dominant ideological rhetoric of Eurocentric otherness as "tough" and in need of aggressive approaches to its "taming" and control. This leads us to consider the wider import of Black hair's "sensitivity" as the political signifier of Black authenticity and Afro-centric sensibilities that must be protected.

As a primary sign of Black politics and aesthetic pride, natural hair has been positioned as vulnerable to attack by the ideology, politics, and practice of white supremacy's "straight hair rule"; this entails that one must take care that one's psyche has not been colonized by this aesthetic regime of power/knowledge. The legendary South African trumpeter Hugh Masekela while at Rhodes University in South Africa to accept an honorary doctorate refused to take pictures with women who wore weaves and extensions, and later commented at a press conference, "We spend about a billion rand on other people's hair each year. I don't know where to begin on this issue."[49] We also see the persistent hierarchical ideology of "natural Black hair" as a signifier of political consciousness in bell hooks's condemnation of American singer-songwriter Beyoncé Knowles-Carter as a "terrorist" in a "New School" discussion entitled, *Are you still a slave: liberating the Black female body*. hooks held forth on Beyoncé's appearance on the cover of *Time* magazine's celebration of the 100 most influential people that hooks asserted exemplified "imperialist, white supremacist, racist patriarchal" imaging of the female body. Doubting Beyoncé's agency in the creation of the image that, of course, included her wearing a blonde wig/weave/hair, hooks argued that Beyoncé's look was in no way "liberatory"; rather, the singer had colluded in her own "construction as a slave."[50]

Within the Black Atlantic, natural hair has always been located as vulnerable organic matter—delicate, sensitive, prone to damage from heat, chemicals, breakage, traction baldness, weaves, extensions—and as such in need of constant care by professionals. Vulnerable comes from the Late Latin *vulnerabilis* and means to expose to wounding, to harm or attack, whether physically or emotionally, and I would also like to add here, political attack and harm. In this sense, "vulnerability" operates as the affective and visible glue that exists between matter, psyches, epistemologies, and politics. Naomi's and Beyoncé's or Ray's and Simone's or any other young Black woman's appropriation of "natural" braids and styles produced by weaves, extension, or wigs come up against second wave Black feminism's and Black Nationalism's embrace of Black antiracist aesthetics' ideology of "naturalness." However, the relationship between the terms natural, artifice, and political struggle is being reinscribed within the performative arenas of "post-race" sensibilities that offer a spectacular alter/native racial hair politics brought into being through diverse contemporary stylization practices (Figure 7.4).[51]

The previous phenomenology of appearance and the subjective certainties of "race" upon which it relied are also being decentered: we can no longer judge who someone is politically, or assess the quality of their "race" credentials by looking at their hair. Indeed, we should no longer continue to expect that this is possible, or look nostalgically backward to a time when such assumptions seemed unassailable. We have to look at the deeds, political alignments, affective orientations, and political alliances of communities freed from rigid hair-related tropes of naturalness and Black authenticity.

CONCLUSION: DECOLONIZING NATURALNESS

Given the pervasiveness of the discourse on naturalness and its equation with Black authenticity and pride within Black communities across the diaspora, how can we decolonize this discourse? There have been some intimations of how it is that women's hair practices themselves decolonize the ideology of natural hair through a process of normalization and the inculcation of taste according to new systems of status recognition.[52] We could say that there has been a progressive process of what Édouard Glissant defined as "creolization."[53] Martinican poet, writer, and literary critic, Glissant's "relational poetics" conceptualized a process whereby the aesthetic and the political, the self and the social, could be brought together in understanding Caribbean culture and identity as one made up of diverse interlocking networks of meaning. Glissant rejected paradigms of cultural sterility in favor of a transformative vision of "opacity" as "opposed to the 'fake clarity' of universal models."[54]

Creolization does not universalize Black hair, but rather creates an understanding of naturalness through evolving and sometimes fleeting hair-stylization trends, practices, and technologies and "brings into relation" hitherto disparate constituencies, for example, hair of African descent, Indian hair in weaves, or blonde synthetic hair extensions from China.

FIGURE 7.4: Girl looks on proudly, Notting Hill Carnival, United Kingdom, 1994. Photo: PYMCA/UIG via Getty Images.

Such hair creolization is at once a suturing and a translation that allows subjects to be in several locations at once. Both rooted and open, it produces new ideologies of natural hair linked to multiple Black identifications that incorporate the collective and the individual. Glissantian relational hair poetics leads to contemporary understandings of fakeness/naturalness as integral to Black political sensibilities that take us beyond identifications that insist on showing their "roots" toward an alter/native Black hair-styling genealogy. This does not mean a loss of Black identity, or a renunciation of the essential Black self; it is rather about a distancing from the essentialist natural/unnatural binary. To decolonize such a binary is to go beyond the dissection of bodies forged by Black antiracist aesthetics only in opposition to whiteness by engaging with a much more fluid, alter/native politics of Black hair difference. In Glissant's metaphorical terms it is "not merely an encounter, a shock ... but a new and original dimension allowing each person to be there and elsewhere."[55]

Defined by the rejection of another's humanity, racism in "an anti-Black world" for Lewis Gordon is not confined to the violent discourses of white supremacy.[56] We must therefore attend to—by this I mean listen to, visualize, care for, look after—the enduring "fungibility"[57] of hair whether straight, curly, kinky, woven, wigged, colored, "real," or "fake" to performatively produce an inclusive politics of Blackness. Attending to Black hair's differences has much to tell us about building new political alliances for twenty-first-century, post-second wave Black feminist, and "post-race" times. Here, "post" does not mean past but implies the emergence of new sensibilities focused on questioning the taken-for-granted-ness of Black hair within a neoliberal racialization in which consumption holds the promise of "making us who we want to be."[58] Within such a context natural/unnatural Black hair exists within a relational "to and fro" of vulnerability and power. Breaking from normative Black naturalness discourses produces an aesthetic as well as a political and epistemological break. This break challenges the primacy of hooks's and Masekela's hegemonic second wave Black feminist/Black Nationalist aesthetics and orientates us to the possibilities of new and diverse racialized aesthetic sensibilities within "post-race" neoliberal discourses on individualism, choice and empowerment.[59] For example, in South Africa the dictates of fashion mean that "Brazilian" and "Caribbean" weaves are "in" so no matter what they may look like on your head, how they frame your face and affect your skin tone, they have to be worn to show well-heeled, stylish, modern femininity.

Mercer argues that "when hairstyling is critically evaluated as an aesthetic practice inscribed in everyday life, *all* black hairstyles are political in that they each articulate responses to the panoply of historical forces which have invested this element of the ethnic signifier with both symbolic meaning and significance."[60] Going beyond the "race" governmentality of "natural hair" repositions post-second wave feminist Blackness as a site of political possibility and aesthetic transformation, and opens up readings of global Black hair stylizations which have nothing to do with white aesthetic supremacy. Instead, these stylizations enable the emergence of a new Black feminist politico-aesthetic where subjective Blackness is not refuted or maintained at a distance, nor whiteness as arbiter of aesthetics and taste denied. In this decolonial move, enabled by the possibilities of stylization technologies and products, we have the inculcation of new tastes in what Jamaicans would call a "fashion ova style" aesthetic politics.[61] Natural hair is a cultural signifier whose reading can no longer be limited to hair that is just washed, and conditioned, moisturized and combed/brushed/locked/twisted/canerowed/plaited. It is a cultural text now extended to include hair that has been straightened, or colored, or that has had locks and braids woven into it, no matter how "impossibly" voluminous or long, or blonde the hair happens to be.

CHAPTER EIGHT

Class and Social Status

GERALDINE BIDDLE-PERRY

ROOTS

In the autumn of 1999, then Mrs., now Lady Pauline Prescott, and her husband John, UK deputy prime minister and MP for Hull, emerged from a chauffeur-driven limousine having been driven a mere 250 yards from their hotel to the annual Labour Party Conference.[1] When asked why the couple had chosen to take the car rather than walk, Mr. Prescott laughed off criticism, quipping that it was for security reasons and because his wife "didn't like to have her hair blown about." Ex-hairdresser Pauline's fastidious attention to her hair and self-evident enjoyment of the benefits of high office were portrayed by the British press of all political shades in largely negative terms as either a confirmation or a betrayal of her working-class roots or both. Pauline's "big hair" became inextricably linked to the perception of "Two Jags"[2] John's proletarian credentials as somewhat undermined by a penchant for flash and his declaration that "We are all middle class now" on the eve of Labour's landslide victory in the 1997 general election.

Some years later, in a two-part BBC TV documentary *Prescott: The Class System and Me* presented by John, the symbolic social status of Pauline's coiffure continued to fascinate.[3] However, in some quarters of the right-wing press, once biting critique was now replaced by grudging admiration for Pauline's obvious ease with her expensive lifestyle. Quentin Letts writing in the *Daily Mail* recast the so-called "Cleopatra of Hull" as someone driven by "the simple desire found in all the best people to make the best of herself ... it could be said every single hair knows its place," an expression that Letts would not "dare apply to her chippy husband lest he took it the wrong way."[4]

Hair-styling practices are rarely explicitly acknowledged as a significant element in the constitution of class and consequentially of class-based stereotypes. Imbued with notions of individual consumer agency, more abstract concepts of "taste" frequently operate as a useful form of aesthetic condescension and, as here, as a way of overcoming potentially problematic understandings of class discrimination, but also inequality and conflict. How one's hair is styled instead frequently contributes to what social historian Beverley Skeggs argues is the assignation of "class through moral euphemism, rarely naming it directly, hence relying on the process of interpretation to do the work of association."[5] Whether viewed in celebratory or derogatory terms, the Prescotts' negotiation of their biological and cultural roots—indeed John too has been the subject of some criticism for resorting to hair dye—and its critical reception raises a number of key issues around the relationship that exists between hair and class identity.

Firstly, the idea of class itself as a viable category of analysis in the modern age is not without difficulties. Over the course of the historical period this volume encompasses there has been a progressive intellectual shift away from understanding class in terms of rigid systems of social stratification based on income and occupation, toward a much more fluid typology based on consumer "lifestyles."[6] Class, it is argued, should no longer be analyzed as a singular, abstract variable that defines status.[7] Rather, theoretically and in concrete material terms it should be understood as just one part of a range of other competing determinants—race, gender, sexuality, age, ethnicity—by which people articulate a modern sense of themselves and others.[8] Correlative to this radical cultural and critical turn, moreover, a progressively stylistically diverse fashion system has emerged where systems of identification might be formulated "as much on the basis of attitudes and behavior as socioeconomic grounds."[9] Of course, it is argued, fashionable dress and the display of wealth and power through consumption continue to mark significant divisions between different social groups, but in ways that challenge "traditional notions of status tied to class."[10]

Class in this chapter is not considered as an abstract system of traditional socioeconomic stratification, nor does discussion include systematic analyses of Marxist or Weberian accounts of antagonistic class relationships. Pierre Bourdieu's writings on fashion and the body are useful because they emphasize the material and symbolic cultural dimensions of modern consumption at work in systems of class differentiation.[11] Diverse bodies of consumers, he argues, can be understood as primary actors within a plurality of existing systems of stratification and a hierarchical framework of "distinction" in which all tastes fit.[12] Social hair practices do not in themselves categorize individuals or social groups as belonging to particular classes but following Bourdieu, they clearly function to visibly consolidate a set of principles and codified rules relating to class and status expression and recognition, "imposed by the ordinary experience of occupational, communal and local divisions and rivalries."[13]

The ritual grooming behaviors of modern everyday lives continue to symbolically enact a striving for social status.[14] While these might intersect the various discourses through which modern social bodies are constituted, constructions of class and status clearly continue to inform personal and institutional interpretive and analytical judgments about social identity. How, and where, and by whom one's hair is dressed or styled offers a historically consistent tripartite system of status recognition through which to examine these practices as fundamental to the construction of class-based subjectivities in the modern age.

A CUT ABOVE

Social historian Steven Zdatny describes how, in 1920, a ladies' journal published in a fashionable French seaside resort offered advice to an international social elite on appropriate dress and coiffure for the coming season. Constant changes of attire were suggested that entailed coordinating changes of hairstyle up to eight times daily, from early morning (hair fastened at the nape of the neck with a barrette, soft curled fringe in front with a few over the ears); through *dejeuner* (a simple Grecian chignon); bathing (hidden under a cap with some strategic pieces of postiche); dinner (many fleecy curls around the face and long hair taken up high into a chignon in the style of a large cravat knot); at the ball (middle parting, bandeaux and hair waved in wide undulations and a chignon knotted heavily at the back with a spray of Paradise plumes); until finally bedtime arrived when the hair was to be brushed and carefully combed, and according to length, tied with ribbon or plaited.[15] This relentless dressing and redressing of hair and body recalls a system of conspicuous fashionable consumption and display synonymous with a bourgeois leisure class in the nineteenth century. Yet, published immediately after World War I, the article simultaneously elicits in the reader an image of a society at the zenith of a golden age about to be, quite literally, cut short. As Zdatny observes, every society lady had always had their own favorite *coiffeur*; but after 1920, aristocratic heads and their dressers came to exist in a state of anxiety impelled by constantly changing style trends, but, as significantly, also by innovations in products and hairdressing techniques potentially available to all in a progressively competitive open marketplace. The modern ladies' salon had arrived.[16]

Hair might still be "dressed" at home by one's maid, but it would also have to be cut and styled in new dedicated salons by a new breed of professionals practiced in the "art" of modern coiffure.[17] The arrival of the bob as *the* style of the modern age required frequent attention, at first to maintain the cut's fashionable sharpness, then to keep up with constant style trends in "shingling," that is, hair cut short, and then "Marcel" or permanently waved in endless variations. "The Chic" required waves arranged in a neat formation and was seen as "becoming to the healthy or vivacious girl"; "The Fleur-de Lis" was a "decided advance in beauty … with waves so disposed that the face is becomingly shadowed," while "The Semi-Tousled or Qua Neglige" allowed the hair to be worn long enough to allow permanent waving.[18] The relative expense in time and money inferred in keeping up with these changes, and the arduous nature of nascent hairdressing technology—permanent waving could take up to ten hours—all enhanced the perception of the modern coiffure as a crucial economic and social "investment" for independent, young female consumers.[19] In Edith Wharton's short story "Permanent Wave," the racy protagonist Nalda Craig describes the hairdressing salon of the late 1920s as a "tiled sanctuary" amid the trials and tribulations of a complicated modern love life.[20] Prior to eloping with her lover, and unsure of when she would have another chance of having her "lank, irregular mop … properly done," Nalda seeks out the "wizard fingers" of upmarket coiffure Gaston. For Nalda, the discomforts to be endured were worth it: "being waved gave one as nothing else, not even a new hat, a reassuring sense of security and power." With her "medusa locks clamped in the steel clutch of the waver," Nalda wiles away the hours spent in the thrall of "the interminable waving séance" flicking through "Gaston's supply of picture papers."[21]

The evolutionary nature of modern ladies' hairdressing practice altered the social dynamics that existed between hairdresser and client and conferred a new kind of status on practitioners like the fictional Gaston.[22] Viewed like couturiers, they were seen as uniquely creative innovators and arbiters of good taste, well versed in the latest technological advances and fashion trends. As significantly, they were seen as sensitive to the unique psychological and physiological needs of their female clientele and their hair.[23] The reputations of these "auteurs" and their salons were built on this dialectic of exclusivity: only they understood the intimate "art" of creating a coiffure *individually* designed according to the requirements of the heads, faces, hair textures, and personalities of a socially elite clientele. Perhaps the most famous of the great *coiffeurs* of the day, Polish émigré Antoine "Antek" Cierplikowski but, henceforth, always known simply as "Antoine," promoted the special qualities of his "magic hands" through which passed "the most beautiful curls in the world" (Figure 8.1).[24] A picture of these was even included in his autobiography, where the great man described the demands the interwar rich and famous placed upon them. Lady Mitchelhelm's hair, "light chestnut turning gray," was frequently dyed fuchsia red; when staying in Vienna she insisted one of Antoine's employees made the seventy-two-hour round trip for a forty-five-minute appointment.[25]

Lady Mendl, an important muse of Antoine's, wanted her hair styled differently every day, depending on her mood—sometimes up, sometimes down, sometimes with flowers or bows, sometimes she didn't know what she wanted, sometimes she did, and sometimes she wanted to experiment. Antoine recalled Lady Mendl laughing and explaining to a reporter, "It's just this. My hair-do is as important as the colour scheme I would select for a room. When Antoine does my hair, he probably regards me as I might a familiar room that I am about to redecorate."[26]

Antoine opened his new salon, "The Glass House," in Paris in 1927 with a fashionable "White Ball."[27] Dressed head to toe in white, with his hair dyed white to match, he welcomed 1,400 guests whose invitations had been engraved on squares of crystal; smiling "Antoinettes" (coiffed by Antoine himself) offered cigarettes, while ten uniformed valets served champagne (Figure 8.2).[28] "Antoine de Paris" salons progressively opened in the world's major cities often in upmarket department stores, notably in Saks Fifth Avenue in New York where British-born hairdresser Sydney Guilaroff (later chief stylist at MGM Studios) started work as a young stylist. In the floor-to-ceiling mirrored salon lit by crystal chandeliers, managed by Monsieur De

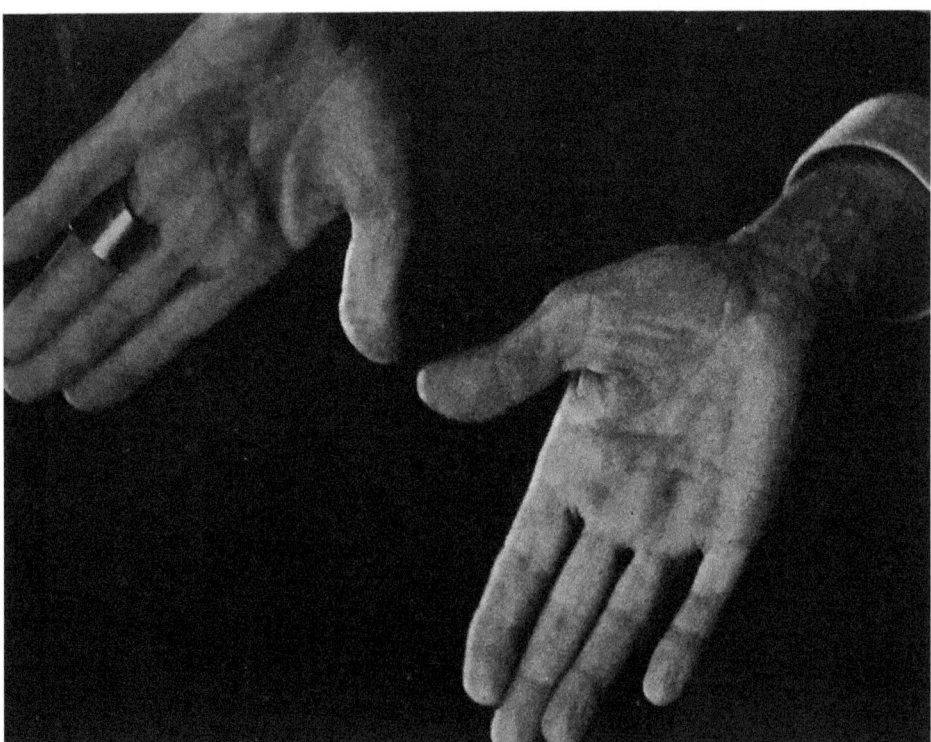

FIGURE 8.1: "Through these fingers have passed the most beautiful curls in the world." The magic hands of "Antoine de Paris" (Antek Cierplikowski). From *Antoine By Antoine*, published by W.H. Allen, 1946.

FIGURE 8.2: "Antoine de Paris" (Antek Cierplikowski) dressed for the White Ball that marked the opening of his salon "The Glass House" in Paris, 1927. From *Antoine By Antoine*, published by W.H. Allen, 1946.

Clairville, sixty European hairdressers dressed in impeccably tailored smocks were each addressed by their first name preceded by "Mr." The wealthy social set whose hair was treated with lotions and perfumes shipped over from France refused to let anyone who wasn't foreign work on their hair, including Guilaroff himself who promptly became "Mr. Sydney."[29] In the art of coiffure, as in the art of couture, the cachet of Paris functioned as a potent symbol of exclusivity.

Philip Crang and Peter Jackson theorize how modern consumerism maps its own geography across local, global, and imaginative sites; *where* people consume is a meaningful part of *what* and how people consume in relation to actual places and "fantasies of elsewhere."[30] The Antoine de Paris salon opened in the Niemen Marcus store in Dallas, Texas, for example, was an exact copy of the one in Cannes, France.[31] From the late nineteenth century the playgrounds of the rich and famous mapped a migratory route of consumerism according to the social and fashionable seasons of Paris, London, Vienna, New York, Deauville, or Cannes, along which a whole service industry grew up devoted to their needs. Gentlemen's barbers and ladies' salons became an important attraction in all the best hotels, top department stores, and in the twentieth century on luxury cruise liners.

In Britain, connotations of modern coiffure craftsmanship and unrivaled personal service were centered on London's Mayfair, an area that since the eighteenth century was synonymous with upmarket fashionable taste and the lifestyles of a social elite. However, in the 1920s, the area had begun to imperceptibly change. Many of the wealthy residents were forced to sell up faced with huge debts for inheritance tax after World War I and losses in successive financial crises and crashes. Their "sedately aristocratic quarters" were replaced with smart shops, hotels, offices and businesses, and small modern service apartments evocative of a new atmosphere of modern consumerism.[32] Design historian Kim Smith examines how Mayfair, long home to the discrete world of London's couture industry, progressively emerged as the epicenter of the modern luxury ladies' hairdressing trade as high-end practitioners opened salons in Grafton, Albemarle, Bond, Dover, and Berkeley Streets, Berkeley Square, and Hay Hill in the southeast corner of the "Mayfair Square Mile."[33] At the height of the Jazz Age, the area became aligned with a generation of "bright young things," fashionable, upper-class men and women, for whom excess and spectacle, particularly in relation to dress and hair styling, were central concepts in the idea of transformation—social, fashionable, and cultural. An avant-garde circle of writers, designers, artists, and socialites who frequented the beauty salons, night clubs, shops, and hotels of modern Mayfair and hosted lavish masquerade and fancy dress parties adopted outré hairstyles that defied aesthetic and social convention—radically short cut hair for women or longer, waved, and very visibly colored hair for men. Cecil Beaton attended one party with his hair dyed platinum blond, while Stephen Tennant appeared with his long blond Marcel waved hair sprinkled with gold dust.[34]

WESTERN EXPANSION

In a British social context, Mayfair and the West End were a site of upper-class indulgence seen as symbolic of new attitudes to consumerism from the late 1920s. However, while grounded in reality, their allure was very much fueled by their mythologizing in sensational romance novels (Figure 8.3 is a typical example), an expanding women's magazine market, and hundreds of yards of column inches in the society and gossip pages popular press all devoted to the latest goings-on of the rich and famous.

FIGURE 8.3: Front cover *Glamour of Mayfair* by Jean Hope, published by Gramol Publications, 1934.

But in the 1930s, such fantasies of being transported to a glamorous "elsewhere" took on a new and wider significance for the status hierarchy and the geography of modern hairdressing. The cinematic construction of "glamour" as a new media aesthetic recast the performance of social status and the spaces of its modern production, reproduction, and consumption.[35] In the golden age of Hollywood, the heads of screen and genealogically titled ladies now equally displayed the credentials of a hairdressing and social elite to challenge the class-based boundaries of the old social order in new ways. Parisian flair via New York or Mayfair retained its cachet for an aristocratic and nouveau-riche clientele, but Hollywood, directly or indirectly, became the fulcrum of style innovation, and through its stars the signifier of a new system of social status and status recognition.

A new kind of modern celebrity hairdresser had also emerged. The Westmore brothers, Perc, Ern, Monte, and Frank, and Sidney Guilaroff became famed for creating the looks, makeup, and hair of all the leading players, and each of them at one time headed up makeup departments of the major studios.[36] In 1917, George Westmore, a wigmaker by trade, opened the first studio makeup department in history in a small corner of the Selig Studio grounds in New York. Here he made Mary Pickford's and later Shirley Temple's long artificial ringlets and pioneered the "graduated" hair cut by layering the athletic Douglas Fairbanks's thick hair to lie flat and sleek against his skull, while his son Monte Westmore gave Valentino his slicked-down hair and long sideburns.[37] Guilaroff recalled in his autobiography how while working at Saks Fifth Avenue he was dubbed by gossip columnists as "the man with the golden shears" after cutting Claudette Colbert's hair and giving the star her "sensational bangs."[38] Soon, all the leading producers and their leading ladies were seeking him out, including Ginger Rogers and, perhaps most famously, Joan Crawford. In 1931, Miss Crawford, then married to Hollywood "royalty" Douglas Fairbanks Jr., desired a new look as much for the media attention as for the hairdo. Guilaroff remembered the day she arrived at Antoine's: "it seemed as if the whole world knew she was coming."[39] Hordes of star-watchers had gathered on Fifth Avenue, and when her limousine pulled up to the curb crowds poured into Saks filling all six elevators. Guilaroff steered Crawford to a private booth in the salon where she left it up to "Mr. Sydney" to do whatever he felt was becoming to her. Guilaroff observed:

> When her lovely dark brunette hair was dry, I removed the pins and started to brush out the curls. I parted her hair on the left and made a single wave on that side, then brushed it back behind her ear to fall in soft, flowing waves. The right side I brushed into a similar single wave, leaving the top of her head sleek and smooth.[40]

The trademark looks created for screen idols by their favorite personal stylists were widely disseminated through their film roles and their constant presence in hugely popular gossip columns in the press media and numerous film magazines devoted to describing every aspect of the cinematic spectacle.[41] Stars also endorsed a rapidly expanding range of new hair-care products and processes developed through innovations in science and technology and a booming interwar chemical industry. A popular beauty guide in 1938 advised:

> Ask your hairdresser to give you a style he thinks will suit you—or choose the film star nearest your own style of beauty, and follow the hairdressing you think suits her best. But be sure she *is* your style. Try to follow Katherine Hepburn when you are more like Sonja Henie, and you will probably find yourself on the eve of an important dance looking more like Nellie Wallace or Mrs Wiggs of the Cabbage Patch.[42]

"Class" was being redefined by beautiful ex-socialites such as Hepburn but particularly ex-showgirls-now-stars like Crawford renowned for being immaculately dressed by designer Adrian in the latest gowns and having her hair styled and restyled by Mr. Sydney to her exacting standards of perfection. Crawford's on-screen performances in films like *The Women* (much of which is set in a beauty salon)[43] further fueled a belief in strategies of ruthless self-management and hard work as a powerful vehicle of social mobility. No longer just spectators, a mainstream audience could also now enjoy having *their* hair styled in the latest fashion in well-equipped "boudoir"-style salons opening up in big cities and out into the suburbs (Figure 8.4).

The noted socialist commentator and novelist, J.B. Priestley famously undertook an *English Journey* in 1934 in order to try to understand the nature of a "new" Britain.[44] Starting out on the first leg of his voyage of cultural discovery Priestley described the Great West Road out of London as looking as if he had "suddenly rolled in to California": "pretty" new factories lined the route producing goods that seemed "to belong to an England of little luxury trades." Meeting with a typical post-World War I entrepreneur on the coach to Camberley in Surrey, he is told of the man's constant search for "an opening" and the next "gold mine" whether it be a tea room in Kent, selling cheap raincoats in Newcastle, or "opening a ladies' hair salon ... in the right district."[45]

The biographies of the "stars" of the hairdressing world offered a similar rags-to-riches narrative of the celebrities whose hair they styled and the films they starred in.

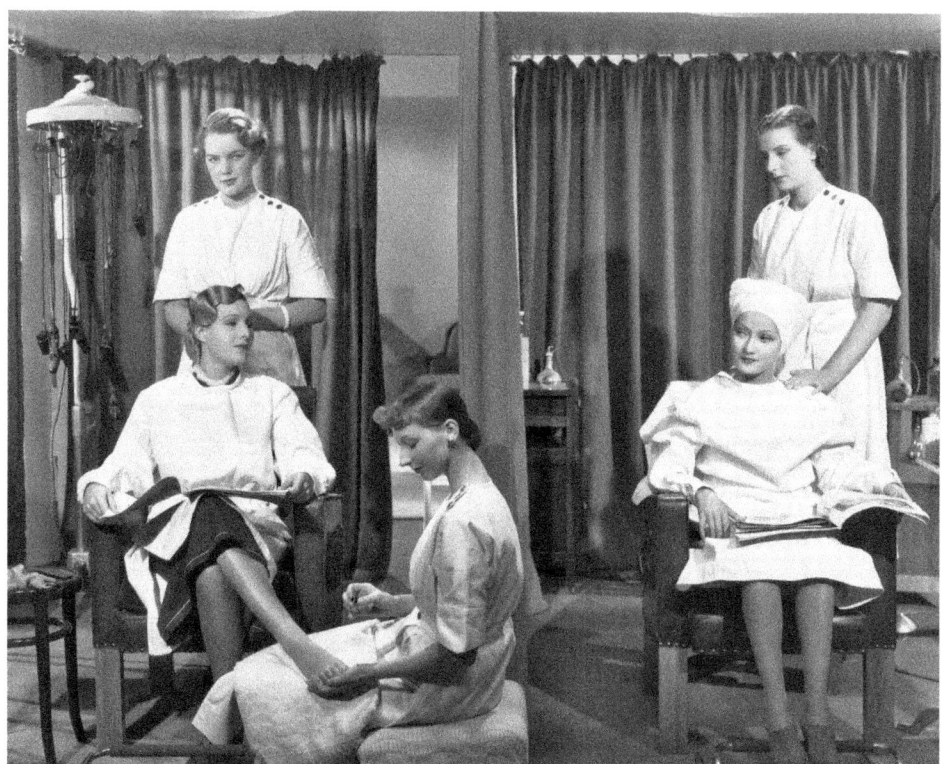

FIGURE 8.4: Two women in a beauty salon getting their hair and nails done, Hollywood, California, ca. 1936.

Antoine's described his poor beginnings in Paris, Guilaroff's his struggle to find work in the big city and contraction of tuberculosis, and Westmore's journey from a one-room barbershop in England to Sunset Boulevard in Los Angeles. However, such stories were not mere fairy tales. Modern hairdressing did offer new opportunities for "improvement" for many working-class men and women for whom domestic service was once the only option. As Steven Zdatny observes, the growth of the modern hairdressing trade in Paris in the 1920s and 1930s was not just about aesthetics; it was also about business. The vogue for short hair generated new patterns of consumption that allowed new avenues of commercial enterprise to emerge.[46] Salon ownership offered an alternative pathway to economic security and upward social mobility for the leading male auteurs of modern hairdressing such as Antoine—but also for the women who poured into the profession after World War I and took up well-paid positions in *coiffure pour dames*.[47] A similar pattern was repeated in Britain. Trade schools such as the one in Barrett Street in London (Figure 8.5) offered young women training and recognized qualifications in the latest hairdressing techniques and a whole range of associated beauty treatments. Opened in 1915, by the 1920s thousands of girls, many from the poorer districts of the East End, had progressed from Barrett Street to careers in top salons all across London's West End, particularly in the new department stores.[48]

In America, the development of modern Black hairdressing practices similarly offered new opportunities for entrepreneurship and economic advancement (Figure 8.6). For

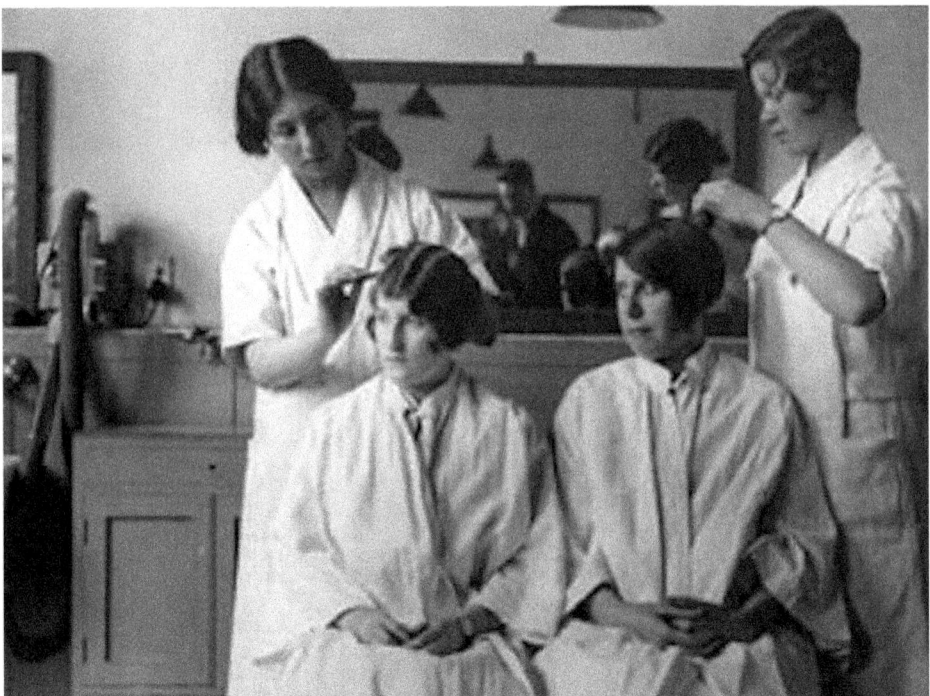

FIGURE 8.5: Women's hairdressing class, Barrett Street Trade School, London, 1928. Photo: Barrett Street Trade School Archive. Reproduced by permission of University of the Arts London: London College of Fashion.

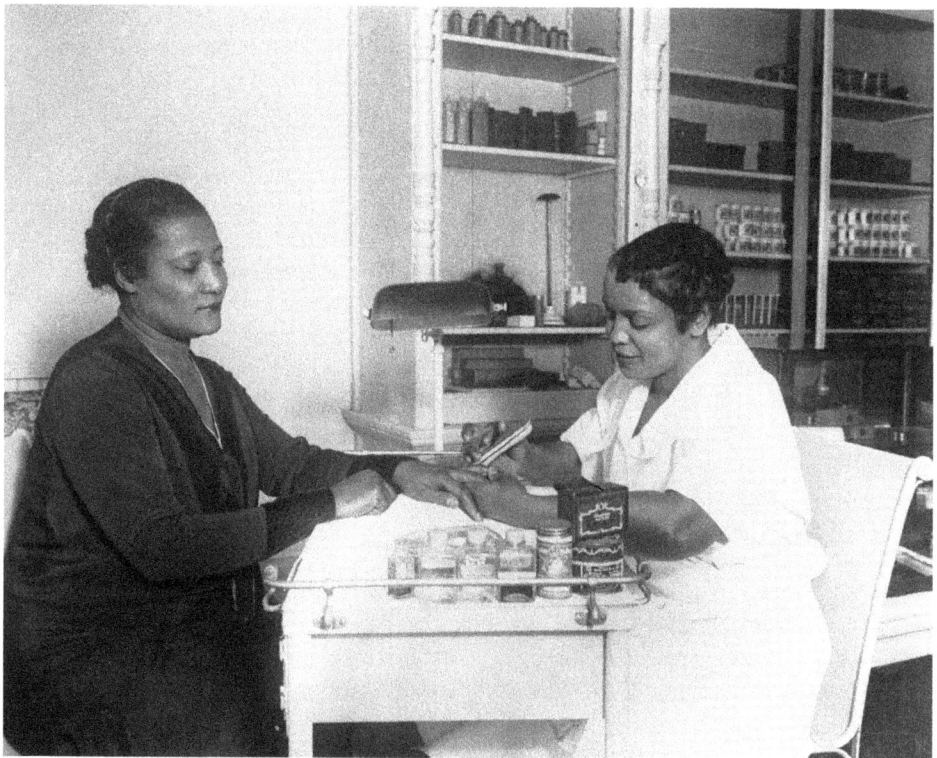

FIGURE 8.6: A beauty salon in Harlem, New York, ca. 1933. Photo: General Photographic Agency/Getty Images.

many Black women, "hair became a means by which [they] could build their fortunes, or at the very least ensure that there would be food on the table every night."[49] In the first decades of the twentieth century, pioneering entrepreneurs such as Annie Turnbo Malone, Madame C.J. Walker, and Sarah Spencer Washington had developed a range of hair-care products and processes that could be administered in new Black beauty salons and sold door-to-door by hundreds of trained agents who kept a percentage of the profits.[50] By 1920, employment in the Black hairdressing trade was increasing rapidly; it was seen to be undermining domestic labor supply in the American South, while in the industrial north numerous salons were opening to meet demand.[51] An important model of Black female entrepreneurship in the twentieth century had been established; employment in the Black hair and beauty industry frequently served as a platform for salon ownership, a move that was viewed as enabling them to experience upward mobility into the middle or upper middle classes.[52]

MOVING UP IN THE WORLD

The constant cycle of innovation, imitation, distinction, and emulation that drives modern industrial capitalism "is manifested nowhere more strikingly than in personal appearance, because dress, hairstyles and makeup are the most obvious signs of affirmation."[53] Mass consumption of distinctly modern hairstyles and strategies of hair care and grooming and of affordable, accessible fashionable clothing played a significant role in correlatively changing systems of status display and recognition. In Britain in the 1930s, the idea that it was no longer possible to judge a person's class by what they wore—or indeed how they styled their hair—became the familiar currency of social observation in the press and popular culture. A cartoon in *Punch* in 1924 satirized the plight of a post-World War I middle class in the guise of "Betty Grant," forced by a lack of domestic servants to pay higher wages for a new maid who could afford to be better dressed than her mistress.[54] Yet, as historian Catherine Horwood points out, as the mythical mill girl gained access to better clothing, then so the demands of middle-class respectability in Britain also generated new strategies of differentiation. Clothes that were *too* new or expensive, or were inappropriately formal or informal, slovenly or smart according to the occasion, combined in a display of agency and taste that the straightened middle and upper middle classes could happily dissociate from.

In the face of what was seen as the relentless progress of modern society and mass consumerism, aesthetic judgments linked to traditional concepts of good and bad physical attributes were incorporated into a new discourse of discrimination in which hairstyles functioned to reveal their wearers' "true" colors. For the suburban middle classes, too tightly curled or exotically or elaborately coiffed "big" hair colored "platinum" blonde, vibrant red, or raven black, fixed one firmly on the lower rungs of the social ladder and in doing so marked one out as a social climber rather than an indigenous native. For consumers of all classes across cultures, the failure to maintain new standards of modern display, evident in a visible lack of professional or personal hair-care regimes (greasy hair, dandruff, telltale dark roots, sharp cuts, shingles, and perms) became symbolic of poverty, fecklessness, and even criminality and prostitution. Under threat from the constant incursion of the mass market, a hierarchy of elite hairstyling was also reformulated through moral judgments informed by a series of tensions between artifice and authenticity, art and commerce that remapped the geography of high-end hairdressing before and, for a short period, after World War II.

Couture fashion and hairstyling enjoyed a "Golden Age" in the 1950s as the two *metiers* incorporated new ideals of body management—hairstyling, cosmetics, perfumes, and manicuring—into a new kind of glamorous femininity. In the world of "haute coiffure," national and international shows, competitions, and demonstrations functioned in the same way as the nascent modern "catwalk" show[55] as a new forum to display the talents of the industry's leading players and the new season's style trends.[56] Hairdressing "auteurs" once again became household names, often appearing alongside their rich and famous clients on the pages and covers of fashionable magazines and the popular press. The extravagant creations of top Mayfair stylist Raymond Bessone, better known as "Mr. Teasie Weasie," were regularly included in Pathé newsreels shown in all major cinemas in Britain before the main feature, and Raymond even hosted his own TV show.[57] In Europe, "Alexandre de Paris" (Louis Alexandre Raimon) who had trained at Antoine's was frequently pictured putting the finishing touches to the hairstyles of stars such as Elizabeth Taylor and Sophia Loren and was famous for styling Grace Kelly's hair for her wedding to Prince Rainier.

Images of the rich and famous complemented frequent features in women's popular and fashion magazines and a booming market in beauty books devoted to advising women on how to achieve the necessary standard of coiffure as part of a carefully coordinated look and lifestyle. Reinforced by the continued allure of French chic, having one's hair professionally styled continued to be equated with affluence and social status. Hair had to be cut and permed every two months, but to successfully maintain the look women had to have their hair "set" in the salon every week. Hair was shampooed, set into a *pli* (derived from the French *mis-en-pli*, meaning to put into position), and finally "dressed" by being brushed out in a coiffure tailored to the client's specific requirements—the defining marker of hairdressing distinction. Leaving the salon, whether in the suburbs or the West End, the finished hairdo sprayed with lacquer to hold it in place served as a highly desirable symbol of its wearer's achievement of a certain economic and social status ... at least for a while.[58]

THE CLASS-LESS SOCIETY

With the benefits of hindsight it would be easy to see the golden age of "big hair" in the 1950s as the zenith of not just outmoded hairdressing practices and processes but also of the class-based system of social stratification these embodied. The stiff styles and time-consuming and constraining rituals of the salon (and the close clipped and shaved conformity of the barbershop) progressively became emblematic of the failures of the authoritarian state and the patriarchal bourgeois culture that sustained it. Hair, while never a mere superficial accessory in the abstract dynamics of social identification and display, assumed a new significance as a potent cultural form for a new generation of young consumers, particularly those involved in various counter and subcultural movements for whom hair became a high visibility strategy of political radicalism. Avant-garde "Beat" artists and writers in America in the late 1950s grew beards and let their hair grow to collar-length; male and female Black civil rights activists in the 1960s left their hair untreated and "nappy" to grow out naturally and styled it into "Afros"; second wave feminists and hippies of both genders in the 1970s went to similar lengths in growing and loosening their hair as a symbol of their liberation from the constraints of patriarchal control. Hair styling as a model of resistance in these examples operated as a powerful vehicle of subjective expression, challenging the imperialist hegemony of western capitalism and patriarchal authority and the normative codes of gender, race, and sexuality that sustained it.

Men's wearing of longer hair and women's rejection of permanent waves and lacquered bouffants offered a continuum of stylistic potential that inspired Vidal Sassoon and a generation of other young creative hairdressers in the 1960s but also changed the attitudes of male consumers. Sassoon revolutionized modern hairdressing practice with his geometric bob and new "boutique" salons opened in what at the time was the down-at-heel environs of the Kings Road, Chelsea. The gender differentiated spaces of the barbershop and ladies' hair salon that the 1920s had initiated were transformed as fashionable men and women had their hair cut and styled at Leonard's in Mayfair, or Sassoon's in Chelsea or Knightsbridge.

An emphasis on youth; the democratization of fashion; a new valorization of working-class roots with the rise of pop music heroes such as the Beatles and East Enders like Sassoon, photographer David Bailey, actor Michael Caine; and the satirizing of an upper-class establishment in film and TV by young middle-class writers and playwrights, all disrupted or challenged traditional concepts of top-to-bottom cultural dissemination and fostered an illusion of a "class-less" society in Britain in the 1960s. However, class is not something like religious faith or fairy dust that can just be forgotten about because *you* no longer believe in it. Useful here is what sociologist Fred Davis identifies as a complex dynamic of status claims and status demurrals expressed through the fashioned body; the former usually involves flaunting what one has, the latter feinting what one lacks.⁵⁹ Davis argues that whatever the motivating force of fashion, much of its inspiration is generated within an essential state of identity ambivalence that springs from the "cross-flows and clashes of the basic cultural categories that structure our lives."⁶⁰

Perhaps because of the particularities of the British class system, questions of class were explicitly drawn in the emergence of some youth subcultures in the postwar period. In the mid-1950s, young, working-class men and teenage boys who had grown up in the shadow of war and postwar austerity appropriated the styles of an upper-class elite to fashion a new look focused on leisure rather than work (which while abundant and relatively well paid was seen as a "dead end"). The so-called "Teddy Boy" combined the eponymous "Edwardian" drape jacket with a "bricolage" of stylistic touches that heavily reflected the influence of American popular culture particularly music: brightly colored suits, ruffled shirts and shoe lace ties, and hair left to grow longer and combed into large pompadours. Rock 'n' roll music, new coffee bars to hang out in, clothing, and a fastidious attention to grooming embodied a growing disenchantment with the culture of respectability that dominated the working and leisured lives of their parents.

Successive subcultural groups emerged for whom the contradistinctions of hair styling remained central to classed subjectivities defined by this complex of style, place, and taste. In the 1970s, working-class "Skinheads" shaved their heads and grew sideburns, and wore checked shirts with jeans with braces and Dr. Marten boots to reconfigure the experience of working-class masculinity, this time in the appropriation of the traditional markers of an increasingly defunct industrial labor force in a Britain ravaged by economic decline and social unrest.

Young male and female Punks took stylistic transgression—in art, music, fashion, makeup, and hairstyling—to extremes to expose the myths of modern capitalism and of a supposedly benign British class system ruled by the monarchy. Do-it-yourself, badly cut and badly dyed hair was formed into vertical spikes, often with any substance that was to hand, in an aggressive, deliberately "antinatural" look, culminating in the ubiquitous Mohican (Figure 8.7). Every aspect of self-presentation was deconstructed to critique not just the normative values of mainstream society, but, by extension, previous sub- and countercultural identities seen as equally defunct markers of British identity (one of the slogans of punk was "Never Trust A Hippie").⁶¹

Punk is seen as triggering some of the most exciting developments in fashion and hair styling in the modern age, but an emphasis on the "look" of transgression swiftly overtook its impact as a vehicle for political change, certainly for the majority of the working, working classes. Punk by its nature despised the mainstream, but its stylistic strategies were often weighted towards the sensitivities of an art school avant-garde rather than the everyday realities of those for whom urban decline and the unemployment queue would be permanent features rather than a passing trend.

As Beverley Skeggs argues, "To engage in the politics of recognition is to convert cultural capital into something more, something that has a wider value than the local cultural arena; something that can be recognized, including powerful others."⁶² In the late 1980s when the film *Working Girl* was released, hair styling and other forms of body management were important elements in strategies of female "power dressing." It was the era of the Young Urban Professional, better known as the "yuppie," and the trend in men's hair styling was toward "a cleaner, stronger and more manly look ... not the short back and sides of years," left fuller on the crown and dressed into shape with the fingers.⁶³ Reminiscent of a 1930s upper-class Oxbridge set captured in films like *Another*

FIGURE 8.7: Young punks Ian Holden ("Angel") and John Vick, May 1982. Photo: Science and Society Picture Library.

Country or *Room With A View*, the style was adopted by city traders—ex-public school boys and working-class oiks—who became the new poster boys of 1980s social aspiration and mobility. In the film, the aspirational main protagonist Tess McGill (Melanie Griffith) asks her best friend Cyn (Joan Cusack) to cut her hair. Asked if she is sure about this, Tess responds: "If you want to be taken seriously, you need serious hair." Having carefully observed the style and deportment of her executive boss Katharine Parker (Sigourney

Weaver), Tess's big, extravagantly blow-dried hair (Figure 8.8) is transformed into a short, discretely layered bob and her tarty clothes, large dangly earrings and rattling jewelry replaced with gray business suits or a demure black cocktail dress and pearls (Figure 8.9). The bewildered Cyn remains content to ramp up the volume with her hair, makeup, and clothes and do her time in the office pool until she gets married.

"Big hair" (worn with short skirts, skimpy tops, very high heels, and lots of makeup) in the United States in some contexts operates as a key signifier of a hypersexualized "white trash" femininity,[64] and in others as signaling one's ethnic identity, for example, many Mexican-American women feel they must keep their hair long, heavily sprayed with full volume curls, and wear heavy makeup despite being aware of the negative connotations this generates outside of their community.[65] Of course, anyone, like *Working Girl*'s Tess, or indeed Lady Prescott with whose big coiffure we began this chapter, can visit the best salons, enjoy the skills of the best stylists, and display the results in all the best

FIGURE 8.8: "Big hair." Melanie Griffith, *Working Girl*, 1988. Moviestore Collection/REX// Shutterstock.

FIGURE 8.9: "You wanna be taken seriously, you need serious hair." Melanie Griffith, *Working Girl*, 1988. Moviestore Collection/REX//Shutterstock.

places. But the successful negotiation of a system that is ultimately dependent on the recognizable characteristics of "others" only reinforces "the how of knowledge, that is 'how' to operationalize knowledge, emotions and performance" in the articulation of classed identity. Body shape and carriage and a repertoire of surface signifiers—clothes, body art, piercings, makeup, and hairstyles—all operate as significant class markers in the construction of a physiognomic indices of "taste" and a corresponding social space, a "marketplace" where symbolic goods are bought and sold from specific subject positions.[66]

CONCLUSION: FAKING IT IN THE MODERN AGE

Class, it is believed, can be consigned to the past along with the hair clippers and curlers, because it is seen as no longer relevant in a new politics of identity motivated by far more powerful vectors of selfhood. However, the body politics of the later twentieth century has created new systems of status recognition within which the traditional tripartite mechanism of hairdressing exclusivity, style–stylist–salon, continues to operate as a discriminatory class-based discourse of identification and recognition. Thus, Skeggs argues, class is in no way in decline in contemporary society. Rather, it is more difficult to pin down because "it is so insinuated in the intimate making of self and culture that it is even more ubiquitous than previously articulated … [with it] leaking beyond the traditional measures of classification."[67] Recent fashionable reimaginings of Victorian bearded patriarchy, or the short back and sides, clean-shaven look of the English upper-class gent, or pastiches of a 1920s "Peaky Blinder" (a member of a criminal gang in Birmingham, West Midlands), or of glamorous feminine domesticity and sexy secretarial looks whose origins are located somewhere in the distant past, all seem to evidence that old systems of status recognition are no longer relevant other than as collection of arbitrary stylistic accessories. However, the historical discourse of class distinction demonstrates how hair's qualities of physiological and social malleability are always emphasized to ambiguously reinforce the boundaries of superior aesthetic judgment while simultaneously reproducing a metonymic pathology of discrimination. Hairstyles continue to carry a heavy symbolic load as a medium by which a classed sense of self and other is legitimatized *because* hair is infinitely manipulative.

Caroline Cox describes how, in the 2000s, fashionable young men in London, inspired by the catwalk looks of session-stylists such as Guido Palau for Gucci and Gianni Scumaci for Vidal Sassoon, began wearing their hair in a style that became known as the "Hoxton Fin" (short at the sides but left long on top and shaped into a center fin). The look, as the name suggests, was seen as characteristic of a particular area of London, a once rundown and working-class East End neighborhood now home to the young and trendy. Cox cites "Vishnoo," an online observer who described fin devotees as "typically called Floyd or Sebastian" with well-paid jobs in the media, who buy all their clothes from Newburgh Street, and have the latest copy of Sleazenation sticking out of the back pocket of their ridiculously low slung Evisu jeans.[68]

Elsewhere, the contemporaneous derogatory construction of figures of the "Essex Girl" and "the Chav" were emerging through a similar system of stylistic and geographically mapped class stereotyping. The former cultural phenomenon was a young woman from a county in southeast England (paradoxically peopled by families with long associations with the East End) objectified in the tabloid press as vulgar, loud, and frequently and excessively drunk, and renowned as dressing in a sexually provocative way, having a very visibly fake tan, and dyed and artificially extended "brassy" blonde long hair; the latter collective term "chav" refers to those seen as belonging to a white, unemployed, underclass of both genders (again originating in the southeast but rapidly becoming more geographically generic), dressed in head to toe counterfeit designer styles, and whose young women and girls were immediately identifiable by their "Croydon face lifts," that is, hair tied back extremely tightly into various buns and high ponytails.

The spectacular expression and the spatial dimensions of hair and its associated styling and grooming practices are ambiguous sites of cultural expression that produce and regulate conformist and subversive social bodies. "High" fashion, "couture" hairdos are no longer solely the privileged preserve of the rich and famous, but they continue to play an important role in the establishment, organization, and maintenance of divisive social boundaries by defining *who* and displaying *what* is of societal value. Katalin Medvedev suggests that attention has progressively shifted to the body itself and the subtle details of exclusive clothing: the cut, the fit, the use of "natural," that is, expensive fabrics and products, the allure of the brand, luxury accessories such as eyeglasses, watches, shoes, and bags. She argues "A stylish haircut, perfect and even teeth, and especially a slender body ... have become more of a class signifier than dress itself."[69]

Hierarchical structures of consumerism have been constructed through understandings of social prestige extant at any one period of time; these continue to elide social differences and inequalities and class conflict through the illusion of fashionable agency. Such illusions have become progressively more complex with a more complex and expanding globalized mass market, greater access for many to new forms of fashionable consumerism, and the influence of new technology and social media networks. But these have initiated new systems of surveillance and judgment that continue to reinforce class-based systems of capital exchange and the construction of a physiognomic index of good and bad taste in which hair and its styling continue to play an important role.

CHAPTER NINE

Cultural Representations

NATHALIE KHAN

HAIR AS FETISH AND DISPLAY IN ART AND QUEER PERFORMANCE: REPRESENTATION, SYMBOL, AND METAPHOR

This chapter focuses on the female wig as commodity and cultural artifact to explore the dialectic nature of hair symbolism, primarily sexual symbolism, in performance and cultural representation. The examples used are not comprehensive; they serve as heuristic devices through which to examine hair as a culturally vital representational form in the modern age. Ideas of psychoanalysis are important to the discussion, particularly the notion of the fetish object in relation to questions of sexual difference.[1] American actor and performer Paul Soileau's reflections on the role of the wig in his construction of the stage persona "Christeene," (Figure 9.1) frames the analysis of key critical approaches to this aspect of hair symbolism.[2] The wig in this context alludes to hair as a performative extension of the sexual self and a potential source of transgression and sexual deviance.[3] Christeene's performance challenges the established binaries of gender and sexuality and the performative dimensions of public and private identities.[4]

In this chapter, the representational aspects of hair and its styling are understood as the product of diverse aesthetic and cultural influences; but this also entails addressing how this relationship was informed by new theoretical approaches to the psychic and social sources of hair's potent sexual symbolism that emerged in the twentieth century.[5] Women's hair as a metaphor for the female body and mass consumerism was increasingly fetishized in literary and visual culture at a time when ideas of the "natural" and the "real" were seen as unstable and under threat of contamination. Different theoretical categories of the fetish—anthropological, sexual, commodity—are situated in this study as a complex of ideas that inform different economies of normative gender and sexual identities in the modern age. These inform an exploration of new forms of art practice and popular cultural representations of hair that challenge shifting sociocultural understandings of ideas of sexual difference and exploiting their performative potential for subversion.

This opens up the discussion to a consideration of the construction and status of the artistic "persona" as an instrumental lynchpin of modern commodity culture.[6] The chapter explores the role of the wig in different artistic strategies of self-presentation and representation that from the 1960s sought to question the boundaries of aesthetic, cultural, and subjective "authenticity" exerted in the performance of private person and

FIGURE 9.1: "'Christeene' leaning over window ledge." Photo: Eli Schmidt. Reproduced by permission of Paul Soileau.

public persona. The work of Andy Warhol and his self-performances as artist and cultural icon are the focus of an analysis of the wider spectacular dimensions of hair symbolism as an integral part of the culture of modern celebrity and its critique.[7] The chapter concludes by returning to Christeene's self-conscious exploitation of hair's symbolic and material ambivalence in strategies of performance and performative identification that question the nature of transgression in contemporary queer politics of the body.

QUEER WIGS: HAIR AND SEXUAL SYMBOLISM

In the hybrid fashion film and music video *Butt Muscle*,[8] the fashion designer Rick Owens and his partner Michele Lami stage intimate acts with "Christeene," a fictional character created by Paul Soileau.[9] The film, which its director Matt Lambert describes as an empowered piece, seeks to challenge normative heterosexuality and gender identity through performance.[10] Christeene's stage persona is rooted in an understanding of identity as one self-consciously constructed through the performance of the body and its dressing, and in particular through wearing a long black wig that, since she first appeared on stage in the video *Fix my Dick* (dir. P J Raval)[11] has become Christeene's performative trademark.[12] *Butt Muscle*, a term referred to in the lyrics as a point where bodies and organs connect physically and metaphorically, explores themes of trust and vulnerability through physiological configurations and poses of bodies and hair that visualize this connection. Soileau observes, "We all seem to enjoy our locks, and it seemed only natural to allow such a strong piece of our aesthetic to mingle together, you know?"[13]

Hair is a highly sexualized cultural signifier: its manipulation and management feature prominently in rituals across cultures articulating social taboos relating to sexual practices and beliefs, and visibly communicating changes in sociosexual status, for example, in initiation ceremonies and rites of passage.[14] Because it is central to the construction of social norms, hair cannot just be seen as solely rooted in biology; the boundaries between the social and the physical, and the essential interrelationship that exists between the two, must be visibly managed.[15] As social anthropologist Mary Douglas points out, each of these bodily experiences (psychic and social) reinforces the categories of the other.[16] Within this exchange, body "dirt"—blood, semen, saliva, excreta, nails, and hair—are seen as "matter out of place," that is, impurities that if left untreated or controlled threaten to pollute and disrupt the social order. During one of the sequences in *Butt Muscle* a stream of urine pours from Christeene onto Rick Owens' face, and in another, Rick Owens' long hair is placed inside Christeene's anus before it is then arranged coming out of her mouth (Figure 9.2).

Hair, in this aspect of the film and media campaign, evokes feelings of both revulsion and desire according to its perception as being either "in" or "out" of place.[17] The erotically charged exchange simultaneously challenges social norms in the intimate physicality of actual sexual bodies, and consolidates them in a symbolic process of incorporation. The performers place themselves in a position of private and public spectacle and repulsion through which bodies and taboos are socially classified and ordered.

Throughout the film, the complex symbolic and material dimensions of hair and its styling are spectacularly exploited to iterate queer identity and sexual desire. Oiled and visibly manipulated like the bodies of the dancers in the performance, Christeene's hair serves as a symbol of femininity while challenging and exploiting the constraints

FIGURE 9.2: "Christeene" with Rick Owens, in *Butt Muscle* (dir. Matt Lambert, 2016). Reproduced by permission of Paul Soileau.

of heteronormative identity. The director Lambert describes how he explicitly used such symbolism to subvert the sexual imagery often used in rap music videos in which femininity is represented as overtly sexualized while queer bodies are portrayed as merely obscene.[18] Soileau too is very aware of the creative possibilities invested in hair's unique malleability and the social penalties at stake in publicly "playing" with one's hair:

> There is an immediate go to action … with Christeene's hair when alone in public. Or being very vulnerable, and that is to take a long strand of the bangs and hold it in both hands pulling and stroking and tilting the head. It's such an awful contradiction of the monster visage and the long childlike hair being stroked. It confuses those around me and I love it.

Psychoanalyst Charles Berg notably theorized how the ease with which hair can be freely played with invites unconscious connections; hair through its unique properties of mutability is invested with repressed sexual potency and, thus, is rendered sacred or taboo.[19] In provocatively "teasing" her hair in this way Christeene reveals the precarity of hair's essentially liminal status *and* the ways in which these unique qualities become key factors in the mechanisms of gendered and sexualized looking.[20] From a Freudian perspective it is this psychodynamic that defines the fetish object. Hair's malleability allows an ambivalent mix of internal and external, psychical and physical strategies of embodiment that offer the potential to overcome the threatening nature of lack, but also the constant possibility of the collapse of such cohesion.

Linked to anthropological understandings of the fetish as a powerful substitute in ritual contexts,[21] Freud's sexual fetish functions to commemorate and disavow the young child's

FIGURE 9.3: "Christeene" in green dress. Photo: Michael Sharkey. Reproduced by permission of Paul Soileau.

last "glance" of the mother's pubic hair.[22] The boy child's sight of the female genitals and lack of a penis invokes the threat of castration and an instantaneous "forgetting" that Freud argues is the psychic foundation of sexual difference.[23] The power of the fetish object lies in its capacity not merely to provide a substitute for such lack but also in the mechanisms of repression that mitigate the horrors of castration the vagina evidences.[24] Thus, Freud's definition of the fetish object as material is useful in this context; he argues, the horror of castration impels a need to "set up a memorial to itself" which quite often takes the form of hair, fur, or feathers.[25]

THE FETISH OBJECT

Both artificial and real, detached from, and an extension of, the constructed and biological "natural" body, the wig as fetishized, fixated object is essential to the performative construction of Christeene and Soileau's intensely personalized physical performances (Figure 9.3). For Soileau, without the wig on his head "Christeene is gone." He describes how he wanted "long and black from the very beginning," and tried other "looks" on Christeene, but "it just falls apart and you lose the character." New wigs arrive silky and smooth in a beautiful gold box so that, "It's a very glamorous kind of Christeene, but the wigs soon begin to find themselves and get nappy and dreaded and beautiful ... in their decline majesty." A battle for autonomy is waged on stage as Soileau "fights with the wig as much as the crowd" and Christeene's hair is thrashed about in its "attempts to fly off his skull."[26]

Janice Miller uses Freudian theory to analyze hair's representational possibilities as both "dead matter" and a source of vitality within the "uncanny" realm that the constant slippage between the two invokes in the cultural imagination.[27] Christeene's wig rests between performances on a multiheaded wig stand alongside wigs belonging to other personae, and a collection of the character's old wigs that have been "turned out to pasture." But in returning it to its stand, Christeene in the guise of the wig becomes somehow reanimated. Soileau observes:

> I always tell it [the wig], good job after a gig or a long tour as I'm putting it on the stand. It becomes her when off my head, or a communicator to her but just for a small bit of praise.

Questions of what constitutes "real" hair are not of course especial to wigs or other hair "additions," rather their objective and subjective physical constructed-ness gives clear material form to what Freud theorizes as a constant state of psychic ambivalence aroused by the fetishized sight of hair. However, Christeene's long, black, smooth wig very visibly objectifies and embodies a series of conflicting fetishistic substitutions in the performance of a constructed and thus consumable identity (Figure 9.4). Just as Freud's mechanisms of psychic substitution and disavowal offer an understanding of how hair as fetish works ritually and socially to "flesh out" subconscious desires, then so Marx's theories of commodity fetishism advance an economic perspective: objects accrue symbolic value through the relations of industrial capitalism that operate to simultaneously render the cost of the transaction invisible.[28] Hair's potent sexual symbolism is harnessed to a critique of the constructed-ness of gender and sexual identities, but this reveals the power of the fetish at work in the different economies of exchange upon which they are contingent for their meaning and value.

FIGURE 9.4: "Christeene" in leather. Photo: Eli Schmidt. Reproduced by permission of Paul Soileau.

FIGURE 9.5: "Christeene" in "bath mat" wig. Photo: Michael Sharkey. Reproduced by permission of Paul Soileau.

Soileau's insights into the ambiguous boundaries of the performative self that are realized in his relationship with Christeene reflect a history of the idea and themes of fetishism that William Pietz argues "persist throughout the various discourses and disciplines that have appropriated the term."[29] The "truth" of the fetish for Pietz, and for Soileau/Christeene, resides in the irreducible *materiality* of an object of intense psychic investment (Figure 9.5). The object's potency endures in its singular capacity for endless repetition of an originating act of identification that orders not just material elements, but desires, beliefs, and narrative structures, and the economic and psychic relations that exist between them.[30]

THE POWER OF HAIR'S SEXUAL SYMBOLISM IN THE MODERN IMAGINATION

This idea of fetishized repetition informed the work of early-twentieth-century French writer and philosopher George Bataille. In his writings on Freud, material objects are conceptualized as both living and dead through the power and paradox of matter as "artificially isolated physical phenomena."[31] Freudian psychoanalysis had a huge impact on contemporary sexual consciousness in the aftermath of the Great War, particularly after his theories were published in French in the 1920s. Together with the revolutionary potential of Marxism to break down the old institutions of state and society, and new approaches to the anthropological study of other cultures, these ideas became influential sources of intellectual and artistic inspiration. Avant-garde writers and artists, like Bataille, many of whom had served in the armed forces or worked as ambulance drivers or in hospitals, drew on the writings of Freud and Marx to probe the interior workings of unconscious instincts and desires and critique the superficialities of modern life as symbolic of a corrupt and defunct social order.[32]

The notion of the fetish informed radically new cultural forms with the potential to challenge the boundaries of self and society, intellectually, theoretically, and aesthetically. The Surrealist movement, of which Bataille was an influential member, attempted to work from the point of view of the unconscious to militate against a rational view of modernity and the bourgeois capitalist impulses that drove it. The metaphorical motifs used by Freud were seen to offer a rich and complex interpretive source through which to transgress the boundaries of conventional representation: the language and "work" of dreams; the Oedipal triangle as the central drama of the psyche; the fetish as a substitute for unconscious desire; and ancient myths and the art and rituals of "primitive," that is, nonwestern cultures. The idea of the fetish as a potent symbol of unconscious drives was seized upon because of the fixated power relations implied in Freudian and Marxist theories of modernity's obsessive isolation of objects from their everyday context.[33] In the *First Surrealist Manifesto*, Andre Breton described the experience of modernity in Marxist terms as one defined by an absolute sense of alienation: "Man, that inveterate dreamer, more and more discontented day by day with his fate, orbits with difficulty around the objects he has been led to make use of."[34]

Surrealists' critiques of modernity sought to subvert the "reality" of the conscious mind and the alienating conditions of industrial capitalism that both Freud and Marx in their different ways critiqued as repressive. Surrealist poets, artists, and writers used "found" detritus such as wire mesh, shoes, hats, scraps of fabric, wood, or industrial machinery, the products of mass manufacturing, and hair in various forms, but also the city itself to "make strange" conventional interpretations of gender and sexuality and indeed art itself as autonomously determined.[35] Meret Oppenheim's iconic piece *Objet: dejeuner en fourrere* (Fur Breakfast) exemplifies how these contradictions and ambiguities could be brought together to explore, directly or indirectly, Freudian psychoanalytic and Marxist political theories of object relations. Shown in an exhibition of Surrealist objects in Paris in 1936, Oppenheim's installation consisted of a cheap cup, saucer, and spoon bought from a department store wrapped in the luxurious and rare silky fur of a Chinese gazelle. The rational and the everyday are transformed through the processes of desire and disavowal that the sight of fur, and the sexual connotations it arouses, set in motion, in Freudian terms, "I know, but all the same." Also shown in the exhibition, Oppenheim's *Fur Gloves with Ten Fingers* similarly offered an unsettling play on feminine and masculine genitalia constructed through random and bizarre juxtapositions of the erotic and the rational to "stand in for" the absurdity of modern life: hard, wooden fingers with shiny red painted nails peep out from the soft gazelle fur gloves.

The conjunction of overlapping categories of fetishism in aesthetic form reinforced hair and its styling as an increasingly salient feature of cultural representation at a time when patriarchal authority and feminine ideals were seen as under threat.[36] Women's short, "bobbed" hair was invested with an exaggerated eroticism in sensational accounts of its barbering in the press and women's magazines; in the work of modern novelists such as F. Scott Fitzgerald; but especially in the expanding spectacle of moving pictures. Avant-garde and popular culture in the 1920s and 1930s could draw on a legacy of metaphorical associations, particularly the sexual overdetermination and growing fetishization of women's hair in Victorian literature and visual culture. In the nineteenth century, the formal presentation of women's hair—loose or tied up, blonde or dark, wild and untamed or overdressed, artificial, or "real"—was a locus for the portrayal of femininity and sexuality as both threatening and reassuring.[37] "False" ringlets, curls, fringes, and other hairpieces were an obligatory addition to the ever more elaborate and ornamented fashions that were the hallmark of bourgeois status display; but as the "additions" increased in size then so they and the bodies they adorned were represented as corrupting, unnatural, and morally suspect.[38] The figure of the golden-haired woman equally provided a rich source of metaphorical ambivalence in the Victorian imagination: linked to feminine sexuality and wealth, long golden hair was linked to the innocent and angelic, or the deceitful and demonic.[39]

The links made between women's hair and sexual innocence or maturity, or corrupting or untainted femininity in all forms of cultural production, were in no way new;[40] but in the twentieth century they were intensified as new meanings of sex altered conceptions of an autonomously determined "natural" identity, and offered possibilities for extending the performances of the embodied self.[41] New representations of an eroticized femininity emerged concomitant with new techniques, codes, and rituals of modern hairdressing, deportment, and display. In the emerging spectacle of interwar cinema, women's cut and visibly artificially colored, waved, and curled hair became a central organizing metaphor of modern sexuality and of sexual difference.[42] An evolving Hollywood glamour aesthetic gave traditional corporeal associations a new impetus: carefully coiffed and visibly artificially achieved blonde-, red-, and dark-haired movie stars were portrayed on and off the screen in terms of a correlative mythology of idealized femininity and its potential subversion, and audiences invited to arbitrate between them.[43]

The spectacular equation of modern hairstyles and modern femininity presented by Hollywood was a complex one: hair was a universally powerful symbol of a natural femininity achieved through the latest techniques in modern hairdressing. Chemically dyed or permanently waved hair became incorporated into a dynamic repertoire of "real" hair and authentic "true" femininity reoriented to the ambiguous opportunities presented and threats posed by mass consumerism and the new systems of status recognition this impelled.

WIGS, STARS, AND CELEBRITY CULTURE: IMAGE, INTIMACY, AND FETISH

Maurizia Boscagli in her account of radical materialism argues that objects, far from being dead or passive, take on a life of their own, and draws on Marxist philosopher and cultural critic Walter Benjamin's account of the sensuality of the commodity as a poetic object, "a new kind of fetish, *whose 'magic' is neither debunked nor brought to reason*" (original emphasis)[44] While Marx polarizes the fetish object as either real or false, she argues, Benjamin is interested in the coded exchange between the two in representations that hybridize the artificial and authentic.[45] Writing in the 1930s, Benjamin's critique of a "commodity producing society" was informed by his interest in Surrealism as a revolt to notions of the modern as rational, ordered, and efficient, particularly in relation to the mythical spaces of bourgeois consumerism. Surrealist images of obsolescent or displaced objects that "made strange" the rationality of their production and conventional representation mediated Benjamin's arguments about the threat posed by photography to the "aura" (ritual value) of the art object,[46] and his focus on the department store as the site of a commodified erotic encounter central to modern culture under capitalism.[47] The dissolution of the "aura" was extended to Benjamin's analysis of the everyday experience of modernity as one defined by a sequential system of distraction and replication analogous with "the rhythm of production on a conveyor belt ... analogous to rhythm of reception in film."[48]

Across the spectrum of interwar cultural life and society, advances in science and technology had resulted in a greater rationalization of a natural body that it was believed had to be scientifically managed and manipulated, both as a source of pleasure and as a commodity. Strategies of modern hair presentation and practice had in response become a key vector in the performance of a sexual self, and in body regimes with the potential to sustain or alter the assumptions of its essential biology. Hollywood cinema and a vast representational media that grew up around it created an eroticized image of femininity as an object of cultural and economic value. Abstracted celebrity bodies elided the economies of labor involved in the production of sexual difference and its commodification. The persona of the screen star had become a new kind of commodity in the modern age, the sum of a series of fragmented "parts" made whole through the substitutive mechanisms of fetishized desire and its disavowal.

In Benjamin's Marxist account, the commodity is a sensual, highly fetishized "magical object" that not only simulates artifice but also mimics the natural.[49] The capacity for replication, so vital to the commodification of the fetish object, blurs the boundaries between the real and the "false"; the material cost of production; and the cultural construction of its value become one as the fetish takes on super "natural" qualities.[50] The implication for this chapter is the ways in which the representational possibilities of this critical dynamic expanded in parallel with new forms of cultural representation in the modern age that explored hair's "magical" metonymic and metaphorical qualities.

In the 1960s, the banalities of modern consumerism and its imagery offered a new generation of artists like Andy Warhol a rich source for questioning the social relevance of art and its institutions and how this was connected to broader questions of capitalist power relations. Warhol's screen printed representations of the products of capitalism—soup cans, boxes of pan scourers, popular cultural icons and contemporary sex symbols—critiqued the construction of bourgeois society and its normative value system through a parody of its strategies of fetishized replication. Warhol was not opposed to consumerism, fashion, glamour, or celebrity; rather the reverse—he wove his fixations with popular culture into his art practice, particularly in his *Celebrity* series of prints and paintings of, for example, Elvis Presley, Jackie Kennedy, Marilyn Monroe, and Elizabeth Taylor.[51]

Warhol and other avant-garde artists and photographers turned modern forms of representation back on themselves to disrupt any conception of identity or its performance as autonomously or essentially determined. American photographer Cindy Sherman, whose early conceptual work in the 1970s is defined through her carefully posed photographs of herself in various "disguises," speaks about her sense of self as both separate from and connected to the images of femininity she performs. Sherman describes the importance of hair and hair styling to the processes of alienation, objectification, and identification that construct them:

> Throughout my life I've tried to keep looking different, so my hair has been all different colors, all lengths and styles. As a result, a lot of these characters look like me in the periods of my life since I shot the *Film Stills*—perhaps unconsciously I've been following them, or at least their hairstyles. Occasionally, I've felt that as I've gotten older I've come to look more like them.[52]

The 1978 cover of the Rolling Stones' album *Some Girls* (Figure 9.6) incorporates black and white reproductions of advertisements for American wigs with graphic images of the faces of band members Bill Wyman, Mick Jagger, and Keith Richards, and others that are left blank.

The wigs, physically cut out from one context and displaced to another, sit uneasily on similarly dislocated cutout heads arranged in repetitive color-coded, price tagged rows that simulate the ads from which the illustrated wigs originate. The disjuncture between ill-fitting cheap wigs and the cultural status of their pop icon wearers is reinforced in an act of collage that both meets and disrupts the expectations of the viewer. Random phrases drawn from advertising and promotional copy are immediately recognizable, but make no sense; and visibly coiffured feminine styles frame the masculine features of the band, further "made up" with lips garishly colored in red and pink. Reduced to a visage of lipstick and hair the icons are reduced to a flat image of mass consumerism. The commodified nature of such an exchange is emphasized when the inner sleeve of the album is pulled out and the wigs are returned through the gaze of the consumer to the iconic heads of stars such as Elizabeth Taylor, Brigitte Bardot, and Jane Fonda from which they were cut.

The link between fashion and celebrity culture portrayed on the *Some Girls* record sleeve clearly references Andy Warhol's work stylistically. However, the connection between Warhol, wigs, and self-image is more than superficial in this context. In representing himself as artist and celebrity icon, Warhol sought to move beyond the boundaries of fine art and contemporary culture. Warhol began wearing a white silver wig in 1963 and documenting his appearance, creating an instantaneously recognizable image of self as artist that acquired the status of icon in its constant replication. In his official

FIGURE 9.6: Rolling Stones' album cover *Some Girls*, 1978. Designed by Peter Corriston. Pictorial Press Ltd./Alamy Stock Photo.

biography of Warhol, Wayne Koestenbaum describes the clash between the wig's function in concealing the artist's progressively balding head and its role in the transformation of person to persona: dressing up became a physiological and psychological necessity, "without the wig, his identity could not be recognizably sustained."[53]

The wig was crucial to Warhol's critique of the distinctions between person, performance, and persona that would become central to postmodern art practice and contemporary critical perspectives on the nature of celebrity culture and its performative constraints and possibilities.[54] The sociologist Chris Rojek has argued that with modern celebrity culture the market inevitably turns the public face of the celebrity into a commodity.[55] However, the study of objects or commodities such as fashionable clothes, wigs, and hairstyles that define the iconic status of an artist or performer reveals a multifaceted network of meanings. The wig simultaneously functions as a symbol of fame and as a means for disguise. Hal Foster has argued, "For the most part, Warhol evoked the mass

FIGURE 9.7: Portrait of Andy Warhol. Moviestore Collection Ltd./Alamy Stock Photo.

subject in two opposite ways: through iconic celebrity and abstract anonymity."[56] Warhol negotiated between the two in constructing an instantly recognizable figure of notoriety through artifice (Figure 9.7).

The role of Warhol's wig in his construction of the artist as celebrity icon embodied a long established symbol marking the boundaries of public and private personae through disguise, but also, crucially, between the artist and the public by operating as a form of protective shield. However, as Jessica Evans and David Hesmondhalgh suggest in their discussion of postmodern media and celebrity culture, spheres such as the public and private and the boundaries between art and entertainment have increasingly "become merged and have come to share the same values and norms of behaviour".[57] Celebrities, such as Warhol, offer peculiarly powerful affirmations of belonging, recognition, and meaning in the midst of the lives of their audiences through cultural representation—although their public image and performance of self as persona are rarely challenged. One exception took place on October 30, 1985, in New York, when Warhol's wig was snatched from his head during a public book signing at the Rizzoli bookstore in New York's SoHo.[58] Newspaper coverage refers to a "young woman" at the scene who fled after throwing the wig over the balcony to an accomplice, before disappearing. According to Warhol's diary entries, staff at the bookstore asked if he wanted to stop the event, but Warhol decided to cover his head with a hood and continue to sign copies of his book, *America*.

Neither Warhol's diary, newspaper accounts, nor biographers reveal the identity of the young woman who snatched Warhol's wig: she disappeared from view surrounded by myth and denial. Warhol described the shame of his public exposure as both emotionally traumatic as well as physically painful.

> She was really pretty, nice looking well-dressed girl. They had her cornered for a while and then let her go. It was too unusual. I guess these people had gone telling everybody they were going to do it, because people later said they'd heard things. It was shocking. It hurt. Physically. And it hurt that nobody had warned me.[59]

Feelings of shame play an important part in the construction of iconic celebrity, aroused not by the possibility of *what* might be exposed (in this case Warhol's balding pate) but rather by the act of *being* exposed itself.[60] Recognition and anonymity take on ideological dimensions in constructing and maintaining the links between consumer capitalism, democracy, and individualism while revealing the ambivalent power structures that police the precarious material and symbolic boundaries that surround celebrity status. The wig's removal embodied a shift of power: the artist's persona was demystified and a sense of shame violently invoked—an experience made all the more visceral in relation to Warhol's earlier attempted assassination and critical wounding by Valerie Solanas in 1968.[61]

WIGS AND THE POLITICAL DIMENSIONS OF THE PRIVATE SPHERE

The ritualistic repetition of normative heterosexuality as described by feminist theorist Judith Butler[62] can be applied to an understanding of Andy Warhol's use of his iconic self-fashioned hairstyle, as well as the ritualistic use of wigs in Christeene's performance with which this chapter began. In 1981, Warhol joined forces with his long-term collaborator Christopher Makos on a series of portraits inspired by Man Ray's photographs of fellow artist Marcel Duchamp's alter ego, Rrose Sélavie (a pun on the French axiom on love, *Eros, c'est la vie*). Taken in the 1920s and drawing on Dada's ironical ersatz aesthetic, Duchamp plays with different combinations of clothes, wigs, and makeup to offer alternative feminized versions of himself as man and artist. Warhol's portraits of himself similarly combined subtle gestures and poses with theatrically applied thick makeup and various wigs, "a cute black pageboy, a Farrah-like mane of brown, a blond wave."[63] In his introduction to the 2001 exhibition catalogue, Makos speaks about visiting a New York wig shop with Warhol:

> The owner himself showed us several hairpieces and escorted us into private rooms, where Andy tried them on. We had trouble deciding which was best, so he bought five different wigs that were used in the final shoots. It was amazing to realize how a new hairstyle—whether a man's hairpiece or a traditional woman's wig—could really "alter" one's image. This is where the phrase and final concept for *Altered Images* originates—our visit to the 57th Street wiggery.[64]

Amelia Jones discusses the way the figure of the artist is represented through gendered performance:

> As self-determined objects of spectatorial desire, male body artists negotiate masculinity from a position of femininity. Their sartorial self-presentation, then, plays a crucial role in their complex and ambivalent relationship to dominant codes of masculinity.[65]

Jones's arguments are, however, based on psychoanalyst John Flügel's writings in the 1930s on the motivations of fashionable change that defined fashion as narcissistic and, hence, feminine.[66] Therefore, Jones depicts Warhol's performance as "visibly queer" and his deployment of wigs in terms of "various states of drag."[67] However, Makos makes clear that *Altered Images* is not a series of photographs of the artist cross-dressing but a portrait of the artist using feminine codes of cultural representation. As Jones argues, the "vestimentary codes of artistic subjectivity" might indeed be questioned.[68] Warhol continues to perform his masculinity through the use of its performative props: jeans, shirt, and tie. But by posing as Warhol as artist in *Altered Images*, the act of drag is ambiguous and open to question: the "feminine" wig becomes a mere vehicle for the artist's pose and a form of feminized disguise that operates as a replicating act of self-creation and branding. Critical theorist Jean Baudrillard has stated, "the celebrity is an effective means for the commodification of the self."[69] Narcissistic self-display is not gendered in this context: Warhol's multiple and ambiguous performances of self as iconic persona in *Altered Images* embodied in his wigs mean all that remains is an "image that is altered."[70]

The wig as a form of icon creation operates through symbolic social codes whose function lies beyond mere disguise or as a form of protective barrier. Self-image and social systems rely on dynamic forces that constitute identity. Hair is a metaphor of consumer culture and its mechanisms of subjugation; it plays on the fetishized nature of gender as social construct and the artificial nature of sexual difference. As an object, Andy Warhol's wig calls attention to gender divides but equally plays a role in dissolving them. As identity formations rely on a highly individual process of being in the world, so countercultural formations challenge and play on the notion of gender as constructed through performative action. Wigs, however much they might be rooted in the identity and self-image of the wearer, have the capacity to transform. In this way they can play on and challenge mainstream bourgeois society and the heteronormative value systems that patrol them.

The self-conscious exploitation of the wig's symbolic ambivalence plays an important role in the construction of what Butler describes as queer identity. However, in the representational context of queer body politics, the notion of the interchangeability of public and private persona—so central within contemporary celebrity culture—arguably needs to be addressed from an alternative theoretical perspective. The integral relationship between public and private personae promotes modes of identification

FIGURE 9.8: "Christeene" in flight. Photo: Eli Schmidt. Reproduced by permission of Paul Soileau.

and intimacy through the mechanisms of fetishism, of objects, and of the commodified bodies of celebrities;[71] but the private sphere plays a particular role within queer theory and materialism, where culture is produced and challenged through representation, public statements, and performance. Eve Kosofsky Sedgwick problematizes the issue and refers to a culture of silence that poses its own risks and ultimately reinforces social norms and stereotypes.[72] The concept of intimacy itself, she argues, needs to be radicalized and become part of public discourse. This argument has been developed further by linking it to the heteronormative conventions of intimacy in Lauren Berlant and Michael Warner's examination of the changed possibilities of identity and queer politics.[73]

Queer theorist Rosemary Hennessy too speaks about the mechanisms of capitalism at work in the formation of gender and the materialization of sex roles.[74] Her definition offers ways to understand the function of material objects in the creation of cultural meaning. Christeene's live performances, as well as her appearance in Matt Lambert's film *Butt Muscle* and her collaborations with Rick Owens and Michele Lamy, as discussed at the beginning of this chapter, play not simply on notions of abjection and fragmentation of the body theorized in Julia Kristeva's essay "Powers of Horror,"[75] but also offer a critical space which is both cultural and economic (Figure 9.8). Christeene's skin, made to appear bruised, her grotesque makeup, and her trademark long black wig left unkempt, oiled, and matted do not reference the glamour, intricacy, or indeed detail of conventional and stylized wigs or hair extension common in drag performance (Figure 9.9). No real effort seems to have gone into creating the style. Instead the wig appears messy, not unlike trash, which has a long history in avant-garde performance. Nor does the long hair entirely represent femininity, as would be the case in drag and/or female impersonation. Instead one can argue that Christeene's choice of dress, makeup, and wig are gestures towards a different way of thinking about representation and the economy of performativity in terms of capitalism and excess.

By playing on both the material qualities of the wig and hair as a source of unity, *Butt Muscle* problematizes the idea of "transgression as image" that informed previous representations of hetero- and homoerotic exploitations of hair's ambivalent psychodynamism. For Paul Soileau, the concept of transgression is, he argues, of little importance in his work:

> There are elements to the definition of "transgressive" that just don't fit any longer. This simple need to outrage or violate ... to violate a command a moral code, to offend and sin. These are all very negative terms that call to mind a need for punishment or atonement. The work that I do is 100% celebratory. It's easy to plop down a headline that reads shock and awe and moral violation instead of actually trying to open your mind and explain what is really going on. I think the same can be said for queer actions and politics.[76]

Soileau's work seeks to overcome the constraints the term "transgression" imposes in conforming to what Butler describes as the normative matrix of inclusion and exclusion through which such a concept is constructed, and controlled.[77] Instead, Christeene's character offers a new form of cultural representation, a celebratory space that seeks to operate outside the command of such codes.

FIGURE 9.9: "Christeene" with bruises in pink dress. Photo: Eli Schmidt. Reproduced by permission of Paul Soileau.

FIGURE 9.10: "Christeene's" wig on a stand. Photo: Michael Sharkey. Reproduced by permission of Paul Soileau.

CONCLUSION

This chapter has explored the mechanisms at work in the construction of self through cultural representations in which hair's unique material and symbolic qualities are always "in play." The ability to manipulate our hair or view that of others as an external expression of internal desires and drives is situated as an exchange—psychic, sexual, material—that attempts to make sense of ourselves in a way that is specific to a particular milieu, a time and a place and yet always in a state of flux. Theoretical perspectives on fetishized object relations inform the analyses of cultural representations in the modern age that in different ways exploit hair's unique qualities of malleability and transformation and probe the psychic and social boundaries of things and self (Figure 9.10).

At its core, the chapter looks at the performative possibilities offered in fashioned hair and stylized wigs at the intersection of popular culture and queer performance. How has hair's potent sexual symbolism been harnessed to critiques of the constructed-ness of gender and sexual identities? How do these confront the political role of the public and private image imbricated in both the critical study of celebrity culture and the discourse on queer performance? If no longer an extension of heteronormative body codes and conventions; nor a form of disguise or artifice; in questioning the idea of a natural, private, and intimate body no longer hidden from display, hair in the form of wigs in this context subverts heterosexuality as a position of economic privilege and the ideologies and institutions that define both normative and transgressive cultural representation of sex and intimacy.

NOTES

Introduction

1. See Frank Westmore's biography (with Muriel Davidson), *The Westmores of Hollywood* (Philadelphia: J.B. Lippincott Company, 1976); see also Sydney Guilaroff's autobiography, *Reflections of Hollywood's Favorite Confidant* (Santa Monica, CA: W. Quay Hays, 1996).
2. Alf Hiltebeitel, "Introduction: Hair Tropes," in *Hair: Its Power and Meaning in Asian Cultures*, eds. Alf Hiltebeitel and Barbara D. Miller (Albany: State University of New York Press, 1998), 2.
3. Ibid.

Chapter One

1. Mary Douglas, *Purity and Danger: An Analysis of the Concepts of Pollution and Taboo* (London: Routledge and Kegan Paul, 1966).
2. In 2004, France banned the wearing of conspicuous religious symbols, including the Muslim face veil (*niqab*). As of April 2011, France became the first country where it is illegal to cover one's face with a veil or any other kind of mask in public. Veils that do not cover the face (scarves and chador) are still allowed.
3. See Carol Delaney, "Untangling the Meanings of Hair in Turkish Society," *Anthropological Quarterly* 67, no. 4 (1994): 159–72; and Faegheh Shirazi, "Men's Facial Hair in Islam: A Matter of Interpretation," in *Hair: Styling, Culture and Fashion*, eds. Geraldine Biddle-Perry and Sarah Cheang (Oxford: Berg, 2008).
4. Paul Hershman, "Hair, Sex and Dirt," *Man*, New Series 9, no. 2 (1974): 276.
5. Christopher Hallpike, "Social Hair," *Man*, New Series 4, no. 2 (1969): 256–64.
6. Edmund R. Leach, "Magical Hair," *Journal of the Royal Anthropological Institute* 88, no. 2 (1958): 147–64.
7. Hallpike, "Social Hair," 257.
8. Hindu tantric tradition asserts that some ascetics mastered the ability to concentrate their seminal fluids into their heads.
9. Karen Lang, "Shaven Heads and Loose Hair: Buddhist Attitudes towards Hair and Sexuality," in *Off With Her Head!: The Denial of Women's Identity in Myth, Religion and Culture*, eds. Howard Eilberg-Schwarz and Wendy Doniger (Berkley: University of California Press, 1995), 32–53, 33; also Patrick Olivelle, "Hair and Society: Social Significance of Hair in South Asian Traditions," in *Hair: Its Power and Meaning in Asian Cultures*, eds. Alf Hiltebeitel and Barbara D. Miller (Albany: State University of New York Press, 1998).
10. Alf Hiltebeitel, "Introduction: Hair Tropes," in *Hair: Its Power and Meaning*, eds. Hiltebeitel and Miller, 2, 6.
11. Olivelle, "Hair and Society," 19.
12. Delaney, "Untangling the Meanings," 167.

13. Pandurang Vaman Kane, *History of Dharmasastra*, vol. II, pt. I (Pune: Bhandarkar Oriental Research Institute, 1941), 260–4, 260. Available at: https://archive.org/details/historyofdharmas029210mbp.
14. In *Viramitrodaya Samskara Prakasa*, vol. 1, 296.
15. Ibid., 15.
16. Shirazi, "Men's Facial Hair."
17. Ibid., 121.
18. Hallpike, "Social Hair."
19. Olivelle, "Hair and Society," 26.
20. One who has been initiated into the Sikh faith. The *khalsa* are described by Guru Gobind Singh as: "He who keeps alight the unquenchable torch of truth, and never swerves from the thought of One God; he who has full love and confidence in God and does not put his faith, even by mistake, in fasting or the graves of Muslim saints, Hindu crematoriums, or Jogis places of sepulcher; he who recognizes the One God and no pilgrimages, alms-giving, non-destruction of life, penances, or austerities; and in whose heart the light of the Perfect One shines,—he is to be recognised as a pure member of the Khalsa," 33 Swaiyyas.
21. Hew McLeod, "The Five Ks of the Khalsa Sikhs," *Journal of the American Oriental Society* 128, no. 2 (2008): 325–31.
22. In some Sikh sects—such as those that follow Yogi Bhajan many of whom reside in the United States—female practitioners will also wear a turban.
23. Michael J. Kister, "'The Crowns of This Community' ... Some Notes on the Turban in the Muslim Tradition," *Jerusalem Studies in Arabic and Islam* 24 (2000): 218.
24. Ibid., 222. This is further exemplified in the various styles of head coverings worn by Muslim men, some of which can be viewed at: http://old.seattletimes.com/news/nation-world/crisis/theregion/turbans.html.
25. This refers to a legal pronouncement on an issue of Islamic law written by a religious legal expert (*muti*) for the purposes of clarifying the perspective of the Muslim faith on a particular issue.
26. F.J. Harahap, "The Fatwa of Muhammad Bin Ja"far Al Kattani Concerning the Wearing of the Turban," *Islamic Quarterly* 42, no. 3 (1998): 191.
27. Yedida Kalfon Stillman, *Arab Dress: From the Dawn of Islam to Modern Times*, ed. Norman Stillman (Leiden: Brill, 2000), 12.
28. Ibid., 193.
29. Ingrid Pflüger-Schindlbeck, "On Symbolism of Hair in Islamic Societies: An Analysis of Approaches," *Anthropology of the Middle East* 1, no. 2 (2006): 84.
30. Christian Bromberger, "Hair: From the West to the Middle East through the Mediterranean," *Journal of American Folklore* 121, no. 482 (2007): 381.
31. Delaney, "Untangling the Meanings," 161.
32. Olivelle, "Hair and Society," 16.
33. Hershman, "Hair Sex and Dirt," 282.
34. See Pflüger-Schindlbeck, "On the Symbolism of Hair," for a discussion of the symbolic connection between notions of veiling and pollution in Islam.
35. The Arabic word "*adha*," while translated in this version to mean "illness," may also translate to mean "impurity" or "pollution." A further clue on the polluting factor of women's hair may come from an interpretation of a *hadith* recorded in the *Book on Dry Ablution*. The narration from Aisha states, "The Prophet entered upon her, and a freed

slave girl of hers concealed herself. The Prophet asked: 'Have your periods begun?' She said, 'Yes.' He tore a piece of his turban and said: 'Cover your head with this.'"

36. Hanna Papanek, "Purdah in Pakistan: Seclusion and Modern Occupations for Women," in *Separate Worlds*, eds. Hanna Papanek and Gail Minault (Columbia, MO: South Asia Books, 1982).
37. Orat Hayyim, 16:8.
38. The women's modesty laws in dress also require that the neck (below and including the collarbone), the upper arms (including the elbow), and the knees of married women be covered both in public and within the confines of her own house. These dress rules continue to be followed in the Orthodox community. For an extensive discussion, see Rabbi Getsel Ellinson, *Women and the Mitzvot: Vol. 2, The Modest Way*, trans. Raphael Blumberg (Jerusalem: Einer Library, 1992).
39. This conspicuous display of a desire for nonnatural hair is a minority practice and the wigs worn are often conservative in style and made from synthetic fibers in contrast to most sheitel-wearing women whose aim is to find the perfect, that is, most "natural" looking, wig. See Emma Tarlo, *Entanglement: The Secret Lives of Hair* (London: One World Publications, 2016), 110.
40. Ibid., 276.
41. Angela King, "The Prisoner of Gender: Foucault and the Disciplining of the Female Body," *Journal of International Women's Studies* 5, no. 2 (2004): 29–39.
42. Stillman, *Arab Dress*.
43. Eilberg-Schwartz, "Introduction: The Spectacle of the Female Head." This collection of essays examines myth, fictional narratives, and religious and medical treatises to explore what is at stake for women rendered "headless" and thus deprived of speech, sight, subjectivity, and agency.
44. Lisa Ahmed, *Women and Gender in Islam: Historical Roots of a Modern Debate* (New Haven, CT: Yale University Press, 1992), 235.
45. Bromberger, "Hair: From the West to the Middle East," 385.
46. Beth Graybill and Linda B. Arthur, "The Social Control of Women's Bodies in Two Mennonite Communities," in *Religion, Dress and the Body*, ed. Linda B. Arthur (Oxford: Berg, 1999).
47. Hermione Harris, *Yoruba in Diaspora: An African Church in London* (New York: Palgrave Macmillan, 2006).
48. Barbara Metcalf, *Making Muslim Space in North America and Europe* (Berkley: University of California Press, 1996), 17.
49. Pnina Werbner, "Fun Spaces: On Identity and Social Empowerment among British Pakistnis," *Theory, Culture and Society* 13, no. 40 (1996): 53–80.
50. Johanna Lessinger, *From the Ganges to the Hudson* (Boston, MA: Allyn and Bacon, 1995).
51. Responsum 1990, see https://ccarnet.org/responsa/narr-20-23/.
52. For a comprehensive list of articles on the subject, see https://www.jofa.org/library/subject/69.
53. Ray Mosher Feinstein ruled that women might show a hand's breadth of hair.
54. Barbara D. Miller, "The Disappearance of the Oiled Braid: Indian Adolescent Female Hairstyles in North America," in *Hair: Its Power and Meaning in Asian* Cultures, eds. Hiltebeitel and Miller.
55. Ibid., 269.
56. Ibid., 261.
57. Ibid., 277.

58. Bromberger, "Hair: From the West to the Middle East," 381.
59. Shirazi, "Men's Facial Hair in Islam," 118.
60. Stephen R. Warner, "Immigration and Religious Communities in the United States," in *Gatherings in Diaspora: Religious Communities and the New Immigration*, eds. R.S. Warner and J.G. Wittner (Philadelphia: Temple University Press, 1998), 3–34, 3.
61. Rivkah Lambert Adler, *Breaking Israel News*, April 1, 2016.
62. Emma Tarlo, "Meeting Through Modesty: Jewish-Muslim Encounters on the Internet," in *Modest Fashion: Styling Bodies, Mediating Faith*, ed. Reina Lewis (London: I.B.Tauris, 2013), 80.
63. Lewis, *Modest Fashion*, 222. Known as "The Head Covering Movement."
64. Read more at: http://www.breakingisraelnews.com/64780/why-christian-women-taking-up-jewish-practice-hair-wrapping-jewish-world/#p0FZkdV4D3p2bLdT.99; image at: http://www.breakingisraelnews.com/wp-content/uploads/2016/04/penina-taylor-300x275.jpg.
65. Aheda Zanetti, "I Created the Burkini to Give Women Freedom, Not to Take It Away," *The Guardian*, August 4, 2016. Available online: https://www.theguardian.com/commentisfree/2016/aug/24/i-created-the-burkini-to-give-women-freedom-not-to-take-it-away. For more information on the burkini, visit: www.burqini.com.
66. Kristina Rodulfo, "Anniesa Hasibuan Becomes First Designer to Present NYFW Collection with Hijabs," *Elle*, September 14, 2016. Available online: http://www.elle.com/fashion/news/a39249/anniesa-hasibuan-first-nyfw-runway-collection-with-hijabs/.
67. Lewis, *Modest Fashion*.
68. Ibid., 2.
69. Ibid.
70. Pnina Werbner, "Veiled Intentions in Pure Space: Shame and Embodied Struggles among Muslims in Britain and France," *Theory and Society*, Special Issue, "Authority and Islam," 24, no. 2 (2007): 161–86.
71. Reina Lewis, "Fashion Forward and Faith-tastic! Online Modest Fashion and the Development of Women as Religious Interpreters and Intermediaries," in *Modest Fashion*, ed. Lewis.
72. 'Conde Nast to launch Vogue Arabia', *Vogue* Paris, n.d. Available online: http://en.vogue.fr/fashion/fashion-news/articles/conde-nast-international-launches-vogue-arabia/43938.
73. Bromberger, "Hair: From the West to the Middle East," 382.
74. Clarissa De Waal, *Everyday Iran: A Provincial Portrait of the Islamic Republic* (London: I.B. Tauris, 2015), 122.
75. Robert W. Heffner, "Multiple Modernities: Christianity, Islam and Hinduism in a Globalizing Age," *Annual Review of Anthropology* 27 (1998): 93.

Chapter Two Part I

1. Carol Delaney, "Untangling the Meanings of Hair in Turkish Society," *Anthropological Quarterly* 67, no. 4 (1994): 159–72; Patrick Olivelle, "Hair and Society: Social Significance of Hair in South Asian Traditions," in *Hair: Its Power and Meaning in Asian Cultures*, eds. Alf Hiltebeitel and Barbara D. Miller (Albany: State University of New York Press, 1998).
2. Delaney, "Untangling the Meanings," 167.
3. Christian Bromberger, *Trichologiques: Une Anthropologie des Cheveux et des Poils* (Montrouge: Bayard, 2010), 235.
4. Edmund Leach, "Magical Hair," *Journal of the Royal Anthropological Institute* 88, no. 2 (1958): 147–64.

5. Paul Hershman, "Hair, Sex and Dirt," *Man*, New Series 9, no. 2 (1974): 247–98.
6. Gananath Obeyesekere, *Medusa's Hair: An Essay on Personal Symbols and Religious Experience* (Chicago: University of Chicago Press, 1981), 13.
7. John Borneman and Abdellah Hammoudi, eds., *Being There: The Fieldwork Encounter and the Making of Truth* (Berkeley: University of California Press, 2009).
8. Delaney, *Untangling the Meanings*, 167.
9. Alf Hiltebeitel, "Introduction," in *Hair: Its Power and Meaning in Asian Cultures*, eds. Alf Hiltebeitel and Barbara D. Miller (Albany: State University of New York Press, 1998), 9.
10. Georg Simmel, "Fashion," in *On Individuality and Social Forms*, ed. D. Levine (Chicago: University of Chicago Press, 1971), 303.
11. Ibid., 323.
12. Bromberger, *Trichologiques*, 235.
13. Simmel, "How Is Society Possible?," in *On Individuality and Social Forms*, ed. D. Levine (Chicago: University of Chicago Press, 1971), 17.
14. Marcel Mauss, "Techniques of the Body," in *Incorporations*, eds. Jonathan Crary and Sanford Kwinter (New York: Zone, 1992 [1936]): 455–77.
15. Victoria Sherrow, *Encyclopedia of Hair: A Cultural History* (Westport, CT: Greenwood Press. 2006), 63–4.
16. Bromberger, "Trichologiques"; Delaney, "Untangling the Meanings."
17. Delaney, "Untangling the Meanings," 164.
18. In 2008, the Turkish government moved to allow university women to wear headscarves used to conceal their hair. Arguments for and against this shift reflect different views on secular and religious expressions of public identity as well as ideas about gender roles in Turkish society. See Alev Çinar, "Subversion and Subjugation in the Public Sphere: Secularism and the Islamic Headscarf," *Signs* 33, no. 4 (2008): 891–913; Sabrina Tavernise, "For Many Turks, Headscarf's Return Aids Religion and Democracy," *New York Times*, February 9, 2008.
19. Mary Douglas, *Natural Symbols: Explorations in Cosmology* (London: Barrie & Rockliff the Cresset Press, 1970), 89.
20. Ibid., 69.
21. See Ingrid Banks, *Hair Matters: Beauty, Power and Black Women's Consciousness* (New York: New York University Press, 2000); Maxime Leeds Craig, *Ain't I a Beauty Queen?: Black Women, Beauty, and the Politics of Race* (New York: Oxford University Press, 2002); Robin D.G. Kelley, "Nap Time: Historicizing the Afro," *Fashion Theory* 1, no. 4 (1997): 339–52, 341; Noliewe M. Rooks, *Hair Raising: Beauty, Culture and African American Women* (Piscataway, NJ: Rutgers University Press, 2000). Both Craig, *Ain't I a Beauty Queen?* and Kelley, "Nap Time" examine the history of the emergence of the Afro as an African American hairstyle as early as the 1960s, while Banks, *Hair Matters* focuses on the role of hair in African American women's cultural and political identities. Rooks, *Hair Raising* combines these approaches through an examination of African American women's concepts of identity and beauty in relation to hairstyles and the marketing of hair products.
22. Kelley, "Nap time," 341.
23. Craig, *Ain't I a Beauty Queen?*, 4.
24. Ibid., 36.
25. Ibid.
26. Julia Thompson, "Cuts and Culture in Kathmandu," in *Hair: Its Power and Meaning in Asian Cultures*, eds. Alf Hiltebeitel and Barbara D. Miller (Albany: State University of New York Press, 1998), 229, 239.

27. Ibid., 250.
28. Gerald F. Murray and Marina Ortiz, *Pelo Bueno/Pelo Malo: Estudio Antropologico de los Salones de Belleza en la République Dominicana* (Santo Domingo: Fondo para el Financiamento de la Microempresa Inc., 2012).
29. Ibid., 6.
30. Ibid., 21.
31. This underlying racial tension surfaced recently when, in June 2015, government officials of the Dominican Republic announced plans to deport people of Haitian origin to Haiti; see Azam Ahmed and Sandra E. Garcia, "Dominican Plan to Expel Haitians Tests Close Ties," *New York Times*, July 4, 2015. Available online: www.nytimes.com (accessed July 18, 2015).
32. Brad Weiss, *Street Dreams and Hip Hop Barbershops: Global Fantasy in Urban Tanzania* (Bloomington: Indiana University Press, 2009), 4.
33. Nancy Cromwell, "Contemporary African Folk Art: Barbershop Signs and Hairstyles," *African Arts* 8, no. 4 (1975): 77.
34. Weiss, *Street Dreams*, 89.
35. Arnold van Gennep, *The Rites of Passage* (Chicago: University of Chicago Press, 1960 [1908]), 166–7.
36. Daniela Bognolo, "Histoire d'un Doute: La Femme à Tête Rasée chez les Lobi du Burkina Faso/A Prolonged Uncertainty: Women with Shaven Heads among the Lobi of Burkina Faso," in *Parures de Tête—Hairstyles and Headdresses*, eds. Christiane Falgayrettes-Leveau and Iris Hahner (Paris: Éditions Dapper, 2003), 154.
37. Henry J. Drewal, "Coiffures chez les Yoruba/Headdresses and Hairstyles Among the Yoruba," in *Parures de Tête—Hairstyles and Headdresses*, eds. Falgayrettes-Leveau and Hahner, 170–203; Marilyn Houlberg, "Social Hair: Tradition and Change in Yoruba Hairstyles in Southwestern Nigeria," in *The Fabrics of Culture: The Anthropology of Clothing and Adornment*, eds. Justine Cordwell and Ronald Schwarz (The Hague: Mouton, 1975), 349–97; Babatunde Lawal, "Orilonise: The Hermeneutics of Head and Hairstyles Among the Yoruba," in *Hair in African Art and Culture*, eds. Roy Sieber and Frank Herreman (New York: Museum of African Art, 2000).
38. Lawal, "Orilonise," 96.
39. Houlberg, "Social Hair," 377.
40. Gananath Obeyesekere, *Medusa's Hair: An Essay on Personal Symbols and Religious Experience* (Chicago: University of Chicago Press, 1981), 65.
41. Frank Dikotter, "Hairy Barbarians, Furry Primates, and Wild Men: Medical Science and Cultural Representations of Hair in China," in *Hair: Its Power and Meaning in Asian Cultures*, eds. Alf Hiltebeitel and Barbara D. Miller (Albany: State University of New York Press, 1998), 56–7.
42. James L. Watson, "Living Ghosts: Long-Haired Destitutes in Colonial Hong Kong," in *Hair: Its Power and Meaning in Asian Cultures*, eds. Hiltebeitel and Miller, 187.
43. Timothy Ryback, "Evidence of Evil," *The New Yorker*, November 15, 1993, 68–81.
44. Van Gennep, "Social Hair."
45. In this case, while a man and woman may marry, the wife's position in her husband's family is not fixed until she gives birth.
46. Bognolo, "Histoire d'un Doute," 152.
47. Carol Laderman, *Wives and Midwives: Childbirth and Nutrition in Rural Malaysia* (Berkeley: University of California Press, 1983), 151.

48. Ibid., 185.
49. Eiluned Edwards, "Hair, Devotion and Trade in India," in *Hair: Styling, Culture and Fashion*, eds. Geraldine Biddle-Perry and Sarah Cheang (Oxford: Berg, 2008), 153.
50. I was told by one Indian-American man that he had his child's hair cut for the *muskan sanskar* ritual in the United States; he kept the hair and later took it to India where he threw it in the Ganges River.
51. Edwards, "Hair, Devotion and Trade," 153.
52. Elishe Renne, "Wives, Chiefs, and Weavers: Gender Relations in Bunu Yoruba Society," (PhD diss., New York University, 1990), 156.
53. Selina Ching Chan and Simin Xu, "Wedding Photographs and the Bridal Gaze in Singapore," *New Zealand Journal of Asian Studies* 9, no. 2 (2007): 89.
54. Ibid., 92; see also Erving Goffman, *The Presentation of Self in Everyday Life* (Harmondsworth: Penguin, 1971), 57–8.
55. Bognolo, "Histoire d'un Doute," 157–8.
56. Roy Sieber, "A Note on Hair and Mourning Especially in Ghana," in *Hair in African Art and Culture*, eds. R. Sieber and F. Herreman (New York: Museum of African Art, 2000).
57. Ibid., 91.
58. Pamela Church Gibson, "Concerning Blondeness: Gender, Ethnicity, Spectacle and Footballers' Waves," in *Hair: Styling, Culture and Fashion*, eds. Biddle-Perry and Cheang, 148.
59. Olivelle, "Hair and Society," 40.

Chapter Two Part II

1. This was the first time Fitzgerald's name had appeared on the front cover of the magazine to which he contributed for most of his life.
2. Francis Scott Fitzgerald, "Bernice Bobs Her Hair," *Flappers and Philosophers* (New York: Charles Scribner & Sons, 1959), 118.
3. Ibid., 132.
4. Ibid., 136.
5. Ibid., 138.
6. Ibid.
7. Caroline Cox, *Good Hair Days* (London: Quartet Books, 1999), 38.
8. See Edmund Leach, "Magical Hair," *Journal of the Royal Anthropological Institute* 88, no. 2 (1958): 147–64; Charles R. Hallpike, "Social Hair," *Man*, New Series 4, no. 2 (1969): 147–54; Wendy Cooper, *Hair: Sex, Society, Symbolism* (New York: Stein & Day, 1971).
9. Cox, *Good Hair Days*; Richard Corson, *Fashions in Hair: The First Five Thousand Years* (London: Peter Owen, 1995).
10. Joanne Entwistle, *The Fashioned Body: Fashion, Dress and Modern Social Theory* (London: Routledge, 2000), 34.
11. Ibid., 39.
12. Gilles Lipovetsky, *The Empire of Fashion: Dressing Modern Democracy* (Princeton, NJ: Princeton University Press, 1987), 6.
13. Mary Douglas, *Purity and Danger* (London: Routledge, 1966), 116.
14. Ibid., 41.
15. Alf Hiltebeitel, "Introduction: Hair Tropes," in *Hair: Its Power and Meaning in Asian Culture*, eds. Alf Hiltebeitel and Barbara D. Miller (Albany: State University of New York Press, 1998), 5.

16. Douglas, *Purity and Danger*, 41.
17. Ibid., 43.
18. Mary Douglas, *Natural Symbols: Explorations in Cosmology* (New York: Pantheon Books, 1982), 72.
19. Cooper, *Hair: Sex, Society, Symbolism*; see also Anthony Synnott, *The Body Social: Symbolism, Self and Society* (London: Routledge, 1993).
20. Corson, *Fashions in Hair*, 611.
21. Karen Stevenson, "Hairy Business: Organising the Gendered Self," in *Gendered Bodies*, eds. Ruth Halliday and John Hassard (London: Routledge, 2001), 145.
22. Marcel waving was a system of applying heated iron tongs to hair to create a series of *ondulations*; it was developed by Marcel Grateau in Paris in the late nineteenth century and popular until the 1930s, see Corson, *Fashions in Hair*.
23. Stephen Gundle, *The Glamour System* (Basingstoke: Palgrave Macmillan, 2006); Ellen Tremper, *I'm No Angel, the Blondee in Fiction and in Film* (Charlottesville: University of Virginia Press, 2006).
24. Richard Dyer, *White* (London: Routledge, 1997), 92.
25. Gundle, *The Glamour System*, 81–3.
26. Ibid., 70.
27. Ibid., 181.
28. Tremper, *I'm No Angel*, 131, 142.
29. Stephen Gundle, *Glamour: A History* (Oxford: Oxford University Press, 2008), 90.
30. "Blondee Loveliness needs Great Care," *Washington Post*, May 19, 1935, 10.
31. Dyer, *White*, 77–8; Cox, *Good Hair Days*, 160; Tremper, *I'm No Angel*, 128.
32. Sandra Gillman, *Making the Body Beautiful: A Cultural History of Aesthetic Surgery* (Princeton, NJ: Princeton University Press, 1999), 22.
33. Kathy Peiss, *Hope in a Jar: The Making of America's Beauty Culture* (New York: Henry Holt, 1998).
34. Dyer, *White* see also Joel Kovel, *White Racism: A Psychohistory* (New York: Columbia University Press, 1988).
35. The ethical, political, and historical dimensions of Michel Foucault's conception of governmentality are developed in his formulation of "bio-politics," a way of understanding how the modern sovereign state and a modern sense of selfhood are mutually constructed as autonomously and institutionally determined but also enacted through the body; see Thomas Lemke "The Birth of Bio-politics: Michel Foucault's Lectures at the College de France on Neo-liberal Governmentality," *Economy and Society* 30, no. 2 (2001): 190–207.
36. Designed by English philosopher and social theorist Jeremy Bentham in the late eighteenth century, Foucault saw the revolutionary structure as a way of "obtaining power of mind over mind" and thus equally applicable to the construction of hospitals, schools, asylums, and so on.
37. In *Discipline and Punish* (Harmondsworth: Penguin Books, 1977), Michel Foucault uses Bentham's panopticon and the disciplinary power of state and self-regulation implied in the constant visibility of the inmate to explore the apparatus of modern social formations and the construction of modern subjectivities, that is, "He who is subjected to a field of visibility ... inscribes in himself the power relation in which he simultaneously plays both roles; he becomes the principle of his own subjection" (202).
38. Ibid., 177.

39. See Geraldine Biddle-Perry, "Hair, Gender and Looking," in *Hair: Styling, Culture and Fashion*, eds. Geraldine Biddle-Perry and Sarah Cheang (Oxford: Berg, 2007), 98.
40. Foucault, *Discipline and Punish*, 129.
41. Ibid., 139.
42. Ibid.
43. See Hallpike, "Social Hair"; see also Alton Philips, "The Erotic Life of Electric Hair Clippers: A Social History," in *Practicing Culture*, eds. Craig Calhoun and Richard Sennett (London: Routledge, 2007).
44. Judy Attfield, "Barbie and Action Man: Adult Toys for Girls and Boys, 1959–93," in *The Gendered Object*, ed. Pat Kirkham (Manchester: Manchester University Press, 1996), 81–2.
45. Roland Barthes, *The Pleasure of the Text*, trans. Richard Miller (New York: Hill and Wang, 1973), 53.
46. Jo B. Paoletti and Carol L. Kregloh, "The Children's Department," in *Men and Women: Dressing the Part*, eds. Valerie Steel and Claudia Brush Kidwell (Washington, DC: Smithsonian Institution Press, 1989), 36.
47. Ann DuCille, *Skin Trade* (Cambridge, MA: Harvard University Press, 1996), 55, and see in particular chap. 10: "Toy Theory: Black Barbie and the Deep Play of Difference."
48. Attfield, "Barbie and Action Man," 84.
49. Mattel Inc. Toymakers, *Life Magazine*, November 25, 1966.
50. Joy Eliot, "The Afro: Black and Beautiful," *Washington Post*, August 19, 1968.
51. DuCille, *Skin Trade*, 34.
52. See Ayana D. Byrd and Lori L. Tharps, *Hair Story: Untangling the Roots of Black Hair in America* (New York: St. Martin's Press, 2001)
53. Hallpike, "Social Hair."
54. DuCille, *Skin Trade*.
55. Cox, *Good Hair Days*, 159.
56. Ibid., 216–17.
57. Bruce Tyler, "Black Hairstyles: Cultural and Socio-political Implications," *The Western Journal of Black Studies* 14, no. 4 (1990): 235–50.
58. Robin D.G. Kelley, "Nap Time: Historicizing the Afro," *Fashion Theory* 1, no. 4 (1997): 341.
59. See Kobena Mercer, *Welcome to the Jungle: New Positions in Black Cultural Politics* (London: Routledge, 1994); Mercer contends that "*all* black hairstyles are political" because they are all responses to historical signifiers of racial difference that have dictated what black hair should or should not mean (104). For Mercer, "the *diversity* of contemporary black hair styles is something to be proud of and valued as an aspect of Africa's 'gift' to modernity" (53); see also his "Black Hair/Style Politics," *New Formations* 3 (Winter, 1997): 33–54.
60. Maxine Craig, "The Decline of the Conk; or, How to Read a Process," *Fashion Theory* 1, no. 4 (1997): 399–420.
61. Shirley Tate contests the historical binary between "natural" and "unnatural" Black beauty that has come to dominate the antiracist aesthetics of the Black Atlantic diaspora. She argues: "Our hair [also] takes the shape of what it is supposed to do on the body on which it sits. It is supposed to be Black and appear as a natural extension of that racialized body, whether it is straight, curly, twisted, locksed, rowed, chiney bumped, shaved, dyed, afroed, or the height of a dancehall diva's. A Black hair style is performative": *Black Beauty: Aesthetics, Stylization, Politics* (Farnham: Ashgate, 2009), 49.

62. Carol Tulloch, "Resounding Power of the Afro Comb," in *Hair: Styling, Culture, Fashion*, eds. Biddle-Perry and Cheang, 126.
63. Celia Lury, *Consumer Culture* (Cambridge: Polity Press, 1996), 256.
64. For a discussion on the importance of style to the construction of British subcultural identities, see Dick Hebdige, *Subculture: The Meaning of Style* (London: Routledge, 1979), and of skinheads in particular see pp. 53–9.
65. Shaun Cole, "Hair and Male (Homo)sexuality: Up Top and Down Below," in *Hair: Styling, Culture, Fashion*, eds. Biddle-Perry and Cheang.

Chapter Three

1. Gilbert Foan, ed., *The Art and Craft of Hairdressing* (London: The New Era Publishing Co., 1931).
2. Ibid., 143.
3. Ibid., 141.
4. Drake Stutesman, "The Silent Screen, 1895–1927," in *Costume, Makeup and* Hair, ed. Adrienne McLean (London: I.B. Tauris, 2016), 44.
5. Foan, *The Art and Craft*, 143.
6. Gilles Lipovetsky, *The Empire of Fashion: Dressing Modern Democracy* (Princeton, NJ: Princeton University Press, 1994), 91–2.
7. Geraldine Biddle-Perry and Sarah Cheang, " Hair," in *Berg Encyclopedia of World Dress and Fashion: Global Perspectives*, eds. Joanne B. Eicher and Phyllis G. Tortora (Oxford: Berg, 2010). *Bloomsbury Fashion Central*. Available online: http://dx.doi.org/10.2752/BEWDF/EDch10311 (accessed February 2, 2017).
8. American feminist activist Charlotte Perkins Gilman (1880–1935) campaigned about the practicality, comfort, and health benefits of short hair, arguing it was representative of women's move towards equality.
9. Karen Stevenson, "Hairy Business. Organizing the Gendered Self," in *Contested Bodies*, eds. R. Holliday and J. Hassard (London: Routledge, 2001), 140–1.
10. Elizabeth Wilson, *Adorned in Dreams: Fashion and Modernity* (London: Virago, 1985), 157.
11. Carolyn van Wycks, "To Bob or Not to Bob Hair—The Major Dilemma Facing Women in 1924," *Photoplay*, April 1924: 32.
12. Elizabeth Wissinger, *This Year's Model: Fashion, Media and the Making of Glamour* (New York: New York University Press, 2015), 70.
13. *Flaming Youth* (1923), [Film] Dir. John Francis Dillion, USA: Associated First National.
14. Stutesman, "The Silent Screen," 44.
15. *It* (1927), [Film] Dir. Clarence G. Badger and Josef von Sternberg, USA: Paramount Pictures.
16. *Pandora's Box* (1929), [Film] Dir. Georg Wilhelm Pabst, Germany: Pabst-Film. *Diary of a Lost Girl* (1929) [Film] Dir. Georg Wilhelm Pabst, Germany: Pabst-Film.
17. Stutesman, "The Silent Screen," 45.
18. National Hair Goods Co. advertisement in *Photoplay*, January 1921: 117.
19. Hermo Hair Lustr advertisement in ibid., 120.
20. In one article Jean Harlow confesses; "Very few people who admire blonde hair realise that every little speck of dust or grime appears on the surface as clearly as it would on a white dress or coat," Brillow hair shampoo was her personal product endorsement. Brigid Keenan, *The Women We Wanted to Look Like* (New York: St. Martin's Press, 1977), 79.

21. Stevenson, "Hairy Business," 142. In the early 1920s there were approximately 11,000 hair salons in the United States; this had tripled by the era of the "post-bob" in the 1930s and by 1951 there were 127,000 hair and beauty salons. Ibid., 150.
22. *Photoplay*, April 1924. The article estimated that the price of the style would average at US $5 for the cut and US $2 a week to maintain it, a minimum of US $107 a year.
23. Foan, *The Art and Craft*, 137.
24. Ibid., 143.
25. "Aureole" was created by the French chemist Eugène Schueller who developed chemical hair colorants and sold these to hairdressers. Schueller responded to fears over the safety of these synthetic dyes by renaming his company the "The French Harmless Hair Dye Company" that would later become L'Oréal.
26. Prof. L Hall, "Hell's Angel," *Photoplay*, January 1931, 75. *Hell's Angel* (1930), [Film] Dir. Howard Hughes, USA: United Artists.
27. Lou Taylor and Elizabeth Wilson, *Through the Looking Glass: A History of Dress from 1860 to the Present Day* (London: BBC Books, 1989), 99.
28. Charles Eckert, "The Carole Lombard in Macy's Window," in *Fabrications: Costume and the Body*, eds. Jane Gaines and Charlotte Herzog (New York: Routledge, 1990). Lipovetsky, *The Empire of Fashion*, 55.
29. Christopher Breward, *The Culture of Fashion: A New History of Fashionable Dress* (Manchester: Manchester University Press, 1995), 187.
30. Eckert, "The Carole Lombard."
31. Sydney Guilaroff, *Reflections of Hollywood's Favorite Confidant* (Santa Monica, CA: W Quay Hays, 1996), 49.
32. Vidal Sassoon, *Sorry I Kept You Waiting* (London: Cassell, 1968).
33. Dylan Jones, *Haircuts: Fifty Years of Styles and Cuts* (London: Thames and Hudson, 1990), 53.
34. Caroline Cox and Lee Widdows, *Hair and Fashion* (London: V & A Publications, 2005), 89.
35. *The Wild Affair* (1965), [Film] Dir. John Krish, UK: Seven Arts Productions.
36. The image circulated within the pages of fashion editorial before the film's later release date in 1965. See Melanie Williams, "Making the Cut," in *Transformation and Tradition in Sixties British Cinema*. Available online: 60sBritishCinema.wordpress.com (accessed November 5, 2015).
37. In 1967, Vidal Sassoon's pixie crop for Mia Farrow's role in *Rosemary's Baby* reimagined the "garçonne" cut of the 1920s.
38. Caroline Cox, *Good Hair Days: A History of British Hairstyling* (London: Quartet Books, 1999), 124.
39. "Vidal Sassoon: Czar of the Scissors," *Sunday Times Magazine*, January 24, 1965, 45.
40. See Martin Harrison, *Appearances: Fashion Photography Since 1945* (London: Jonathan Cape, 1991) and Hilary Radner, "On the Move: Fashion Photography and the Single Girl in the 1960s," in *Fashion Cultures: Theories, Explorations and Analysis*, eds. Stella Bruzzi and Pamela Church Gibson (London: Routledge, 2000).
41. Brigid Keenan, "Fashion is Dead Long Live Clothes," *Nova*, September 1968, 36.
42. Penny Vincenzi, "Profile of a Profile," *Nova*, May 1972, 76.
43. Laird Borrelli, "Dressing Up and Talking about It: Fashion Writing in *Vogue* from 1968–1993," *Fashion Theory: The Journal of Dress Body and Culture* 1, no. 3 (1997): 255.
44. Caroline Baker, "Old-time Favourites," *Nova*, December 1973, 72.
45. Pip Newberry, "Hair Today," *Nova*, September 1973, 90.

46. Valerie Steele, "Anti-Fashion: The 1970s," *Fashion Theory: The Journal of Dress Body and Culture* 1, no. 3 (1997): 280.
47. Rosetta Brooks, "Sighs and Whispers in Bloomingdales: A Review of a Mail-Order Catalogue," in *Zoot Suits and Second Hand Dresses: An Anthology of Fashion and Music*, ed. Angela McRobbie (London: Macmillan, 1989), 187.
48. Newberry, "Hair Today," 90.
49. Ibid.
50. "Paris News," *Vogue* USA, August 1980, 24.
51. "Hair Now: Fall Report," *Vogue* USA, August 1980, 24.
52. "Hair with a New Sense of Line," *Vogue* USA, January 1980, 167.
53. Ibid., 166.
54. Cox and Widdows, *Hair and Fashion*, 89.
55. Shari Sims, "Hair from the 1970s to 2000," *Fashion Photography Archive* (London: Bloomsbury, 2015). *Bloomsbury Fashion Central*. Available online: http://dx.doi.org/10.5040/9781474260428-FPA195 (accessed March 2, 2017).
56. Wissinger, *This Year's Model*, 99.
57. Ibid., 63.
58. Ibid., 99–100.
59. Lou Stoppard, "Hair for the Catwalk," in *Hair by Sam McKnight: A Companion Volume*, eds. Tim Blanks and Sam McKnight (London: Somerset House, 2017), 45.
60. Becky Conekin, "The Model: Transforming Image Through Hair," in *Hair by Sam McKnight*, eds. Blanks and McKnight, 52.
61. Stoppard, "Hair for the Catwalk," 45.
62. Sam McKnight quoted in Katy Young, "No Blondes—Karl Lagerfeld's Hair Rules for Chanel Haute Couture," *The Telegraph*, July 18, 2015. Available online: https://www.telegraph.co.uk/beauty/hair/Chanel-Couture-hair/.
63. Ibid.
64. Sam McKnight, "modern Retro", in *Hair by Sam McKnight*, ed. Tim Blanks (London: Rizzoli International Publications, 2016), 153.

Chapter Four

1. John Heskett, *Industrial Design* (London: Thames & Hudson Reprint, 1980), 190.
2. Anthony M. Mills and Mark P. Mills, "The Invention of the War Machine: Science, Technology and the First World War," *The New Atlantis* 42 (2014): 22.
3. Richard Corson, *Fashions in Hair: The First 5000 Years* (London: Peter Owen, 1965).
4. Caroline Cox, *Good Hair Days* (London: Quartet Books, 1999).
5. Wendy Cooper, *Hair, Sex, Society, Symbolism* (London: Aldus Books, 1971).
6. Anthony Synnott, "Shame and Glory: A Sociology of Hair," *The British Journal of Sociology* 38, no. 3 (September, 1987): 381–413; also see Synnott, *The Body Social: Symbolism, Self and Society* (London: Routledge, 1993).
7. William A. Camfield, "The Machinist Style of Francis Picabia," *The Art Bulletin* 48, no. 3/4 (September–December, 1966): 314; emphasis in original.
8. *Thoroughly Modern Millie* (1967), [Film] Dir. George Roy Hill, USA, Universal Pictures.
9. Steven Zdatny, "The Boyish Look and the Liberated Woman: The Politics and Aesthetics of Women's Hairstyles," *Fashion Theory* 1, no. 4 (1997): 367.
10. Zhang Zhen, "An Amorous History of the Silver Screen: The Actress as Vernacular Embodiment in Early Chinese Film Culture," in *A Feminist Reader in Early Cinema*, eds.

Jennifer M. Bean and Diane Negra (Durham, NC: Duke University Press, 2002), 522. With reference to the on-screen haircut it was possibly in one of two films made in 1926: either *Child Labourer* or more probably *The Movie Actress*.
11. Synnott, "Shame and Glory," 408.
12. Cheryl Buckley, *Designing Modern Britain* (London: Reaktion Books, 2007), 55.
13. Elizabeth Wilson, *Adorned in Dreams: Fashion and Modernity* (London: Virago, 1985).
14. Anne Massey, *Hollywood Beyond the Screen* (Oxford: Berg, 2000), 26.
15. Christine Moneera Laennec, "The 'Assembly Line Love Goddess': Women and the Machine Aesthetic in Fashion Photography 1918–1940" in *Bodily Discursions: Genders, Representations, Technologies*, eds. Deborah S. Wilson and Christine M. Laennec (Albany: State University of New York Press, 1997), 81.
16. Briony Fer, "The Language of Construction," in *Realism, Rationalism and Surrealism: Art between the Wars*, eds. B. Fer, D. Batchelor, and P. Wood (New Haven, CT: Yale University Press, 1993), 139.
17. Penny Sparke, *A Century of Design: Design Pioneers of the 20th Century* (London: Mitchell Beasley, 1999), 30.
18. Karen Stevenson, "Hairy Business: Organising the Gendered Self," in *Gendered Bodies*, eds. Ruth Halliday and John Hassard (London: Routledge, 2001), 142.
19. Lou Taylor and Elizabeth Wilson, *Through the Looking Glass: A History of Dress from 1860 to the Present Day* (London: BBC Publications, 1989), 81.
20. Wilson, *Adorned*, 168.
21. Arnold Shaw, *The Jazz Age: Popular Music in the 1920s* (Oxford: Oxford University Press, 1987), 9.
22. Guilia Pivetta, *The Barber Book* (London: Phaidon, 2014), 76.
23. Dene October, "The Big Shave: Modernity and Fashions in Men's Facial Hair," in *Hair: Styling, Culture, and Fashion*, eds. Geraldine Biddle-Perry and Sarah Cheang (Oxford: Berg, 2008), 68.
24. Ibid.
25. Kim Smith, "From Style to Place: The Emergence of the Ladies' Hair Salon in the Twentieth Century," in *Hair: Styling, Culture, Fashion*, eds. Biddle-Perry and Cheang, 55–67, 57–8.
26. Joshua Galvin and Daniel Galvin, *Hair Matters* (London: Macmillan Publishers, 1985), 72.
27. Ibid., 73.
28. "Instruments for Craftsmen," *Hairdressers' Journal*, April 16, 1959, 39–61.
29. Stevenson, "Hairy Business," 142.
30. Ibid., 143.
31. Massey, *Hollywood Beyond the Screen*, 67.
32. Anna Cottrell, "Deathless Blondes and Permanent Waves: Women's Hairstyles in Interwar Britain," *Literature and History* 25, no. 1 (2016): 23, 25.
33. Ibid., 25.
34. Steven Zdatny, "Fashion and Class Struggle: The Case of Coiffure," *Social History* 18, no. 1 (January, 1993): 58.
35. Cox, *Good Hair*, 148, 150.
36. Barbara Brookes and Catherine Smith, "Technology and Gender: Barbers and Hairdressers in New Zealand, 1900–1970," *History and Technology* 25, no. 4 (December, 2009): 375.
37. Maxine Craig, "The Decline and Fall of the Conk; or, How to Read a Process," *Fashion Theory* 1, no. 4 (1997): 403.

38. Ayana D. Byrd and Lori L. Tharps, *Hair Story: Untangling the Roots of Black Hair in America* (New York: St. Martin's Press, 2001).
39. Ibid., 34.
40. Noliwe M. Rooks, *Hair Raising: Beauty, Culture and African American Women* (New Brunswick, NJ: Rutgers University Press, 1996), 49.
41. Craig, "The Decline and Fall," 404.
42. Byrd and Tharps, *Hair Story*, 31–5.
43. Cottrell, "Deathless Blondes," 23.
44. Sylvia Katz, *Classic Plastics: From Bakelite to High-Tech* (London: Thames & Hudson, 1984), 10.
45. Jessica Gross, "Who Made That Dryer?" *New York Times*, July 19, 2013.
46. Cox, *Good Hair*, 60–1.
47. Victoria Sherrow, *Encyclopedia of Hair: A Cultural History* (Westport, CT: Greenwood Press, 2006), 10.
48. P.G. Gugenheim, "How Hair Dyes Work," *Hairdressers Journal*, June 5, 1958, 31–2. The word "para" is an abbreviation of two chemical compounds, para phenylene diamine (a derivative of aniline) and para toluylene (a derivative of phenazine) which in various combinations would create a range of colors from black to orange-red.
49. Cox, *Good Hair*, 158.
50. Kim Smith, "Strands of the Sixties: A Cultural Analysis of the Design and Consumption of the New London West End Hair Salons c.1954–1975" (PhD thesis, University of East London, 2014), 190.
51. Lois Banner, "The Creature from the Black Lagoon: Marilyn Monroe and Whiteness," *Cinema Journal* 47, no. 4 (Summer, 2008): 11.
52. Massey, *Hollywood Behind the Scenes*, 67.
53. Susannah Handley, *NYLON: The Manmade Fashion Revolution. A Celebration of Design from Art Silk to Nylon and Thinking Fibres* (London: Bloomsbury, 1995), 25.
54. Harlow had already become an international star before appearing in the film *Platinum Blonde* in 1931. The legendary director Howard Hughes, who was remaking an earlier silent film (*Gallagher*), retitled it, having decided upon this name to reflect Harlow's hair color.
55. Harlow's hair color was in fact achieved through a dangerous mixture of chemicals, later established by her hairdresser as a weekly solution of ammonia, chlorox bleach, and Lux soap flakes to create the color. Numerous theories have suggested that this eventually caused her death but these have been refuted with the evidence that she died of kidney failure. Cox, *Good Hair*, 161.
56. Handley, *NYLON*, 48.
57. Geraldine Howell, *Wartime Fashion: From Haute Couture to Homemade* (London: Bloomsbury Academic, 2012), 154.
58. Pat Kirkham, "Beauty and Duty: Keeping Up the Home Front," in *War Culture: Social Change and Changing Experience in World War Two Britain*, eds. Pat Kirkham and David Thoms (London: Lawrence & Wishart, 1995).
59. Jackie Stacey, *Star Gazing: Hollywood Cinema and Female Spectatorship* (London: Routledge, 1994).
60. Smith, *Strands of the Sixties*, 105.
61. Raymond [Bessone], *Raymond: The Outrageous Story of the Hairstylist "Teasie Weasie"* (London: Wyndham Publications, 1976), 128.
62. Smith, *Strands of the Sixties*, 138.

63. Ibid., 218–21.
64. Penny Sparke, *As Long As It's Pink: The Sexual Politics of Taste* (London: Pandora, 1995), 183.
65. Handley, *NYLON*, 54.
66. Galvin and Galvin, *Hair Matters*, 94.
67. Museum of London, *The Crime Museum Uncovered* (Exhibition: October 9, 2015–April 10, 2016).
68. Guggenheim, "How Hair Dyes Work," 41.
69. Cox, *Good Hair*, 165.
70. Ibid.
71. "Britain Enjoying World's Biggest Colour Boom, London Guild Told," *Hairdressers' Journal*, June 2, 1960, 43.
72. "Colour Sales Leap," *Hairdressers' Journal*, April 26, 1962, 28.
73. US Patent Office #256,801, Filed, February 16, 1939.
74. Smith, *Strands of the Sixties*, 158.
75. In the UK, a colloquial abbreviation of "duck's arse" so called because of its shape, also known as duck's tail or ducktail.
76. Cox, *Good Hair*, 183.
77. Ibid., 185.
78. Grant McCracken, *Big Hair: A Journey into the Transformation of Self* (Toronto: Viking, 1995), 31.
79. Susan Brownmiller, *Femininity* (New York: Linden Books, 1984), 34.
80. Vidal Sassoon, *Vidal: The Autobiography* (London: Pan Macmillan, 2010).
81. Michael Gordon, *Hair Heroes* (New York: Bumble and Bumble, 2002), 240.
82. Sassoon, *Vidal*.
83. Galvin and Galvin, *Hair Matters*, 94.
84. Cox, *Good Hair*, 241.
85. Gordon, *Hair Heroes*, 145–7.
86. Smith, *Strands of the Sixties*, 206–9.
87. Ibid., 212.
88. Galvin and Galvin, *Hair Matters*, 108.
89. Smith, *Strands of the Sixties*, 214.
90. Galvin and Galvin, *Hair Matters*, 17–18.
91. Craig, "The Rise and Fall," 401–2.
92. Central to such debate is a consideration of race and gender as embodied in hair styling and grooming processes and practices seen as either assimilationist or nationalist according to the level of hair alteration involved, or alternatively seeing all such practices as offering a complex set of meanings that defy reductive politicized polarities of Black consciousness. See Ingrid Banks, *Hair Matters: Beauty Power and Black Women's Consciousness* (New York: New York University Press, 2000), 53–4; Kobena Mercer, *Welcome to the Jungle: New Positions in Black Cultural Studies* (New York: Routledge, 1994); and Shirley Tate, *Black Beauty: Aesthetics, Stylization, Politics* (London: Routledge, 2007).
93. Robin D.G. Kelley, "Nap Time: Historicizing the Afro," *Fashion Theory* 1, no. 4 (1997): 319–46, 346.
94. Carol Tulloch, "Resounding Power of the Afro Comb," in *Hair: Styling, Culture, Fashion*, eds. Biddle-Perry and Cheang, 128.
95. Ibid., 132–3.
96. Banks, *Hair Matters*, 54.

97. Byrd and Tharps, *Hair Story*, 62.
98. Mercer, *Welcome to the Jungle*, 124.
99. Carol Tulloch, "Rebel Without a Pause," in *Chic Thrills: A Fashion Reader*, eds. Juliet Ash and Elizabeth Wilson (London: Pandora, 1992), 91.
100. Synnott, "Shame and Glory," 381.
101. Anon., "Then and Now," *American Salon*, October 2015, 82.
102. Deborah Arthurs, "It's the New Wave! Say Goodbye to Frumpy Perms—The New Digital Perm is the Secret to Getting Curls Like Kate Middleton," *Daily Mail*, November 15, 2011.
103. Elizabeth Paton, "Dyson Wants to Create a Hair Dryer Revolution," *New York Times*, April 27, 2015.
104. Jeffery L. Meikle, "Plastics in the American Machine Age: 1920–1950," in *The Plastics Age: From Modernity to Post-Modernity*, ed. Penny Sparke (London: Victoria and Albert Museum, 1990), 46.

Chapter Five

1. Respondent 1151, *Response to April 1939 Directive on Personal Appearance* (n.d.), Mass Observation Archives, via *Mass Observation Online* (MOA-MOO), http://www.massobs.org.uk/accessing_material_online.htm (accessed September 29, 2014).
2. Kurt Stein, *Hair: A Human History* (New York: Pegasus Books, 2016), xiii.
3. Kathy Peiss, *Hope in a Jar: The Making of America's Beauty Culture* (New York: Metropolitan Books, 1998), 3–8. On this emerging beauty culture, see Ana Carden-Coyne, *Reconstructing the Body: Classicism, Modernism, and the First World War* (Oxford: Oxford University Press, 2009); Michael Hau, *The Cult of Health and Beauty in Germany: A Social History, 1890–1930* (Chicago: University of Chicago Press, 2003); Mary Lynn Stewart, *For Health and Beauty: Physical Culture for Frenchwomen, 1880s–1930s* (Baltimore: Johns Hopkins University Press, 2001); and Ina Zweiniger-Bargielowska, *Managing the Body: Beauty, Health, and Fitness in Britain, 1880–1939* (Oxford: Oxford University Press, 2010).
4. Geoffrey Jones, "Blonde and Blue eyed? Globalizing Beauty," *Economic History Review* 61, no. 1 (2008): 126–9.
5. Caroline Cox, *Good Hair Days: A History of British Hairstyling* (London: Quartet Books, 1999), 66.
6. On this process in France, see Steven Zdatny, *Fashion, Work, and Politics in Modern France* (New York: Palgrave Macmillan, 2006).
7. Cox, *Good Hair*, 1–11; and Julie Willett, *Permanent Waves: The Making of the American Beauty Shop* (New York: New York University Press, 2000), 14–16.
8. Jackson Lears, *Fables of Abundance: A Cultural History of Advertising in America* (New York: Basic Books, 1994), 169–72.
9. On the importance of psychological mindsets, see Mathew Thomson, *Psychological Subjects: Identity, Culture, and Health in Twentieth-Century Britain* (Oxford: Oxford University Press, 2006).
10. Lears, *Fables of Abundance*, 323–9.
11. Steven Zdatny, "The French Hygiene Offensive of the 1950s: A Critical Moment in the History of Manners," *Journal of Modern History* 84 (December 2012): 897–932.
12. Thomas Richards, *The Commodity Culture in Victorian England: Advertising and Spectacle* (Stanford, CA: Stanford University Press, 1990), 226.

13. Valerie Steele, *Fashion and Eroticism: Ideals of Feminine Beauty from the Victorian Era to the Jazz Age* (New York: Oxford University Press, 1985), 19.
14. Carole Tobin, "Fashioning the American Man: The Arrow Collar Man, 1907–1931," in *Material Strategies: Dress and Gender in Historical Perspective*, eds. Barbara Burman and Carole Turbin (Oxford: Blackwell Publishing, 2003), 100–22.
15. Harry Johnston, *The Backward People and Our Relations with Them* (London: Humphrey Milford/Oxford University Press, 1920), 21.
16. See Sarah Cheang, "Roots: Hair and Race," in *Hair: Styling, Culture, and Fashion*, eds. Geraldine Biddle-Perry and Sarah Cheang (Oxford: Berg, 2008), 27–42.
17. Leonard Sloane, "Advertising: The Breck Girl—Not Just a Pretty Face," *New York Times*, August 17, 1977, 76, via *ProQuest Historical Newspapers: The New York Times (PHN: NYT)*. Available online: http://search.proquest.com.ezproxy.uvm.edu/hnpnewyorktimes/advanced?accountid=14679 (accessed February 18, 2017).
18. Christopher Oldstone-Moore, *Of Beards and Men: The Revealing History of Facial Hair* (Chicago: University of Chicago Press, 2015), 218.
19. Ibid., 215; Dene October, "The Big Shave: Modernity and Fashion in Men's Facial Hair," in *Hair: Styling, Culture, Fashion*, eds. Biddle-Perry and Cheang, 68–9.
20. Richard Corson, *Fashions in Hair: The First Five Thousand Years* (London: Peter Owen, 1971), 611.
21. Advertisement in Faye Brookman, "Hair Care Products," in *The Advertising Age Encyclopedia of Advertising*, vol. 2, eds. John McDonough and the Museum of Broadcast Communications, Karen Egolf, and Jaqueline V. Reid (New York: Fitzroy Dearborn), 706.
22. Cox, *Good Hair*, 55.
23. Ayana D. Byrd and Lori L. Tharps, *Hair Story: Untangling the Roots of Black Hair in America* (New York: St. Martin's Press, 2001), 31.
24. Susannah Walker, *Style and Status: Selling Beauty to African American Women, 1920–1975* (Lexington: University Press of Kentucky, 2007), 51–5.
25. Advertisement for Poro, *Pittsburgh Courier*, April 11, 1931. Quoted in Walker, *Style and Status*, 27.
26. "Don't Let Your Daily Dip Cause 'Dry Hair'," *Picture Post* 3, no. 10 (June 10, 1939): 65, via *Picture Post Historical Archive* (PPHA). Available online: http://find.galegroup.com.ezproxy.uvm.edu/pipo/start.do?prodId=PIPO&userGroupName=vol_b92b (accessed February 18, 2017).
27. Paul R. Deslandes, "Selling, Consuming, and Becoming the Beautiful Man in Britain: The 1930s and 1940s," in *Consuming Behaviours: Identity, Politics, and Pleasure in Twentieth-Century Britain*, eds. Erika Rappaport, Sandra Trudgen Dawson, and Mark J. Crowley (London: Bloomsbury, 2015), 54.
28. Respondent 1129, *Response to 1939 Directive* (April 19, 1939), MOA-MOO.
29. William L. Schultz, "Shulton Toiletries' War Program: Nimble Package Changes, More Ads," *Sales Management* 50 (May 15, 1942): 30. Quoted in Peiss, *Hope in a Jar*, 254.
30. "Gray Hair-The Heartless Dictator" (1943), *Ad*Access, John W. Hartman Center for Sales, Advertising, and Marketing History, Duke University Libraries*. Available online: (http://library.duke.edu/digitalcollections/adaccess_BH0382/ (accessed February 16, 2017).
31. Angela G. Liljequist, "'Soft, Glossy Tresses': Shampoo, Advertisements, White Women's Hair, and the Late and Post-World War II Domestic Ideal" (PhD diss., University of Kansas, 2015), 65–89.

32. "Highlight Your Hair with a Natural Silken Sheen," *Picture Post* 40, no. 4 (July 24, 1948): 2; "Wishing It Won't Make It So...," *Picture Post* 41, no. 2 (October 9, 1948): 4, via *PPHA*.
33. Zdatny, "The French Hygiene Offensive," 913.
34. Cox, *Good Hair*, 170.
35. Liljequist, "Soft Glossy Tresses," 70.
36. "Which is Your Type of Hair?" *Picture Post*, 54, no. 9 (March 1, 1952): 7 via *PPHA*.
37. "JERIS Wins the Lead, Handsomer Hair" (1953), *Ad*Access*.
38. Cox, *Good Hair*, 172–3.
39. "The Most Beautiful Hair in the World is Kept at its Loveliest … with Lustre-Crème Shampoo" (1952), *Ad*Access*.
40. Cox, *Good Hair*, 175.
41. Ibid., 168, 173; and Liljequist, "Soft Glossy Tresses," 72–3.
42. Cox, *Good Hair*, 187.
43. "Frisée Comme Une Caniche? Non: Ondulée Naturellement" (1950), Author's Personal Collection.
44. "Does She … or Doesn't She?" (1960) in *Mid-Century Ads*, ed. Jim Heimann (Cologne: Taschen, 2015), 299.
45. Grant McCracken, *Big Hair: A Journey into the Transformation of Self* (Woodstock, NY: Overlook Press, 1996), 52–5.
46. Willett, *Permanent Waves*, 156, 158.
47. "Hair Like Yours Needs a Shampoo Like Ours. Wella Balsam Shampoo," *Playboy* 20, no. 3 (March 1973), 189.
48. McCracken, *Big Hair*, 125–46.
49. On these developments, see Cox, *Good Hair*, 228–30; and Carol Dyhouse, *Glamour: Women, History, Feminism* (London: Zed Books, 2010), 136–8.
50. Sally Brampton, "Making Your Hair Stand on End," *Observer*, February 28, 1982, 43, via *ProQuest Historical Newspapers: The Guardian and the Observer* (PHN: GO) (accessed February 18, 2017).
51. Respondent C2834, *Response to a Mass Observation Directive on Hair and Hairdressing* (2001), Mass Observation Archive (MOA) 2/1/62/1/1.
52. Respondent B1426, *Response to a Mass Observation Directive* (2001).
53. Geraldine Biddle-Perry and Sarah Cheang, "Introduction: Thinking About Hair," in *Hair: Styling, Culture, Fashion*, eds. Biddle-Perry and Cheang, 10–11.
54. Zdatny, *Fashion, Work, and Politics*, 62.
55. Mary Louise Roberts, *Civilization Without Sexes: Reconstructing Gender in Postwar France, 1917–1927* (Chicago: University of Chicago Press, 1994), 46–62; and Zdatny, *Fashion, Work, and Politics*, 65.
56. Irene Guenther, *Nazi Chic? Fashioning Women in the Third Reich* (Oxford: Berg, 2004), 72.
57. Laura Doan, "Passing Fashions: Reading Female Masculinities in the 1920s," *Feminist Studies* 24, no. 3 (Fall 1998): 672–5.
58. Zdatny, *Fashion, Work, and Politics*, 64.
59. "A Dreadful Prospect for the Bobbed," *Manchester Guardian* (September 24, 1924), 9, via *PHN: GO*.
60. Roberts, *Civilization Without Sexes*, 63; and Zdatny, *Fashion, Work, and Politics*, 64.
61. "Our Own Correspondent, Student Rowdies in Vienna," *Manchester Guardian*, June 7, 1925, 8, via *PHN: GO*.

62. Doan, "Passing Fashions," 683.
63. Ibid., 695–7.
64. Respondent 1206, *Response to April 1939 Directive*, MOA-MOO.
65. Victoria De Grazia, *How Fascism Ruled Women: Italy, 1922–45* (Berkeley: University of California Press, 1991), 211–14.
66. Guenther, 53, 71–2, 76, 106, 120.
67. Ibid., 275.
68. Doriane Gomet, "From Punishment to Death: Body Practices for Deported Women in Nazi Camps," *International Journal of the History of Sport* 30, no. 9 (2013): 934–49.
69. Lee Kennett, *G.I.: The American Soldier in World War II* (New York: Charles Scribner & Sons, 1987), 24–41.
70. War Department, *Basic Field Manual Soldier's Handbook* (Washington, DC: United States Government Printing Office, 1941), 206–7.
71. SOEForce 136, "A Bit Blown-Up: A Soldier's Haircut" (2003), *WW2 People's War: An Archive of World War Two Memories—Written by the Public, Gathered by the BBC*. Available online: http://www.bbc.co.uk/history/ww2peopleswar/stories/24/a2105524.shtml (accessed February 17, 2017).
72. Lulu Hansen, "Female Denouncers: Women's Social Transgression During the German Occupation of Denmark, 1940–45," *Women's History Magazine* 67 (Fall 2011): 11–16, 12.
73. Michael Curtis, *Verdict on Vichy: Power and Prejudice in the Vichy France Regime* (New York: Arcade Publishing, 2002), 257.
74. From Alain Brossat, *Les Tondues: Un Carnaval Moche* (Paris: Édition Manya, 1992), 157. Quoted in Claire Duchen, "Crime and Punishment in Liberated France: The Case of *les femmes tondues*," in *When War Was Over: Women, War, and Peace in Europe, 1940–1956*, eds. Claire Duchen and Irene Bandhauss-Schöffmann (London: Leicester University Press, 2000), 246.
75. Lynne Luciano, *Looking Good: Male Body Image in Modern America* (New York: Hill and Wang, 2001), 42.
76. NSA, HCC (C546) F2483-F2487, Oral History of Sandy Martin, *Hall Carpenter Collection*. Quoted in Rebecca Jennings, *Tomboys and Bachelor Girls: A Lesbian History of Post-War Britain* (Manchester: Manchester University Press, 2007), 120.
77. Alix Ginter, "Appearances Can Be Deceiving: Butch-Femme Fashion and Queer Legibility in New York City, 1945–1969," *Feminist Studies* 42, no. 3 (2016): 622. Ginter has questioned the extent to which butch femme identities were totally contingent on the embrace of "male styles" (noting that some women played with markers of femininity like the skirt to express a kind of conformist butch identity), but also evidences how the styling and grooming of hair were central to the articulation of butch identities.
78. Cox, *Good Hair*, 199–200. On the musical *Hair*, see Arthur Marwick, *The Sixties: Cultural Revolution in Britain, France, Italy, and the United States, c. 1958–c.1974* (Oxford: Oxford University Press, 1998), 357–8; and William J. Rorabaugh, *American Hippies* (New York: Cambridge University Press, 2015), 78.
79. Germaine Greer, *The Female Eunuch* (London: MacGibbon and Kee, 1970), 27. Quoted in Cox, *Good Hair*, 256.
80. Bebe Moore Campbell, "What Happened to the Afro?" *Ebony* 37 (June 1982): 79–84. Quoted in Willett, *Permanent Waves*, 176.
81. Rorabaugh, *American Hippies*, 97, 88.

82. Allan Peterkin, *One Thousand Beards: A Cultural History Facial Hair* (Vancouver: Arsenal Pulp Press, 2001), 136. Quoted in Shaun Cole, "Hair and Male (Homo) Sexuality: 'Up Top and Down Below'," in *Hair: Styling, Culture, Fashion*, eds. Biddle-Perry and Cheang, 81–97, 89.

Chapter Six

1. Judith Butler, *Gender Trouble: Feminism and the Subversion of Identity* (New York: Routledge, 1990).
2. Judith Butler, *Bodies That Matter: On the Discursive Limits of "Sex"* (London: Routledge, 1993), 230.
3. Anthony Synnott, *The Body Social: Symbolism, Self and Society* (London: Routledge, 1993).
4. Ibid., 104–5.
5. Karin Lesnik-Oberstein, ed., *The Last Taboo: Women and Body Hair* (Manchester: Manchester University Press, 2006).
6. Rebecca Herzig, *Plucked: A History of Hair Removal* (New York: New York University Press, 2015); Meredith Suzanne Dault, "The Last Triangle: Sex, Money, and the Politics of Pubic Hair" (MA thesis, Department of Cultural Studies, Queen's University, 2011).
7. Candace West and Don Zimmerman, "Doing Gender," *Gender and Society* 1, no. 2 (1987): 125–51.
8. Suzanne J. Kessler and Wendy McKenna, *Gender: An Ethnomethodological Approach* (Chicago: University of Chicago Press, 1985); Kristen Schilt and Laurel Westbrook, "Doing Gender, Doing Heteronormativity: 'Gender Normals,' Transgender People, and the Social Maintenance of Heterosexuality," *Gender and Society* 23, no. 4 (2009): 440–64; Kristen Schilt, "'A Little Too Ironic': The Appropriation and Packaging of Riot Grrrl Politics by Mainstream Female Musicians," *Popular Music and Society* 26, no. 1 (2006): 5–16.
9. Kristen Schilt, *Just One of the Guys? Transgender Men and the Persistence of Gender Inequality* (Chicago: University of Chicago Press, 2011).
10. Virginia Valian, *Why So Slow? The Advancement of Women* (Cambridge, MA: MIT Press, 1999).
11. Faegeh Shirazi, "Men's Facial Hair in Islam: A Matter of Interpretation," in *Hair: Styling, Culture and Fashion*, eds. Geraldine Biddle-Perry and Sarah Cheang (Oxford: Berg, 2008).
12. Kristen Barber, "Remembering Leonard Nimoy, Feminist Photographer," *Feminist Reflections*, March 5, 2015. Available online: https://thesocietypages.org/feminist/2015/03/05/remembering-leonard-nimoy-feminist-photographer/ (accessed July 27, 2016).
13. Christopher Oldstone-Moore, *Of Beards and Men: The Revealing History of Facial Hair* (Chicago: University of Chicago Press, 2016), 279.
14. Ibid., 280.
15. Synnott, *The Body Social*, 123.
16. Ibid., 124.
17. See for example, Kimberly Battle-Walters, *Sheila's Shop: Working-Class African American Women Talk About Life, Love, Race, and Hair* (Lanham, MD: Rowman & Littlefield, 2004); Tiffany M. Gill, *Beauty Shop Politics: African American Women's Activism in the Beauty Industry* (Champaign: University of Illinois Press, 2010); Adia Harvey Wingfield, *Doing Business with Beauty: Black Women, Hair Salons, and the Racial Enclave Economy*

(Lanham, MD: Rowman & Littlefield, 2008); Lanita Jacobs-Huey, *From the Kitchen to the Parlor: Language and Becoming in African American Women's Hair Care* (New York: Oxford University Press, 2007).
18. Tanisha Ford, *Liberated Threads: Black Women, Style, and the Global Politics of Soul* (Chapel Hill: University of North Carolina Press, 2015); Jacobs-Hue, *From the Kitchen*.
19. Audre Lorde, "Age, Race, Class and Sex: Women Redefining Difference," in *Sister Outsider: Essays and Speeches*, eds. Audre Lorde et al. (Trumansburg, NY: Crossing Press, 1984), 288.
20. Stephanie Shaw, "Black Clubwomen's Movement," in *The Reader's Companion to U.S. Women's History*, eds. Wilma Mankiller et al. (Boston, MA: Houghton Mifflin, 1999).
21. Maxine Leeds Craig, *Ain't I a Beauty Queen? Black Women, Beauty, and the Politics of Race* (New York: Oxford University Press, 2002); Tiffany Gill, "'I Had My Own Business ... So I Didn't Have to Worry': Beauty Salons, Beauty Culturists, and the Politics of African American Female Entrepreneurship," in *Beauty and Business: Commerce, Gender, and Culture in Modern America*, ed. Philip Scranton (New York: Routledge, 2001); Susannah Walker, "Black is Profitable: The Commodification of the Afro, 1960–1975," in *Beauty and Business: Commerce, Gender, and Culture in Modern America*, ed. Philip Scranton (New York: Routledge, 2001); Kevin Gaines, *Uplifting the Race: Black Leadership, Politics, and Culture in the Twentieth Century* (Chapel Hill: University of North Carolina Press, 1996); Evelyn B. Higginbotham, *Righteous Discontent: The Women's Movement in the Black Baptist Church, 1880–1920* (Cambridge, MA: Harvard University Press, 1993).
22. A'lelia Bundles, "Madam C.J. Walker: 'Let Me Correct the Erroneous Impression that I Claim to Straighten Hair,'" in *Tenderheaded: A Comb-Bending Collection of Hair Stories*, eds. Juliet Harris and Pamela Johnson (New York: Pocket Books, 2001); Noliwe M. Rooks, *Hair Raising: Beauty, Culture, and African American Women* (New Brunswick, NJ: Rutgers University Press, 1996).
23. Malia McAndrew, "A Twentieth Century Triangle Trade: Selling Black Beauty at Home and Abroad, 1945–1965," *Enterprise & Society* 11, no. 4 (2010): 798.
24. Willett, *Permanent Waves*.
25. Patricia Hill Collins, *Black Sexual Politics: African Americans, Gender, and the New Racism* (New York: Routledge, 2004).
26. Higginbotham, *Righteous Discontent*; Elizabeth Johnson, *Resistance and Empowerment in Black Women's Hair Styling* (Farnham: Ashgate, 2013); see also Michelle Mitchell, *Righteous Propagation: African Americans and the Politics of Racial Destiny after Reconstruction* (Chapel Hill: University of North Carolina Press, 2004).
27. Robert Lang and Maher Ben Moussa, "Choosing to Be 'Not a Man': Masculine Anxiety in Nouri Bouzid's Rih Essed/ Man of Ashes," in *Masculinity Bodies, Movies, Culture*, ed. Peter Lehman (New York: Routledge, 2001), 81–94.
28. Malcolm X and Alex Haley, *The Autobiography of Malcolm X* (New York: Grove Press, 1965), 64.
29. A member of a Chicano or Mexican-American subculture who wore zoot suits and "ducktail" hairstyles and spoke a form of slang called Caló. *Pachucos* were popularly assumed to be gangsters.
30. Luis Alvarez, *The Power of the Zoot: Youth Culture and Resistance during World War II* (Berkeley: University of California Press, 2009).
31. Catherine Ramirez, *The Woman in the Zoot Suit: Gender, Nationalism, and the Cultural Politics of Memory* (Durham, NC: Duke University Press, 2009).
32. Ibid.

33. Mauricio Mazon, *The Zoot-Suit Riots: The Psychology of Symbolic Annihilation* (Austin: University of Texas Press, 2010); Ramirez, *The Woman in the Zoot Suit*.
34. Elizabeth Wilson, *Adorned in Dreams: Fashion and Modernity* (London: Virago, 1985), 198; Stuart Cosgrave, "The Zoot Suit and Style Warfare," *History Workshop Journal* 18 (1984): 82.
35. Cosgrave, "The Zoot Suit," 87.
36. Malcolm X cited in Wilson, *Adorned in Dreams*, 199.
37. Craig, *Aint I a Beauty Queen*, 18.
38. Kobena Mercer, "Black Hair/Style Politics," *New Formations*, no. 3 (1987): 33–54, see also *Welcome to the Jungle: New Positions in Black Cultural Studies* (Cambridge, MA: The MIT Press, 1994).
39. Ingrid Banks, *Hair Matters: Beauty, Power, and Black Women's Consciousness* (New York: New York University Press, 2000); see also Rooks, *Hair Raising*.
40. Angela Davis, "Afro Images: Politics, Fashion, and Nostalgia," *Critical Inquiry* 21, no. 1 (1994): 42.
41. Mercer, *Welcome to the Jungle*; see also Shirley Anne Tate, *Black Beauty: Aesthetics, Stylization, Politics* (Farnham: Ashgate, 2009).
42. Shirley A. Tate, *Black Beauty: Aesthetics, Stylization, Politics* (Farnham: Ashgate, 2009).
43. Butler, *Bodies That Matter*, 225–6.
44. Lynne Luciano, *Looking Good: Male Body Image in Modern America* (New York: Hill and Wang, 2006).
45. Willett, *Permanent Waves*.
46. Luciano, *Looking Good*.
47. Michael Kimmel, *Manhood in America: A Cultural History* (New York: Oxford University Press, 1996).
48. Kristen Barber, "The Well-Coiffed Man: Class, Race, and Heterosexual Masculinity in the Hair Salon," *Gender & Society* 22, no. 4 (2008): 455–78; Barber, "Remembering Leonard Nimoy"; "Styled Masculinity: Men's Consumption of Salon Hair Care and the Construction of Difference," in *Exploring Masculinities: Identity, Inequality, Continuity and Change*, eds. C.J. Pascoe and Tristan Bridges (Oxford: Oxford University Press, 2015); Barber, "The Man Bun as Cultural Appropriation," *Feminist Reflections*, October 22, 2015. Available online: https://thesocietypages.org/feminist/2015/10/22/man-buns-as-cultural-appropriation/ (accessed July 27, 2016); Barber, *Styling Masculinity: Gender, Class, and Inequality in the Men's Grooming Industry* (New Brunswick, NJ: Rutgers University Press, 2016).
49. Kris Paap, *Working Construction: Why White Working-Class Men Put Themselves—and the Labor Movement—in Harm's Way* (Ithaca, NY: Cornell University Press, 2006).
50. Amanda Jade Martin, *Trend Alert: The Man Bun—Chimere Cisse, London*, January 15, 2014. Available online: https://stylehunter.com/hair-trends/trend-alert-the-man-bun-chimere-cisse-london/ (accessed February 27, 2017).
51. Barber, *The Man Bun*.
52. Dick Hebdige, *Subculture: The Meaning of Style* (London: Routledge, 1979).
53. Lauren Langman, "Punk, Porn and Resistance: Carnivalization and the Body in Popular Culture," *Current Sociology* 56, no. 4 (2008): 657.
54. Dawn H. Currie, Deirdre M. Kelly, and Shauna Pomerantz, *"Girl Power": Girls Reinventing Girlhood* (New York: Peter Lang, 2005).

55. Schilt, "A Little Too Ironic."
56. Cisgender refers to "individuals who have a match between the gender they were assigned at birth, their bodies, and their personal identity" (Schilt and Westbrook, "Doing Gender," 461).
57. The "wave" is helpful in thinking about shifts in feminist movement ideologies, but scholars have problematized the metaphor for missing the overlaps of feminist generations and the impact of organizations that have not explicitly used "feminist" rhetoric—such as those run by women of color. See, for example, Claire R. Snyder, "What is Third Wave Feminism? A New Directions Essay," *Signs* 34, no. 1 (2008): 175–96; Jo Reger, *Everywhere and Nowhere: U.S. Feminist Communities in the 21st Century* (New York: Oxford University Press, 2012), and Reger, "Micro Cohorts, Feminist Generations and the Making of the Toronto SlutWalk," *Feminist Formations* 26, no. 1 (2014): 49–69.
58. Wilson, *Adorned in Dreams*, 201.
59. Butler, *Bodies That Matter*.
60. Pamela Church Gibson, "Concerning Blondeness: Gender, Ethnicity, Spectacle and Footballers' Waves," in *Hair*, eds. Biddle-Perry and Cheang, 141–8.
61. Jess Butler, "For White Girls Only? Postfeminism and the Politics of Inclusion," *Feminist Formations* 25, no. 1 (2013): 35–58.
62. Collins, *Black Sexual Politics*; Craig, *Ain't I a Beauty Queen?*; Banks, *Hair Matters*; Higginbotham, *Righteous Discontent*.
63. Stephen A. Crockett, "Toronto Server Sent Home Because Her Natural Hair Wouldn't Lie Down," *The Root*. Available online: https://www.theroot.com/toronto-server-sent-home-because-her-natural-hair-would-1790854666 (accessed May 21, 2018).
64. Ashley Mears, *Pricing Beauty: The Making of a Fashion Model* (Berkeley: University of California Press, 2011); bell hooks, *Aint I a Woman: Black Women and Feminism* (New York: Routledge, 1978), see also bell hooks, *Black Looks: Race and Representation* (Boston, MA: South End Press, 2014); Evelyn Nakano Glenn, "Yearning for Lightness: Transnational Circuits in the Marketing and Consumption of Skin Lighteners," *Gender & Society* 22, no. 3 (2008): 281–302.
65. Stephanie Smith, "Essence Panel Explore Beauty Purchasing," *Women's Wear Daily*. Available online: http://wwd.com/beauty-industry-news/color-cosmetics/essence-panel-explores-beauty-purchasing-2139829/.
66. Produced by Jeff Stilson (2009).
67. Eiluned Edwards, "Hair, Devotion and Trade in India," in *Hair*, eds. Biddle-Perry and Cheang, 149–66.
68. Ibid.
69. Ayana Byrd and Lori L. Tharps, *Hair Story: Untangling the Roots of Black Hair in America* (New York: St. Martin's Press, 2014).
70. See http://www.indianhairs.com.
71. For example, Nirmal Kumar Chandra, *The Retarded Economies: Foreign Domination and Class Relations in India and Other Emerging Nations* (Oxford: Oxford University Press, 1988).
72. Edwards, "Hair and Devotion."
73. Judith Halberstam, *Female Masculinity* (Durham, NC: Duke University Press, 1998).

Chapter Seven

1. See especially Frantz Fanon, *Black Skins, White Masks* (London: Pluto Press, 1986). Fanon's seminal text explores the psychodynamics of Black oppression and resistance formulated in and through the experiences of colonization. For a more recent approach following the tradition of Fanon's phenomenological approach to the construction of black subjectivities through a dynamic exchange of racialized gazes, see George Yancy, *Black Bodies, White Gaze: The Continuing Significance of Race* (Lanham, MD: Rowan & Littlefield, 2008).
2. For Fanon the exposure of the "timeless truth" of racist power relations was not enough, this merely created stalemate; the real task of resistance he argues was to disclose the mechanics of oppression, not to collect facts and stories about behavior, but to find their meaning, *Black Skin, White Masks*, 129.
3. Stuart Hall and Sut Jhally, Transcript of "The Floating Signifier" (1996). Available online: https://www.mediaed.org/assets/products/407/transcript_407.pdf (accessed January 19, 2016).
4. Kobena Mercer, *Welcome to the Jungle: New Positions in Black Cultural Politics* (London: Routledge, 1994); Ayana d. Byrd and Lori L. Tharps, *Hair Story: Untangling the Roots of Black Hair in America* (New York: St. Martin's Press, 2001); Shirley A. Tate, *Black Beauty: Aesthetics, Stylization, Politics* (Farnham: Ashgate, 2009).
5. Noliewe M. Rooks, *Hair Raising: Beauty, Culture and African American Women* (Piscataway, NJ: Rutgers University Press, 2000); Ingrid Banks, *Hair Matters: Beauty, Power and Black Women's Consciousness* (New York: New York University Press, 2000); Adia H. Wingfield, *Doing Business with Beauty: Black Women, Hair Salons and the Racial Enclave Economy* (Lanham, MD: Rowman and Littlefield, 2008); Tiffany M. Gill, *Beauty Shop Politics: African American Women's Activism in the Beauty Industry* (Urbana, IL: University of Chicago Press, 2010).
6. Frank B. Wilderson III, *Red, White and Black: Cinema and the Structure of US Antagonisms* (Durham, NC: Duke University Press, 2008).
7. Sara Ahmed, *The Cultural Politics of Emotion* (Edinburgh: Edinburgh University Press, 2004), 2.
8. Paul C. Taylor, "Malcolm's Conk and Danto's Colors: Or Four Logical Petitions Concerning Race, Beauty, Aesthetics," in *Beauty Matters*, ed. Peg Zeglin Brand (Bloomington: Indiana University Press, 2000).
9. Fanon, *Black Skin, White Masks*, 92.
10. Barry Chevannes, *Rastafari: Roots and Ideology* (Syracuse, NY: Syracuse University Press, 1994).
11. Eiluned Edwards, "Hair, Devotion and Trade in India," in *Hair: Styling, Culture and Fashion*, eds. Geraldine Biddle-Perry and Sarah Cheang (Oxford: Berg 2008), 149–66.
12. Chevannes, *Rastafari*; see also Shirley Tate and Ian Law, *Caribbean Racisms: Connections and Complexities in the Racialization of the Caribbean Region* (Basingstoke: Palgrave Macmillan, 2015).
13. Foucault developed the key concept of "governmentality" in a series of lectures in the late 1970s. He brought together questions raised in *Discipline and Punish: The Birth of the Modern Prison*, trans. Alan Sheridan (1975; London: Pantheon Books, 1977) and *History of Sexuality Vol. 1*, trans. Robert Hurley (London: Allen Lane, 1976) in an analysis of the interrelationship between technologies of self and the institutional technologies of state power that mutually constituted the formation of the modern state and the modern subject. Shirley Tate in *Black Beauty*, explores these links in the context of race and the everyday

experiences of Black women in negotiating paradoxically appropriate "fake" and "natural" hairstyles and techniques. Black beauty on an everyday level in Foucauldian terms offers a spectacular "cultural translation" that "make us question not only the boundaries of Black beauty but ... the necessity for visibility and recognition of our *dis-identification* from 'beauty comes from within,'" 23.
14. Tate, *Black Beauty*, 7.
15. Sarah Cheang, "Roots: Hair and Race," in *Hair*, eds. Biddle-Perry and Cheang, 27–42.
16. Wilderson, *Red, White and Black*.
17. Ibid., 7.
18. Ginetta Candelario, *Black Behind the Ears: Dominican Racial Identity from Museums to Beauty Shops* (Durham, NC: Duke University Press, 2005).
19. Davarian Baldwin, "From the Washtub to the World: Madame C.J. Walker and the 'Recreation' of Race Womanhood, 1900–1935," in *The Modern Girl Around the World: Consumption, Modernity and Globalization*, ed. The Modern Girl Around The World Research Group (Durham, NC: Duke University Press, 2008), 55–76.
20. A'Lelia Bundles, "Let Me Correct the Erroneous Impression that I Claim to Straighten Hair," in *Tender Headed: A Comb-bending Collection of Hair Stories* (New York: Pocket Books, 2001).
21. For a comprehensive critical assessment of the wider political and cultural historical significance of Madame C. Walker's entrepreneurial enterprise and its effect on an expanding Black beauty industry, see Byrd and Tharps, *Hair Story*.
22. By the 1930s, the Apex Co. of Atlantic City, New Jersey had eclipsed Madame Walker's dominance in the Black hair-care industry. The company was founded by a young hairdresser Sarah Spencer Washington, a shrewd businesswoman who worked in her salon during the day and sold her products door-to-door at night. Apex became one of the United States' leading Black manufacturers and Washington's empire came to encompass a laboratory, beauty colleges in twelve states, and some 35,000 agents all over the world; see Kathy Peiss, *Hope in a Jar: The Making of America's Beauty Industry* (New York: Metropolitan Books, 1998), 235–7.
23. Bundles, "Let Me Correct the Erroneous Impression."
24. Ever since taking office, Michelle Obama's hairstyles and styling techniques have been the object of much debate online and in the popular press; for example, for a discussion of conservative negative reactions to Michelle and Malia "stepping out unstraightened" on holiday and of complexities of what now constitutes "good hair" for contemporary Black women in the United States, see Catherine Saint Louis, "Black Hair, Still Tangled in Politics," *New York Times*, August 26, 2009. Available online: www.nytimes.com/2009/08/27/fashion/27SKIN.html). For further debates on the problems associated with being "relaxed" and the thoughts of Obama's hairdresser Johnny Wright, see Kimberley Walker, "HAIR: Black Women's Right to Remain Relaxed," *EBONY*, August 29, 2012. Available online: www.ebony.com/style/hair-black-womens-right-to-remain-relaxed-122#axzz40Yuw7dg.
25. See Kobena Mercer, "Black Hair/Style Politics," *New Formations*, no. 3 (1987): 33–54; Mercer in this article addresses the complex dynamics of Black hair styling and politics across the diaspora through a series of historical "style wars"; he argues, the diversity of Black styles is something to be proud of, "an inventive, improvisational aesthetic that should be valued as an aspect of Africa's gift to modernity," 53.
26. Tate, *Black Beauty*.
27. This is a term for "race mixing."

28. See Patricia De Santana Pinho, *Mama Africa: Remembering Blackness in Bahia*, trans. E. Langdon (Durham, NC: Duke University Press, 2010); Kia Lilly Caldwell, *Negras In Brazil: Re-envisioning Black Women, Citizenship and the Politics of Identity* (New Brunswick, NJ: Rutgers University Press, 2006).
29. Ahmed, *Cultural Politics of Emotion*, 120.
30. Tate, *Black Beauty*, 52.
31. Carol Tulloch, "Resounding Power of the Afro Comb," in *Hair*, eds. Biddle-Perry and Cheang, 132.
32. Byrd and Tharps, *Hair Story*, 61.
33. Angela Y. Davis, "Afro Images: Politics, Fashion and Nostalgia," *Critical Inquiry* 21, no. 1 (Autumn 1994), 42.
34. The deracination of Black hairstyles and practices seen as the sign of autonomous Black femininity dominates online discussion; for posts generated by model and social reality star Kylie Jenner's cornrows, see, for example, Laura Cochran, "Kylie Jenner's Cornrows and the Racial Politics of Hair," *The Guardian*, July 13, 2015. Available online: https://www.theguardian.com/fashion/shortcuts/2015/jul/13/kylie-jenner-cornrows-racial-politics-hair.
35. bell hooks, *Black Looks: Race and Representation* (Boston, MA: South End Press, 1992).
36. Byrd and Tharps, *Hair Story*, 62.
37. Chevannes, *Rastafari*.
38. Tate, *Black Beauty*, 46–52.
39. Jamelia, "Jamelia: BBC3 'Whose Hair Is It Anyway?'" [video], 57:23. Available online: https://vimeo.com/68778551 (accessed January 10, 2016); for discussion of the wider culture of hair sacrifice in India, see also Edwards, "Hair Devotion and Trade."
40. Jamelia, "Whose Hair."
41. Carolyn Cooper, *Soundclash: Jamaican Dancehall Culture at Large* (Basingstoke: Palgrave, 2004).
42. Simedele Dosekun, "Fashioning Spectacular Femininities in Nigeria: Post-feminism, Consumption and the Transnational" (Unpublished PhD thesis, King's College, London, 2015).
43. Cooper, *Soundclash*.
44. Pinho, *Mama Africa*; *Ebony Goddess- 24a Black Beauty Night Ilê Ayê* (2003), Dir. Angela Figueiredo. Documentary film. (DVD).
45. Figueiredo, *Ebony Goddess*.
46. Ibid.
47. Caldwell, *Negras in Brazil*; Pinho, *Mama Africa*.
48. Julee Wilson, "Naomi Campbell Hair: Supermodel Exposes Huge Bald Spot," Huffington Post, August 9, 2012. Available online: http://www.huffingtonpost.com/2012/08/09/naomi-campbell-hair-exposes-bald-spot_n_1761999.html (accessed October 10, 2015).
49. City Press, "I Don't Take Pics with Girls Who Wear Weaves," *News 24*, April 19, 2015. Available online: http://www.news24.com/Archives/City-Press/I-dont-take-pics-with-girls-who-wear-weaves-20150429 (accessed January 10, 2016).
50. Hillary Crosley Coker, "What bell hooks Really Means When She Calls Beyoncé a 'Terrorist'," *Jezebel*, May 9, 2014. Available online: http://jezebel.com/what-bell-hooks-really-means-when-she-calls-beyonce-a-t-1573991834 (accessed September 3, 2015); see also: "Are You Still a Slave", *The New School* [video], 1:55:41. Available online: https://livestream.com/accounts/1369487/events/2940187.
51. Michel-Rolf Truillot, *Global Transformations: Anthropology and the Modern World* (Basingstoke: Palgrave Macmillan, 2003).

52. It is important to acknowledge how this commodification of the "natural" also enables the development of particular types of Black hyper-femininities and also speaks unequivocally of class and economic status; only those with a significant disposable income can afford human hair because of the cost, for example, Russian hair costs £2,000 for a full head weave (Jamelia, "Whose Hair"). Space prevents further discussion here, but class, sexuality, location, and historical moment need to be addressed as important factors with which Black women struggle within a wider politics of appearance; see Tate, *Black Beauty*; and Tate and Law, *Caribbean Racisms*.
53. Édouard Glissant, *Poetics of Relation*, trans. B. Wing (Ann Arbor: University of Michigan Press, 1997).
54. Ibid., 29, 90.
55. Ibid., 3.
56. Lewis Gordon, *Fanon: A Critical Reader* (London: Routledge, 1997).
57. Wilderson in *Red, White and Black* uses the concept of "fungibility" to locate the construction of the Black body as the antithesis of the human subject (p. 9). The term infers an understanding of the properties of a good or commodity and the commodity itself—for Fanon the value and properties of a slave—are liable to mutual substitution. In this slave relation the Black body as a fungibile object is created through structures of whiteness that eradicate Black subjectivity (p. 45).
58. Rosalind Gill and Christina Scharff, "Introduction," in *New Femininities: Postfeminism, Neoliberalism and Subjectivity*, eds. Rosalind Gill and Christina Scharff (Basingstoke: Palgrave Macmillan, 2011).
59. Ibid.
60. Mercer, *Welcome to the Jungle*, 104.
61. Donna Hope, *Man Vibes: Masculinities in Jamaican Dancehall* (Kingston: Ian Randle Publishers, 2010).

Chapter Eight

1. John, Baron Prescott of Kingston upon Hull was made a life peer and entered the House of Lords in 2010.
2. Prescott was pointedly referred to in the popular media as "Two Jags" in reference to his private ownership of a Jaguar car and his use of another as a ministerial car.
3. BBC TV, "Prescott: The Class System and Me," First Broadcast October 27, 2008.
4. Quentin Letts, "The Cleopatra of Hull: Why Pauline Prescott is in a Class of Her Own," *Daily Mail*, November 7, 2008. Letts's accusation of John Prescott being "chippy" is a euphemism for his having a "chip on his shoulder," that is, a resentment against those who it is believed consider themselves higher up the social scale.
5. Beverly Skeggs, "The Making of Class and Gender through Visualizing Moral Subject Formation," *Sociology* 39, no. 5 (December 2005): 963.
6. See in particular Mike Featherstone, *Consumer Culture and Postmodernism* (Los Angeles, CA: Sage Publications, 2007); Celia Lury, *Consumer Culture* (Cambridge: Polity Press); Don Slater, *Consumer Culture and Modernity* (Cambridge: Polity Press, 1996).
7. Anthony Giddens, *Modernity and Self-Identity: Self and Society in the Modern Age* (Cambridge: Polity Press, 1991).
8. Stuart Hall, "Introduction: Who Needs Identity," in *Questions of Cultural Identity*, eds. Stuart Hall and Paul Du Gay (London: Sage Publications, 1996).

9. Joanne Finkelstein, *The Fashioned Self* (London: Wiley, 1991), 122.
10. Joanne Entwistle, *The Fashioned Body: Fashion, Dress and Modern Social Theory* (Cambridge: Polity Press, 2000), 133.
11. Pierre Bourdieu, "Cultural Reproduction and Social Reproduction," first published 1973. Available online: https://www.scribd.com/doc/39994014/Bourdieu-1973-Cultural-Reproduction-and-Social-Reproduction.
12. Pierre Bourdieu, "The Forms of Capital," in *Handbook of Theory and Research for the Sociology of Education*, ed. John Richardson (New York: Greenwood, 1986).
13. Pierre Bourdieu, *Distinction: A Social Critique of the Judgement of Taste*, trans. Richard Nice (Cambridge, MA: Harvard University Press, 1987), 7.
14. Dennis W. Rook, "The Ritual Dimension of Consumer Behavior," *Journal of Consumer Research* 12, no. 3 (1985): 251–64.
15. Steven Zdatny, *Hairstyles and Fashion: A Hairdresser's History of Paris, 1910–1920* (London: Bloomsbury Academic, 1999), 192.
16. Ibid., 188.
17. Kim Smith, "From Style to Place: The Emergence of the Ladies' Hair Salon in the Twentieth Century," in *Hair: Styling, Culture, Fashion*, eds. Geraldine Biddle-Perry and Sarah Cheang (Oxford: Berg, 2008), 55–67, 57–8.
18. Gilbert A. Foan, *The Art and Craft of Hairdressing* (London: The New Era Publishing Co., 1931), 174–5.
19. Richard Corson, *Fashions in Hair: The First 5000 Years* (London: Peter Owen, 1965); Caroline Cox, *Good Hair Days* (London: Quartet Books, 1999).
20. Edith Wharton, "Permanent Wave," in *The World Over* (New York: D. Appleton-Century, 1936).
21. Ibid., 114–17.
22. This character is probably based on the real-life fashionable coiffure "Antoine" (Antek) Cierplikowski. Wharton, renowned for her understanding of the nuances of New York high society, also spent the last decades of her life in Paris and so would have been well aware of the cachet attached to Antoine's "magic fingers" and of having one's hair done in luxurious "Antoine de Paris" salons in both cities.
23. Cox, *Good Hair Days*, 99.
24. Antoine, *Antoine By Antoine* (London: W.H. Allen and Co., 1946).
25. Ibid., 124.
26. Ibid., 129.
27. Beverley Nichols, British author and playwright, recalled how in 1927 "white parties" were all the rage in the upper-class London social scene of which he was a part: *All I Could Never Be* (London: Weidenfeld and Nicolson, 1949), 32.
28. Antoine, *Antoine By Antoine*, 107.
29. Sydney Guilaroff, *Reflections of Hollywood's Favorite Confidant* (Santa Monica, CA: W. Quay Hays, 1996).
30. Philip Crang and Peter Jackson, "Geographies of Consumption," in *British Cultural Studies: Geography, Nationality and Identity*, eds. David Morley and Kevin Robins (Oxford: Oxford University Press, 2001).
31. Antoine, *Antoine By Antoine*, 175.
32. Christopher Breward, "Fashion's Front and Back: 'Rag trade' Cultures and Cultures of Consumption in Post-war London c. 1945–1970," *The London Journal* 31, no. 1 (June 2006): 15–40.

33. Kim Smith, "Strands of the Sixties: A Cultural Analysis of the Design and Consumption of the New London West End Hair Salons c. 1954–1975" (PhD thesis, University of East London, 2014), 125–6.
34. David J. Taylor, *Bright Young People: The Lost Generation of London's Jazz Age* (New York: Farrar, Straus and Gilroy, 2007).
35. Stephen Gundle, *The Glamour System* (Basingstoke: Palgrave Macmillan, 2006).
36. For a personal account of the evolutionary nature of studio hairdressing, see Frank Westmore's biography (with Muriel Davidson), *The Westmores of Hollywood* (Philadelphia: J.B. Lippincott Company, 1976); and Sydney Guilaroff's autobiography, *Reflections of Hollywood's Favorite Confidant*.
37. Westmore, *The Westmores of Hollywood*, 15–17.
38. Guilaroff, *Hollywood's Favorite Confidant*, 44.
39. Ibid., 47.
40. Ibid., 49.
41. Carole Dyehouse, *Glamour: Women, History, Feminism* (London: Zed Books, 2010).
42. Beryl M. Cross, *Modern Girls' Beauty Book* (London: Sir Isaac Pitman & Sons, 1938), 75.
43. *The Women* (1934), [Film] Dir. George Cukor.
44. J.B. [John Boynton] Priestley, *English Journey* (Leipzig: Tauchnitz, 1934), 9.
45. Ibid., 12. Priestley describes the man thus: "Like so many men in business, he was at heart a pure romantic. The type has always been with us, and more or less fantastic specimens of it have found their way into literature as Micawber or Mr. Polly. He was the kind of man who comes into a few hundred pounds in his early twenties, begins to lose money readily, but contrives to marry another few hundreds, then begins to lose them, but is rescued by the death of an aunt who leaves him another few hundreds … Even in these days, there are still a few thousand like him up and down the country, especially in growing towns and new suburbs."
46. Steven Zdatny, "Fashion and Class Struggle: The Case of coiffure," *Social History* 18, no. 1 (January 1993): 52–72.
47. Ibid.
48. Joan Edwards, "The Barrett Street Trade School," *Costume* 18, no. 1 (2017): 83–5.
49. Ayana D. Byrd and Lori L. Tharps, *Hair Story: Untangling the Roots of Black Hair in America* (New York: St. Martin's Press, 2001), 31.
50. Aida M Harvey, "Personal Satisfaction and Economic Improvement: Working-Class Black Women's Entrepreneurship in the Hair Industry," *Journal of Black Studies* 38, no. 6 (2008): 900–15.
51. Byrd and Tharps, *Hair Story*, 82.
52. Harvey, "Personal Satisfaction," 932.
53. Gilles Lipovetsky, *The Empire of Fashion: Dressing Modern Democracy* (Princeton, NJ: Princeton University Press, 1987), 33.
54. Catherine Horwood, *Keeping Up Appearances: Fashion and Class Between the Wars* (Stroud: The History Press, 2005).
55. The use of the term "catwalk" or indeed "runway" to refer to the narrow platform upon which fashion mannequins walked to display the latest collections only became part of the vernacular in the 1940s—although such shows still took place behind the closed doors of individual couture houses.
56. Stanley G. Flitman, *The Craft of Ladies' Hairdressing* (London: Butterworth & Co., 1959).
57. "The Latest Creations from London Hairstylist Raymond," *Pathé News*, 1955. Available online: http://www.britishpathe.com/video/hair-styles-beware-other-colour-pics-share-this-1.

58. Smith, *Strands of the Sixties*.
59. Fred Davis, *Fashion, Culture and Identity* (Chicago: University of Chicago Press, 1992), 54, 58.
60. Ibid.
61. Caroline Cox, "White Hair: Styling the London Man," in *London: From Punk to Blair*, eds. Joe Kerr and Andrew Gibson (London: Reaktion Books, 2003), 75.
62. Beverly Skeggs, "The Making of Class and Gender through Visualizing Moral Subject Formation," *Sociology* 39, no. 5 (2005): 965–82.
63. Cox, "White Hair," 76.
64. Sherry Beth Ortner, "Reading America: Preliminary Notes in Class and Culture," in *Recapturing Anthropology*, ed. Richard G. Fox (Santa Fe, NM: School of American Research, 1991).
65. Rose Weitz, *Rapunzel's Daughters: What Women's Hair Tells About Women's Lives* (New York: Farrah, Straus and Giroux, 2004), 124–5.
66. Chris Haylett, "'This is About Us, This Is Our Film': Personal and Popular Discourses of 'Underclass'," in *Cultural Studies and the Working Class: Subject to Change*, ed. Sally Munt (London: Routledge 1997), 64–6.
67. Skeggs, "The Making of Class and Gender," 969.
68. Cox "White Hair," 78.
69. Katalin Medvedev, "Social Class and Clothing," in *The Berg Companion to Fashion*, ed. Valerie Steele (Oxford: Bloomsbury Academic, 2010).

Chapter Nine

1. Sigmund Freud, *Introductory Lectures on Psychoanalysis*, vol. 1 (London: Pelican Freud Library, 1973); "Three Essays on the Theory of Sexuality" and "Fetishism," (1905) in *On Sexuality*, vol. 7 (London, Pelican Freud Library, 1977).
2. Interview Nathalie Khan: Paul Soileau, January 21, 2017.
3. Mary Douglas, *Purity and Danger: An Analysis of Concepts of Pollution and Taboo* (London: Routledge and Kegan Paul, 1998).
4. Ivan Crozier offers a useful discussion on differences between performance and performativity in "Performing the Western Sexual Body after 1920," in *A Cultural History of the Human Body in the Modern Age*, ed. Ivan Crozier (London: Bloomsbury Academic, 2010), 43–71, 46–8.
5. Notably Charles Berg, *The Unconscious Significance of Hair* (London: George Allen and Unwin, 1936); Edmund Leach, "Magical Hair," *Journal of the Royal Anthropological Institute* 88, no. 2 (1958): 147–64; Christopher Hallpike, "Social Hair," *Man*, New Series 9, no. 2 (1969): 256–64.
6. Maurizia Boscagli, *Stuff Theory, Everyday Objects, Radical Materialism* (London: Bloomsbury, 2014).
7. Ellis Cashmore, *Celebrity Culture* (London: Routledge, 2006); Chris Rojek, *Celebrity* (London: Reaktion Books, 2001); *Presumed Intimacy: Parasocial Interaction in Media, Society and* Celebrity *Culture* (London: John Wiley and Sons, 2016).
8. *Butt Muscle* (2017), [Film] Dir. Matt Lambert.
9. Other characters created by Paul Soileau include Rebecca Havemeyer.
10. Film-maker and director Matt Lambert discusses motivation, process, and collaboration with Rick Owens and Christeene in an interview with Thom Bettridge in 032c available at https://032c.com/buttmuscle.
11. Available online: https://imvdb.com/video/christeene/fix-my-dick.

12. For a detailed discussion addressing differences between individual performance and performativity, see Irene Rafanell, "Durkheim and the Performative Model: Reconfiguring social Objectivity," in *Sociological Objects: The Reconfiguration of Social Theory*, eds. Geoff Cooper, Andrew King, and Ruth Retti (Farnham: Ashgate, 2009); Rafanell extends Judith Butler's understanding of gender performativity; see Judith Butler, *Gender Trouble* (London: Routledge, 1990). Performativity for Rafanell is a collective negotiation that gives objects and things the appearance of an external reality with power over the individual performance of practices and idealized expressions of identity. Thus, Rafanell emphasizes the role of this causal relationship as the context in which self-referential acts of subjective identification are negotiated, socially sanctioned, and performatively produced.
13. Interview Khan: Soileau.
14. Berg, *The Unconscious Significance of Hair*; and Leach, "Magical Hair."
15. Gananath Obeyesekere's study of modern matted-hair ascetics in Sri Lanka, *Medusa's Hair: An Essay on Personal Symbols and Religious Experience* (Chicago: University of Chicago Press, 1981) overcomes previous divisions between psychoanalytical and sociological viewpoints (see note 14 above) by making connections between hair symbolism's unconscious origins and its operational vitality. This is further developed by Patrick Olivelle's rereading of Obeyesekere's theories hair as a "natural symbol" that provokes the work of culture, see "Hair and Society: Social Significance of Hair in South Asian Traditions," in *Hair: Its Power and Meaning in Asian Cultures*, eds. Alf Hiltebeitel and Barbara D. Miller (Albany: State University of New York Press, 1998).
16. Douglas, *Purity and Danger*, 65.
17. Ibid., 50.
18. Lambert, interview with Thom Bettridge.
19. Berg, *The Unconscious Significance of Hair*, 74–5.
20. See Geraldine Biddle-Perry, "Hair, Gender, and Looking," in *Hair, Styling, Culture and Fashion*, eds. Geraldine Biddle-Perry and Sarah Cheang (Oxford: Berg, 2008).
21. James George Frazer, 1890, *The Golden Bough: A Study in Magic and Religion* (London: Wordsworth, 1993). Frazer describes hair and nail clippings or other types of physical matter as forming a "sympathetic connexion" between a person and those involved in, for example, healing rituals or vengeful magic in the belief that the spirit resided in this remnant of the living or dead body (p. 143).
22. Sigmund Freud, "The Sexual Aberrations" (1905), in *On Sexuality* (Penguin Freud Library vol. 7, Harmondsworth: Penguin Books, 1977), 153, 155.
23. Sigmund Freud, "Fetishism" (1905), in *On Sexuality* (Penguin Freud Library vol. 7, Harmondsworth: Penguin Books, 1977).
24. Ibid., 352.
25. Ibid., 354.
26. Interview, Khan: Soileau.
27. Janice Miller, "Hair without a Head, Disembodiment and the Uncanny," in *Hair, Styling, Culture*, eds. Geraldine Biddle-Perry and Sarah Cheang (Oxford: Berg, 2008), 183.
28. Karl Marx, *Das Kapital: A Critique of Political Economy*, vol. I, pt. I, "The Process of Capitalist Production" (1867) (New York: Cosimo Classics, 2007).
29. William Pietz, "The Problem of the Fetish, I," *RES* 9 (1985): 7.
30. Ibid., 10.
31. Briony Fer, "Surrealism, Myth and Psychoanalysis," in *Realism, Rationalism, Surrealism: Art between the Wars*, eds. Briony Fer, David Batchelor, and Paul Wood (New Haven, CT:

Yale University Press, 1993), 170. See also Georges Bataille, "The Pineal Eye," in *Visions of Excess: Selected Writings, 1927–1939*, ed. Allan Stoekl (Minneapolis: University of Minnesota Press, 1985).
32. Fer, "Surrealism, Myth and Psychoanalysis."
33. Ibid., 172–3.
34. André Breton, *Manifestoes of Surrealism*, trans. Richard Seaver and Helen R. Lane (Ann Arbor: University of Michigan Press, 1969), 32.
35. Fer, "Surrealism, Myth and Psychoanalysis," 210–12.
36. Karen Stevenson, "Hairy Business: Organising the Gendered Self," in *Contested Bodies*, eds. Ruth Holliday and John Hassard (London: Routledge, 2001); see also Kim Smith, "From Style to Place: The Emergence of the Ladies' Hair Salon in the Twentieth Century," in *Hair, Styling, Culture and Fashion,* eds. Biddle-Perry and Cheang 57–67.
37. For a detailed analysis of the antecedents of the gold hair tradition and its centrality to Victorian art and fiction, see Elisabeth G. Gitter, "The Power of Women's Hair in the Victorian Imagination," *PMLA* 99, no. 5 (1984): 936–54. For a more complex critical analysis of hair as an important cultural form in the nineteenth century and the wider social context of its increasing fetishization, see Galia Ofek, *Representations of Hair in Victorian Literature and Culture* (Farnham: Ashgate, 2009).
38. Ofek, *Representations of Hair.*
39. Gitter, "The Power of Women's Hair."
40. Marina Warner, *From the Beast to the Blonde: On Fairy Tales and Their Tellers* (New York: Farrar, Straus and Giroux, 1995) is a seminal work exploring the symbolic tropes of hair that dominate legends, myths, and fairy stories and situating their origins and meanings in a social historical context.
41. Ivan Crozier, "Performing the Western Sexual Body after 1920," in *A Cultural History of the Human Body in the Modern Age*, ed. Ivan Crozier (London: Bloomsbury, 2010), 43.
42. Graeme Turner, *Understanding Celebrity* (London: Sage, 2004).
43. Richard Dyer, *Stars* (London: British Film Institute, 1979).
44. Boscagli, *Stuff Theory*, 48, 49.
45. Ibid., 53.
46. Walter Benjamin, "The Work of Art in the Age of Mechanical Reproduction" (1936), in *Illuminations* (London: Fontana, 1973).
47. Walter Benjamin, *Charles Baudelaire: A Lyric Poet in the Era of High Capitalism* (London: New Left Books, 1973).
48. Benjamin, "The Work of Art," 132.
49. Walter Benjamin, *The Arcades Project*, trans. Howard Eiland and Kevin McLaughlin (Cambridge, MA: Harvard University Press, 1999).
50. Ibid. 69.
51. Pamela Church Gibson, *Fashion and Celebrity Culture* (London: Berg, 2012).
52. Cindy Sherman cited in Johanna Burton, *Cindy Sherman (October Files # 6)* (Cambridge, MA: MIT Press, 2006), 195.
53. Wayne Koestenbaum, *Andy Warhol: A Biography* (New York: Open Road, 2015).
54. Trevor Fairbrother, "Skulls," in *The Work of Andy Warhol*, ed. Gary Garrels (Seattle, WA: Bay Press, 1989); Simon Watney, "Photography and AIDS," *Ten 8*, no. 26 (1989): 14–26; see also Rojek, *Celebrity* (London: Sage, 2001).
55. Rojek, *Celebrity*, 53.

56. Hal Foster, "Death in America," in *October: The Second Decade, 1986–1996, Vol. 76*, eds. Rosalind E. Krauss et al. (Cambridge, MA: MIT Press, 1997), 367.
57. Jessica Evans and David Hesmondhalgh, eds., *Understanding Media: Inside Celebrity* (Maidenhead: Open University Press, 2005), 16.
58. Andy Warhol, *The Warhol Diaries*, ed. Pat Hackett (New York: Warner Books, 1989). Warhol referred to the incident several times in his diary. It was also reported by Liz Smith in her celebrity column in the *Daily News* on November 1, 1985.
59. Ibid.
60. Church Gibson, *Fashion and Celebrity Culture*; Rojek, *Celebrity*.
61. Solanas, a writer and radical women's rights activist, shot and critically wounded Warhol on June 3, 1968, upset after Warhol had lost a script for her play, *Up Your Ass*.
62. Butler, *Gender Trouble*.
63. Amelia Jones, "Dis/Playing the Phallus: Male Artists Perform Their Masculinities," *Art History* 17, no. 4 (December 1994): 546–84. Jones here is referring to the iconic hairstyle worn by actress Farrah Fawcett-Majors in the late 1970s consisting of a long feather cut with blonde highlights and bouncy, blow-dried curls.
64. Christopher Makos, *Andy* (New York: Perseus, 2001), 12.
65. Amelia Jones, *Body Art/Performing the Subject* (Minneapolis: University of Minnesota Press, 1995), 19.
66. John Flügel, *The Psychology of Clothes* (London: Hogarth Press, 1930). Flügel's study while groundbreaking in recognizing the symbolic and social significance of clothes is now considered very much of its time. He explains male and female dress and differences between them in terms of psychic drives but his argument relies on contemporary gender assumptions and reductive equations made between fashion, superficiality, and femininity as somehow essential.
67. Jones, *Performing the Subject*, 70–1.
68. Ibid., 25.
69. Jean Baudrillard, *The System of Objects*, trans. James Benedict (London: Verso, 2005), 96.
70. Makos, *Andy*, 64.
71. See Church Gibson, *Fashion and Celebrity Culture*; Rojek, *Celebrity*; Graeme Turner, *Understanding Celebrity*.
72. Eve Sedgwick, *The Epistemology of the Closet* (Berkeley: California University Press, 1990).
73. Lauren Berlant and Michael Warner, "Sex in Public," in *The Routledge Queer Studies Reader*, eds. Donald E. Hall and Annamarie Jagose (London: Routledge, 2013).
74. Rosemary Hennessy, "The Material of Sex," in *The Routledge Queer Studies Reader*, eds. Hall and Jagose, 134–49.
75. Julia Kristeva, *Powers of Horror: An Essay on Abjection*, trans. Leon S. Rodriguez, (New York: Columbia University Press, 1982).
76. Interview, Khan: Soileau.
77. Judith Butler, *Bodies That Matter* (London: Routledge, 1994).

BIBLIOGRAPHY

Ahmed, Leila. *Women and Gender in Islam: Historical Roots of a Modern Debate*. New Haven, CT: Yale University Press, 1992.

Ahmed, Sara. *The Cultural Politics of Emotion*. Edinburgh: Edinburgh University Press, 2004.

Alvarez, Luis. *The Power of the Zoot: Youth Culture and Resistance during World War II*. Berkeley: University of California Press, 2009.

Antoine. *Antoine By Antoine*. London, W.H. Allen, 1946.

Baduel, C., and C. Meillassoux. "Modes et Codes de la Coiffure Ouest-Africaine." *L'Ethnographie* 69, no. 1 (1975): 13–59.

Baldwin, Davarian. "From the Washtub to the World: Madame C.J. Walker and the Recreation of Race Womanhood, 1900–1935." In *The Modern Girl Around The World: Consumption, Modernity and Globalization*, edited by The Modern Girl Around The World Research Group, 55–76. Durham, NC: Duke University Press, 2008.

Banks, Ingrid. *Hair Matters: Beauty Power and Black Women's Consciousness*. New York: New York University Press, 2000.

Banner, Lois. "The Creature from the Black Lagoon: Marilyn Monroe and Whiteness." *Cinema Journal* 47, no. 4 (Summer 2008): 4–29.

Barber, Kristen. "Remembering Leonard Nimoy, Feminist Photographer." *Feminist Reflections*, March 5, 2015. Available online: https://thesocietypages.org/feminist/2015/03/05/remembering-leonard-nimoy-feminist-photographer/. Accessed July 27, 2016.

Barthes, Roland. *The Pleasure of the Text*. Translated by Richard Miller. New York: Hill and Wang, 1973.

Bataille, Georges. "The Pineal Eye." In *Visions of Excess: Selected Writings, 1927–1939*. Translated by Allan Stoekl. Edited by Allan Stoekl et al., 79–90. Minneapolis: University of Minnesota Press, 1985.

Battle-Waters, Kimberly. *Sheila's Shop: Working-Class African American Women Talk About Life, Love, Race, and Hair*. Lanham, MD: Rowman & Littlefield, 2004.

Baudrillard, Jean. *The System of Objects*. Translated by James Benedict. London: Verso, 2005.

Benjamin, Walter. *Charles Baudelaire: A Lyric Poet in the Era of High Capitalism*. London: New Left Books, 1973.

Benjamin, Walter. "The Work of Art in the Age of Mechanical Reproduction" (1936). In *Illuminations*, edited by Hannah Arendt, 211–44. London: Fontana, 1973.

Benjamin, Walter. *The Arcades Project*. Translated by Howard Eiland and Kevin McLaughlin. Cambridge, MA: Harvard University Press, 1999.

Berlant, Lauren, and Michael Warner. "Sex in Public." In *The Routledge Queer Studies Reader*, edited by Donald E. Hall and Annamarie Jagose, 165–79. London: Routledge, 2013.

Biddle-Perry, Geraldine. "Hair, Gender, and Looking." In *Hair, Styling, Culture, and Fashion*, edited by Geraldine Biddle-Perry and Sarah Cheang, 97–111. Oxford: Berg, 2008.

Biddle-Perry, Geraldine, and Sarah Cheang. "Introduction: Thinking About Hair." In *Hair: Styling, Culture, and Fashion*, edited by Geraldine Biddle-Perry and Sarah Cheang, 3–12. Oxford: Berg, 2008.

Biddle-Perry, Geraldine, and Sarah Cheang. "Hair." In *Berg Encyclopedia of World Dress and Fashion: Global Perspectives*, edited by Joanne B. Eicher and Phyllis G. Tortora. Oxford: Berg, 2010. *Bloomsbury Fashion Central*. Available online: http://dx.doi.org/10.2752/BEWDF/EDch10311 (accessed February 2, 2017).

Bognolo, D. "Histoire d'un doute: La Femme a Tête Rasée chez les Lobi dur Burkina Faso/A Prolonged Uncertainty: Women with Shaven Heads among the Lobi of Burkina Faso." In *Parures de Tête—Hairstyles and Headdresses*, edited by C. Falgayrettes-Leveau and I. Hahner 147–70, Paris: Éditions Dapper, 2003.

Borrelli, Laird. "Dressing Up and Talking about It: Fashion Writing in *Vogue* from 1968–1993." *Fashion Theory: The Journal of Dress Body and Culture* 1, no. 3 (1997): 247–59.

Boscagli, Maurizia. *Stuff Theory, Everyday Objects, Radical Materialism*. London: Bloomsbury, 2014.

Bourdieu, Pierre. "The Forms of Capital." In *Handbook of Theory and Research for the Sociology of Education*, edited by John Richardson, 241–58. New York: Greenwood Press, 1986.

Bourdieu, Pierre. *Distinction: A Social Critique of the Judgement of Taste*. Translated by Richard Nice. Cambridge, MA: Harvard University Press, 1987.

Breton, André. *Manifestoes of Surrealism*, Translated by Richard Seaver and Helen R. Lane. Ann Arbor: University of Michigan Press, 1969.

Breward, Christopher. *The Culture of Fashion: A New History of Fashionable Dress*. Manchester: Manchester University Press, 1995.

Breward, Christopher. "Fashion's Front and Back: Rag Trade Cultures and Cultures of Consumption in Post-war London c. 1945–1970." *The London Journal* 31, no. 1 (June 2006): 15–40.

Bromberger, Christian. "Hair: From the West to the Middle East through the Mediterranean." *Journal of American Folklore* 121, no. 482 (2007): 379–99.

Bromberger, Christian. *Trichologiques: Une Anthropologie des Cheveux et des Poils*. Paris: Bayard Presse, 2010.

Brookes, Barbara, and Catherine Smith. "Technology and Gender: Barbers and Hairdressers in New Zealand, 1900–1970." *History and Technology* 25, no. 4 (December, 2009): 365–86.

Brookman, Faye. 'Hair Care Products." In *The Advertising Age Encyclopedia of Advertising*, Vol. 2, edited by John McDonough and the Museum of Broadcast Communications, Karen Egolf, and Jaqueline V. Reid. New York: Fitzroy Dearborn, 2002.

Brooks, Rosetta. "Sighs and Whispers in Bloomingdales: A Review of a Mail-Order Catalogue." In *Zoot Suits and Second Hand Dresses: An Anthology of Fashion and Music*, edited by Angela McRobbie. London: Macmillan, 1989.

Brownmiller, Susan. *Femininity*. New York: Linden Books, 1984.

Buckley, Cheryl. *Designing Modern Britain*. London: Reaktion Books, 2007.

Bundles, A'lelia. "Madam C.J. Walker: 'Let Me Correct the Erroneous Impression that I Claim to Straighten Hair'." In *Tenderheaded: A Comb-Bending Collection of Hair Stories*, edited by Juliet Harris and Pamela Johnson, 2–11. New York: Pocket Books, 2001.

Burton, Johanna. *Cindy Sherman (October Files # 6)*. Cambridge, MA: MIT Press, 2006.

Butler, Jess. "For White Girls Only? Postfeminism and the Politics of Inclusion." *Feminist Formations* 25, no. 1 (2013): 35–58.

Butler, Judith. *Gender Trouble: Feminism and the Subversion of Identity*. New York: Routledge, 1990.

Butler, Judith. *Bodies That Matter: On the Discursive Limits of Sex*. London: Routledge, 1993.

Byrd, Ayana D., and Lori L. Tharps. *Hair Story: Untangling the Roots of Black Hair in America*. New York: St. Martin's Press, 2001.

Caldwell, Kia Lilly. *Negras In Brazil: Re-envisioning Black Women, Citizenship and the Politics of Identity*. New Brunswick, NJ: Rutgers University Press, 2006.

Camfield, William A. "The Machinist Style of Francis Picabia." *The Art Bulletin* 48, no. 3/4 (September-December 1966): 28–51.

Candelario, Ginetta. *Black Behind the Ears: Dominican Racial Identity from Museums to Beauty Shops*. Durham, NC: Duke University Press, 2005.

Carden-Coyne, Ana. *Reconstructing the Body: Classicism, Modernism, and the First World War*. Oxford: Oxford University Press, 2009.

Cashmore, Ellis. *Celebrity Culture*. London: Routledge, 2006.

Chan, S. C., and S. Xu. "Wedding Photographs and the Bridal Gaze in Singapore." *New Zealand Journal of Asian Studies* 9, no. 2 (2007): 87–103.

Cheang, Sarah. "Roots: Hair and Race." In *Hair: Styling, Culture, and Fashion*, edited by Geraldine Biddle-Perry and Sarah Cheang, 27–42. Oxford: Berg, 2008.

Chevannes, Barry. *Rastafari: Roots and Ideology*. Syracuse, NY: Syracuse University Press, 1994.

Chundra, Nirmal Kumar. *The Retarded Economies: Foreign Domination and Class Relations in India and Other Emerging Nations*. Oxford: Oxford University Press, 1988.

Çinar, Alev. "Subversion and Subjugation in the Public Sphere: Secularism and the Islamic Headscarf." *Signs* 33, no. 4 (2008): 891–913.

Cole, Shaun. "Hair and Male (Homo)sexuality: Up Top and Down Below." In *Hair: Styling, Culture, and Fashion*, edited by Geraldine Biddle-Perry and Sarah Cheang, 81–97. London: Berg 2008.

Collins, Patricia Hill. *Black Sexual Politics: African Americans, Gender, and the New Racism*. New York: Routledge, 2004.

Conekin, Becky. "The Model: Transforming Image Through Hair." In *Hair by Sam McKnight: A Companion Volume*, edited by Sam McKnight and Tim Banks, London: Somerset House, 2017.

Cooper, Carolyn. *Soundclash: Jamaican Dancehall Culture at Large*. Basingstoke: Palgrave, 2004.

Cooper, Wendy. *Hair, Sex, Society, Symbolism*. London: Aldus Books, 1971.

Corson Richard. *Fashions in Hair: The First 5000 Years*. London: Peter Owen, 1965.

Cosgrave, Stuart. "The Zoot Suit and Style Warfare." *History Workshop Journal* 18 (1984): 77–90.

Cox, Caroline. *Good Hair Days: A History of British Hairstyling*. London: Quartet Books, 1999.

Cox, Caroline. "White Hair: Styling the London Man." In *London: From Punk to Blair*, edited by Joe Kerr and Andrew Gibson, 77–85. London: Reaktion Books, 2003.

Cox, Caroline, and Lee Widdows, *Hair and Fashion*. London: V & A Publications, 2005.

Craig, Maxine Leeds. "The Decline and Fall of the Conk; or, How to Read a Process." *Fashion Theory* 1, no. 4 (1997): 399–420.

Craig, Maxine Leeds. *Ain't I a Beauty Queen? Black Women, Beauty, and the Politics of Race*. New York: Oxford University Press, 2002.

Crang, Philip, and Peter Jackson. "Geographies of Consumption." In *British Cultural Studies: Geography, Nationality and Identity*, edited by David Morley and Kevin Robins, 329–39. Oxford: Oxford University Press, 2001.

Cromwell, Nancy. "Contemporary African Folk Art: Barbershop Signs and Hairstyles." *African Arts* 8, no. 4 (1975): 77.

Cross, Beryl. *Modern Girls' Beauty Book*. London: Sir Isaac Pitman & Sons, 1938.

Crozier, Ivan. "Performing the Western Sexual Body after 1920." In *A Cultural History of the Human Body in the Modern Age*, edited by Ivan Crozier, 43–71. London: Bloomsbury, 2010.

Currie, Dawn H., Deirdre M. Kelly, and Shauna Pomerantz. *Girl Power: Girls Reinventing Girlhood*. New York: Peter Lang, 2005.

Curtis, Michael. *Verdict on Vichy: Power and Prejudice in the Vichy France Regime*. New York: Arcade Publishing, 2002.

CW Television Network. "Cedric's Barber Battle," 2015. Available online: http://www.cwtv.com/shows/cedrics-barber-battle/. Accessed July 6, 2015.

Danforth, Loring. *The Death Rituals of Rural Greece*. Princeton, NJ: Princeton University Press, 1982.

Dault, Meredith Suzanne. "The Last Triangle: Sex, Money, and the Politics of Pubic Hair." MA thesis, Department of Cultural Studies, Queen's University, 2011.

Davis, Angela. "Afro images: Politics, Fashion and Nostalgia." *Critical Inquiry* 21, no. 1 (Fall 1994): 37–45.

Davis, Fred. *Fashion, Culture and Identity*. Chicago: University of Chicago Press, 1992.

De Grazia, Victoria. *How Fascism Ruled Women: Italy, 1922–45*. Berkeley: University of California Press, 1991.

De Waal, Clarissa. *Everyday Iran: A Provincial Portrait of the Islamic Republic*. London: I.B. Tauris, 2015.

Delaney, Carol. "Untangling the Meanings of Hair in Turkish Society." *Anthropological Quarterly* 67, no. 4 (1994): 159–72.

Deslandes, Paul R. "Selling, Consuming, and Becoming the Beautiful Man in Britain: The 1930s and 1940s." In *Consuming Behaviours: Identity, Politics, and Pleasure in Twentieth-Century Britain*, edited by Erika Rappaport, Sandra Trudgen Dawson, and Mark J. Crowley, 53–70. London: Bloomsbury, 2015.

Dikotter, Frank. "Hairy Barbarians, Furry Primates, and Wild Men: Medical Science and Cultural Representations of Hair in China." In *Hair: Its Power and Meaning in Asian Cultures*, edited by Alf Hiltebeitel and Barbara D. Miller, 51–74. Albany: State University of New York Press, 1998.

Doan, Laura. "Passing Fashions: Reading Female Masculinities in the 1920s." *Feminist Studies* 24, no. 3 (Fall 1998): 672–5.

Douglas, Mary. *Purity and Danger: An Analysis of the Concepts of Pollution and Taboo*. London: Routledge & Kegan Paul, 1966.

Douglas, Mary. *Natural Symbols: Explorations in Cosmology* New York: Pantheon Books, 1982.

Drewal, H. "Coiffures chez les Yoruba/Headdresses and Hairstyles Among the Yoruba." In *Parures de Tête—Hairstyles and Headdresses*, edited by C. Falgayrettes-Leveau and I. Hahner, 170–203, Paris: Editions Dapper, 2003.

Duchen, Claire. "Crime and Punishment in Liberated France: The Case of *les femmes tondues*." In *When War Was Over: Women, War, and Peace in Europe, 1940–1956*, edited by Claire Duchen and Irene Bandhauss-Schöffmann, 233–51. London: Leicester University Press, 2000.

DuCille, Ann. *Skin Trade*. Cambridge, MA: Harvard University Press, 1996.
Dyehouse, Carol. *Glamour: Women, History, Feminism*, London: Zed Books, 2010.
Dyer, Richard. *Stars*. London: British Film Institute, 1979.
Dyer, Richard. *White*. London: Routledge, 1997.
Eckert, Charles. "The Carole Lombard in Macy's Window." In *Fabrications: Costume and the Body*, edited by Jane Gaines and Charlotte Herzog, 100–21. New York: Routledge, 1990.
Edwards, Eiluned. "Hair, Devotion and Trade in India.," In *Hair: Styling, Culture, and Fashion*, edited by Geraldine Biddle-Perry and Sarah Cheang, 149–66. Oxford: Berg, 2008.
Edwards, Joan. "The Barrett Street Trade School." *Costume* 18, no. 1 (2017): 83–5.
Ellinson, Rabbi Getsel. *Women and the Mitzvot: Vol. 2, The Modest Way*. Translated by Raphael Blumberg. Jerusalem: Einer Library, 1992.
Entwistle, Joanne. *The Fashioned Body: Fashion, Dress and Modern Social Theory*. Cambridge: Polity Press, 2000.
Evans, Jessica, and David Hesmondhalgh, eds. *Understanding Media: Inside Celebrity*. Maidenhead: Open University Press, 2005.
Fairbrother, Trevor. "Skulls." In *The Work of Andy Warhol*, edited by Gary Garrels. Seattle: Bay Press, 1989.
Fanon, Frantz. *Black Skins, White Masks*. London: Pluto Press, 1986.
Featherstone, Mike. *Consumer Culture and Postmodernism*. Los Angeles: Sage Publications, 2007.
Fer, Briony. "The Language of Construction." In *Realism, Rationalism and Surrealism: Art between the Wars*, edited by Briony Fer, David Batchelor, and Paul Wood. New Haven, CT: Yale University Press, 1993.
Finkelstein, Joanne. *The Fashioned Self*. London: Wiley, 1991.
Fitzgerald, Francis Scott. "Bernice Bobs Her Hair" (1920). In *Flappers and Philosophers*, edited by F. Scott Fitzgerald. New York: Charles Scribner & Sons, 1959.
Flitman, Stanley. *The Craft of Ladies' Hairdressing*. London: Butterworth & Co., 1959.
Flugel, John. *The Psychology of Clothes*. London: Hogarth Press, 1930.
Foan Gilbert, ed. *The Art and Craft of Hairdressing*. London: The New Era Publishing Co., 1931.
Ford, Tanisha. *Liberated Threads: Black Women, Style, and the Global Politics of Soul*. Chapel Hill: University of North Carolina Press, 2015.
Foster, Hal. "Death in America." In *October: The Second Decade, 1986–1996*, edited by Rosalind E. Krauss et al., 348–75. Cambridge, MA: MIT Press, 1997.
Foucault, Michel. *Discipline and Punish: The Birth of the Modern Prison*. Translated by Alan Sheridan. London: Pantheon Books, 1977.
Foucault, Michel. *History of Sexuality, Vol. I. An Introduction*. Translated by Robert Hurley. London: Allen Lane, 1978.
Frazer, James George. *The Golden Bough: A Study in Magic and Religion* (1890). London: Wordsworth, 1993.
Freud, Sigmund. *New Introductory Lectures on Psychoanalysis* (1915). Vol. 2, Penguin Freud Library, Penguin Books, 1973.
Freud, Sigmund. "Fetishism." In *On Sexuality* (1905). Vol. 7, Penguin Freud Library, 352–4. Harmondsworth: Penguin Books, 1977.
Freud, Sigmund. "Three Essays on the theory of Sexuality." In *On Sexuality* (1905), Vol .7, Penguin Freud Library. Harmondsworth: Penguin Books, 1977.
Gaines, Kevin. *Uplifting the Race: Black Leadership, Politics, and Culture in the Twentieth Century*. Chapel Hill: University of North Carolina Press, 1996.

Galvin, Joshua, and Daniel Galvin. *Hair Matters*. London: Macmillan Publishers, 1985.

Gibson, Pamela Church. "Concerning Blondeness: Gender, Ethnicity, Spectacle and Footballers' Waves." In *Hair: Styling, Culture, and Fashion*, edited by Geraldine Biddle-Perry and Sarah Cheang, 141–9. Oxford: Berg, 2008.

Gibson, Pamela Church. *Fashion and Celebrity Culture*. London: Berg, 2012.

Giddens, Anthony. *Modernity and Self-Identity: Self and Society in the Modern Age*. Cambridge: Polity Press, 1991.

Gill, Rosalind, and Christina Scharff. "Introduction." In *New Femininities: Postfeminism, Neoliberalism and Subjectivity*, edited by Rosalind Gill and Christina Scharff, 1–19. Basingstoke: Palgrave Macmillan, 2011.

Gill, Tiffany. "'I Had My Own Business ... So I Didn't Have to Worry': Beauty Salons, Beauty Culturists, and the Politics of African American Female Entrepreneurship." In *Beauty and Business: Commerce, Gender, and Culture in Modern America*, edited by Philip Scranton, 169–94. New York: Routledge, 2001.

Gill, Tiffany. *Beauty Shop Politics: African American Women's Activism in the Beauty Industry*. Champaign: University of Illinois Press, 2010.

Gillman, Sandra. *Making the Body Beautiful: A Cultural History of Aesthetic Surgery*. Princeton, NJ: Princeton University Press, 1999.

Gitter, Elisabeth G. "The Power of Women's Hair in the Victorian Imagination." *PMLA* 99, no. 5 (1984): 936–54.

Glenn, Evelyn Nakano. "Yearning for Lightness: Transnational Circuits in the Marketing and Consumption of Skin Lighteners." *Gender & Society* 22, no. 3 (2008): 281–302.

Glissant, Édouard. *Poetics of Relation*. Translated by B. Wing. Ann Arbor: University of Michigan Press, 1997.

Goffman, Erwin. *The Presentation of Self in Everyday Life*. Harmondsworth: Penguin, 1971.

Gomet, Doriane. "From Punishment to Death: Body Practices for Deported Women in Nazi Camps." *International Journal of the History of Sport* 30, no. 9 (2013): 934–49.

Gordon, Lewis. *Fanon: A Critical Reader*. London: Routledge, 1997.

Gordon, Michael. *Hair Heroes*. New York: Bumble and Bumble, 2002.

Graybill, Beth, and Linda B. Arthur. "The Social Control of Women's Bodies in Two Mennonite Communities." In *Religion, Dress and the Body*, edited by Linda B. Arthur, 9–30. Oxford: Berg, 1999.

Greer, Germaine, *The Female Eunuch*. London: MacGibbon and Kee, 1970.

Gugenheim, P. "How Hair Dyes Work," *Hairdressers Journal*, June 5, 1958: 31–2.

Guilaroff, Sydney. *Reflections of Hollywood's Favorite Confidant*. Santa Monica, CA: W. Quay Hays, 1996.

Gundle, Stephen. *The Glamour System*. Basingstoke: Palgrave Macmillan, 2006.

Hahner, Iris. "Le Langage des Coiffures/The Language of Hairstyles and Headdresses." In *Parures de Tête—Hairstyles and Headdresses*, edited by Christiane Falgayrettes-Leveau and Iris Hahner, 60–117. Paris: Éditions Dapper, 2003.

Halberstam, Judith. *Female Masculinity*. Durham, NC: Duke University Press, 1998.

Hall, Stuart. "Introduction: Who Needs Identity." In *Questions of Cultural Identity*, edited by Stuart Hall and Paul Du Gay, 1–18. London: Sage Publications, 1996.

Hallpike, Charles R. "Social Hair." *Man*, New Series 4, no. 2 (1969): 256–64.

Handley, Susannah. *NYLON: The Manmade Fashion Revolution. A Celebration of Design from Art Silk to Nylon and Thinking Fibres*. London: Bloomsbury, 1995.

Hansen, Lulu. "Female Denouncers: Women's Social Transgression During the German Occupation of Denmark, 1940–45." *Women's History Magazine* 67 (Fall 2011): 11–16.

Harahap, F.J. "The Fatwa of Muhammad Bin Ja'far Al Kattani Concerning the Wearing of the Turban." *Islamic Quarterly* 42, no. 3 (1998): 188–99.

Harris, Hermione. *Yoruba in Diaspora: An African Church in London*. New York: Palgrave Macmillan, 2006.

Harvey, Aida M. "Personal Satisfaction and Economic Improvement: Working-Class Black Women's Entrepreneurship in the Hair Industry." *Journal of Black Studies* 38, no. 6 (2008): 900–15.

Hau, Michael. *The Cult of Health and Beauty in Germany: A Social History, 1890–1930*. Chicago: University of Chicago Press, 2003.

Haylett, Chris. "'This is About Us. This Is Our Film': Personal and Popular Discourses of Underclass." In *Cultural Studies and the Working Class: Subject to Change*, edited by Sally Munt, 69–82. London: Routledge 1997.

Hebdige, Dick. *Subculture: The Meaning of Style*. London: Routledge, 1979.

Heffner, Robert W. "Multiple Modernities: Christianity, Islam and Hinduism in a Globalizing Age." *Annual Review of Anthropology* 27 (1998): 83–104.

Hennessy, Rosemary. "The Material of Sex." In *The Routledge Queer Studies Reader*, edited by Donald E. Hall and Annamarie Jagose. London: Routledge, 2013.

Hershman, Paul. "Hair, Sex and Dirt." *Man*, New Series 9, no. 2 (1974): 274–98.

Herzig, Rebecca. *Plucked: A History of Hair Removal*. New York: New York University Press, 2015.

Heskett, John. *Industrial Design*. London: Thames & Hudson, 1980.

Higginbotham, Evelyn B. *Righteous Discontent: The Women's Movement in the Black Baptist Church, 1880–1920*. Cambridge, MA: Harvard University Press, 1993.

Hiltebeitel, Alf. "Introduction: Hair Tropes." In *Hair: Its Power and Meaning in Asian Culture*, edited by Alf Hiltebeitel and Barbara D. Miller, 1–11. Albany: State University of New York Press, 1998.

hooks, bell. *Ain't I a Woman? Black Women and Feminism*. New York: Routledge, 1978.

hooks, bell. *Black Looks: Race and Representation*. Boston, MA: South End Press, 2014.

Hope, Donna. *Man Vibes: Masculinities in Jamaican Dancehall*. Kingston: Ian Randle Publishers, 2010.

Horwood, Catherine. *Keeping Up Appearances: Fashion and Class Between the Wars*. Stroud: The History Press, 2005.

Houlberg, M. "Social Hair: Tradition and Change in Yoruba Hairstyles in Southwestern Nigeria." In *The Fabrics of Culture: The Anthropology of Clothing and Adornment*, edited by J. Cordwell and R. Schwarz, 349–97. The Hague: Mouton, 1975.

Howell, Geraldine. *Wartime Fashion: From Haute Couture to Homemade*. London: Bloomsbury Academic, 2012.

Jacobs-Huey, Lanita. *From the Kitchen to the Parlor: Language and Becoming in African American Women's Hair Care*. Oxford: Oxford University Press, 2007.

Jennings, Rebecca. *Tomboys and Bachelor Girls: A Lesbian History of Post-War Britain*. Manchester: Manchester University Press, 2007.

Johnson, Elizabeth. *Resistance and Empowerment in Black Women's Hair Styling*. Farnham: Ashgate, 2013.

Johnston, Harry. *The Backward People and Our Relations with Them*. London: Humphrey Milford and Oxford University Press, 1920.

Jones, Amelia. *Body Art/performing the Subject*. Minneapolis: University of Minnesota Press, 1995.

Jones, Dylan. *Haircuts: Fifty Years of Styles and Cuts*. London: Thames and Hudson, 1990.

Jones, Geoffrey. "Blonde and Blue eyed? Globalizing Beauty." *Economic History Review* 61, no. 1 (2008): 125–54.

Kane, Pandurang Vaman. *History of Dharmasastra*, vol. II, pt I. Pune: Bhandarkar Oriental Research Institute, 1941. Available online: https://archive.org/details/historyofdharmas029210mbp.

Katz, Sylvia. *Classic Plastics: from Bakelite to High-Tech*. London: Thames & Hudson, 1984.

Kaustenbaum, Wayne. *Andy Warhol: A Biography*. New York: Open Road, 2015.

Keenan, Brigid. *The Women We Wanted to Look Like*. New York: St. Martin's Press, 1977.

Kelley, Robin D.G. "Nap Time: Historicizing the Afro." *Fashion Theory* 1, no. 4 (1997): 339–52.

Kennett, Lee. *G.I.: The American Soldier in World War II*. New York: Charles Scribner & Sons, 1987.

Kessler, Suzanne J., and Wendy McKenna. *Gender: An Ethnomethodological Approach*. Chicago: University of Chicago Press, 1985.

Kimmel, Michael. *Manhood in America: A Cultural History*. New York: Oxford University Press, 1996.

King, Angela. "The Prisoner of Gender: Foucault and the Disciplining of the Female Body." *Journal of International Women's Studies* 5, no. 2 (2004): 29–39.

Kirkham, Pat. "Beauty and Duty: Keeping Up the Home Front." In *War Culture: Social Change and Changing Experience in World War Two Britain*, edited by Pat Kirkham and David Thoms, 13–28. London: Lawrence & Wishart, 1995.

Kister, Michael J. "'The Crowns of This Community' … Some Notes on the Turban in the Muslim Tradition." *Jerusalem Studies in Arabic and Islam* 24 (2000): 217–45.

Kristeva, Julia. *Powers of Horror: An Essay on Abjection*. Translated by Leon S. Rodrigez. New York: Columbia University Press, 1982.

Laderman, C. *Wives and Midwives: Childbirth and Nutrition in Rural Malaysia*. Berkeley: University of California Press, 1983.

Laennec, Christine Moneera. "The Assembly Line Love Goddess: Women and the Machine Aesthetic in Fashion Photography 1918–1940." In *Bodily Discursions: Genders, Representations, Technologies*, edited by Deborah S. Wilson and Christine Moneera Laennec, 81–102. Albany: State University of New York Press, 1997.

Lang, Karen. "Shaven Heads and Loose Hair: Buddhist Attitudes towards Hair and Sexuality." In *Off With Her Head!: The Denial of Women's Identity in Myth, Religion and Culture*, edited by Howard Eilberg-Schwarz and Wendy Doniger, 32–53. Berkeley: University of California Press, 1995.

Lang, Robert, and Maher Ben Moussa. "Choosing to Be Not a Man: Masculine Anxiety in Nouri Bouzid's Rih Essed/Man of Ashes." In *Masculinity Bodies, Movies, Culture*, edited by Peter Lehman, 81–94. New York: Routledge, 2001.

Langman, Lauren. "Punk, Porn and Resistance: Carnivalization and the Body in Popular Culture." *Current Sociology* 56, no. 4 (2008): 657–77.

Lawal, B. (2000), "Orilonise: The Hermeneutics of Head and Hairstyles Among the Yoruba." In *Hair in African Art and Culture*, edited by Roy Sieber and Frank Herreman, 92–109. New York: Museum of African Art.

Leach, Edmund. "Magical Hair." *Journal of the Royal Anthropological Institute* 88, no. 2 (1958): 147–64.

Lears, Jackson. *Fables of Abundance: A Cultural History of Advertising in America.* New York: Basic Books, 1994.

Lemke, Thomas. "The Birth of Bio-politics: Michel Foucault's Lectures at the College de France on Neo-liberal Governmentality." *Economy and Society* 30, no. 2 (2001): 190–207.

Lesnik-Oberstein, Karin. ed. *The Last Taboo: Women and Body Hair.* Manchester: Manchester University Press, 2006.

Lessinger, Johanna. *From the Ganges to the Hudson.* Boston, MA: Allyn and Bacon, 1995.

Lewis, Reina. "Fashion Forward and Faith-tastic! Online Modest Fashion and the Development of Women as Religious Interpreters and Intermediaries." In *Modest Fashion: Styling Bodies, Mediating Faith*, edited by Reina Lewis, 41–66. Oxford: I.B. Taurus.

Lipovetsky, Gilles. *The Empire of Fashion: Dressing Modern Democracy.* Princeton, NJ: Princeton University Press, 1987.

Lorde, Audre. "Age, Race, Class and Sex: Women Redefining Difference." In *Sister Outsider: Essays and Speeches,* edited by Audre Lorde et al. Trumansburg, NY: Crossing Press, 1984.

Luciano, Lynne. *Looking Good: Male Body Image in Modern America.* New York: Hill and Wang, 2001.

Lury, Celia. *Consumer Culture.* Cambridge: Polity Press, 1996.

Makos, Christopher. *Andy.* New York: Perseus, 2001.

Marwick, Arthur. *The Sixties: Cultural Revolution in Britain, France, Italy, and the United States, c. 1958–c.1974.* Oxford: Oxford University Press, 1998.

Marx, Karl. *Das Kapital: A Critique of Political Economy*, vol. I. New York: Cosimo Classics, (1867/2007).

Massey, Anne. *Hollywood Beyond the Screen.* Oxford: Berg, 2000.

Mauss, Marcel. "Techniques of the Body" (1936). In *Incorporations*, edited by Jonathan Crary and Sandford Kwinter, 455–77. New York: Zone, 1992.

Mazon, Mauricio. *The Zoot-Suit Riots: The Psychology of Symbolic Annihilation.* Austin: University of Texas Press, 2010.

McAndrew, Malia. "A Twentieth Century Triangle Trade: Selling Black Beauty at Home and Abroad, 1945–1965." *Enterprise & Society* 11, no. 4 (2010): 784–807.

McCracken, Grant. *Big Hair: A Journey into the Transformation of Self.* Toronto: Viking, 1995.

McKnight, Sam, and Tim Blanks, *Hair by Sam McKnight.* London: Rizzoli International Publications, 2016.

McLeod, Hew. "The Five Ks of the Khalsa Sikhs." *Journal of the American Oriental Society* 128, no. 2 (2008): 328–31.

Mears, Ashley. *Pricing Beauty: The Making of a Fashion Model.* Berkeley: University of California Press, 2011.

Medvedev, Katalin. "Social Class and Clothing." In *The Berg Companion to Fashion*, edited by Valerie Steele. Oxford: Bloomsbury Academic, 2010.

Meikle, Jeffery. "Plastics in the American Machine Age: 1920–1950." In *The Plastics Age: from Modernity to Post-Modernity*, edited by Penny Sparke, 40–53. London: Victoria and Albert Museum, 1990.

Mercer, Kobena. *Welcome to the Jungle: New Positions in Black Cultural Politics.* London: Routledge, 1994.

Mercer, Kobena. "Black Hair/Style Politics." *New Formations* 3 (Winter, 1997): 33–54.

Metcalf, Barbara. *Making Muslim Space in North America and Europe.* Berkeley: University of California Press, 1996.

Miller, Barbara D. "The Disappearance of the Oiled Braid: Indian Adolescent Female Hairstyles in North America." In *Hair: Its Power and Meaning in Asian Cultures*, edited by Alf

Hiltebeitel and Barbara D. Miller, 259–81. Albany: State University of New York Press, 1998.

Miller, Janice. "Hair without a Head, Disembodiment and the Uncanny." In *Hair, Styling, Culture, and Fashion*, edited by Geraldine Biddle-Perry and Sarah Cheang, 183–93. Oxford: Berg, 2008.

Mills, Anthony M., and Mark P. Mills. "The Invention of the War Machine: Science, Technology and the First World War." *The New Atlantis* 42 (2014): 3–25.

Mitchell, Michelle. *Righteous Propagation: African Americans and the Politics of Racial Destiny after Reconstruction*. Chapel Hill: University of North Carolina Press, 2004.

Motherzone. "The Traditions of Mundan Sanskar in India." Motherzone website, 2015. Available online: http://www.motherszone.com/culture/mundan-sanskar/. Accessed June 27, 2015.

Murray, Gerald F., and Marina Ortiz. *Pelo Bueno/Pelo Malo: Estudio Antropologico de los Salones de Belleza en la República Dominicana*. Santo Domingo: Fondo para el Financiamento de la Microempresa Inc., 2012.

Nichols, Beverley. *All I Could Never Be*. London: Weidenfeld and Nicolson, 1949.

Obeyesekere, Gananath. *Medusa's Hair: An Essay on Personal Symbols and Religious Experience*. Chicago: University of Chicago Press, 1981.

October, Dene. "The Big Shave: Modernity and Fashions in Men's Facial Hair." In *Hair: Styling, Culture, and Fashion*, edited by Geraldine Biddle-Perry and Sarah Cheang, 67–79. Oxford: Berg, 2008.

Ofek, Galia. *Representations of Hair in Victorian Literature and Culture*. Farnham: Ashgate, 2009.

Oldstone-Moore, Christopher. *Of Beards and Men: The Revealing History of Facial Hair*. Chicago: University of Chicago Press, 2015.

Olivelle, Patrick. "Hair and Society: Social Significance of Hair in South Asian Traditions." In *Hair: Its Power and Meaning in Asian Cultures*, edited by Alf Hiltebeitel and Barbara D. Miller, 11–51. Albany: State University of New York Press, 1998.

Ortner, Sherry Beth. "Reading America: Preliminary Notes in Class and Culture." In *Recapturing Anthropology*, edited by Richard G. Fox, 163–89. Santa Fe, NM: School of American Research, 1991.

Paap, Kris. *Working Construction: Why White Working-Class Men Put Themselves—and the Labor Movement—in Harm's Way*. Ithaca, NY: Cornell University Press, 2006.

Paoletti, Jo B., and Carol L. Kregloh. "The Children's Department." In *Men and Women: Dressing the Part*, edited by Claudia Brush Kidwell and Valerie Steel, 22–41. Washington, DC: Smithsonian Institution Press, 1989.

Papanek, Hanna. "Purdah in Pakistan: Seclusion and Modern Occupations for Women." In *Separate Worlds*, edited by Hanna Papanek and Gail Minault, 190–216. Columbia, MO: South Asian Books, 1982.

Peiss, Kathy. *Hope in a Jar: The Making of America's Beauty Culture*. New York: Metropolitan Books, 1998.

Peterkin, Allan. *One Thousand Beards: A Cultural History Facial Hair*. Vancouver: Arsenal Pulp Press, 2001.

Pfluger-Schindlbeck, Ingrid. "On Symbolism of Hair in Islamic Societies: An Analysis of Approaches." *Anthropology of the Middle East* 1, no. 2 (2006): 72–88.

Philips, Alton. "The Erotic Life of Electric Hair Clippers: A Social History." In *Practicing Culture*, edited by Craig Calhoun and Richard Sennett, 193–215. London: Routledge, 2007.

Pietz, William. "The Problem of the Fetish, I." *RES* 9 (1985): 5–17.

Pinho, Patricia de Santana. *Mama Africa: Remembering Blackness in Bahia*. Translated by E. Langdon. Durham, NC: Duke University Press, 2010.

Pivetta, Guilia. *The Barber Book*. London: Phaidon, 2014.

Priestley, J.B. [John Boynton]. *English Journey*. Leipzig: Tauchnitz, 1934.

ProBeautyKit. "Barber Poster-African American Men." 2015. Available online: http://www.probeautykit.com/index.php?main_page=index&manufacturers_id=2. Accessed July 6, 2015.

Rafanell, Irene. "Durkheim and the Performative Model: Reconfiguring social Objectivity." In *Sociological Objects: The Reconfiguration of Social Theory*, edited by Geoff Cooper, Andrew King, and Ruth Retti, 59–66. Farnham: Ashgate, 2009.

Ramirez, Catherine. *The Woman in the Zoot Suit: Gender, Nationalism, and the Cultural Politics of Memory*. Durham, NC: Duke University Press, 2009.

Raymond [Bessonne], *Raymond: The Outrageous Story of the Hairstylist "Teasie Weasie."* London: Wyndham Publications, 1976.

Reger, Jo. *Everywhere and Nowhere: U.S. Feminist Communities in the 21st Century*. Oxford: Oxford University Press, 2012.

Reger, Jo. "Micro Cohorts, Feminist Generations and the Making of the Toronto SlutWalk." *Feminist Formations* 26, no. 1 (2014): 49–69.

Renne, Elisha. "Wives, Chiefs, and Weavers: Gender Relations in Bunu Yoruba Society." PhD diss., New York University, 1990.

Richards, Thomas. *The Commodity Culture in Victorian England: Advertising and Spectacle*. Stanford, CA: Stanford University Press, 1990.

Roberts, Mary Louise. *Civilization Without Sexes: Reconstructing Gender in Postwar France, 1917–1927*. Chicago: University of Chicago Press, 1994.

Rojek Chris. *Celebrity*. London: Reaktion Books, 2001.

Rojek, Chris. *Presumed Intimacy: Parasocial Interaction in Media, Society and Celebrity Culture*. London: John Wiley and Sons, 2016.

Rook, Dennis W. "The Ritual Dimension of Consumer Behavior." *Journal of Consumer Research* 12, no. 3 (1985): 251–64.

Rooks, Noliwe M. *Hair Raising: Beauty, Culture and African American Women*. New Brunswick, NJ: Rutgers University Press, 1996.

Rorabaugh, William J. *American Hippies*. New York: Cambridge University Press, 2015.

Ryback, T. "Evidence of Evil." *The New Yorker*, November 15, 1993, 68–81.

Sassoon, Vidal. *Sorry I Kept You Waiting*. London: Cassell, 1968.

Sassoon, Vidal. *Vidal: The Autobiography*. London: Pan Macmillan, 2010.

Schilt, Kristen. "A Little Too Ironic: The Appropriation and Packaging of Riot Grrrl Politics by Mainstream Female Musicians." *Popular Music and Society* 26, no. 1 (2006): 5–16.

Schilt, Kristen, and Laurel Westbrook. "Doing Gender, Doing Heteronormativity: Gender Normals, Transgender People, and the Social Maintenance of Heterosexuality." *Gender and Society* 23, no. 4 (2009): 440–64.

Schilt, Kristen. *Just One of the Guys? Transgender Men and the Persistence of Gender Inequality*. Chicago: University of Chicago Press, 2011.

Sedgwick, Eve. *The Epistemology of the Closet*. Berkeley: California University Press, 1990.

Shaw, Arnold. *The Jazz Age: Popular Music in the 1920s*. Oxford: Oxford University Press, 1987.

Shaw, Stephanie. "Black Clubwomen's Movement." In *The Reader's Companion to U.S. Women's History*, edited by Wilma Mankiller et al., 62–3. Boston, MA: Houghton Mifflin, 1999.

Sherrow, Victoria. *Encyclopedia of Hair: A Cultural History*. Westport, CT: Greenwood Press, 2006.

Shirazi, Faegeh. "Men's Facial Hair in Islam: A Matter of Interpretation." In *Hair: Styling, Culture, and Fashion*, edited by Geraldine Biddle-Perry and Sarah Cheang, 111–23. Oxford: Berg, 2008.

Sieber, Roy. "A Note on Hair and Mourning Especially in Ghana." In *Hair in African Art and Culture*, edited by Roy Sieber and Frank Herreman, 88–91. New York: Museum of African Art, 2000.

Simmel, Georg. "Fashion." In *On Individuality and Social Forms*, edited by D. Levine, 294–323. Chicago: University of Chicago Press, 1971.

Simmel, Georg. "How is Society Possible?" In *On Individuality and Social Forms*, edited by D. Levine, 3–22. Chicago: University of Chicago Press, 1971.

Sims, Shari. "Hair from the 1970s to 2000." In *Fashion Photography Archive*. London: Bloomsbury, 2015.

Skeggs, Beverly. "The Making of Class and Gender through Visualizing Moral Subject Formation." *Sociology*, 39, no. 5 (December 2005): 965–82.

Slater, Don. *Consumer Culture and Modernity*. Cambridge: Polity Press, 1996.

Smith, Kim. "From Style to Place: The Emergence of the Ladies' Hair Salon in the Twentieth Century." In *Hair: Styling, Culture, and Fashion*, edited by Geraldine Biddle-Perry and Sarah Cheang, 55–67. Oxford: Berg, 2008.

Smith Kim. "Strands of the Sixties: A Cultural Analysis of the Design and Consumption of the New London West End Hair Salons c.1954–1975." PhD thesis, University of East London, 2014.

Snyder, Claire R. "What is Third Wave Feminism? A New Directions Essay." *Signs* 34, no. 1 (2008): 175–96.

Sparke, Penny. *As Long as It's Pink: The Sexual Politics of Taste*. London: Pandora, 1995.

Sparke, Penny. *A Century of Design: Design Pioneers of the 20th Century*. London: Mitchell Beasley, 1999.

Stacey, Jackie. *Star Gazing: Hollywood Cinema and Female Spectatorship*. London: Routledge, 1994.

Steele, Valerie. *Fashion and Eroticism: Ideals of Feminine Beauty from the Victorian Era to the Jazz Age*. New York: Oxford University Press, 1985.

Steele, Valerie. "Anti-Fashion: The 1970s." *Fashion Theory: The Journal of Dress Body and Culture* 1, no. 3 (1997): 279–96.

Stein, Kurt. *Hair: A Human History*. New York: Pegasus Books, 2016.

Stevenson, Karen. "Hairy Business: Organising the Gendered Self." In *Gendered Bodies*, edited by Ruth Halliday, and John Hassard, 137–53. London: Routledge, 2001.

Stewart, Mary Lynn. *For Health and Beauty: Physical Culture for Frenchwomen, 1880s-1930s*. Baltimore: Johns Hopkins University Press, 2001.

Stillman, Yedida K. *Arab Dress: A Short History from the Dawn of Islam to Modern Times*. Leiden: Brill, 2000.

Stoppard, Lou. "Hair for the Catwalk." In *Hair by Sam McKnight: A Companion Volume*. London: Somerset House, 2017.

Stutesman, Drake. "The Silent Screen, 1895–1927." In *Costume, Makeup and Hair*, edited by Adrienne McLean, 21–47. London: I.B. Tauris, 2016.

Synnott, Anthony. "Shame and Glory: A Sociology of Hair." *The British Journal of Sociology*, 38, no. 3 (September 1987): 381–413.

Synnott, Anthony. *The Body Social: Symbolism, Self and Society*. London: Routledge, 1993.

Talbot, P.A. *In the Shadow of the Bush*. London: Heinemann, 1912.

Tarlo, Emma. "Meeting Through Modesty: Jewish-Muslim Encounters on the Internet." In *Modest Fashion: Styling Bodies, Mediating Faith*, edited by Reina Lewis, 67–90. London: I.B. Tauris, 2013.

Tarlo, Emma. *Entanglement: The Secret Lives of Hair*. London: One World Publications, 2016.
Tate, Shirley Anne. *Black Beauty: Aesthetics, Stylization, Politics*. Farnham: Ashgate, 2009.
Tate, Shirley Anne, and Ian Law. *Caribbean Racisms: Connections and Complexities in the Racialization of the Caribbean Region*. Basingstoke: Palgrave Macmillan, 2015.
Tavernise, Sabrina. "For Many Turks, Headscarf's Return Aids Religion and Democracy." *New York Times*, February 9, 2008.
Taylor, David J. *Bright Young People: The Lost Generation of London's Jazz Age*. New York: Farrar, Straus and Gilroy, 2007.
Taylor, Lou, and Elizabeth Wilson. *Through the Looking Glass: A History of Dress from 1860 to the Present Day*. London: BBC Books, 1989.
Taylor, Paul C. "Malcolm's conk and Danto's Colors: Or Four Logical Petitions Concerning Race, Beauty, Aesthetics." In *Beauty Matters*, edited by Peg Zeglin Brand, 57–64. Bloomington: Indiana University Press, 2000.
Thompson, Julia J. "Cuts and Culture in Kathmandu." In *Hair: Its Power and Meaning in Asian Cultures*, edited by Alf Hiltebeitel and Barbara D. Miller, 219–58. Albany: State University of New York Press, 1998.
Thomson, Mathew. *Psychological Subjects: Identity, Culture, and Health in Twentieth-Century Britain*. Oxford: Oxford University Press, 2006.
Tobin, Carole. "Fashioning the American Man: The Arrow Collar Man, 1907–1931." In *Material Strategies: Dress and Gender in Historical Perspective*, edited by Barbara Burman and Carole Turbin, 100–22. Oxford: Blackwell Publishing, 2003.
Tremper, Ellen. *I'm No Angel, the Blondee in Fiction and in Film*. Charlottesville: University of Virginia Press, 2006.
Truillot, Michel-Rolf. *Global Transformations: Anthropology and the Modern World*. Basingstoke: Palgrave Macmillan, 2003.
Tulloch, Carol. "Rebel Without a Pause." In *Chic Thrills: A Fashion Reader*, edited by Juliet Ash and Elizabeth Wilson, 84–101. London: Pandora, 1992.
Tulloch, Carol. "Resounding Power of the Afro Comb." In *Hair: Styling, Culture, and Fashion*, edited by Geraldine Biddle-Perry and Sarah Cheang, 123–41. London: Berg 2008.
Turner, Graeme. *Understanding Celebrity*. London: Sage, 2004.
Tyler, Bruce. "Black Hairstyles: Cultural and Socio-political Implications." *The Western Journal of Black Studies* 14, no. 4 (1990): 235–50.
Valian, Virginia. *Why So Slow? The Advancement of Women*. Cambridge, MA: MIT Press, 1999.
Van Gennep, Arnold. *The Rites of Passage*. Chicago: University of Chicago Press, [1908] 1960.
Walker, Susannah. "Black is Profitable: The Commodification of the Afro, 1960–1975." In *Beauty and Business: Commerce, Gender, and Culture in Modern America*, edited by Philip Scranton, 254–77. London: Routledge, 2001.
Walker, Susannah. *Style and Status: Selling Beauty to African American Women, 1920–1975*. Lexington: University Press of Kentucky, 2007.
Warner, Marina. *From the Beast to the Blonde: On Fairy Tales and Their Tellers*. New York: Farrar, Straus and Giroux, 1995.
Warner, R. Stephen. "Immigration and Religious Communities in the United States." In *Gatherings in Diaspora: Religious Communities and the New Immigration*, edited by R. Stephen Warner and Judith G. Wittner, 3–34. Philadelphia: Temple University Press, 1998.
Watney, Simon. "Photography and AIDS." *Ten 8*, no. 26 (1989): 14–26.

Watson, James L. "Living Ghosts: Long-Haired Destitutes in Colonial Hong Kong." In *Hair: Its Power and Meaning in Asian Cultures*, edited by Alf Hiltebeitel and Barbara D. Miller, 177–93. Albany: State University of New York Press.

Weiss, Brad. *Street Dreams and Hip Hop Barbershops: Global Fantasy in Urban Tanzania*. Bloomington: Indiana University Press, 2009.

Werbner, Pnina. "Fun Spaces: On Identity and Social Empowerment among British Pakistnis." *Theory, Culture and Society* 13, no. 40 (1996): 53–80.

Werbner, Pnina. "Veiled Intentions in Pure Space: Shame and Embodied Struggles among Muslims in Britain and France." *Theory and Society*, Special Issue, "Authority and Islam" 24, no. 2 (2007): 161–86.

West, Candace, and Don Zimmerman. "Doing Gender," *Gender and Society* 1, no. 2 (1987): 125–51.

Westmore, Frank. *The Westmores of Hollywood*. Philadelphia: J.B. Lippincott Company, 1976.

Wharton, Edith. "Permanent Wave." In *The World Over*, edited by Edith Wharton. New York: D. Appleton-Century Inc., 1936.

Wilderson III, Frank B. *Red, White and Black: Cinema and the Structure of US Antagonisms*. Durham, NC: Duke University Press, 2008.

Willett, Julie. *Permanent Waves: The Making of the American Beauty Shop*. New York: New York University Press, 2000.

Williams, Melanie. "Making the Cut." In *Transformation and Tradition in Sixties British Cinema*. Available online: 60sBritishCinema.wordpress.com. Accessed November 5, 2015.

Wilson, Elizabeth. *Adorned in Dreams: Fashion and Modernity*. London: Virago, 1985.

Wingfield, Adia Harvey. *Doing Business with Beauty: Black Women, Hair Salons, and the Racial Enclave Economy*. Lanham, MD: Rowman & Littlefield, 2008.

Wissinger, Elizabeth. *This Year's Model: Fashion, Media and the Making of Glamour*. New York: New York University Press, 2015.

X, Malcolm, and Alex Haley, *The Autobiography of Malcolm X*. New York: Grove Press, 1965.

Yancy, George. *Black Bodies, White Gaze: The Continuing Significance of Race*. Lanham, MD: Rowan & Littlefield, 2008.

Zdatny, Steven. "Fashion and Class Struggle: The Case of coiffure" *Social History* 18, no. 1 (January 1993): 52–72.

Zdatny, Steven. "The Boyish Look and the Liberated Woman: The Politics and Aesthetics of Women's Hairstyles." *Fashion Theory* 1, no. 4 (1997): 367–98.

Zdatny, Steven. *Hairstyles and Fashion: A Hairdresser's History of Paris, 1910–1920*. London: Bloomsbury Academic, 1999.

Zdatny, Steven. 'The French Hygiene Offensive of the 1950s: A Critical Moment in the History of Manners." *Journal of Modern History* 84 (December 2012): 897–932.

Zhen, Zhang. "An Amorous History of the Silver Screen: The Actress as Vernacular Embodiment in Early Chinese Film Culture." In *A Feminist Reader in Early Cinema*, edited by Jennifer M. Bean and Diane Negra, 501–30. Durham, NC: Duke University Press, 2002.

Zweiniger-Bargielowska, Ina. *Managing the Body: Beauty, Health, and Fitness in Britain, 1880–1939*. Oxford: Oxford University Press, 2010.

CONTRIBUTORS

Kristen Barber is Associate Professor of Sociology at Southern Illinois University, Carbondale, USA, where she is also Faculty Affiliate in the Women, Gender, and Sexuality Studies Program. Barber's research looks at the intersections of race, class, gender, and sexuality with an emphasis on culture, work, consumption, and social inequalities. Her book *Styling Masculinity: Gender, Class, and Inequality* (2016) is an empirical examination of the men's grooming industry, with a focus on the labor of women hairstylists responsible for convincing men the salon experience can support their identities and privileges. Her articles on this project can be found in: *Gender & Society* and *Contexts*. Barber's current research shifts gears to consider men's participation in feminist protest. This work has been published in the journals *Contexts* and *Mobilization*.

Alice Beard is an academic and design historian and has held positions at Kingston University, the Royal College of Art, and the University of the Arts, UK. Her teaching and research is focused on fashion media and the intersections between fashion, design, text, and photography. She is particularly interested in magazine cultures and using oral history and object analysis to reconstruct production and consumption histories. Her publications include articles for *Fashion Theory: The Journal for Dress, Body & Culture* on fashion photography and fashion curation. She contributed book chapters on 1970s fashion editor Caroline Baker for *Fashion Media: Past and Present* (eds. Bartlett, Cole, and Rocamora, 2012), and on styling and the construction of a fashionable "look" in *Hair: Styling, Culture and Fashion* (eds. Biddle-Perry and Cheang, 2008). Beard curated "Beauty Queens: Smiles, Swimsuits and Sabotage" (2004) and "Remembering *Nova* Magazine 1965–1976" (2006) at The Women's Library, London. Alice Beard was awarded a PhD for her history of *Nova* magazine from Goldsmiths, University of London, UK in 2014.

Geraldine Biddle-Perry is a cultural historian and lectures in Cultural Studies and Fashion History and Theory at University of the Arts London (UAL) Central Saint Martins and University of East London, UK. Her work considers questions of self in relation to the self-conscious fashioning of modern bodies through popular consumerism. Central to her approach is the interrogation of the assumptions of class and gender that underpin the construction of mainstream fashionable identities. Biddle-Perry coedited with Dr. Sarah Cheang *Hair: Styling, Culture and Fashion* (2008), a notable collection of essays, looking at the symbolic and social significance of hair; coorganized an international symposium "Hair Stories: Practice, Theory and Culture" at the V&A Museum (2009); and was cocurator of "Unlocking the Look: From Hair Cut to Hair Couture," London College of Fashion (LCF) Fashion Space Gallery. She has published journal articles on fashion and oral history, club cycling and social aspiration in the nineteenth century, the history of sports and leisure retailing in Britain, and of British Olympic ceremonial uniforms. She is author of *Dressing for Austerity: Aspiration, Leisure and Fashion in Postwar Britain* (2017).

Hanna Cody currently serves as an End Trafficking Fellow with UNICEF USA's End Trafficking Project. Based in New York City, she serves as a grassroots and national spokesperson for children and educates communities on issues of child trafficking as it occurs both globally and locally. Leveraging UNICEF USA's initiatives, she engages student, faith-based, and community groups to take action against child trafficking. Hanna has previously served as a legislative intern on gender and security for the US Senate Foreign Relations Committee as well as a research and knowledge management intern for the UN Women's Political Participation Unit. While at UN Women, she conducted original research on women's heads of state and government, assisted in the development of a guide on violence against women in elections, and supported the methodological development of Sustainable Development Goal Indicator 5.5.1.b on women's participation in local government. Hanna graduated as Valedictorian of her class at Rollins College, Winter Park, Florida, USA, with her university's first honors bachelor's degree in gender studies.

Paul R. Deslandes is Associate Professor and Chair of the Department of History at the University of Vermont. His research focuses on the study of masculinity, sexuality, and the history of visual culture, fashion, and beauty. Deslandes has published a number of essays, book chapters, and reviews in journals including the *Journal of British Studies, Gender and History, Journal of Women's History*, and *History Compass* as well as collections such as *British Queer History, Consuming Behaviours*, and the *Routledge History of Sex and the Body: 1500 to the Present*. He is also the author of *Oxbridge Men: British Masculinity and the Undergraduate Experience, 1850–1920* (2005). He is currently completing a new book titled *The Culture of Male Beauty in Britain: From the First Photographs to David Beckham* and is the series editor for a forthcoming collection of essays (to be published by Bloomsbury) on *The Cultural History of Beauty*. Deslandes has served as the Executive Secretary for the North American Conference on British Studies and is highly active in a number of other scholarly organizations including the American Historical Association.

Yudit Kornberg Greenberg is the George D. and Harriet W. Cornell Endowed Chair of Religion, and Founding Director of the Jewish Studies Program at Rollins College in Winter Park, Florida, USA. Dr. Greenberg is the author and editor of books and articles in modern and contemporary Jewish thought, comparative religion, women and religion, and cross-cultural views of love and the body, including the two-volume *Encyclopedia of Love in World Religions* (2008), *From Spinoza to Levinas: Hermeneutical, Ethical, and Political Issues in Modern and Contemporary Jewish Philosophy* (2009), *The Body in Religion: Crosscultural Perspectives* (2017), and *Dharma and Halacha: Comparative Studies in Hindu-Jewish Philosophy and Religion* (2018). Dr. Greenberg served as cochair of the Comparative Study of Hinduisms and Judaisms Group at the American Academy of Religion from 2004 to 2011, and is on the Editorial Board of the *Journal of the American Academy of Religion*.

Chelsea Johnson is a PhD candidate and Provost's Doctoral Fellow in Sociology at the University of Southern California, USA. Her interests lie at the intersection of race, class, gender, and the body. Her work to date explores how race and class identities shape feminist praxis, embodiment, and political expression, focusing primarily on the experiences of middle-class and/or upwardly mobile women of African descent. Her doctoral research examines the natural hair movement to theorize the relationships between black beauty, black business, and black politics in an increasingly global, digital, and commercialized field of race and gender relations. This work has enabled her to conduct funded ethnography in the United States, South Africa, Brazil, and the Netherlands. Previously, Chelsea researched how black women's college experiences challenge liberal feminist critiques of sport and notions of empowerment. Through an ethnographic study of athletes at a Historically Black College for women, she published "Cheerleading at the Intersection of Race, Class, and Gender," *Sociology of Sport Journal*'s honorable mention for Best Article of 2015. Chelsea is a graduate of Spelman College, the International De-colonial Black Feminism School, and the Black European Summer School.

Nathalie Khan teaches fashion history and theory at Central Saint Martins and London College of Fashion, UK. She is also a guest lecturer at NYU London, UK, Sotheby's Institute of Art in New York, USA, and La Cambre Mode[s] in Brussels, Belgium. Curatorial practice includes a project titled *I Know Simply Thatced the Sky Will Last Longer Than I*, with the Belgian visual artist Pierre Debusschere during the 28th International Festival of Fashion and Photography (2013). Khan is a leading theorist and writer on contemporary fashion media and the impact of new technology on the traditional catwalk show, fashion film, and photography.

Royce Mahawatte is Senior Lecturer in Cultural Studies at Central Saint Martins, University of the Arts London and a member of the faculty at NYU London, UK. Selected publications: *George Eliot and the Gothic Novel* (2013) and "Horror in the Nineteenth Century 1820–1900" in *A Literary History of Horror* (2017) and "The Sad Fortunes of 'Stylish Things': George Eliot and the Languages of Fashion" in *Communicating Transcultural Fashion Narratives* (2018). His research interests are Victorian fiction, the Gothic, and cultures of fashion and the body. He is currently working on a monograph about the male body and Victorian writing.

Elisha P. Renne is Professor Emerita in the Department of Afroamerican and African Studies (DAAS) and in the Department of Anthropology, University of Michigan, Ann Arbor, USA. Her interests include African ethnology and infectious disease; fertility and reproductive health; gender relations; religion and social change; and the anthropology of cloth. Renne's current research focuses on textile manufacturing and cotton production in northern Nigeria as well as local development projects in northeastern Ghana. She is the author of *Cloth That Does Not Die* (1995); *Population and Progress in a Yoruba Town* (2003); *The Politics of Polio in Northern Nigeria* (2010); *Veils, Turbans, and Islamic Reform in Northern Nigeria* (in press); and is the editor of *Veiling in Africa* (2013). She has also published articles in several journals, which include *Africa, African Arts, American Anthropologist, Anthropology Today, Journal of the Royal Anthropological Institute, Material Religion, Population and Development Review, RES, Social Science & Medicine,* and *Textile History*.

Kim Smith is Senior Lecturer in Fashion History and Theory at University of East London. A design historian, her doctoral research examined the design of West End hairdressing salons in the 1960s, the consumption of luxury hairdressing and the interaction between clients, hairdressers, and the hair trade community. Smith contributed a chapter on the history of the ladies' hairdressing salon to *Hair: Styling, Culture and Fashion* (ed. Biddle-Perry and Cheang, 2008) and has presented numerous conference papers based on her research: "Heady Days: Mayfair's Hairdressing 'Goldrush' into the New Frontier of Postwar Britain" examined the expansion of exclusive Mayfair salons after World War II at the *London and the Nation* conference in 2015; "From Brixton to Mayfair: the Professionalisation of Black Hairdressing in Mid-Twentieth Century Britain" was presented at the *Personal, Fashionable and Archival Spaces of Hair* symposium at Somerset House in 2016 and explored the influence of popular Trinidadian pianist Winifred Atwell. This latter paper is the basis for an article to be included in a special issue of *Fashion Theory* (forthcoming).

Shirley Anne Tate is Professor of Race and Education and Director of the Centre for Race, Education and Decoloniality (CRED) in the Carnegie School of Education, Leeds Beckett University, UK, and Research Associate in the Centre for Critical Studies in Higher Education Transformation at Nelson Mandela University, South Africa. Her area of research is Black diaspora studies broadly and her research interests are institutional racism, the body, affect, beauty, "race" performativity, and Caribbean decolonial studies while paying attention to the intersections of "race" and gender.

INDEX

abjection 116
acculturation 118
advertising 4–5, 83, 94–9, 103, 172
aesthetics 137–8, 154
African Americans 29–32, 39, 80, 90, 95, 107–8, 116
African hair practices 136
"Afro" hairstyle 5–6, 29–30, 39, 90, 94, 104, 107–8, 117–19, 126–7, 131, 134–5, 138, 155
Agyemfra, Akua 125
Ahmed, Leila 17
American Salon (journal) 91
Andrews, Julie 3, 76
Antoine de Paris 64, 145–52
Arusha 31
Asante ethnic group 38
assimilation 118
Auschwitz 33–4
"authenticity" 135–9, 163

Bailey, David 155
Baird, Beatrice 133
Bakelite 82, 86
Baker, Caroline 69
Baker, Josephine 76–7
baldness 97, 104, 138, 173, 175
Bampton, Sally 102
Banks, Ingrid 90
barber shops 19, 29, 31, 78–9, 102, 155
Bardot, Brigitte 69, 172
Barrett Street Trade School 152
Bataille, George 169
Baudrillard, Jean 176
Bauhaus movement 89
beards 11–13, 19, 28, 39, 78, 112–14, 155
Beaton, Cecil 148
"beehive" hairstyle 87
Beetham's (company) 94
Benjamin, Walter 171
Berg, Charles 166
Berlant, Lauren 177
Berman, Bonnie 71
Bessone, Raymond 84–5, 88, 154
Beyoncé. *See* Knowles-Carter, Beyoncé

biblical texts 12, 15
Biddle-Perry, Geraldine (editor) 58, 103
"big hair" 87, 102, 143, 154–5, 158
birth 35
Bizumić, Nikola 78
black hair and black hairstyles 6, 80, 90–1, 129–41, 152–3
Blackmon, Larry 91
"blackness" 129–31, 134, 141
Black Power movement 135
black pride 118
Black Widows (gang) 117
bleaching of hair 4, 62
blocos afro 137
blonde hair 62, 83
Blondell, Joan 4
"blue stockings" 59
"bobbed" hair 2–5, 27, 58–62, 65–8, 71–3, 76, 79, 88, 95, 102, 104, 111, 126, 145
Bobbed Hair (film) 60
body politics 19
Bolam, Mark 121
Borelli, Laird 68
Boscagli, Maurizia 171
bouffant hairstyle 102, 155
Boughessa, Faiza 22
Bourdieu, Pierre 144
bourgeois society 155, 171–2
"boutique" salons 155
Bow, Clara 59–61
Bowie, David 69, 121
braided hair 30
natural 137–8
Brazil 133–4, 137–8
"Breck Girl" campaign 95
Breton, Andre 169
Breward, Christopher 64
"brickwork" technique 89
Bromberger, Christian 22
Brooks, Louise 3, 60–1, 64
Brownmiller, Susan 87–8
Brylcreem 97
Buckley, Cheryl 76
"buns" 120–1. *See also* "man buns"
Burkina Faso 32–5, 38

"burkini" design 20–1
Burstein, Caroline 71
business opportunities 152–3
"butch" identity 106–7
Butler, Judith 111, 123–4, 175–8
Butt Muscle (film) 164–5, 177–8
"buzz cuts" 71, 80, 91

Caine, Michael 155
Campbell, Bebe Moore 107–8
Campbell, Naomi 138–9
Candelario, Ginetta 132
capitalism 153, 155, 167–72, 177
Carangi, Gia 70
carnival 137
Carter, Madam 114
Carvalho, Taís 137
Castle, Irene 59
celebrity culture 3–4, 172–7, 180
Chanel, Coco 58
Chanel (fashion house) 64
Charles, Caroline 69
"the Chav" 160
Cheang, Sarah 58, 103
Chelsea 155
Chen Yinghuang 33
"Chic" hairstyle 145
chignons 65
children's hair 11–12, 27, 32
Christianity 17
Cierplikowski, Antek 145. *See also* Antoine de Paris
cinema 57–64, 83–4, 150, 154
civil rights activists 155
Clairol 98, 101
class distinctions 4, 143–4, 151, 154–61
   in Britain 156
class-less society 155–9
Cleaver, Kathleen 118
Coddington, Grace 65–7
coiffing 111, 120
Colbert, Claudette 4, 64, 150
Collier's magazine 94
Collis, Michael 71
colonialism 23, 126
colorants 4, 62
color of hair 85, 89–91
combs 80, 86–7, 90, 96, 132, 134
   hot 82
commodification of women's bodies and hair 93, 125–6
commodity fetishism 167
concentration camps 33–4, 39, 105

consciousness of hair 84
conspicuous consumption 145
constipation 99
consumer culture 176
consumer goods 4, 98
consumerism 3–4, 32, 59, 82, 84, 91, 107, 154, 161, 163, 171–2
Cooper, Carolyn 136
Cooper, Wendy 75
Corriston, Peter 173
Corson, Richard 75
cosmetics 80, 119–20
Coupe Sauvage hairstyle 88
covering the head 13–20, 27–9, 112
Cox, Caroline 65, 75, 95, 160
Craig, Maxine 29–30
Crang, Philip 148
Crawford, Joan 64, 150–1
"creolization" 139–40
crew cuts 99
cropped hair 58–9, 77, 99, 104. *See also* "Eton crops"
croquinole 84
curled hair 132, 170
Cusack, Joan 157
cutting of hair 15–16, 26–9, 32, 65, 154–5

dandruff 97–100
Davis, Angela 118–19, 135
Davis, Fred 155–6
Dean, John Denman 86
death, associations with 38, 83
De Clairville, Monsieur 146–8
Delaney, Carol 25–9
Delevingne, Cara 71
Dengel, Veronica 99
Denman styling brush 86
department stores 171
Derek, Bo 90
Deyn, Agyness 71
Diary of a Lost Girl (film) 60
diasporas 19
Dietrich, Marlene 68
dirun obitan 35–6
domestic service 152–3
Dominican Republic 30, 39, 132, 134
Donovan, Terence 65
Doronin, Vladislav 138
Douglas, Mary 165
dreadlocks 32, 118, 130, 134, 138
dress codes 9
Du Bois, W.E.B. 115, 132
Duchamp, Marcel 175

Du Pont Corporation 84
dyeing of hair 83, 85, 90, 124
Dyson Supersonic blow-dryer 91

Ebony Goddess pageant 137–8
electric clippers 78, 90
elite hairdressing 154
"English cut" 88
entrepreneurship 152–3
eroticism 165, 170–1
"Essex girl" figure 160
"Eton crops" 58, 67, 76–7
eugenics 95
Evans, Jessica 174
expenditure on hair care 125
exports 125

Facebook 19
The Face (television program) 138
Factor, Max 63, 138
Fairbanks, Douglas 150
Fanon, Frantz 129–30
fashion 4, 22–3, 26, 32, 57–8, 64, 70, 105, 124, 176
    definition of 58
fashionability 69
fashion statements 69
fatwas 13
femininity 3–4, 39, 57, 63, 67, 76, 79, 83–4, 102, 104, 113–18, 154, 166, 170–1, 178
    active 59–60
    black 6, 114–16, 132
feminism 130, 133, 155
fetishism 5, 103, 127, 163, 166–72, 176, 179
Figueiredo, Angela 137
Filberg-Schwartz, Howard 17
First World War 3, 27, 75, 84, 104
Fitzgerald, Scott 2, 170
Flaming Youth (film) 59
"flappers" 3, 58–9, 77, 111, 126
Fleur de Lis hairstyle 145
Flügel, John 176
Foan, Gilbert 57, 62
Fonda, Jane 172
Ford Model "T" 27
Foster, Hal 173–4
Foucault, Michel 131
Francis, Kay 4
French, Freddy 86
Freud, Sigmund (and Freudian theory) 166–70

Frieda, John 88
fundamentalism, religious 19, 23
"Funki-Dreds" hairstyle 91

Galvin, Daniel 88–91
Galvin, Joshua 88
Garbo, Greta 68
gbe obitan 35–6
gender differences in hairdressing 79
gender politics 111, 123–6
Ghana 38
Ghanem, Khaoula 22
Gibson, Charles Dana (and the "Gibson Girl") 59, 94–5
Gillette safety razor 95
Ginter, Alex 106
glamour 4, 59, 62, 84, 102, 149–50, 154, 170
"glass ceiling" 112
The Glass House, Paris 146–7
Glissant, Édouard 139–41
Glynn, Elinor 59
"golden age" of hairdressing 154–5
golden hair 170
Goldwin, Samuel 64
Goodson, Saufeeya 22
Gordon, Lewis 141
Gow, James 105
gray hair 98, 108–9
Greer, Germaine 107
Griffith, Melanie 157–9
grooming 4, 7, 62, 93–7, 101–5, 130, 144, 156
    military 125
Guether, Irene 105
Guilaroff, Sydney 64, 146–52

hair brushes 86, 99
Hairdressers' Weekly Journal (British) 93
hairdressing professionals, changes in the role of 3–4, 7, 57–8, 64–7, 71, 75–81, 145, 152
hair dryers 82, 88, 91
hairlessness 112
Hair (musical) 106
hairpieces 6, 72
hairstyle changes in the course of a day 144–5
the *hajj* 11, 14, 28
Hall, L. 62–3
Hall, Radclyffe 77, 104
Hall, Stuart 129
Hallpike, C. 10, 12
Harahap, F.J. 13

INDEX

Harlow, Jean 4, 62–4, 83
Harry, Debbie 70
Hasibuan, Anniesa 21
Hasidism 12, 16
hats 16
haute couture 58, 64–5, 84, 154
Hawley, Wanda 60
"healthy" hair 4–5, 94–9
Held, John 77
Hell's Angel (film) 62
Henie, Sonja 150
Hennessy, Rosemary 177
Hepburn, Katherine 150–1
Hermo *Hair-Lustr* 62–3
Hershman, Paul 10, 25
Hesch, Gottlieb 60
Hesmondhalgh, David 174
Heston, Charlton 100
"High-Top Fade" hairstyle 91
hijab wearing 17, 20–2, 112
Hiltebeitel, Alf 6, 26
Hilton, Paris 124
Hinduism 10–15, 18, 32, 35, 125
hippies 108, 119–20, 126–7, 155–6
hire purchase 58
Hokkaido 33
Holden, Ian 157
Hollywood 4, 59–64, 83–4, 150, 170–1
home hairdressing 62–5, 69, 101, 145
hooks, bell 138–9
Hornby, Lesley. *See* "Twiggy"
Horwood, Catherine 154
House of Westmore 4
Houtenbos, Christian 70–3
Howorth, Jeny 71
"Hoxton Fin" hairstyle 160
Hulanicki, Barbara 65
Humphreys, Annie 89–91
hygiene 93–109

identity
　British 156
　class-based 159
　construction of 164
　gendered 104–5, 123
　racial or ethnic 30–1, 129–30, 134, 140
　religious 19, 23
　social 26–30, 39–40, 143–4
Iggy Pop 121
Ilê Aiyê 137
India 18–19, 25, 35, 125–6
individuality in matters of fashon 69, 145

initiation ceremonies 11, 165
Iran 22, 27
Ish, Hazon 16
Islam 12–15. *See also* Muslim communities
　political 23
Italy 105

Jackson, Jesse 118
Jackson, Peter 148
Jagger, Mick 172
"Japanese bonnet style" 60
jazz music 77
"Jazzie B" 91
Jeris hair tonic 99–100
Jewish Reform movement 18
"jherri curl" hairstyle 90
Jim Crowism 114
Johnston, Harry Hamilton 95
Jones, Amelia 176
Jones, Grace 70
Jordan, Michael 31
Judaism 11–19, 112–14, 125

Kampf, Günther 60
Kathmandu 30–1, 39
Keegan, Kevin 89
Kelly, Grace 154
Kennan, Brigid 67
Kennedy, Jackie 172
Kimmel, Michael 120
Klein, Calvin 70
KnocksKinksKrazy (KKK) company 80
Knowles-Carter, Beyoncé 138–9
Koestenbaum, Wayne 173
Kristeva, Julia 177
Kwan, Nancy 65

La Creole Laboratories 95
La Garçonne (novel) 76, 104
Lagerfeld, Karl 71
Lambert, Matt 164, 166
Lami, Michele 164, 177
Leach, Edmund 10, 25
Lears, Jackson 94
Lenglen, Mlle. 57
lesbianism 106
Letts, Quentin 143
Lewis, Leonard 67, 88
Lewis, Reina 21
Leyendecker, J.C. 95
Liljequist, Angela 98
Lipovetsky, Gilles 64

Lobi society 34–5, 38
Lombard, Carole 4
long hair 102–8, 119–20, 178
"the Look" 3, 57, 64–5, 71
loose hair 15, 18, 155
Lorde, Andre 114
L'Oréal (company) 101
Loren, Sophia 154
Luciano, Lynne 106
Lustre-Crème shampoo 99

McCracken, Grant 87
McGhee, Rayfield 117
"machine aesthetic" and "machine consciousness" 76–7
McKnight, Sam 71–3
magazines 59, 62–9, 154
Maimonides, Moses 12
Makeba, Miriam 90
Makos, Christopher 175–6
Malaysia 35
Malcolm X 116, 118
malleability of hair 9, 91, 123, 160, 166, 179
Malone, Annie Turnbo 95, 114, 153
"man buns" 120–1, 124
Manchester 18, 135
Manson, Charles 108
marginalization 33
Margueritte, Victor 104
married status 16, 18, 28, 35
Marx, Karl (and Marxism) 167–71
masculinity 13, 78, 95, 99, 112, 116–20, 135, 156
   acquired by women 104
   "crisis" of 120
Masekela, Hugh 138, 141
mass consumption 153–4, 171
Mass Observation 97, 102–5
mass production techniques 64
Mayfair 84, 148–50, 155
Medvedev, Katalin 161
Mendl, Lady 146
Mennonites 17
menstruation 15
Mercer, Kobena 118, 133, 141
metaphorical significance of hair 10–14, 163, 169, 176
Metcalf, Barbara 18
Mexican-American women 158
Michaelson, Leah 19, 21
military discipline 105, 125
Miller, Barbara 18–19
Miller, Janice 167

Minaj, Nicki 124
Mitchelhelm, Lady 146
modesty 14, 17–22, 29, 112
Mohican hairstyle 156
Monroe, Marilyn 172
Moon, Sarah 68
Moore, Colleen 3, 59
Moore, Julianne 72
Morel, Lady Ottoline 77
Morrow, Willie 90
Moss, Kate 71
Muhammed the Prophet 13, 15
mundan sanskar 35
Murray, Gerald 30
Muslim communities 11–19, 23, 27, 29, 112, 114
mustaches 13, 39

National Hair Goods Co. 62
National Socialism. *See* Nazi regime
"natural" hair 7, 106–7, 118, 129–41
"natural" hairstyles 88, 90, 102
Nazi regime 33–4, 39, 105
neocolonialism 17
Nepal 30–1, 39
Nestlé, Carl 80, 91
Newberry, Pip 69
Newton, Huey 108, 118
"new woman" image 27, 58, 77
New York 76, 106, 175
Nigeria 32, 35–6
Nimoy, Leonard 112–13
Notting Hill Carnival 140
Nova magazine 68
Nsoko 38
Nyerere, Julius 31
nylon 85–6

Obama, Michelle 133
Obeyesekere, Gananath 25
Olivelle, Patrick 10, 13, 40
Oppenheim, Meret 170
Ortiz, Martina 30
Owens, Rick 164–5, 177

Pagano, Alfred 63
Palau, Guido 160
Pandora's Box (film) 60
Papanek, Hanna 15
paper patterns for home dressmaking 64
Paradis, Vanesaa 72
Paris 4, 58, 84, 146, 152, 170
Patou, Jean 58, 60–1

INDEX

patriarchy and patriarchal authority 5, 14, 17, 22, 112, 155, 160, 170
Pecheux, Tom 72
Peiss, Kathy 93
Penn, Irving 70
Pentecostal churches 17
performativity 111, 124, 171, 176, 180
permanent wave treatment 62, 80–3, 88, 91, 145, 154–5
Peterkin, Allan 109
photography 67–8, 73, 94, 171
Photoplay (magazine) 59, 62
Pickford, Mary 150
Picture Post 99
Pietz, William 169
pilgrimage to Mecca. *See* [the] *hajj*
Pittsburgh Courier 133
"pixelated" hair 91
"platinum blondes" 83, 154
politically-motivated hair-styling 134
politics of hair and hygiene 103–9
pomades 116
Poro company 95–7
"power dressing" 156
Prescott, John and Pauline 143, 158
Presley, Elvis 106, 172
Priestley, J.B. 151
private and public spheres 174–7
products for hair care 30, 57, 79–80, 84, 93, 97–8, 101, 119–20, 125, 132, 150, 153
propaganda 84
psychoanalysis 163, 169
psychological benefits of hair care 97
pubic hair 166–7
public sphere. *See* private and public spheres
Punch 154
punk movement 121–3, 156–7

Qua Neglige hairstyle 145
Quant, Mary 65–6, 70, 88–9
Queen magazine 67
queer theory 176–7
the Qur'an 12–15

racial differences 129
racial discrimination 29
racism 29, 95, 116, 130–4, 141
Raimon, Alexandre 154
Ram, Shrijana 30
Rastafarianism 130, 132, 135
rationing 84, 116
razors 79, 95
Reagan, Ronald 108

Redding, Jherri 90
red hair 154
Reid, Wallace 63
"relaxers" 116
religion 6–7, 9–23, 112–13, 126
Rendlesham, Claire 67
respectability, culture of 156
Rhodes, Zandra 90
Richards, Keith 172
Richards, Thomas 94
Riot Grrrls 122–3, 127
rites of passage 32–5, 165
rituals 32–5, 125, 165
Roberts, Mary Louise 104
Rock, Chris 125
Rogers, Ginger 150
Rojek, Chris 173
The Rolling Stones 172–3
Rose, Angel 86

St. Laurent, Yves 65
salons 3, 27–30, 39, 62, 75, 78–81, 84, 87, 91, 114, 145, 151–5
Santos, Simone 137–9
Sassoon, Vidal 58, 65–70, 73, 88–90, 102, 155
Saturday Evening Post 96
Schiaparelli, Elia 64
Schilt, Kristen 112
Schneider, Maria 69
Schueller, Eugène 83
scissors 79
Scott's electronic curler 132
Scumaci, Gianni 160
Second World War 64, 83–4, 98, 105–6
secularization 6–7
Sedgwick, Eve Kosofsky 177
self-expression 9
"semi-tousled" hairstyle 145
"session stylists" 70–1, 160
sexuality and sexual difference 10, 14–17, 25–8, 61, 170–1, 176
Shakur, Tupac 31
shampoo 98–9, 102–3, 155
sharia law 12
shaving 10–12
    of heads of wartime collaborators 106
    prohibition of 12
Sherman, Cindy 172
"shingled" hairstyles 79, 145
Shirazi, Faegeh 12
Shiva 10–11
short hair 39–42, 49, 59, 64, 69, 76, 95, 103–6, 111, 148, 152

sideburns 78, 113, 156
Sieber, Roy 38
Sikhism 13, 112
silk 58
Silvikrin 99
Simmel, Georg 26
Simone, Nina 90
Singapore 37–8
"Sisterlocks" 135
Skeggs, Beverley 143, 156, 160
"Skiffle cut" hairstyle 91
"skinheads" 156
skullcaps 13
Slick Chicks 117
Smith, Kim 148
Smith, Will 91
social climbing 154
social control 14
social media 22, 161
social organization 29–32
social practices 26
social status 4, 144, 150, 154–5, 160, 171
Sofer, Hatam 16
Soileau, Paul 163–9, 178
Solanas, Valerie 175
Some Girls (record album) 172–3
Song of Songs 15
Sorbie, Trevor 88
South Africa 141
spectacularization of hair 136
Sri Lanka 32
Stanwyck, Barbara 64
status differentials. *See* social status
Steele, Valerie 69
Stein, Kurt 93
Stevenson, Karen 59
Stewart, Kirsten 72
straightened hair 29–30, 39, 80, 90, 95, 114, 118, 125, 130–4, 138
Stutesman, Drake 59–60
styling of hair 4–7, 17, 22, 27–32, 39, 57–8, 62–5, 73
Sunday Times Magazine 65
Surrealism 5, 169–71
Suter, Eugene 80–1
Swanson, Gloria 62–4
symbolism of hair 5, 10, 13–14, 17–19, 25, 32, 40, 103, 106, 109, 123, 127, 163–7, 170–1, 180
synagogue services 13
Synnott, Anthony 17, 75–6, 91, 111–14
synthetic materials 91

Taliban regime 19
Tanzania 31–2
Tate, Sharon 108
Taylor, Elizabeth 99, 154, 172
Taylor, Penina 19–20
"Teasie Weasie". *See* Bessone, Raymond
technological advances
    in hairdressing 75–6, 80–4, 88–92, 150
    stimulated by warfare 84
Teddy Boys 86–7, 156
Temple, Shirley 150
"ten-inch bobs" 62
Tennant, Stephen 148
Thatcher, Margaret 102
thinning hair 97
thinning shears 79
Thompson, Julia 30
Thompson, Roger 88
Thoroughly Modern Millie (film) 3, 76
Time magazine 139
traction alopecia 138
trade in hair 136
tradition 18, 23
training in hairdressing 152
transgender people 112
Tuaregs 13–14
Tulloch, Carol 134
turbans 13
Turkey 25–9, 39
"Twiggy" 67–8, 71

upsherin ceremony 12
uses of hair 34

Valentino, Rudolf 69, 77, 150
van Gennep, Arnold 32
veiling 9–10, 15–17, 20, 29
Vick, John 157
Victorian culture 160, 170
Vietnam War 120
Villeneuve, Justin 67
Vincenzi, Penny 67
Vionnet, Madame 64
"Vishnoo" 160
Vogue 65, 69–71
Vogue Arabia 22
"vulnerability" 139

Wahl, Leo 78
Walker, C.J. (Madame) 80, 96, 114–15, 132, 153
Walker, Tim 71

Wang Hanlun 76
Warhol, Andy 164, 172–6
Warner, Michael 177
Warner, Stephen 19
washing of hair 95, 97
Washington, Sarah Spencer 153
Waxson, Lindsey 71
Wayne State University 120
Weaver, Sigourney 157–8
"weaves" 125, 136
wedding ceremonies 35–9
Weiss, Paul 31–2
The Well of Loneliness 104
Wells balsam shampoo 102–3
West, Mae 4, 62, 64
Westmore family 4, 59, 64, 150, 152
Westwood, Vivienne 71
Wharton, Edith 145
"wig hats" 72–3
wigs 5, 16, 64, 71, 112, 125, 138, 163, 167, 172–80
The Wild Affair (film) 65
Wilderson, Frank B. 130–1

Willett, Julia 120
Williams, Gertrude 84
Williams, Sandra 29
Wissinger, Elizabeth 59, 70
The Women (film) 151
women's emancipation 57
women's employment 58
Wood, Brent Michael 121
Woodstock Festival 120
Working Girl (film) 157–9
"wrapping" with colored scarves 19
Wrapunzel community 20
Wyman, Bill 172

xenophobia 116

Yoruba people 35–6
youth subcultures 102, 155–6
"yuppies" 156

Zanetti, Aheda 20–1
Zdatny, Steven 104, 144–5, 152
zoot suits 116–17